Myth and the Human
Hans Blumenberg's Theory of Myth

This is the first book-length critical analysis in any language of Hans Blumenberg's theory of myth. Blumenberg can be regarded as the most important German theorist of myth of the second half of the twentieth century, and his *Work on Myth* (1979) has resonated across disciplines ranging from literary theory, via philosophy, religious studies and anthropology, to the history and philosophy of science.

Nicholls introduces Anglophone readers to Blumenberg's biography and to his philosophical contexts. He elucidates Blumenberg's theory of myth by relating it to three important developments in late nineteenth- and early twentieth-century German philosophy (hermeneutics, phenomenology and philosophical anthropology), while also comparing Blumenberg's ideas with those of other prominent theorists of myth such as Vico, Hume, Schelling, Max Müller, Frazer, Sorel, Freud, Cassirer, Heidegger, Horkheimer and Adorno. According to Nicholls, Blumenberg's theory of myth can only be understood in relation to the 'human sciences,' since it emerges from a speculative hypothesis concerning the emergence of the earliest human beings. For Blumenberg, myth was originally a cultural adaptation that constituted the human attempt to deal with anxieties concerning the threatening forces of nature by anthropomorphizing those forces into mythic images.

In the final two chapters, Blumenberg's theory of myth is placed within the post-war political context of West Germany. Through a consideration of Blumenberg's exchanges with Carl Schmitt, as well as by analysing unpublished correspondence and parts of the original *Work of Myth* manuscript that Blumenberg held back from publication, Nicholls shows that Blumenberg's theory of myth also amounted to a reckoning with the legacy of National Socialism.

Angus Nicholls is Chair of the Department of Comparative Literature at Queen Mary University of London, UK, where he teaches German and Comparative Literature. His previous books include *Goethe's Concept of the Daemonic* (2006) and *Thinking the Unconscious* (co-edited with Martin Liebscher, 2010). He is co-editor of *History of the Human Sciences* and of the *Publications of the English Goethe Society*.

Theorists of Myth

Series Editor: Robert A. Segal

Myth and the Human Sciences
Hans Blumenberg's Theory of Myth

Angus Nicholls

Routledge
Taylor & Francis Group

LONDON AND NEW YORK

First published 2015
by Routledge
711 Third Avenue, New York, NY 10017

and by Routledge
2 Park Square, Milton Park, Abingdon, Oxfordshire OX14 4RN

First issued in paperback 2016

Routledge is an imprint of the Taylor and Francis Group, an informa business

© 2015 Taylor & Francis

The right of Angus Nicholls to be identified as author of this work has been asserted by him/her in accordance with sections 77 and 78 of the Copyright, Designs and Patents Act 1988.

Library of Congress Cataloging-in-Publication Data

Nicholls, Angus (Angus James), 1972–
 Myth and the human sciences : Hans Blumenberg's theory of myth / by Angus Nicholls. — First [edition].
  pages cm. — (Theorists of myth ; 16)
  Includes bibliographical references and index.
 1. Blumenberg, Hans. 2. Myth. I. Title.
  B3209.B834N53 2014
  201'.3092—dc23
  2014032874

ISBN 13: 978-1-138-23670-7 (pbk)
ISBN 13: 978-0-415-88549-2 (hbk)

Typeset in Sabon
by Apex CoVantage, LLC

for Walter F. Veit

Origin of Man now proved.—Metaphysic must flourish.—He who understands baboon ~~will~~ *would do more towards metaphysics than Locke.*

Charles Darwin, *Notebook M,* 1838

We now have here before us, in the application of the theory of evolution of Darwinism, in the broadest sense, to man, a blunder of the first order.

Hans Blumenberg, *Description of Man,* 2006

Contents

Note on Sources

RELATED PUBLICATIONS

Elements of the argument in this book also appear in the following publications:

Angus Nicholls, "Das Spannungsverhältnis von Wissenschaft und Mythologie in Deutschland um 1800 und in Großbritannien um 1850–1900," 133–56, in *Wissenschaftsgeschichte als Begriffsgeschichte. Terminologische Umbrüche im Entstehungsprozess der modernen Wissenschaften*, eds. Michael Eggers and Matthias Rothe (Bielefeld: Transcript 2009).
Angus Nicholls, "The *Fremdling* of Teleology: On Roger Smith's *Being Human*," in *History of the Human Sciences* 23, no. 5 (2010): 194–201.
Angus Nicholls and Felix Heidenreich, "Nachwort der Herausgeber," 83–146, in Hans Blumenberg, *Präfiguration: Arbeit am politischen Mythos* (Berlin: Suhrkamp, 2014).
Angus Nicholls "The Goethe Complex: Hans Blumenberg on *Das Dämonische*," 97–119, in *Das Dämonische. Schicksale einer Kategorie der Zweideutigkeit nach Goethe*, ed. Lars Friedrich, Eva Geulen and Kirk Wetters (Munich: Fink, 2014).

WORKS BY HANS BLUMENBERG

Works by Hans Blumenberg are referenced according to the German and, where available, the English editions. Quotes from works by Blumenberg that are already published appear in English translation only; quotes from the Blumenberg *Nachlass* appear in English in the main text and in German in the notes. Unless otherwise noted, all translations of Blumenberg's works are my own.

WORKS BY OTHER GERMAN LANGUAGE AUTHORS

All German language primary sources are referenced according to the German and, where available, the English editions. Unless otherwise noted, all translations of German works are my own.

ABBREVIATIONS OF FREQUENTLY CITED
WORKS BY HANS BLUMENBERG

AAR	"Anthropologische Annäherung an die Aktualität der Rhetorik" (1971), in *Wirklichkeiten, in denen wir Leben: Aufsätze und eine Rede* (Stuttgart: Reclam, 1986) (cited according to WWL, see below): 104–36 ["An Anthropological Approach to the Contemporary Significance of Rhetoric," trans. Robert M. Wallace, in *After Philosophy: End or Transformation*, eds. Kenneth Baynes, James Bohman, and Thomas McCarthy (Cambridge, MA: MIT Press, 1987), 429–58].
AM = WOM	*Arbeit am Mythos.* (Frankfurt am Main: Suhrkamp, 1979) [*Work on Myth*, trans. Robert M. Wallace (Cambridge, MA: MIT Press, 1985)].
ÄMS	*Ästhetische und metaphorologische Schriften* [*Aesthetic and Metaphorological Writings*], ed. Anselm Haverkamp (Frankfurt am Main: Suhrkamp, 2001).
BDM	*Beschreibung des Menschen* [*Description of Man*], ed. Manfred Sommer (Frankfurt am Main: Suhrkamp, 2006).
BG	*Begriffe in Geschichten* [*Concepts in Stories*], (Frankfurt am Main: Suhrkamp, 1998).
BSB	*Hans Blumenberg/Carl Schmitt, Briefwechsel*, eds. Alexander Schmitz and Marcel Lepper (Frankfurt am Main: Suhrkamp, 2007).
BTB	*Hans Blumenberg/Jacob Taubes, Briefwechsel 1961–1981 und weitere Materialien*, eds. Herbert Kopp-Oberstebrink and Martin Treml (Berlin: Suhrkamp, 2013).
EMS	*Ein mögliches Selbstverständnis: Aus dem Nachlaß* [*A Possible Self-Understanding: From the Nachlaß*] (Stuttgart: Reclam, 1997).
GKW = GCW	*Die Genesis der kopernikanischen Welt.* 3 vols. 1975 (Frankfurt am Main: Suhrkamp, 1981). [*The Genesis of the Copernican World*, trans. Robert M. Wallace (Cambridge, MA: MIT Press, 1989)]
HA	*Höhlenausgänge* [*Cave Exits*] (Frankfurt am Main: Suhrkamp, 1989).
LDN = LMA	*Die Legitimität der Neuzeit.* Erneuerte Ausgabe, 1966 (Frankfurt am Main: Suhrkamp, 1996) [*The Legitimacy of the Modern Age*, trans. Robert M. Wallace (Cambridge, MA: MIT Press, 1985).]
LW	*Die Lesbarkeit der Welt* [*The Legibility of the World*] (Frankfurt am Main: Suhrkamp, 1981).

LZ   *Lebenszeit und Weltzeit* [*Lifetime and World-Time*] (Frankfurt am Main: Suhrkamp, 1986).

OD   *Die ontologische Distanz. Eine Untersuchung über die Krisis der Phänomenologie Husserls* [*The Ontological Distance. An Investigation into the Crisis of Husserl's Phenomenology*]. Unpublished Habilitation diss., University of Kiel, 1950. References are based on the second manuscript copy held in the *Deutsches Literaturarchiv* Marbach under the following title: *Die ontologische Distanz. Eine Untersuchung zur Krisis der philosophischen Grundlagen der Neuzeit* [*The Ontological Distance. An Investigation of the Crisis of the Philosophical Foundations of the Modern Age*].

PF   *Präfiguration: Arbeit am politischen Mythos* [*Prefiguration: Work on Political Myth*], eds. Angus Nicholls and Felix Heidenreich (Berlin: Suhrkamp, 2014).

PZM = PM   *Paradigmen zu einer Metaphorologie*, 1960 (Frankfurt am Main: Suhrkamp, 1997). [*Paradigms for a Metaphorology*, trans. Robert Savage (Ithaca, NY: Cornell University Press, 2010).]

QSE   *Quellen, Ströme, Eisberge* [*Springs, Streams, Icebergs*], eds. Ulrich von Bülow and Dorit Krusche (Frankfurt am Main: Suhrkamp, 2012).

SMZ = SWS   *Schiffbruch mit Zuschauer. Paradigma einer Daseinsmetapher* (Frankfurt am Main: Suhrkamp, 1979). [*Shipwreck with Spectator: Paradigm of a Metaphor for Existence*, trans. Steven Rendall (Cambridge, MA: MIT Press, 1997).]

SÜF = CCR   *Die Sorge geht über den Fluss* (Frankfurt am Main: Suhrkamp, 1987). [*Care Crosses the River*, trans. Paul Fleming (Stanford, CA: Stanford University Press, 2010).]

TDL   *Theorie der Lebenswelt* [*Theory of the Life-World*], ed. Manfred Sommer (Frankfurt am Main: Suhrkamp, 2010).

TDU   *Theorie der Unbegrifflichkeit.* [*Theory of Non-Conceptuality*], ed. Anselm Haverkamp (Frankfurt am Main: Suhrkamp, 2007).

VP   *Die Verführbarkeit des Philosophen* [*The Seducibility of the Philosopher*], (Frankfurt am Main: Suhrkamp, 2005).

VS   *Die Vollzähligkeit der Sterne* [*The Completeness of the Stars*] (Frankfurt am Main: Suhrkamp, 1997).

WST   "Wirklichkeitsbegriff und Staatstheorie" ["The Concept of Reality and the Theory of the State"], in *Schweizer Monatshefte* 48 (1968–9): 121–46.

WWL   *Wirklichkeiten, in denen wir leben: Aufsätze und eine Rede* [*Realities in Which We Live: Essays and a Speech*] (Stuttgart: Reclam, 1986).

WWM   "Wirklichkeitsbegriff und Wirkungspotential des Mythos" ["The Concept of Reality and the Effective Potential of Myth"], in *Terror und Spiel. Probleme der Mythenrezeption* (Poetik und Hermeneutik 4), ed. Manfred Fuhrmann (Munich: Fink, 1971, 11–66).

ZSZ   *Zu den Sachen und zurück* [*To the Things and Back Again*], ed. Manfred Sommer (Frankfurt am Main: Suhrkamp, 2002).

ABBREVIATIONS OF MATERIALS FROM THE BLUMENBERG *NACHLASS*

KMZ   "Kein Mythos des XX. Jahrhunderts" ["No Myth of the Twentieth Century"]

RM   "Remythisierungen" ["Remythicizations"] (AMY IV)

COPYRIGHT ACKNOWLEDGEMENTS

Foreword

Robert A. Segal

Several years ago I was invited to speak at a conference on myth and literature at the University of Freiburg. Only at the conference did I discover the
stature of Hans Blumenberg. All or almost all of the other papers, which
numbered perhaps two dozen, were on Blumenberg. Happily, mine was too,
but only by coincidence. I learned that Blumenberg is a preeminent authority on myth and literature in the German-speaking world. The cultural
divide between the German-speaking world, where Blumenberg is very well
known, and the English-speaking world was confirmed for me.

In the English-speaking world knowledge of Blumenberg comes above all
from the translations of and detailed introductions to three of his fat tomes
by Robert M. Wallace: *Work on Myth, The Legitimacy of the Modern Age*,
and *The Genesis of the Copernican World*. All three were originally published (or published in revised form) in German in the 1970s and were published in translation by MIT Press in the 1980s in a series on Studies in
Contemporary German Social Thought, edited by Thomas McCarthy. Of
the three works, *Work on Myth* is the best known. There have also been not
a few essays and at least one book in English on Blumenberg, but until now
there has been no book in English, or in any language, focused on Blumenberg's theory of myth.

Angus Nicholls's book places Blumenberg's theory within his whole philosophy. Nicholls is enviably familiar with Blumenberg's staggering corpus,
not least the items, many of them unpublished, in Blumenberg's *Nachlass*.
(Blumenberg did not suffer from writer's block.) Nicholls is an intellectual
historian. For him, Blumenberg's views, however original, did not arise *ex
nihilo*. They arose in reaction to what might be called several concentric
circles. Nicholls takes Blumenberg's intellectual roots all the way back to the
eighteenth and nineteenth centuries. He begins with Vico. The many other
figures he considers—most but, like Vico, not all of them German—include
Michaelis, Heyne, Feder, Meiners, Hume, Herder, Kant, Schlegel, Schelling,
Hegel, Max Müller, Nietzsche, Tylor, Frazer, and Dilthey. At least a few of
these figures will likely be unknown to most Anglophone readers—and were
so to me.

Nicholls then turns to twentieth-century thinkers—above all Husserl, Heidegger, Cassirer, Scheler, Plessner, Alsberg, Rothacker, and Gehlen. All of these thinkers were concerned with the broad topic of the nature of human beings and with the only slightly less broad topic of the nature of the humanities vis-à-vis the sciences. Hence the title of Nicholls's book: *Myth and the Human Sciences*.

When Nicholls turns to the tradition inaugurated by Scheler in particular, he introduces a narrower way of categorizing Blumenberg's interests: that of philosophical anthropology, which, as Nicholls makes clear, is philosophy rather than fieldwork anthropology. Alsberg, Plessner, Rothacker, and Gehlen incorporated biological perspectives into philosophical anthropology. Here human beings, not just our forebears but even humans today, are preoccupied with survival in a harsh and indifferent world. Myth becomes a 'survival mechanism'—a view of religion as a whole, not just of myth, also found in the work of some current cognitivists, beginning with Stewart Guthrie's *Faces in the Clouds* (1993). At the same time Blumenberg and those who influenced him rejected the seeming attempt of Darwin, and later of evolutionary psychology, to reduce culture to biology. The biological approach forged most of all by Alsberg firmly distinguishes cultural evolution, which gives human beings the technological power to control the environment considerably, from physical evolution, which animals undergo. Survival of the fittest for humans means survival of the most adroit.

The third and narrowest circle with which Nicholls associates Blumenberg's biography is that of National Socialism, in the throes of which Blumenberg grew up and by which he was persecuted. Nicholls argues that despite Blumenberg's apparent disavowal of politics, his theory of myth offers a critique of National Socialism. Where, notably, Ernst Cassirer turned his approach to myth from a conceptual, philosophical one to an overtly political one, Blumenberg's political approach was not so overt, at least not until much later and, as Nicholls reveals, is to be found mostly in texts that were not published during his lifetime. Yet far from striving to transcend his times, as his philosophizing might be taken to mean, he was positioning himself politically within his times.

Nicholls covers an exceptionally large number of issues. To cite just a single example, he analyzes the centrality for Blumenberg of language, not least of metaphor. Another topic Nicholls considers is the relationship for Blumenberg of myth and science. I myself use this topic as a key way of classifying modern theorists of myth.

In the nineteenth century, if one can generalise, myth was commonly taken to be the 'primitive' counterpart to science, which was assumed to be entirely modern. Myth originated and functioned to do for 'primitive' peoples what science now does for moderns: account for all events in the physical world. One could not consistently hold both kinds of explanations, and moderns, who were *defined* as scientific, were logically obliged to abandon myth. The rise of science spelled the death of myth.

The leading Anglophone exponents of this nineteenth-century view of myth were the pioneering anthropologist E.B. Tylor, whose main work, *Primitive Culture*, was published in 1871, and the classicist and fellow pioneering anthropologist J.G. Frazer, whose key work, *The Golden Bough*, was first published in 1890. For Tylor, myth provides knowledge of the world as an end in itself. For Frazer, the knowledge that myth provides is a means to control over the world, above all for securing food. For both Tylor and Frazer, the events explained or affected by myth are ones in the external world, such as rainfall and death, rather than ones in the social world, such as marriage and war. Myth is the 'primitive' counterpart to natural, not social, science. It is the counterpart to biology, chemistry, and physics rather than to sociology, anthropology, psychology, and economics. For Tylor, myth is the exact counterpart to scientific theory. For Frazer, myth is the exact counterpart to applied science.

Myth, which is part of religion, attributes rain to a decision by a god. Science attributes it to impersonal, meteorological processes. For Tylor and Frazer, the explanations are incompatible because both are direct. In myth, gods operate not behind or through impersonal forces but in place of them. God does not set meteorological processes in motion but instead likely dumps accumulated buckets of water on a designated spot below. Therefore one cannot stack the mythic explanation atop the scientific explanation, crediting science with the direct explanation and crediting myth with the indirect explanation. Rather, one must choose between them. Because moderns by definition have science, the choice has already been made. They must give up myth, which is not merely outdated but false. Moderns who still cling to myth have failed either to recognize or to concede the incompatibility of it with science.

The biggest difficulty for the nineteenth-century view of myth as the primitive counterpart to science was the inability to account for the continued presence of myth. If myth does no more than science, why is it still around? If myth is incompatible with science, how is it still around? Tylor and Frazer would surely reply that whatever remains is not myth, and exactly because it is not serving a scientific-like function. But that reply presupposes, of course, that the function of myth can only be scientific-like.

Twentieth-century theories of myth can be divided into three groups. First are those theories which maintain that myth, while still about the world, is not an explanation of the world, in which case its function diverges from that of science. The true function of myth can range from acceptance of the world to escape from the world. The preeminent theorists here are the anthropologist Bronislaw Malinowski and the historian of religions Mircea Eliade, both of whom still read myth literally. Second are those theories which maintain that myth is not to be read literally, in which case the subject matter of myth is not the physical world. The true subject matter of myth can range from the impact of the physical world on human beings to human beings themselves. The leading theorists here are the New Testament scholar

Rudolf Bultmann, the scholar of Gnosticism Hans Jonas, and the French secular existentialist Albert Camus, interpreter of the myth of Sisyphus. All of them ignore the function of myth and confine themselves to the proper reading of myth. Third and most radical are those theories which maintain both that myth is not an explanation and that myth is not to be read literally. Here fall, above all, Freud and Jung. As much as the two differ from each other, both deem the subject matter of myth to be the human mind and deem the function of myth to be the experience of that mind. Blumenberg includes Malinowski, Jonas, and especially Freud in his analysis of myth.

In my opinion, Blumenberg is very much a twentieth-century theorist of myth, less because he reads myth other than literally and more because he takes the function of myth to be other than scientific. Blumenberg maintains that the survival of myth alongside science proves that myth has *never* served the same function as science. As Nicholls shows, Blumenberg concentrates on what he calls the 'significance,' or function, rather than the origin, by which he means the historical, one-time origin. For Blumenberg, myth serves to alleviate anxiety about the world rather than to explain the world—an argument that rests partly on his definition of explanation as ultimate rather than recurrent origin.

One ramification of the nineteenth-century view of myth as scientific-like is the downplaying of myth as literature. True, both Tylor and Frazer take for granted that a myth is a story. But they deem myth a causal explanation of events in the physical world that merely happens to take the form of a story. Of course, myth may tell the story of how a god becomes responsible for rain and exercises that responsibility. But what counts is the information itself, not the way it is conveyed.

The opposite is true of Blumenberg, for whom myth alleviates anxiety and provides orientation precisely through the telling of stories. The 'significance' of the story depends on the way in which it is told and how it is adapted to the changing needs and concerns of the audience. Blumenberg's theory of myth crosses into the territory of literary theory and, through his detailed readings of Goethe, predominantly German literary history. As a literary scholar and a specialist in Goethe, Nicholls is well qualified to guide the reader through these complex fields.

The prologue to this volume carries the intriguing title 'A Story About the Telling of Stories.' For Tylor and Frazer, myth is an explanation that only incidentally takes the form of a story. For Blumenberg, myth is always a story and therefore not an explanation. The function, or 'work' of myth—that of making humans feel 'at home in the world' rather than explaining the world—requires us to see myth as a story (WOM, 113; AM, 127). On this point, as on so many other points, Nicholls provides the most incisive, the most detailed, and the most pellucid analysis of Blumenberg's theory of myth to date.

Acknowledgements

The majority of this book was researched and written between October 2011 and March 2013, during which time I was Alexander von Humboldt Fellow at the *Deutsches Literaturarchiv* in Marbach am Neckar and at the *Institut für Literaturwissenschaft* at the University of Stuttgart. I would firstly like to thank the Alexander von Humboldt Foundation for having made my research stay in Germany possible. Ulrich von Bülow (DLA Marbach), Philip Ajouri (Stuttgart) and Sandra Richter (Stuttgart) kindly supported my Humboldt application and hosted my research stay in Germany. Benjamin Specht (Stuttgart) taught me a great deal about Blumenberg on metaphor. Dorit Krusche (DLA Marbach) provided me with invaluable advice concerning the Hans Blumenberg *Nachlass*. Most importantly of all, I would like to thank Bettina Blumenberg for allowing me to quote from and paraphrase manuscripts and correspondence in her father's *Nachlass*, and for discussing with me her father's life and works.

I have benefited from conversations and correspondence with many scholars working on Hans Blumenberg and related themes. Felix Heidenreich has been my constant and untiring interlocutor on all things Blumenbergian since October 2011—his deep insights into Blumenberg's works have marked this study indelibly. Robert Savage's extensive knowledge of Blumenberg's works, and especially his research on Blumenberg and Alsberg, have influenced my approach to Blumenberg's theory of myth. Manfred Sommer was an invaluable source of information concerning Blumenberg's early career at the University of Kiel. Rüdiger Zill pointed me to many issues and connections in Blumenberg's works that I would not otherwise have identified, while also providing me with very significant help in interpreting the Blumenberg *Nachlass*. Petra Boden was extremely generous in sharing with me her knowledge concerning the research group on Poetics and Hermeneutics. Pini Ifergan alerted me to important issues concerning Hans Blumenberg and Erich Rothacker. Eva Geulen provided me with insights into Blumenberg's relation to philosophical anthropology. Robert Buch and Daniel Weidner invited me to a very informative conference on Blumenberg at the *Zentrum für Literatur- und Kulturforschung* in Berlin. My fellow Humboldtian in Stuttgart, Lynn Wolff, informed many aspects of this book with her insights into post-war German culture. Jerome Carroll, Paul Fleming, Robert Gillett, Rüdiger Görner, Astrid Köhler, Melissa Schuh and Henning Trüper provided me with helpful comments on the manuscript.

Robert Segal played an instrumental role in helping me to place this study within the Routledge series, *Theorists of Myth*, while also reading the manuscript with great care. At Routledge, I would like to thank Denise File, Margo C. Irvin, Kathleen Laurentiev, Stacy Noto, Laura Stearns and Lauren Verity and for their excellent support. Three anonymous referees thought that this project was worth publishing; whoever they are, I thank them.

I especially wish to thank my colleagues in the Departments of German and Comparative Literature at Queen Mary University of London, for their support, and I thank the College for granting me the research leave that enabled me to write this book. As ever, I thank Soe Tjen Marching for far too many things to mention here.

A. N.
London, October 2014

Prologue
A Story about the Telling of Stories

If, as a prominent contemporary theorist of myth has recently stated, myths are stories that relate something significant about the origin of things, about gods, or about essential features of a culture or a belief system (whether theological or not),[1] then we might claim that a story, also explaining something significant, has repeatedly been told about myth. This appealing narrative of progress has been told from roughly the sixth century BC until the present. Whether this story about myth is itself a myth is perhaps the primary question posed by this study, and by its subject: the philosopher and theorist of myth Hans Blumenberg (1920–96). Blumenberg is also the subject of stories, but before we come to them in Chapter 1 of this volume, let us first consider the basic tale about myth as it has been told and retold over the ages.

Myths, so the old story goes, are inventions of the ancients that are reprehensible in moral terms, since they depict the gods as behaving immorally, and in any case involve fallacious anthropomorphic projections, conceiving of the gods only in human form (Xenophanes 570–470 BC). In this sense myths are mostly unreliable, and one of our main tasks is to establish which elements of them are fantastical and false, and which are true (Hecataeus of Miletus, 550–476 BC). Within the context of the state, these unreliable stories tend to appeal to the irrational parts of the soul, so we should carefully censor them, if not ban them altogether (Plato, 424–348 BC, *Republic* 595b, 605b). And since the ideal and unchanging truths of philosophy exist beyond the transient and corruptible physical world that we inhabit, statements about our physical world should not be accepted at face value and must carefully be tested in order to determine whether they offer a merely probable and therefore unreliable account (*eikos mythos*) or a reliable account (*eikos logos*) of how things stand (Plato, *Timaeus*, 29b–d). Granted, it may be the case that some ancient knowledge is preserved in myths, and we may also enjoy having these myths told to us; in fact, the joy and wonder arising from myths may prepare our minds for philosophical inquiry (Aristotle, 384–322 BC, *Metaphysics*, 1074b, 982b). But while these fables might have passed for knowledge in the old days, they are of little practical use now, in comparison with the truer accounts to be found in philosophy and geography (Strabo, 64 BC–AD 24, *Geography*, 1.19).

The scepticism of the classical philosophers concerning myths can also be found in the Christian tradition, which advises us not to "give heed to fables [*muthois*; i.e., myths] and endless genealogies"; instead we must "refuse profane old wives' fables" and turn to God (1 Timothy, 1:4; 4:7). The New Testament is thus not to be taken as a collection of "cunningly devised fables [*muthois*]" about a man named Jesus Christ; rather it is a true account told by "eyewitnesses of his majesty" (2 Peter, 1:16).[2] Yet when the more radical thinkers of the French Enlightenment, such as Paul Henri Thiry d'Holbach (1723–89) turned against these self-same religious texts and the teachings derived from them, they characterised them as mere developments of the mythologies of ancient Greece and Rome, now designed to secure and reinforce the corrupt powers of the Church.[3] In the earlier stages of the Enlightenment, such myths had already been described, with reference to classical sources as well as to contemporary so-called primitive cultures of the purportedly 'New World,' as "errors of the human spirit" (Bernard le Bovier de Fontenelle, 1657–1757); but in the late Enlightenment they began to be associated with Christianity too.[4]

Yet even if myths are errors of the human spirit that have been superseded by the rationality of the modern age, an educated person still needs to know about them. Or so, at least, runs the argument of the article on "Mythology" in volume 10 of the French *Encyclopaedia* (1765). Mythology, by which is meant "fabled history of the gods, the demigods, and heroes of antiquity," along with "everything connected with pagan religion," is a "confused mixture of the fancies of the imagination, the dreams of philosophy, and the dreams of earliest history." For this reason it is not to be mistaken for history proper, and the more or less arbitrary processes of variation, elaboration and retelling associated with myths mean that the corpus of Western mythology is a "shapeless, disorganised mass, yet pleasing in its particulars." The pleasing element of mythology consists in the fact that it "constitutes the most extensive field in the study of literature," and for this reason the "study of mythology is a necessity for painters, sculptors, and particularly poets." Indeed, it is the "wellspring of their works," from which they draw the ornaments that not only appear in literature, but also adorn palaces, galleries, ceilings and gardens.[5]

Although these various treatments of myth[6]—spanning from the pre-Socratics, via Plato and Aristotle, to the New Testament and finally the Enlightenment—do not make exactly the same arguments, they nevertheless concur in one essential claim: myth is a stage in human cultural development that is primitive, misleading and often fallacious, and should therefore be left behind if one is to achieve philosophical rationality, to acquire the correct (usually monotheistic) religious beliefs, or to attain the practical advantages of scientific modernity. Myths may indeed be beguiling and even beautiful, but ultimately they are backward and therefore need to be discarded by humanity as objects of conviction, just as a child emerges from the immature habits of its infancy. This claim—that myth belongs to an earlier phase in culture that can completely be surmounted—is directly challenged by Hans Blumenberg in *Work on Myth* (*Arbeit am Mythos*, 1979).

The stories that have been told about myth are deeply related to the question of the essence or function of the human being. If, for example, the function of the human being is to exercise the rational faculties in pursuit of the good (Aristotle, *Nichomachean Ethics*, I.13), then overcoming the initial wonders of myth is an expression of this function. "What is the human being?" (*Was ist der Mensch?*) is also the final question that Immanuel Kant includes, in his *Logic* (1800, see A25), alongside his other three key questions: "What can I know? What should I do? What may I hope for?" Kant suggestively claims that these first three questions—which define the disciplines of metaphysics, ethics, and religion, respectively—all relate to the final anthropological question of what it is to be human.[7] And his implicit answer to this question is already to be found in his *Anthropology from a Pragmatic Point of View* (*Anthropologie in pragmatischer Hinsicht*, 1798): the human being is determined by a series of physiological inclinations (the needs for food, shelter, and sex), which we should come to understand so that they can be surmounted through the pragmatic exercise of reason in ethics.

Many twentieth-century German thinkers were dissatisfied both with Kant's framing of the question concerning the human being and with his answer to it. In his essay "On the Idea of Man" ("Zur Idee des Menschen," 1914), Max Scheler pointedly answers and does not answer Kant's question by claiming that the essence of humans lies precisely in their indefinability. Paul Alsberg, in his *Puzzle of Humanity* (*Das Menschheitsrätsel*, 1922), claims that our pre-human ancestors first became human when they began to use stone projectiles as a means of self-defence—a form of mediation through distance that presaged later technologies, along with language and conceptual thought. According to Helmuth Plessner's account in *The Stages of the Organic and Man* (*Die Stufen des Organischen und der Mensch*, 1929), to be human means to be 'eccentric' in the sense of being only weakly pre-determined by instincts and therefore open to making artificial and self-reflexive adaptations. In *Kant and the Problem of Metaphysics* (*Kant und das Problem der Metaphysik*, 1929), Martin Heidegger suggests that Kant's fourth and final question merely diverts us from the task of outlining a fundamental ontology, a task that Heidegger had attempted two years earlier in *Being and Time* (*Sein und Zeit*, 1927). Ernst Cassirer offers a revised version of Aristotle's answer by stating, in his *Philosophy of Symbolic Forms* (*Philosophie der symbolischen Formen*, 3 vols., 1923–9) and in his *Essay on Man* (1944), that the human being is not simply a rational animal, but also a symbol-producing animal. Arnold Gehlen, in *Man: His Nature and Place in the World* (*Der Mensch: Seine Natur und seine Stellung in der Welt*, 1940), proposes that the human being is a 'creature of deficiencies' (*Mängelwesen*), and compensates for its lack of biological adaptations through the development of technology, culture, and institutions. While Erich Rothacker argues, in his *Problems of Cultural Anthropology* (*Probleme der Kulturanthropologie*, 1942), that insofar as humans actively create and respond to their own cultural as opposed to natural environments, they must be understood as cultural beings (*Kulturwesen*).

Hans Blumenberg's story about the human being takes over elements of those told by Scheler, Alsberg, Plessner, Heidegger, Cassirer, Gehlen, and Rothacker. But perhaps his most direct response to Kant's anthropological question can be found in the posthumously published text *Description of Man* (*Beschreibung des Menschen*, 2006): "the human being is the discounted popular version of reason" (BDM, 501). This response, which implies that in practice reason is always less than it theoretically pretends to be, also tells us something about Blumenberg's attitude to myth: myths are attempts to deal with pressing questions that arise from the very nature of the human situation. The function of these myths is not to answer these questions directly and theoretically in the manner of science, but to tell stories which respond to the questions by assuaging the need for them to be asked in the first place: "myth does not need to answer questions; it makes something up, before the question becomes acute and so that it does not become acute" (WOM, 197; AM, 219). And even if some of the old reassurances provided by myth may be left behind in the name of scientific rationality, it may still be the case that the original questions to which myth responds do not go away, but are simply 'reoccupied' (*umbesetzt*, see LMA, 65; LDN, 75). As Blumenberg states in *Work on Myth*: "theory sees in myth an ensemble of answers to questions, such as it is itself, or wants to be. That forces it, while rejecting the answers, to acknowledge the questions" (WOM, 27; AM, 34).

Like many of the original questions addressed by myth, the question "What is the human being?" has also not gone away. If Kant's fourth question has proven so difficult to answer in a satisfying way, what does this tell us about the human sciences? The human sciences are faced with an irreducible problem because human nature is not an empirical thing. This is the argument with which Roger Smith begins a recent study on the history of the human sciences.[8] Smith's opening gamut is not an exercise in mystification. Human 'nature' is not a stable empirical object precisely because human beings are *both* biological *and* cultural beings that have continually to decide—from within the limitations of their own historical and cultural standpoints—what it means to be human. And it is precisely here where the difficulties begin. When I attempt to understand other human beings, I must necessarily do so on the basis of my own self-understanding. Yet because my consciousness is conditioned by a history and by a culture that can never be completely external objects for me, precisely because I am *in* them, I can never achieve full self-transparency when it comes to understanding myself and my relation to other human beings. Writing in the early 1970s, in a late contribution to the German tradition of philosophical anthropology, Hans Blumenberg described this epistemological situation as follows:

> Man has no immediate, no purely 'internal' relation to himself. His self-understanding has the structure of 'self-externality.' Kant was the first to deny that inner experience has any precedence over outer experience; we are appearance to ourselves, the secondary synthesis of a primary multiplicity, not the reverse. The substantialism of identity is destroyed; identity must be realized, it becomes a kind of accomplishment, and accordingly there is a pathology of identity. What remains as the subject matter of anthropology is a 'human nature' that has never been 'nature' and never will be.
>
> (AAR, 456; WWL, 134)

One possible way around this problem described by Blumenberg is precisely to *objectify* the human being by way of what Smith critically refers to as biological reduction.[9] According to this view, the human being would be nothing more than an organism that has evolved through natural selection, and whose thinking and cultures might be reduced to the biological sciences of the brain. Such a view would also claim that Darwin did away with the central problem of the human sciences, that of values or teleology, which had seen humans defining themselves according to a range of divine and human purposes that could not be measured by the methods of the natural sciences, and which were therefore unscientific. Blumenberg's most sustained attempts to confront some of these fundamental questions of the human sciences were written during the early and middle stages of the 1970s, prior to *Work on Myth*, and are brought together by Manfred Sommer in the second part of *Description of Man*. The outcome of this confrontation is to be found in *Work on Myth*, and it is at once problematic and compelling. Blumenberg's theory of myth is based upon a speculative account of anthropogenesis, and amounts to a quasi-Darwinian theory of culture that arises from a critique of Darwin. It is a theory of myth that is inseparable from Blumenberg's answer, which is a hypothetical and therefore less than final answer, to Kant's fourth question, which is *the* fundamental question of the human sciences.

NOTES

1. Robert Segal, *Myth: A Very Short Introduction* (Oxford: Oxford University Press, 2004), 4–5.
2. *The Bible, Authorized King James Version with Apocrypha*, introd. Robert Carroll and Stephen Prickett (Oxford: Oxford University Press, 1988), 258, 260, 290.

3. Paul Henri Baron d'Holbach, *Système de la Nature* (London, 1770), Part II, Chapter 2 "De la mythologie et de la théologie"; see also the section on Holbach in *The Rise of Modern Mythology*, ed. Burton Feldman and Robert D. Richardson, Jr. (Bloomington: University of Indiana Press, 1972), 177–84.

4. Bernard le Bovier de Fontenelle, *De l' origine des fables*, ed. J.R. Carré (1724; Paris: Alcan, 1942), 32, 40.

5. Louis de Jaucourt, "Mythology," in *The Encyclopedia of Diderot & d'Alembert Collaborative Translation Project*, trans. Nelly S. Hoyt and Thomas Cassirer (Ann Arbor: MPublishing, University of Michigan Library, 2003), http://hdl.handle.net/2027/spo.did2222.0000.162 (accessed February 14, 2012). Originally published as "Mythologie," in *Encyclopédie ou Dictionnaire raisonné des sciences, des arts et des metiers*, vol. 10 (Paris, 1765), 924–7.

6. For a comprehensive account of the history of the concept of myth in Western thought, see the following two articles by Axel Horstmann: "Mythos, Mythologie," in *Historisches Wörterbuch der Philosophie*, 13 vols., ed. Joachim Ritter et al. (Basel: Schwabe, 1971–2007), 6:218–318; "Der Mythosbegriff vom frühen Christentum bis zur Gegenwart," *Archiv für Begriffsgeschichte* 23, no. 1 (1979): 7–54, 197–245. The brief overview provided above is in part based upon Horstmann's analysis.

7. Immanuel Kant, *Logik*, in *Werke in sechs Bänden*, ed. Wilhelm Weischedel, 7th ed., 6 vols. (Darmstadt: Wissenschaftliche Buchgesellschaft, 2011), 3:447–8.

8. Roger Smith, *Being Human: Historical Knowledge and the Creation of Human Nature* (New York: Columbia University Press, 2007), 1.

9. Smith, *Being Human*, 6. For a further discussion of this notion of biological reduction, see Julian Nida-Rümelin, "Naturalismus und Humanismus," in *Evolution in Natur und Kultur*, ed. Volker Gerhardt and Julian Nida-Rümelin (Berlin: De Gruyter, 2010), 4–14; here: 5, 9.

1 Hans Blumenberg
An Introduction

Hans Blumenberg was an interpreter of literary fiction—which Plato referred to as myths—who was at the same time a professional philosopher. The agonistic struggle between literature and philosophy announced in Plato's attack on the myth-makers in Book Ten of the *Republic* is a theme to which Blumenberg implicitly devoted his attention from the very beginning of his career, most explicitly in *Paradigms for a Metaphorology* (*Paradigmen zu einer Metaphorologie*, 1960), in which the so-called literary device of metaphor is seen as conditioning the existence of philosophical concepts. Blumenberg's interpretations of 'Goethe' in Part IV of *Work on Myth*, which in their sheer audacity make this most culturally over-burdened of German authors once more fresh and exciting, show his keen awareness of the fact that the stories which an author writes may become intertwined with the stories about his or her life. 'Goethe' means not just the real historical person named Johann Wolfgang Goethe who lived from 1749–1832, but also the biographical anecdotes, conversations, and legends, many of which are neither completely true or false, which accompany and to some extent even define the works. "Is there another life that we have ever seen spread out before us in such multifarious relation to reality and illusion?" asks Blumenberg in *Work on Myth* (WOM, 399–400; AM, 435). And his subsequent analysis shows that the distinction between Goethe and 'Goethe,' between reality and its semi-fictional reconstruction, is not altogether an easy one to make.

In a moment of ironic and not-so-private megalomania, Hans Blumenberg once fantasised about the day upon which a telegram would arrive at his house, informing him that half of humanity had read one of his books. His imagined response: "What are the other half doing?"[1] Blumenberg would surely not have compared himself with Goethe, but his ambitions, like his longer books, were not modest. Would the educated reading public have been likely to read, say, a tome of 827 pages devoted to the cave metaphor in Western thought? This is the challenge laid down by *Cave Exits* (*Höhlenausgänge*, 1989), the last of Blumenberg's long studies. The other massive works by Blumenberg—*The Legitimacy of the Modern Age* (*Die*

Legitimität der Neuzeit 1966/1974), *The Genesis of the Copernican World* (*Die Genesis der kopernikanischen Welt*, 1975), *Work on Myth* (*Arbeit am Mythos*, 1979), and *The Legibility of the World* (*Die Lesbarkeit der Welt*, 1981), *Lifetime and World-Time* (*Lebenszeit und Weltzeit*, 1986)—are equally daunting in their erudition and their tendency towards anecdote and digression.

A good deal of this might be put down to Blumenberg's working methods, probably in use since the 1940s, which consisted of transcribing quotations from primary sources onto index-cards, titled according to the various projects upon which he was working simultaneously at any given time. Some index cards also have cut-out passages from newspaper or journal articles pasted onto them, or are accompanied by related images from magazines. These index cards would then thematically be assembled and worked through during the phase of writing, before being marked with a red pen as *erledigt*, or 'used.' At least since the 1960s, Blumenberg's writing process consisted of speaking—both with the assistance of his index cards and also freely—into a tape recorder or Dictaphone, the transcript of which would later be typed up by his secretary, before finally being edited by hand by Blumenberg himself. In terms of method, Blumenberg was a 'materialist,' not in the philosophical sense of being focused on the physical world, but in the sense that his arguments seem to have been built from the ground up, based on his astonishingly wide reading of primary sources from all periods of Western culture. This pile of material now lies in the bunkers of the German Literary Archive (*Deutsches Literaturarchiv*) in Marbach am Neckar, the home of Blumenberg's *Nachlass* (papers and manuscript remains), in which circa 30,000 index cards can be found.[2]

As one of Blumenberg's closest interlocutors—Henning Ritter (1943–2013),[3] former editor of the humanities pages of the *Frankfurter Allgemeine Zeitung*—recently observed, all of this has become the stuff of legend, even of literary fiction. In an article that describes Blumenberg as "the great unknown of German philosophy," Ritter reflects on the ways in which the anthropological insights of Blumenberg's published works have been applied to his life. Such as when Blumenberg's study at his home in Altenberge, near Münster—to which he increasingly retreated during the latter stages of his career, and where he would work through his index cards at night "like Marcel Proust, insulated from the external world"[4]—is compared by Odo Marquard to the cave, described in *Cave Exits* as the sanctum of culture in which prehistoric humans sought refuge from the dangers of the open savannah. Blumenberg's night-owl tendencies even extended, according to Marquard, to only sleeping six nights per week in order to make up for the lost years of National Socialism, during which university study was forbidden to him. And Marquard relates this habit to the central phenomenological theme of Blumenberg's *Lifetime and World-Time*: that once we take departure from the certainties and routines of everyday pre-theoretical existence as embodied in Edmund Husserl's concept of the life-world, we become increasingly aware of the vast expanse of world-time and of the brevity of our lives in comparison to it.[5]

Further parallels between Blumenberg's philosophical anthropology and his biography have been noted. Such as when Henning Ritter interprets Blumenberg's desire not to be photographed (only two public photos of him exist) in relation to the theme of seeing and being seen, characterised by Blumenberg in *Description of Man* as the central anthropological factor in the development of our distant ancestors when they moved onto the open savannah as their forested habitat shrank (BDM, 777). Or the alacrity with which Blumenberg, the defender of the achievements of scientific modernity in *The Legitimacy of the Modern Age*, used the technology of the Dictaphone in order to compose his works, for it is technology and more broadly culture—again distantly embodied in the first stone purportedly thrown by our pre-human ancestor to defend himself, a primordial scene of self-assertion that is also restaged in *Description of Man*—that for Blumenberg make us human. It is not coincidental, then, that the novel loosely based on Blumenberg and an entirely fictional circle of his students in Münster, Sibylle Lewitscharoff's *Blumenberg* (2011), makes much of Blumenberg's legendary nightshifts, and begins with the following sentence: "Blumenberg had just taken hold of a new cassette, in order to place it into the Dictaphone."[6]

Thus, the irony of Henning Ritter's feature article on Blumenberg (which is accompanied by a large photograph of the man), is that Blumenberg is now anything but unknown: today he counts among the most renowned philosophers in Germany, is the subject of a critically acclaimed novel, and features regularly in German newspapers. It seems that Blumenberg's late retreat from public life, a less extreme version of that undertaken by Thomas Pynchon or J.D. Salinger in the United States, has even added something to his allure. Yet outside of Germany and especially in the Anglophone world, his profile does not begin to approach that of his immediate forbears and contemporaries like Theodor W. Adorno, Hans-Georg Gadamer or Jürgen Habermas.

Research on Hans Blumenberg remains in its infancy in both the German-speaking and the Anglophone worlds. In recent years, a series of German-language monographs have outlined Blumenberg's position within the history of German philosophy—some of them provide an overview at an introductory level,[7] while others go into much greater philosophical depth.[8] Important edited volumes have also examined Blumenberg's writings and intellectual legacy in general,[9] as well as particular themes in his work such as those of philosophical anthropology[10] and the theory of metaphor.[11] Other studies have focused upon Blumenberg's importance for theological discourses.[12] There is only one existing monograph on Blumenberg in English: Elizabeth Brient's *The Immanence of the Infinite*, which focuses primarily on the theological dimensions of Blumenberg's theory of modernity as outlined in the *Legitimacy of the Modern Age*.[13] No comprehensive introduction to Blumenberg's works exists in English, with the closest approximations being Robert M. Wallace's highly informative introductions to his monumental translations of three key works by Blumenberg.[14] A further general introductory essay by Wallace (concentrating primarily on *Work on Myth*), as well as four special issues of Anglophone journals, may provide the Anglophone reader with some general orientation.[15]

A major recent development in Blumenberg research has been the acquisition of his *Nachlass* by the German Literary Archive in Marbach am Neckar, which has led to a number of important book publications based on *Nachlass* materials. While a general introduction to all of Blumenberg's works is far beyond the scope and primary focus of the present study, Chapters 1 and 7 endeavour to offer an overview of important institutional and political aspects of his life and academic career. Blumenberg poses a particular problem for a purely theoretical or philosophical approach to intellectual history. This is because his early life coincided with and was indelibly marked by the years of National Socialism (1933–45), as well as by the subsequent post-war efforts to deal with that period both institutionally and philosophically. There is no sense in which Blumenberg's thought in general, and his theory of myth in particular, can be reduced to purely historical or biographical readings. But at the same time, Blumenberg's thought and especially his theory of myth cannot be separated from this historical context, especially since myth is one of the most politically loaded notions in modern German thought. Blumenberg scholarship has until now by and large neglected to historicise Blumenberg's works in both institutional and political terms, and the image of 'Blumenberg' as the withdrawn and reticent scholar depicted by Henning Ritter, Odo Marquard, and Sibylle Lewitscharoff might suggest that philosophy or theory can take place in the hermetic confines of one's study, unaffected by history and institutional politics.

This, indeed, may at times have even been Blumenberg's wish. Writing to his friend Hans Jonas in 1955 in an attempt to convince Jonas to return to Germany, Blumenberg remarked that it is "easier to be finished with the past here than abroad," referring to the "successful overcoming of the ideological residuum" of National Socialism.[16] As both Chapter 7 and Chapter 8 of this volume will demonstrate, it is doubtful in the extreme whether this 'residuum' had in any way been 'overcome' in Germany by 1955. Indeed, in *Work on Myth* and elsewhere, Blumenberg often takes up positions in relation to political debates marked by the legacy of National Socialism without necessarily always naming or citing his interlocutors. This is the case with respect to his near contemporaries in the tradition of German philosophical anthropology—especially Erich Rothacker and Arnold Gehlen—as well as with regard to thinkers associated with the Frankfurt School, such as Theodor Adorno and Jürgen Habermas, not to mention those who are very explicitly associated with the politics of National Socialism, such as Carl Schmitt. Our task will therefore be to investigate the philosophical networks and debates within which Blumenberg's writing on myth is situated, which means that Blumenberg's historical context is of the utmost importance.

What experiences did Blumenberg undergo during the period of National Socialism? What were the institutional circumstances of Blumenberg's early research career? What are the key aspects of Blumenberg's theory of myth? Do they continue to deserve serious consideration today, and if so, why? And how might Anglophone readers approach this most eminently German of writers and thinkers? These are some of the questions to be addressed in this opening chapter.

ONE LIFE, ONE IDENTITY?

Hans Josef Konrad Blumenberg was born in 1920 in the Hanseatic city of Lübeck, near Hamburg, most famously known as the hometown of Thomas Mann. Blumenberg attended the same school as Thomas Mann, the prestigious Katharineum *Gymnasium*, from which he graduated as dux (*Klassenprimus*) in 1939. Upon graduating, Blumenberg decided against addressing his classmates during the final graduation ceremony—an honour normally afforded to the top-ranked student of the year—for fear of not being allowed to do so. This fear, which is to be seen in the context of the Nuremberg racial laws passed by the National Socialist regime in 1935, emerged from Blumenberg's awareness of his mother's Jewish ancestry. Accordingly Blumenberg's speech was, at his request, read out by one of his classmates.[17] Blumenberg's father, Josef Carl Blumenberg, who was born in 1880 and baptised as a Catholic,[18] worked as a successful art-publisher (*Kunstverleger*) in Lübeck. In 1919 Josef Carl married Else Schreier, who was born of German Jewish parents in 1882, and who later converted to Protestantism.

On Blumenberg's high-school leaving certificate he expresses the intention to study Catholic theology.[19] Blumenberg was baptised as a Catholic, but his choice of further study may also have been determined as much by political circumstances as by choice. Since university study had been forbidden to him under the Nazi regime, Blumenberg's best chance of gaining a philosophical education was provided by the Catholic philosophical-theological colleges that he attended, first in Paderborn (from the summer semester of 1939 until the winter semester 1939–40) and subsequently in Frankfurt am Main (from the winter semester 1939–40 until the summer semester of 1940). Yet due to the extreme anti-Semitic political climate of the time, even these institutions also eventually denied him the opportunity to further his education.[20]

After returning to Lübeck to assist with his father's art-publishing business located at the family home, which he had helped to rebuild following the Allied bombing of the city on Palm Sunday of 1942, Blumenberg's situation became increasingly difficult. The National Socialist regime firstly assigned him as a compulsory worker to the aeroplane manufacturer Dornier in Lübeck. From April 1943, Blumenberg was employed as a purchasing officer by Drägerwerk AG,[21] a large-scale producer of gasmasks and other medical products that still exists to this day and that was of extreme importance to the German war effort. It was owing to this employment, and to the efforts of the prominent industrialist Dr. Heinrich Dräger (Director of the Drägerwerk), that Blumenberg was able to avoid being sent to a concentration camp. Dräger's ability to protect valued workers, such as Blumenberg, can in part be attributed to his willingness strategically to collaborate with the National Socialist regime. Dräger joined the NSDAP in 1933, while also eventually allowing the forced employment of over five hundred female political prisoners at a Drägerwerk production facility in Hamburg-Wandsbek. Dräger was initially categorised as a 'follower' or *Mitläufer* in two denazification hearings held at Plön and Lübeck during 1947, before being 'exonerated' in 1948.[22]

But even Heinrich Dräger was only able to protect Blumenberg until February 1945, when Blumenberg was sent to a National Socialist work camp at Zerbst in Saxony-Anhalt. At Zerbst, according to the account that Blumenberg provided to his local authorities near Hamburg in 1946, he experienced the brutality of the National Socialist regime: fourteen-hour workdays, completely insufficient nutrition, surveillance with dogs, terribly cramped sleeping quarters, and arbitrary punishments carried out in the open air during winter.[23] It was apparently Dräger's intervention that enabled Blumenberg and other former employees of the *Drägerwerk* to be released from Zerbst,[24] and for the remaining months of the war Blumenberg was hidden in the Lübeck family home of his future wife, Ursula.[25] In a text published from the *Nachlass*, Blumenberg appears to suggest that his wife's father, the man who agreed to hide him and who may therefore have saved his life, was a National Socialist *Blockwart* or *Blockleiter*: a party member designated to undertake surveillance of a particular neighbourhood.[26] Thus, as in the case with respect to Dräger, it seems to have been the assistance of an NSDAP member that enabled Blumenberg to survive the final months of the war. One of Blumenberg's only direct reflections on these experiences can be found in a letter that he wrote to Heinrich Dräger on 8 December 1945:

> You have taken me, as the so-called half-Jew, deprived of all rights and reputation, excluded from the continuation of university study, to whom every development of his capabilities has been refused [. . .] into your factory, even though only difficulties and disadvantages for your firm could be expected to follow from this, on account of the ever more radical surveillance of the party.[27]

According to Hans Blumenberg's daughter, Bettina, Heinrich Dräger also gave 6,000 *Reichsmarks* to Blumenberg immediately following the war, which then enabled Blumenberg to finance the writing of his doctoral dissertation.[28]

Despite this litany of injustices, humiliations and terrors, there seems never to have been any question of Blumenberg leaving Germany. And what followed was a sparkling academic career in the new Federal Republic, beginning with a dissertation on medieval scholastic philosophy in Kiel and followed by a *Habilitation* on the phenomenology of Edmund Husserl,[29] which initially led to an extraordinary Professorship in Hamburg (1958–60), and then to full Professorial appointments in Gießen (1960–5), Bochum (1965–70), and finally Münster (1970–85). Unlike other fellow German philosophers with Jewish backgrounds who had survived the war and who went on to careers in post-war Germany—here one thinks in particular of Max Horkheimer (1895–1973), Karl Löwith (1897–1973), and Theodor Adorno (1903–69)—Blumenberg never undertook an explicit and extended examination of National Socialism and the Holocaust in his published works.[30] One difference between Blumenberg and these thinkers is that while Horkheimer, Löwith and Adorno were able to leave Germany during the period of National Socialism, Blumenberg stayed behind.

Obliquely addressing the post-war German process of coming to terms with history (incorporated in the term *Vergangenheitsbewältigung*), Blumenberg once wrote:

> Every human has only *one* life, and it is for this reason that he resists the impertinence of the 'coming to terms with the past' [*Bewältigung der Vergangenheit*] that is demanded of him. The politically unified crowd of people, of which this coming to terms is more rightfully demanded, may only have one life, but this does not stand for a *single* identity. Hence, in history this identity is searched for without avail.[31]

This passage and others like them to be found in the *Nachlass* collection *A Possible Self-Understanding* (*Ein mögliches Selbstverständnis*, 1997) remain abstract and therefore resistant to strictly autobiographical interpretations. The "politically unified crowd" is not necessarily the German people, and the individual who resists coming to terms with the past is not necessarily a German, or, for that matter, Hans Blumenberg. If one *were* to hazard an autobiographical reading of this passage, then it would suggest that for Blumenberg, the legacy of National Socialism was, rather understandably, characterised by an extreme ambivalence and complexity. Coming to terms with the past, such a reading would suggest, *is* an important political task for the German people. But since the 'the German people'—a people that includes Hans Blumenberg and many others like him—does not amount to a single identity, this coming to terms will always be deeply problematic. This is precisely because the supposedly homogenous post-war 'German people' were made up of both perpetrators and victims of National Socialism as well as of endless finer gradations between those two categories.

THE HISTORY OF CONCEPTS, POETICS AND HERMENEUTICS

One of the main philosophical contexts for Blumenberg's early career is to be found in a project on the History of Concepts (*Begriffsgeschichte*), which was the original brainchild of Erich Rothacker and which was later funded by the German Research Foundation (*Deutsche Forschungsgemeinschaft*) under the leadership of Hans-Georg Gadamer. Rothacker had founded the journal *Archive for the History of Concepts* (*Archiv für Begriffsgeschichte*) in 1955 as a means of researching key concepts in the history of philosophy. The editorship of the journal was later taken over by Gadamer, who also successfully applied for funding from the German Research Foundation to stage a series of conferences in which such key concepts would be investigated. Blumenberg was an original member of the resulting Senate Commission for the History of Concepts (*Senatskommission für Begriffsgeschichte*) and gave a legendary two-hour lecture at its first conference in 1958, which was later summarised by Blumenberg under the title of "Theses Towards a Metaphorology" ("Thesen zu einer Metaphorologie").[32] According to Margarita Kranz, this was the only lecture staged at any of the seven conferences of the *Senatskommission* between 1958 and 1966 programmatically to address the history of concepts,[33] and it did so controversially insofar as it suggested that absolute metaphors (to be explained in Chapter 5 of this volume) may precede and underlie concepts in the process of philosophical theory formation, being an "insuperable basic inventory (*Grundbestand*) of philosophical language."[34] This 'metaphorological' approach to the history of concepts did not go on to establish itself in the later meetings of *Senatskommission*, although the publication that emerged from this lecture— *Paradigms for a Metaphorology*—was published by Rothacker in the *Archiv für Begriffsgeschichte* in 1960 and has become (not least on account of its brevity) one of Blumenberg's most widely-read works.[35]

As a result of the German Research Foundation's dissatisfaction with Gadamer's leadership of the project, the *Senatskommission* was discontinued in 1966. Blumenberg had also been unhappy with the organisation of the *Senatskommission*, complaining to the German Research Foundation that after the first conference in 1958 he was the only person punctually to have provided a condensed version of his lecture for circulation among participants. It is probably for this reason that Blumenberg ceased attending the meetings of the *Senatskommission* after its third meeting in 1962 and then officially resigned from the group in 1965.[36] But Rothacker's original vision of *Begriffsgeschichte* was later realised in the thirteen volumes of the *Historical Lexicon of Philosophy* (*Historisches Wörterbuch der Philosophie*, 1971– 2007),[37] which offers the most comprehensive history of key philosophical concepts in German, and perhaps even in any language, and which was initially edited by Joachim Ritter (1903–74), whom Blumenberg would go on to succeed as Professor of Philosophy at the University of Münster in 1970.

The *Senatskommission* is now seen as one of the first attempts undertaken in the new Federal Republic to create a large interdisciplinary research project in the humanities. Its apparent problems and failures must have been fresh in Blumenberg's mind when he took up a Professorship at the University of Gießen in 1960 and later decided to found another research group with his new colleagues there: the Romanist Hans Robert Jauss (1921–97) and the Germanist Clemens Heselhaus (1912–2000). Jauss traces their first discussion concerning the research group Poetics and Hermeneutics (*Poetik und Hermeneutik*) to the platform of a church-tower in Upper Hessen, during a faculty excursion in 1961.[38] The outcome of this initial conversation would go on to serve as a model for interdisciplinary research collaborations in the new Federal Republic, involving such key figures as the journalist and sociologist Siegfried Kracauer (1889–1966), the historian Reinhart Koselleck (1923–2006), the Professor of English Wolfgang Iser (1926–2007), the philosopher Dieter Henrich (1927–), the philosopher of religion Jacob Taubes (1923–87), and the renowned comparatist Peter Szondi (1929–71). The two most prominent literary scholars in the group—Iser and Jauss—had studied hermeneutics with Gadamer in Heidelberg and are now associated with the so-called Constance School of Reception Theory in literary studies. Even though Odo Marquard (who himself joined Poetics und Hermeneutics in 1965) has described Blumenberg as having been the most dominant philosopher in the group, Blumenberg stopped attending its meetings in 1974,[39] and is said to have even suggested that the group cease holding conferences altogether and function by correspondence alone.[40]

When Blumenberg is considered as a theorist of both metaphor and of myth, it is important to recognise that his early ideas on both subjects were developed in the interdisciplinary group situations of the *Senatskommission* and the research group on Poetics und Hermeneutics. In the latter case, Blumenberg's essay "The Concept of Reality and the Effective Potential of Myth" ("Wirklichkeitsbegriff und Wirkungspotential des Mythos," see WWM) was delivered at a Poetics und Hermeneutics meeting held in the politically charged year of 1968. And as Marquard himself has pointed out, the image of Blumenberg working in splendid isolation and recording his books onto a Dictaphone in his study-cave in Altenberg—now popularised by Sibylle Lewitscharoff's novel—offers a rather one-sided portrait of an academic career which, at least in its early phases, saw Blumenberg being at the very centre of new developments in the humanities in the young Federal Republic.[41] Alongside his activities in the *Senatskommission* and in the research group on *Poetik und Hermeneutik*, Blumenberg was a member of the Mainz Academy of the Science and Literature (*Mainzer Akademie der Wissenschaften und der Literatur*), served in the Senate of the German Research Foundation, and also belonged to the commission formed in 1965 by the sociologist Helmut Schelsky (1912–84) that led to the founding of the University of Bielefeld.[42] At least partly due to the mediating efforts of Jacob Taubes,[43] Blumenberg became one of the most prominent philosophers published—alongside names such as Adorno, Benjamin, and Habermas—by Suhrkamp Verlag, arguably the most influential academic publishing house in the *Bundesrepublik*. In Taubes's opinion, expressed in a letter written to the president of the *Freie Universität* in Berlin in 1977, Blumenberg was the most important philosopher then teaching in Germany.[44]

BLUMENBERG ON MYTH, PROVISIONALLY SPEAKING

In *Work on Myth*, Hans Blumenberg outlines a philosophical anthropology—to be explained and contextualised in Chapter 4 of this volume—that consists in reading the history of Western thought as a story of human self-assertion against what he calls 'the absolutism of reality.' In its earliest form, this absolutism corresponds with the notion that our pre-human ancestors may have lacked sufficient physical and instinctual adaptations that would have enabled them to deal effectively with changes in their habitat. Without the automatism of such crucial adaptations, these pre-humans were purportedly at a complete loss: they simply did not know what to do and were overwhelmed by anxiety. This hypothesis concerning the human being as a 'creature of deficiencies' (*Mängelwesen*) is taken over by Blumenberg not only from the prominent philosophical anthropologist Arnold Gehlen, but also from lesser-known figures in the tradition of German philosophical anthropology such as Paul Alsberg, a debt that is outlined by Blumenberg in *Description of Man*. This image of the human being is also deeply embedded in Western philosophy prior to the twentieth century, and earlier versions of it can be found in Herder (see Chapter 2 of this volume) and even in Plato's *Protagoras* (see Chapter 5). As we shall see in Chapter 4, Blumenberg arguably tones down this *Mängelwesen* hypothesis by using it only *functionally* rather than *ontologically*, suggesting that while it may not be empirically provable, it may at the same time be philosophically effective in explaining the origins of culture.

The key moment in Blumenberg's openly speculative account of primeval human beings arises when they had to face their predators on the open savannah. The question asked of these pre-humans on this historical occasion of occasions was 'How will you survive, despite your weakness?' The answer was: 'through culture.' Culture, primordially symbolised by the first stone weapon hurled by this maladapted weakling at his aggressor (BDM, 575), is to be understood as an "emergency program to compensate for deficiencies in biological equipment" (BDM, 552). Culture emerges from reflection and from reason, and reason, too, was in its earliest form nothing more than a compensatory "makeshift remedy" (*Notbehelf*) that enabled primordial humans to survive their perilous situation (BDM, 490). Here the implication is that if our pre-human ancestor had not resorted to culture as a means of self-preservation, then human beings may not have come to be at all, since for Blumenberg the human being is the "*being that could have failed and can still fail*" (BDM, 524, emphasis in the original). Neverthe-less, once this compensatory mode of behaviour demonstrated its selective advantages and took root in human behaviour, cultural development was set upon its historical path, and eventually no longer served the purposes of survival alone. In this way, "what initially was successful only as compensa-tion" developed into "the most sublime of cultural achievements" (BDM, 490).

The reworking of myths through being told and retold is one such cul-tural achievement. Myths may have initially helped the 'creatures of defi-ciency' to cope with their paralysing fears, before going on to entertain them through the long, dark nights. When confronted, for example, with the terrors of thunder and lightning, the human being's telling of stories endowed these natural phenomena with fictive explanations that rendered them familiar and approachable: "panic and paralysis," defined by Blumen-berg as the "two extremes of anxiety behaviour," were thereby "dissolved by the appearance of calculable magnitudes to deal with and regulated ways of dealing with them" (WOM, 6; AM, 12). Even if these magnitudes were fictive, they were also psychologically effective, allowing questions about existence to be forestalled and even 'answered' in what were evidently pro-visional but therapeutic ways.

Questions asked of humans and answered by them form the core of Blu-menberg's account of intellectual history, not only in *Work on Myth* but also in the *Legitimacy of the Modern Age*. There the 'absolutism of reality' finds a new cultural guise in the theological absolutism of the late medieval period, which was "not concerned with the reality of the world and its significance for human consciousness but with preserving the full range of God's pos-sibilities" (LMA, 159; LDN, 178). This meant conceiving of a completely unrestricted God who had created the world and who could therefore also destroy the world at any given moment for no apparent reason. This created a situation in which humans were omitted "entirely from the determination of the world's meaning" and in which "the world no longer possessed an accessible order" (LMA, 171; LDN, 194). To use a term on which Blumen-berg wrote an entry for a prominent theological lexicon published in 1959, such a situation was one of *contingence* (*Kontingenz*): "one of the few con-cepts of specifically Christian descent in the history of metaphysics."[45] A contingent world would be a world that, according to the dictates of God, *could or could not be* at any given moment, just as the pre-human being either could or could not have survived the primordial occasion of anthro-pogenesis sketched above.[46] In the face of the radical theological contingency of the late medieval period, humans had two choices: either to continue praying to an apparently hidden and arbitrary God in the hope of salvation, or to undertake what Blumenberg calls "immanent self-assertion" (*imman-ente Selbstbehauptung*, LMA, 137; LDN, 150). The central achievement of what Blumenberg calls the 'modern age' (*Neuzeit*), was to follow the sec-ond path and to develop the "existential program" (*Daseinsprogramm*) of "self-assertion" by way of scientific rationality. Drawing again on Gehlen's vision of humans as 'creatures of deficiency' (LMA, 138; LDN, 151), Blumenberg argues that scientific modernity produces hypotheses that can only be verified by humans, irrespective of the existence of any divinity (LMA, 199–200; LDN, 229). This power to "foresee events, to anticipate them, to alter or to produce them, proves to be the 'self-assertive' sense of the incipient modern science" (LMA, 209; LDN, 238).

A key feature of Blumenberg's accounts of both prehistoric and modern cultures is this notion of self-assertion undertaken by insufficiently adapted, self-conscious and therefore anxious human beings within situations of radical contingency. The forms that such self-assertion takes may be either fictive and speculative (in the case of myth) or empirical and actual (in the case of both stone technology and modern science), and the needs that they serve, or the questions to which they respond, may change according to particular historical contexts. It was, for example, precisely the existential question posed by the theological context of the late Middle Ages—how to survive the capricious dictates of an omnipotent and incalculable God—that gave rise to the answers provided by scientific modernity (LMA, 48; LDN, 59). The notion of progress peculiar to scientific modernity does not, therefore, represent a secularisation of Christian eschatology. Rather, scientific modernity provides new answers to, and in this sense "reoccupies" (*umbesetzt*) a question posed by Christian theology: 'How are we to be saved?' The old answer was 'through prayer, right action and God's grace,' while the new answer was 'through rationality and exercising control over nature.' Here the old theological contents do not undergo a "transposition" (*Umsetzung*) into a new historical context. Instead, the old questions to which they responded are subjected to a "reoccupation" (*Umbesetzung*) in which they are filled with entirely new content (LMA, 65; LDN, 75). The answers provided serve similar world-orienting *functions*, but their *substances* are fundamentally opposed. This distinction between function and substance in intellectual history has been attributed to Blumenberg's reading of Ernst Cassirer.[47] Thus the modern "idea of method" is not to be understood as a "transformation of the divine salvation plan," but rather as the establishment of a "disposition of the subject [. . .] to take part in a process that generates knowledge in a transsubjective manner" (LMA, 33; LDN, 42).

In *Work on Myth*, Blumenberg draws upon similar arguments to those outlined in the *Legitimacy of the Modern Age*. The original aim of myth is to provide humans with existential orientation, which means eliminating incomprehensibility and arbitrariness by naming and rendering knowable those threatening natural powers that are unnamed and indefinite (WOM, 42–3; AM, 49–50). Here one might ask how myth is to be differentiated from religion on the one hand and from scientific rationality on the other, since they also provide humans with orientation. Myth certainly responds to questions that are later taken up or 'reoccupied' by theological discourses—such as 'Why do bad things happen to some people and not to others?'—but unlike theology, it does not provide answers to these questions. The preferred mode of myth is that of the fateful decree rather than the homily: "myths do not answer questions; they make things unquestionable" and in this sense "myth is [. . .] not a theology because the punishing god does not explain himself" (WOM, 126, 599; AM, 142, 649). Nevertheless, one might claim, as Robert Segal has done in his critique of Blumenberg,[48] that making things unquestionable still means providing answers or explanations, even if they are not rational. Or as Blumenberg put it in an early theoretical reflection on this subject, myth "is not capable of producing a controlled relation between question and answer."[49] As will be seen in Chapter 8 of this volume, the potential danger of myth, according to Blumenberg, lies precisely in its seductive capacity to forestall the need to answer questions in rational and transparent ways. In that sense, forestalling the need to answer questions by telling stories also means 'answering' them.

It is also true to suggest that both myth and scientific rationality share the aim of explaining the world, and that an abstract opposition between myth and rationality, between *mythos* and *logos*, is a false opposition (WOM, 27; AM, 34). Yet rationality or "theory," as Blumenberg tends to call it, is "the better adapted mode of mastering the episodic *tremenda* of recurring world events," in that testable scientific hypotheses receive repeated verifications from external reality (WOM, 26; AM, 33). Science therefore reoccupies and to some degree even surpasses (*überbieten*) the explanatory position of myth by taking over questions originally addressed by myth and by providing more convincing and reliable answers to them (WOM, 27; AM, 34). Yet this does not mean that myth can completely be resolved or overcome by science. As long as there are aspects of reality that are "not transparent for human beings," myths will remain, and if myths "were an expression of the lack of science [. . .] they would have been disposed of automatically at the latest when science, with its increasing powers of accomplishment, made its entrance" (WOM, 274; AM, 303). It may be the case, too, that science and technology can in fact create conditions—such as global warming or nuclear Armageddon—that pose new 'absolutist' threats to human survival and that may therefore be initially dealt with in mythic terms. As Blumenberg shows in *The Genesis of the Copernican World*, science is a double-edged sword. The discovery that the earth was not the centre of the universe was liberating and self-empowering for human understanding on the one hand, yet disappointing on the other (GCW, 81; GKW, 1:99). Revealed by Copernicus to be dwelling on a planet located at the margins, human beings discovered they were "not the addressee[s] of the cosmic performance" (GCW, 572; GKW, 3:665). Now they needed their myths more than ever before, and Blumenberg accordingly interprets the resurgence of both the subject and of myth in German idealism and romanticism respectively as a resistance against the cosmic demotion forced upon humans by Copernicus (GCW, 77–80; GKW, 1:94–8).

The survival of myth in the modern age demonstrates that, despite and sometimes *because* of the superior explanatory powers of science, humans still need 'significance' (*Bedeutsamkeit*) as a component of their world-orientation.[50] As we shall see, this key term is subjected to a variety of definitions by Blumenberg, perhaps the most helpful of which is the following: "Significance [. . .] arises as a result of the representation of the relationship between the resistance that reality opposes to life and the summoning up of energy that enables one to measure up to it" (WOM, 75; AM, 86). The deeds of Prometheus are therefore 'significant' on account of his powers of self-assertion and cunning in his dealings with the absolutism of Zeus, and because of his daring procurement of fire for human beings. Thus, wherever the interests of human beings appear to be threatened by external reality, there is potential for significance. What is perceived as being significant varies according to historical and cultural needs and circumstances, and myth, which is "the servicing of the need for significance," gains its traction by tying "acute experiences and important current events into the context of long familiarity" (WOM, 95; AM, 108–9). This is why the constellation of events that led to Goethe's "Prometheus" drama fragment and poem being associated with the pantheism controversy in the late German Enlightenment is so important for Blumenberg in *Work on Myth* (see WOM, 403–29; AM, 438–66, and also Chapter 6 of this volume), demonstrating how an old story can gain new meaning when it is linked to heated contemporary debates through slight changes being made to its narrative core. The crucial alteration made by Goethe in the drama fragment was to transform the hierarchical relation between Zeus and Prometheus (that of god and titan) into one between a father and his rebellious son, which made the myth highly significant for the theological debates of Goethe's age.

The example of Goethe's "Prometheus" brings the historicism of Blumenberg's philosophical anthropology into view. Myths, writes Blumenberg, "are distinguished by a high degree of constancy in their narrative core and by an equally pronounced capacity for variation" (WOM, 34; AM, 40). We recognise from the title of Goethe's poem, and from its characters and some aspects of its plot, that we are dealing with the Prometheus story of antiquity. This sense of constancy, permanence and cultural authority that is ascribed to a myth like that of Prometheus is referred to by Blumenberg as its "pregnance" (*prägnanz*)—a key concept that Blumenberg takes from Erich Rothacker, this time from the latter's *Philosophical Anthropology* (*Philosophische Anthropologie*, 1964). Yet while Rothacker believes that the "singular durability" of these "imprinted forms" may slowly be eroded by time,[51] Blumenberg sees pregnance as a factor that is both resistant to *and* produced by time (WOM, 69; AM, 79). We know that a myth has authority and pregnance because it has resisted the negative cultural inertia of forgetting, because it has survived countless rounds of cultural selection. The longer it prevails, the more pregnance it assumes. And in everyday German, *prägnant* means 'pithy' or 'concise,' which expresses another key aspect of a myth's durability: namely, that it expresses one captivating emotional idea, such as, in the case of Prometheus, the titan who defied Zeus, or in Goethe's variation, the artist-as-genius who defied his Creator by claiming to take on the role of creator himself.

A myth's capacity for survival and constancy is, however, dependent upon change—upon processes of cultural adaptation. The changes made by Goethe to the Prometheus story endowed it with a new meaning and power in the context of the late eighteenth century. The reception of myth arises from this dialectic between the familiarity and authority of the ancient stories on the one hand, and their acquiring contemporary relevance through variation on the other. That which seems relevant and 'significant' to an historically situated audience is seen as expressing a kind of ancient truth, while also being able to speak to their contemporary human needs. In fact, Blumenberg suggests that new historical contexts may even bring out something in a myth that was not already 'in it' in the first place (WOM, 69; AM, 79). In this respect Blumenberg's theory of myth and its central concept of significance (*Bedeutsamkeit*) are deeply influenced by the historicist version of philosophical anthropology elaborated by Erich Rothacker in *Philosophy of History* (*Geschichtsphilosophie*, 1934) and in *Problems of Cultural Anthropology* (*Probleme der Kulturanthropologie*, 1942).

For Rothacker, the human being is not simply a *Mängelwesen* or 'creature of deficiencies,' it is a *Kulturwesen*, or 'cultural being.'[52] Following the example of the biologist-cum-philosopher Jakob Johann von Uexküll,[53] Rothacker underlines the extent to which cultural and not natural factors define the human setting. This point is made through a comparison between animals and humans. The severely limited sensory world of a deaf and blind tick (*Zecke*) is determined by a series of environmental catalysts: light sensors in its skin allow it to climb a bush to particular height; the smell of an approaching animal leads it to release itself from the branch on which it rests; temperature sensors on its body inform it that the animal upon which it has landed is warm-blooded and therefore a potential source of nutrition; its sense of touch helps it to find a clear path to bare skin on the animal's body.[54] Humans, according to Rothacker, are not automatically determined in this way. In being open to the world (*Welt*) and not just to a restricted *Umwelt* (environment) characterised by limited sensory activators, humans selectively create their own cultural settings. The same forest will, for example, be a source of timber for the lumberjack, a hunting ground for the hunter, a cool and shaded wood for the hiker, a hiding place for the fugitive, or an aesthetic object for the poet. The forest's meaning and significance (*Bedeutung*) are a function of culturally determined human interests.[55]

Rothacker's earlier historicist move in his *Philosophy of History*, a move redolent of Wilhelm Dilthey, was to project these individual perspectives and needs onto cultural groups and epochs: that which appears to be relevant, important and worthy of mention within a culture or historical period is a reflection of "human life-plans" and interests particular to that culture or period. The "worldview" (*Weltanschauung*) of a culture or period is thus characterised by the "questions posed" (*Fragestellungen*).[56] So, for example, within the world of the late German Enlightenment, Goethe's "Prometheus" spoke to a culture both questioning the traditional Christian view of the relation between God and humans and preoccupied with the idea of aesthetic genius. In speaking to these interests, the poem was able to enter collective consciousness by penetrating what Rothacker calls the "cultural threshold" (*Kulturschwelle*). This threshold is correlated with the particular "style of life" (*Lebenstil*) and attendant interests of an historical group or period. Seen in this way, "the content of world history is the struggle of human groups to form their lives and worlds," while the task of the philosophy of history is to inquire into the "meaning" (*Sinn*) and "mode of being" (*Seinsform*) of these struggles.[57]

In a text published from Blumenberg's *Nachlass* that was probably written in the second half of the 1970s, in the lead up to *Work on Myth*, Blumenberg adopts, almost completely, Rothacker's characterisation of human consciousness as a form of consciousness defined by historically conditioned interests.[58] He does so by associating Rothacker's notion of human cultural worlds with the phenomenological notion of the life-world or *Lebenswelt*, a term of crucial importance in Blumenberg's works that will be discussed at length in Chapter 4 of this volume. An *Umwelt*, or environment, writes Blumenberg, is characterised by specific catalysts that trigger automatic behaviours in an organism. These catalysts in turn ensure the organism's on-going existence, as in the case of the tick just discussed. The human life-world, by contrast, is defined not by instinctive automatism but by "functional competence" (*Funktionstüchtigkeit*): the series of compensatory cultural behaviours, such as the telling of tales or the use of tools and other technologies that humans have developed in order to orient themselves and survive (TDL, 135). In an earlier essay on the life-world and technology, first delivered as a lecture in 1959, Blumenberg proposes that as long as these adaptive behaviours remain successful und useful, they are taken for granted and are characterised by a certain everydayness, becoming part of an almost unconscious repertoire of beliefs, attitudes, and survival methods. For example, ringing the doorbell when visiting someone's house has become so natural a procedure that it leads to little self-reflection on the part of the user.[59]

In this way Blumenberg argues, contra the position of Heidegger in "The Question Concerning Technology" ("Die Frage nach der Technik," 1954), that technology always already belongs to the human life-world rather than being a later mode of "enframing" (*Gestell*) that obstructs (*verstellt*) a more authentic relation to a romanticised conception of Being. [60] But this everyday life-world can also be disrupted by new threats and "invasions by the unknown" that cannot immediately be assimilated by the existing means at the disposal of consciousness (TDL, 135). These invasions may have natural causes, technological causes, or a combination of both, and in turn require new adjustments to be made. At the most basic level, these threats at least need to be named, before being integrated into the life-world by myth, by metaphor, or by philosophical concepts. Myth, then, may help to repair these tears or breaks in the everydayness of the life-world (TDL, 136). Here one might think of nuclear reactors. As long as they quietly supply us with power, they sink into the life-world and make our lives easier and more efficient. But when they endanger us, as occurred at Fukushima, to name just one recent example, they disrupt this very matter-of-factness of the life-world. The human reaction to Fukushima—a catastrophe with both natural and technological causes that captured the public imagination and was filled with significance—might, as the German author Alexander Kluge has proposed, provide one example of myth reasserting itself in the contemporary world.[61]

In this provisional reading of Blumenberg's theory of myth, we can see the extent to which his version of philosophical anthropology is non-essentialist and historicist. Blumenberg's position certainly refers to the human deficiencies identified by Gehlen and others to explain the beginnings of human culture. But once the process of cultural development is underway, and especially once humans have achieved a certain distance from the threats posed to them by their natural environments, they also achieve a measure of freedom to determine their own historical existence. In Blumenberg's terms this means the freedom to decide how important existential questions should be dealt with, if not always answered. Here Blumenberg is not referring to the substantial or fixed "constants of philosophical anthropology," but rather to the historical "reference-frame conditions" according to which human needs are defined (LMA, 466; LDN, 541–2). Human freedom is admittedly always restricted by the historical questions and cultural forms that humans inherit from previous epochs. But the human ability to reformulate or provide new approaches to these questions, and in so doing to reshape culture, is attested to by the very process that Blumenberg refers to as the 'work on myth.' If humans were entirely fixed in their essence and possibilities, there would literally be no 'work on myth' to be done.

Although Gehlen's *Mängelwesen* idea has often been associated with Blumenberg's reception of philosophical anthropology as expounded from the 1970s onwards,[62] in the course of this study we will also discover that other twentieth-century sources provide equally and perhaps even more important contexts for Blumenberg's theory of myth. Perhaps the most important source of all is the phenomenology of Edmund Husserl and especially the late phenomenological category of the *Lebenswelt* or life-world. Although Husserl is barely discussed at all in the *Legitimacy of the Modern Age* and *Work on Myth*, the idea, common to both texts, that theory and myth respectively arise from human needs or interests, from the need to repair fissures in the everydayness of the life-world, is grounded in Husserl's notion that consciousness is always accompanied by intentionality. As reinterpreted by Blumenberg, intentionality refers to a "system of self-stabilisation and self-regulation" through which emergency repairs to the life-world can be made (BDM, 76). It will also become clear that the late Husserl stands at the centre of Blumenberg's attempts, undertaken in the early to mid-1970s and crucial to the argument of *Work on Myth*, to develop the philosophical anthropology found in part two of *Description of Man*.

The thought of Martin Heidegger exists within the tradition of, yet also critiques, the phenomenology of Husserl. As we shall see in Chapter 4 of this volume, Blumenberg's own position concerning the relation between Husserl and Heidegger is complex and subject to variation over the course of his career. It is certain that Blumenberg's philosophy of technology (*Technik*), as elaborated from 1959 onwards,[63] stood in polemical opposition to that of Heidegger.[64] Blumenberg also privately expressed what might be referred to as a political hostility towards Heidegger's tradition and legacy at the University of Freiburg.[65] What remains clear, however, is that Heidegger's analysis of anxiety (*Angst*) as a category of Being (*Dasein*) in *Being and Time* is a key source for Blumenberg's understanding of human responses to the 'absolutism of reality' (see Chapter 4 of this volume), even if Blumenberg's analysis of anxiety leads him to quite different conclusions from those reached by Heidegger. Similarly, while Ernst Cassirer's emphasis on the epistemological role of myth in part two of his *Philosophy of Symbolic Forms* is certainly an influence upon Blumenberg's notion that *mythos* may serve a rational function and cannot simply be opposed to *logos*, Blumenberg alleges, in *Work on Myth*, that Cassirer mistakenly views myth as "something that has been overcome" (*das Überwundene*) rather than as something that can always return when reality is resistant to human needs or wishes (WOM, 168; AM, 186). This key relation between Blumenberg and Cassirer might also been seen to extend into the period 'after the work on myth' (see Chapter 7 of this volume) when Blumenberg admits that he neglected to explain the apparently successful mobilisation of myth by National Socialism. Such an explanation is attempted by Cassirer in the *Myth of the State* (1946).

WHY BLUMENBERG?

One of the fundamental questions faced by a study of Blumenberg's theory of myth is that of contemporary relevance. Do we now read Blumenberg's theory of myth merely as an important episode in the history of German philosophy and literary theory, perhaps as the last gasp of philosophical anthropology? Or does Blumenberg's theory of myth have a viable future as a mode of thinking about culture?

Within the current landscape of both Anglophone and German literary and cultural theory, Blumenberg may offer a potentially valuable response to Darwinian approaches to literature and culture associated with evolutionary psychology. At the centre of Blumenberg's philosophical anthropology stands his bold claim that the application of the Darwinian theory of evolution to human culture is a "blunder of the first order." Such an application, according to Blumenberg,

> overlooks that man's possibility for existence is biologically defined precisely by his having been able to deactivate the factors of his own development. He succeeded in doing this, in that he compensated for his probably hopeless original situation through the creation of a cultural zone around his own naked body. This cultural zone, filled with tools and all sorts of life-protecting devices of a material and institutional kind, intercepts [*abfangen*] the access of selective mechanisms to the organic system itself. Man is *indirectly* domesticated: he first of all created the enclosure, the domestic animal [*Haustier*] of which he could subsequently become [. . .] The domestication of man is therefore the deactivation and immobilisation of the biological process through which he became what he is, and this state of affairs forbids making any conclusions about his future on the basis of his past.
>
> (BDM, 539)

As strange, exotic and implausible as such a passage might seem to the Anglophone reader schooled in Darwinian natural selection, Blumenberg's critique of Darwin belongs to the mainstream of German philosophical anthropology from Scheler, through Plessner, to Gehlen. The lesser-known thinker who developed this full-frontal critique of Darwin in the most explicit terms was Paul Alsberg, who sees *Körperausschaltung*—the deactivation of human bodily adaptation through the protection, provided by technology, from natural selective pressures—as the anti-Darwinian key to understanding human cultural development.[66] Alsberg plays a central role in Blumenberg's main work of philosophical anthropology—*Description of Man*—and will be a central subject for consideration in Chapter 4 of this volume.

The notion that the use of technology may exert an ameliorating influence on natural selective pressures has precedents in mainstream evolutionary theory, spanning from Alfred Russel Wallace and Darwin to contemporary sources. As we shall see in Chapters 4 and 6 of this volume, the acceptance of such notions is usually not one of total agreement or rejection but rather one of degree. The real questions are to *what extent* humans are buffered from the selective pressures of their environments, and to *what degree* might natural selection be supplemented by cultural selection? When it comes to interpretations of culture, these questions have important implications, and in certain respects Blumenberg's position displays some similarities with the 'dual inheritance model' of human evolution, which argues that different processes of inheritance and selection to those apparent at the purely genetic level can be found in cultural systems. According to this model, culture functions as a "second system of inheritance" that coexists with genetic selection. Even so, the main theorists of this dual inheritance model, Peter J.

Richerson and Robert Boyd, would be likely to class Blumenberg precisely as one of those "humanistic philosophers" who "portray the existence of culture as an emergent phenomenon by which important parts of the human phenotype have escaped the operation of natural selection."[67]

Blumenberg does maintain that human beings were at a certain point successful in making a break with nature to the extent that *cultural selection*—the psychological appeal or significance (*Bedeutsamkeit*) of an element of culture—trumps natural selection in explaining aesthetic phenomena such as myths. In this account, the fact that human beings may originally have been 'creatures of deficiency' who were forced to take recourse to culture becomes itself a potentially captivating story in which human consciousness represents "the triumph of nature over nature" (BDM, 553). It also means that since human nature can no longer exclusively be defined in relation to biological needs, and since the human being itself becomes an open-ended project susceptible of transformation by technology and by surrounding cultural conditions, interpretations of culture must adopt a thorough-going historicism if they are to understand why a piece of culture was attractive and meaningful at a certain period in human history. Blumenberg's tracking of the Prometheus myth across various stages of European modernity, outlined in *Work on Myth*, offers precisely this kind of differentiated historicist interpretation. Indeed, Blumenberg himself made the following declaration in a public lecture delivered in 1974: "I have always felt the accusation of 'historicism' to be honourable."[68]

The German tradition of philosophical anthropology to which Alsberg, Rothacker, Gehlen, and Blumenberg belong has had only a very limited reception in the Anglophone world and has until now played little if any role at all in contemporary Anglophone debates concerning evolutionary interpretations of culture.[69] Without themselves referring directly to this tradition, John Tooby and Leda Cosmides, perhaps the leading figures in propagating the version of evolutionary psychology that has been taken up by some literary scholars in the United States and Germany during the past fifteen years or so, offer an account of human development that directly counters the 'creature of deficiencies' model found in Alsberg, Gehlen, and Blumenberg. "What is special about the human mind," they write,

> is not that it gave up 'instinct' in order to become flexible, but that it proliferated 'instincts'—that is, content-specific problem-solving specializations—which allowed an expanding role for psychological mechanisms that are (relatively) more function-general.[70]

The human mind, they argue, is characterised by a collection of cognitive mechanisms for solving problems or performing tasks—such as mate selection, predator avoidance, tool-making, face recognition, friendship forming, among many others—that were crucial for our ancestors' survival. This mental equipment, which evolved under the high selective pressures of the

Pleistocene age, is said to constitute the universal biological inheritance of modern human beings. In this way, Tooby and Cosmides adopt the very position that Blumenberg would forbid: claiming that when it comes to the human mind the past (i.e., the Pleistocene) explains the present.[71] Such an approach would, in Blumenberg's implicit view, belie the very openness, historicism, and adaptability that are the on-going project of being human.

Scholars such as Joseph Carroll in the United States and Karl Eibl in Germany have in turn used these ideas, as well as similar arguments proposed by Edward O. Wilson in the final chapter of *Sociobiology: The New Synthesis* (1975) and in *On Human Nature* (1979), to propose that both the themes and the functions of literary texts can accurately be interpreted along evolutionist lines.[72] Thus, for example, the human biological universal of "mate selection" is said by Carroll to be the "central behavioural system" that is "activated" in Jane Austen's *Pride and Prejudice*.[73] Or Eibl claims, in a more differentiated and nuanced approach than that advanced by Carroll, that culture and especially narrative constitute an "in-between-world" (*Zwischenwelt*), which enables humans to test out fictional worlds and alternate courses of action in potentially difficult survival situations.[74] While Carroll seems to ignore German philosophical anthropology, Eibl definitely does not. His evolutionary approach to culture includes an explicit rejection of Gehlen's 'creature of deficiencies' hypothesis, accompanied by the assertion that culture emerges from a wealth of instincts rather than from a lack of them.[75] Thus, while some of the arguments made by Eibl—in particular, the notion that culture might originally have been a cognitive coping strategy— do indeed sound similar to positions taken up by Blumenberg in *Work on Myth*, they emerge from an entirely different epistemological background that is deeply informed by evolutionary psychology.

Yet, as we shall see in Chapter 6 of this volume, Blumenberg's position in *Work on Myth* does appear to resemble certain kinds of argumentation to those found in what might be described as the speculative end of recent evolutionary theory—a genre in popular science exemplified by Anglophone writers such as Richard Dawkins and Daniel Dennett. Here the key concept (or perhaps metaphor) that could be related to Blumenberg's ideas about myth is Richard Dawkins's coinage of the 'meme.'[76] In a similar way to the authors of the 'dual inheritance model,'[77] Dawkins claims that "cultural transmission is analogous to genetic transmission in that, though basically conservative, it can give rise to a form of evolution." Just as genes are the replicators that drive natural selection, memes are said to be units of cultural transmission, which compete with one another within cultures or the so-called meme pool. Memes are said to "propagate themselves [. . .] by leaping from brain to brain via a process which, in the broad sense, can be called imitation." Like genes, memes are subject to variation, and may be selected by human cultures, not necessarily on the basis of their capacity to enhance survival, but by dint of what Dawkins refers to as their "psychological appeal." Some examples of memes are "tunes, ideas, catch-phrases, clothes, fashions, ways of making pots or building arches."[78] Similarly, Daniel Dennett's claim, outlined in *Darwin's Dangerous Idea*, that culture "can swamp many—but not all—of the earlier genetic pressures and processes that created it,"[79] at least superficially resembles Blumenberg's position in *Description of Man*, according to which cultural selection by and large took over from natural selection at a certain point in human development.

Like the memes discussed by Dawkins and Dennett, myths, in Blumenberg's account, display both core narrative stability and variation and are subject to imitation and transmission across epochs. As appears to be the case with memes, human cultures shape the processes of selection to which myths are subject. But as Stephen Shennan has pointed out, it is precisely here that key differences between natural and cultural selection need to be stressed. While genetic mutation is "blind" and while organisms cannot consciously influence or control natural selection, cultural variation and selection might to some extent be "purposive" and therefore guided by human agents. [80] Although there may certainly be random variations and copying errors when a meme or myth is inherited, one can also—as Goethe seems to have done in his "Prometheus" poem—*consciously* attempt to rewrite a myth or to refine a piece of technology, even if one cannot control its subsequent effects. Indeed, while in evolutionary biology variation and selection are radically non-teleological and decoupled from one another, in culture there may be situations in which they are deeply conjoined.[81] The reason why a variation made to a myth is 'selected' by a particular culture or group could be put down to *conscious* and *purposive* changes that are made to its content in order to suit a particular historical setting.

These matters will be further explored in Chapter 6 of this volume. For now, a word of caution: these apparent links between Blumenberg and Anglo-American theorists of cultural evolution should certainly not be overstated, since Blumenberg's background in phenomenology is entirely different to their empiricist and natural scientific orientations. Nevertheless, a critical account of Blumenberg's theory of myth must assess its relevance to these contemporary debates on cultural evolution.

STYLE, TRANSLATION, AND THE *NACHLASS*

One of the finest pieces of writing on Blumenberg in English is a short essay by Joseph Leo Koerner on the subject of style. Blumenberg, writes Koerner, is the author of "numerous thick, densely written, almost ludicrously erudite books composed in a German prose style unmatched since Thomas Mann."[82] Koerner is correct to suggest that Blumenberg should, like Nietzsche, be regarded as a literary philosopher for whom the mode of expression and the content expressed are of equal and even inseparable importance.

A clue to Blumenberg's attitude to philosophical style can be found in his ideas concerning rhetoric, as outlined in an important essay originally published in Italian translation in 1971.[83] Blumenberg writes explicitly against the philosophical tradition, dominated by Plato, which sees rhetoric as either an amoral means of persuasion that is deployed regardless of truth content, or—and this is the best case scenario under the Platonic schema—as an ethical means of convincing an audience when one is already in possession of the truth. The ideal of Socratic truth that stands behind this conception of rhetoric represents, according to Blumenberg, an "excessive demand" (*Überforderung*) that was impossible to fulfil in reality (AAR, 431; WWL, 107). If Plato's "realm of Ideas" turns out to be fundamentally inaccessible, and if human beings are "forsaken by evidentness," then an anthropology that has been subsumed by rhetoric would become "the last, and belated, discipline of philosophy" (AAR, 432; WWL, 107). Following Aristotle's critique of the doctrine of Ideas, rhetoric then becomes a means of achieving consensus about what is empirically "real," about "that which everyone thinks really is so" (AAR, 433; WWL, 108).[84] But even Aristotle's position, according to Blumenberg, is misleading: it is not the case that rhetoric merely secures agreement concerning a position that has already been arrived at empirically or logically; rather, rhetoric is the very means of arriving at such a position in the first place. In other words: if human beings find themselves to be located outside of the realm of objective truth, then they are forced to make things up as they go along.

Making things up means telling stories, and to be human means being born into a world in which stories already exist and shape one's worldview: "however certain it is that myths were made up," writes Blumenberg, "we know no one who did it and no moment at which it was done" (WOM, 266; AM, 294). There is, at least for the purposes of human cognition, no time 'before' the stories were told, just as, on the first page of *Cave Exits*, we read that "no consciousness can experience itself as beginning" (HA, 11). This epistemological state of affairs is incorporated into Blumenberg's style, since Blumenberg is an obsessive collector and teller of anecdotes about the history of Western thought.[85] The point is neither to find the beginning, nor to reach the end, which is perhaps why, after 636 pages of anecdotes and exegesis, *Work on Myth* ends with a question: "But what if there were still something to say, after all?" (WOM, 636; AM, 689). Koerner's view that Blumenberg's writings are *metatexts*, in that they are "always becoming the very thing that they describe,"[86] is probably not an accurate description of *all* of Blumenberg's works, but it surely applies to *Work on Myth*, which constructs an epic argument about myth that both unfolds through and circles around fragmentary narratives and asides, while also occasionally being punctuated by authoritative summaries and pronouncements.

In this, Blumenberg is the philosopher as rhapsode—the figure for whom every retelling of the tradition is also a creative mutation or reinvention of it. Writing in 1993, before the existence of the *Nachlass*, Koerner suggested that Blumenberg's tendency suddenly to swerve from "abstract, high theory to local, miniature fact" (or, indeed, to anecdote) was redolent of "a cautious philologist's yellowing notecards" on which "bibliographic tidbits" had been collected.[87] We now know this surmise to be a statement of fact: as Ulrich von Bülow and Dorit Krusche show, Blumenberg's often non-systematic and fragmentary style can be seen as a direct extension of a 'materialist' research method based on a collection of 30,000 index cards.

Blumenberg's rehabilitation of rhetoric self-consciously elaborates a "sceptical destruction" of the Aristotelian teleology according to which the rhetorician simply persuades an audience of a truth that already exists in advance (AAR, 433; WWL, 108–9). And although Blumenberg was not given to signing up to movements or generations, in historical terms his position can be seen as typical of what Helmut Schelsky has termed the "sceptical generation"—those who achieved young adulthood during the period of National Socialism.[88] Odo Marquard has described this 'generational' form of scepticism in a far more biographical way than Blumenberg would ever have done. Initially drawn to the philosophy of history and its association with the post-war left (a position that Blumenberg probably did not share), Marquard came to believe, especially after the events of 1968, that the opposite of totalitarianism is not socialism, but liberal democracy. All claims to philosophical absoluteness, whether from the left or from the right, were therefore to be renounced in favour of a fundamental scepticism, or a radical scaling down, of what philosophy might achieve. Of most interest in this connection are Marquard's comments on philosophical style, which fit Blumenberg's habitus almost exactly: the more philosophy moves in the direction of non-absolute, the more it gives up elaborating false grand theories—in short: the more sceptical it becomes—the more philosophical style matters. Thus "it will no longer suffice," concludes Marquard, "to formulate philosophical sentences that are only true because they are boring."[89]

In *Work on Myth*, Hans Blumenberg's German sentences are rarely boring, and his absolute mastery of the flexibilities within German word order and grammar makes them extremely difficult to render into English while also preserving their playfulness and irony. This is not to criticise the stupendous achievement of Robert M. Wallace—the translator and also (to some extent) the main Anglophone explicator, not only of *Work on Myth*, but also of *The Legitimacy of the Modern Age* and *The Genesis of the Copernican World*. It is to highlight the limitations of translation itself. The different valences of German and English become particularly apparent when Blumenberg's philosophical language gestures towards the inexpressible or pre-verbal, towards beginnings:

> Von den Anfängen zu reden, ist immer des Ursprünglichkeitswahns verdächtig. Zu dem Anfang, auf den konvergiert, wovon hier die Rede ist, will nichts zurück.
>
> (AM, 28)

To speak of beginnings is always to be suspected of a mania for returning to origins. Nothing wants to go back to the beginning that is the
point toward which the lines of what we are speaking of here converge.
(WOM, 21)

Of note here are three things: that in German Blumenberg can express in a
single, almost ridiculously ponderous word (*Ursprünglichkeitswahn*) one
of the central ambiguities of myth: that of not being able to return to the
origin while also needing to speak about it as something that lies far behind
us; that the genitive construction *des Ursprünglichkeitswahns verdächtig*
has an old-fashioned high-literary register which is perhaps suggestive
of an irony that is designed precisely to deflate the ponderousness of the
Ursprünglichkeitswahn—a stylistic twist that eludes the translator; and that
the second sentence, which in German is pithy and elegant, cannot easily
be translated without verbosity, since word order in German sentence construction is far more flexible than it is in English. The Anglophone reader
must therefore be aware that no English-language version of Blumenberg
could ever achieve the stylistic heights and nuances of the German original.

By now a significant number of Blumenberg's longer and shorter works
have appeared in English. These include the three large volumes translated
by Wallace,[90] two shorter works—*Shipwreck With Spectator* (*Schiffbruch
mit Zuschauer*, 1979) and *Paradigms for a Metaphorology*—that provide
fundamental insights into Blumenberg's theory of metaphor,[91] along with a
collection of anecdotes and short pieces that demonstrate the literary dimensions of Blumenberg's thought (*Die Sorge geht über den Fluss/Care Crosses
the River*).[92] On the basis of these translations one could gain an impression
of Blumenberg as a thinker whose primary achievements are in the history
of philosophy, the history of science, and what might generally be termed the
poetics of thought (metaphor and myth). What this Anglophone image of
Blumenberg currently lacks are his important contributions to phenomenology, which are to be found in texts such as *Zu den Sachen und zurück* (*To
the Things and Back Again*, 2002), *Description of Man* (*Beschreibung des
Menschen*, 2006), and *Theorie der Lebenswelt* (*Theory of the Life-World*,
2010).[93] It is significant that these three volumes have all been published
from the *Nachlass* by Manfred Sommer, Blumenberg's former assistant in
Münster and later Professor of philosophy in Kiel, whose own field of specialisation is phenomenology.

On 3 February 1984 Blumenberg wrote the following from Münster to
his old school friend Ulrich Thoemmes:

My books are indeed mostly moonlighting [*Nebenarbeiten*] and do not
emerge from the mainline of philosophy shaped by phenomenology,
which is what I offer to the advanced students here and will still publish after I have been made Emeritus Professor, if the circumstances are
favourable.[94]

If one were to take Blumenberg at his word, then this would mean that *Work on Myth* was something that he wrote just for fun, but did not really belong to the core of his work as a philosopher. This is, of course, only half the truth. Blumenberg's theory of myth in fact emerges from his work on phenomenological anthropology, most of which was undertaken during the early to mid-1970s, and a significant portion of which is to be found in *Description of Man*. That text in particular—and especially its second part, "Contingency and Visibility," probably written in 1976 and 1977—is central to the argument of the present study, in that it offers the most detailed and explicit presentation of the philosophical anthropology that underlies *Work on Myth*. Here it is important to remember that at least some of these *Nachlass* volumes cannot, in any sense, be seen as finished books. In *To the Things and Back Again* we are at least dealing with a text to which Blumenberg himself gave the title, and its parts are published in something resembling the order that he gave to them. But in the cases of *Description of Man* and *Theory of the Life-World* we have 'books' that were never given these titles by Blumenberg himself. *Description of Man* emerged from two separate groups of texts that were written in the mid-1970s and the early 1980s, respectively, but are presented by Manfred Sommer in reverse chronological order in their published form; while *Theory of the Life-World* consists of a combination of both published and unpublished material on the theme of the life-world.[95]

From Blumenberg's correspondence it is clear that a good deal of this unpublished material was central to his self-conception and overall 'project' (if, indeed, he had one) as a philosopher. When, for example, the American scholar David Adams wrote to Blumenberg during the late 1980s and early 1990s concerning his desire to write a dissertation on Blumenberg's works, Blumenberg advised him against this undertaking on the basis that his *oeuvre* was not yet a finished research object, since essential elements of it were then still in preparation. Adams interprets this advice, as well as Blumenberg's implicit references to the *Nachlass* of Ernst Cassirer,[96] as an indication that Blumenberg was already planning his own *Nachlass* at this late stage of his career.[97] The publications that have emerged from the *Nachlass*, especially those edited by Manfred Sommer, certainly lend plausibility to this speculation, as well as adding weight to their interpretative value in relation to the published works.

THE ARGUMENT

The purpose of this study is not merely to offer an internal analysis of Blumenberg's theory of myth. As its title suggests, it also aims to consider the theory of myth as a special problem within the human sciences, and to suggest that Blumenberg's theory of myth is one of the most sophisticated recent elaborations of and responses to that problem. The problem can be delineated as follows: any theory about the function of myth will normally presuppose a theory of the human being, which in turn presupposes providing an answer—even if only a provisional one—to Kant's fourth and final question concerning the human being. Only by addressing Kant's fourth question can one hope to deliver a comprehensive theory of myth. Such an approach demands that Blumenberg's theory of myth be situated within a grander spectrum of theories about the human being in general as well as theories about myth in particular. And in order to do justice to Blumenberg's argument, the term 'human sciences' must encompass not only what in English are regarded as the 'humanities' or in German as the *Geisteswissenschaften*; it must also include palaeoanthropology, human biology, and theories of evolution as they are applied to human beings, as well as more speculative modes of inquiry such as philosophical anthropology and psychoanalysis. These questions are not merely theoretical and historical, since any definition of the human being, and any theory of myth that arises from such a definition, will be likely to have either implicit or explicit political consequences. The relationship between myth and politics is one of the key questions, not only for Blumenberg, but also for other twentieth-century theorists of myth such as Georges Sorel, Carl Schmitt, Ernst Cassirer, Max Horkheimer, and Theodor Adorno. It is, moreover, a question that remains on the agenda of contemporary political thought.[98]

Work on Myth displays a daunting erudition that is always reflexively aware of its own historical position within the theory of myth, and its theory of myth is outlined in relation to seminal thinkers on the subject such as Vico, Schelling, Nietzsche, Cassirer, Heidegger, and Freud, to name but a few. Many of these earlier theorists of myth are discussed in *Work on Myth*, some in passing and some in greater depth, but acknowledging deep similarities between his own approach to myth and those that precede him is not generally part of Blumenberg's habitus. His high expectations of readers might be summed up in the following phrase: 'those who have read as widely as I have will recognise the similarities and differences without them being underlined.' This is even more the case with respect to Blumenberg's position in the history of German philosophy. Although *Work on Myth* contains virtually no direct references to the works of Edmund Husserl, Blumenberg's theory of myth can only be understood in relation to Husserl's late conception of the life-world. Similarly, while the German tradition of philosophical anthropology is another key influence upon *Work on Myth*, this crucial background seems to be treated by Blumenberg as more or less assumed knowledge, and perhaps Blumenberg's main source from palaeoanthropology—the work of Paul Alsberg—is not explicitly mentioned even once in its pages.

In light of these difficult features of *Work on Myth*—especially for Anglophone readers who may not be intimately familiar with the history of German philosophy—some aspects of this book might be described as reconstructive intellectual history in two senses: first, in relating Blumenberg's ideas to those of other thinkers that precede him; and second: in contextu-alising *Work on Myth* in relation to Blumenberg's own broader *oeuvre* and philosophical development. This study is therefore comprised of theoretical chapters that explain the philosophical and anthropological backgrounds to Blumenberg's theory of myth (Chapters 2, 3 and 4), of case studies that demonstrate how the theory works in relation to primary literary sources (Chapters 5 and 6), and of contextualising chapters that evaluate the politi-cal context of Blumenberg's theory of myth and its reception (Chapters 7 and 8).

Chapter 2, for example, endeavours to identify and explain the main eighteenth- and nineteenth-century theorists of myth with whom Blumen-berg is in dialogue in *Work on Myth*, while Chapters 3 and 4 demonstrate the ways in which Blumenberg's theory of myth is embedded within three different but interrelated traditions in early twentieth-century German thought: phenomenology, hermeneutics, and philosophical anthropology. Chapters 3 and 4 in particular have Kant's fourth question—*What is the human being?*—at their heart, since it is Blumenberg's functional and self-consciously hypothetical answer to this fundamental question of the human sciences that underlies his theory of myth. Chapters 5 and 6 then undertake a close examination of Blumenberg's engagement with the Prometheus myth in Western culture, entertaining the possibility that Blumenberg's theory of myth is itself a 'Promethean' theory, and therefore that his theory of myth is itself always implicated in myth. Chapter 7 explores the ambivalent politi-cal context in which *Work on Myth* was written, along with its political reception. Its guiding question is the following one: Is it possible to write a comprehensive theory of myth in Germany after 1945 without addressing the role played by myth in National Socialism? In Chapter 8, the answer to this question will be provided by an extended examination of those explic-itly political parts of the *Work on Myth* manuscripts that Blumenberg chose not to publish during his lifetime.

NOTES

1. Blumenberg, "Sättigungsgrade," in *EMS*, 30. Originally published in the *Neue Zürcher Zeitung*, February 4, 1987 (supplement on the Frankfurt Book Fair).
2. Blumenberg's processes of research and composition are described in detail by Ulrich von Bülow and Dorit Krusche in the Afterword to QSE, 279–85.
3. Ritter offers some observations on his correspondence and telephone con-versations with Blumenberg in "Hans Blumenberg. *Imaginäre Bibliotheke*," in *Verehrte Denker. Porträts nach Begegnungen* (Springe: Klampen Verlag, 2012), 91–107; see especially 103–7.
4. Henning Ritter, "Vom Wunder, die Sterne zu Sehen," *Frankfurter Allgemeine Zeitung*, January 7, 2012, Z1.
5. Odo Marquard, "Entlastung vom Absoluten," in *Die Kunst des Überlebens: Nachdenken über Hans Blumenberg*, ed. Franz Josef Wetz and Hermann

Timm (Frankfurt am Main: Suhrkamp, 1999), 17–27; here: 26. See also Blumenberg, LZ, 99.

6. Sibylle Lewitscharoff, *Blumenberg* (Berlin: Suhrkamp, 2011), 9.
7. Franz Josef Wetz, *Hans Blumenberg: Zur Einführung* (Hamburg: Junius, 2004).
8. Felix Heidenreich, *Mensch und Moderne bei Hans Blumenberg* (Munich: Fink, 2005); Oliver Müller, *Sorge um die Vernunft. Hans Blumenbergs phänomenologische Anthropologie* (Paderborn: Mentis, 2005).
9. Wetz and Timm, *Die Kunst des Überlebens*; Cornelius Borck, ed., *Hans Blumenberg beobachtet. Wissenschaft, Technik und Philosophie* (Freiburg: Alber, 2013). A critical glossary of key terms in Blumenberg's works is also currently in press: Robert Buch and Daniel Weidner, eds., *Blumenberg lesen. Ein Glossar* (Berlin: Suhrkamp, 2014).
10. Rebekka A. Klein, ed., *Auf Distanz zur Natur: Philosophische und theologische Perspektive in Hans Blumenbergs Anthropologie* (Würzburg: Königshausen und Neumann, 2009); Michael Moxter, ed., *Erinnerung an das Humane. Beiträge zur phänomenologischen Anthropologie Hans Blumenbergs* (Tübingen: Mohr Siebeck, 2011).
11. Anselm Haverkamp and Dirk Mende, eds., *Metaphorologie. Zur Praxis von Theorie* (Frankfurt am Main: Suhrkamp, 2009); see also Haverkamp's new critical edition of *Paradigmen zu einer Metaphorologie* (Frankfurt am Main: Suhrkamp, 2013), which includes a lengthy commentary.
12. Peter Behrenberg, *Endliche Unsterblichkeit: Studien zur Theologiekritik Hans Blumenbergs* (Würzburg: Königshausen und Neumann, 1994); Philipp Stoellger, *Metapher und Lebenswelt: Hans Blumenbergs Metaphorologie als Lebensweltthermeneutik und ihr religionsphänomenologischer Horizont* (Tübingen: Mohr Siebeck, 2000).
13. Elizabeth Brient, *The Immanence of the Infinite: Hans Blumenberg and the Threshold to Modernity* (Washington, DC: Catholic University of America Press, 2002).
14. See LMA, xi–xxxi; WOM, vii–xl; GCW, ix–xlviii. See also Robert Savage's informative afterword to his translation of *Paradigmen zu einer Metaphorologie* in PM, 133–46.
15. Robert M. Wallace, "Introduction to Blumenberg," *New German Critique* 32 (1984): 93–108; see also: *History of the Human Sciences* 6, no. 4 (1993); *Annals of Scholarship* 5 (1997); *Thesis Eleven* 104, no. 1 (2011); and *Telos* 158 (Spring, 2012).
16. Hans Blumenberg to Hans Jonas, November 12, 1955, *Hans-Jonas Archiv.* Quoted and translated by Benjamin Lazier in "Hans Jonas, Hans Blumenberg and the Overcoming of the Natural World," *Journal of the History of Ideas* 64, no. 4 (2003): 619–37; here: 622–3. In a letter to Jonas dated January 23, 1961, Blumenberg expresses his disappointment concerning Jonas's decision not to take up a Professorship at the University of Marburg (see BTB, 22). Blumenberg had also previously attempted to secure a post for Jonas at the University of Kiel. See Blumenberg to Taubes, September 18, 1961, and the accompanying commentary in BTB, 21–2.
17. Wetz, *Hans Blumenberg: Zur Einführung*, 11–12.
18. Josef Carl Blumenberg, Geburts- und Taufbescheinigung, Hildesheim, August 4, 1919, Hans Blumenberg Nachlass, *Deutsches Literaturarchiv* Marbach (hereafter DLA Marbach).
19. Hans Blumenberg, Reifezeugnis, March 2, 1939, Katharineum zu Lübeck, Hans Blumenberg Nachlass, DLA Marbach.
20. See Hans Blumenberg, Studentenausweis, Erzbischöfliche philosophisch-theologische Akademie Paderborn, dated 1939; Hans Blumenberg,

Studienbescheinigung der philosophisch-theologischen Hochschule Sankt Georgen, Frankfurt am Main, 1939–40, dated June 16, 1947; Hans Blumenberg, Abgangszeugnis, philosophisch-theologische Hochschule Sankt Georgen, Frankfurt am Main, dated May 9, 1942; Hans Blumenberg, Bescheinigung über Immatrikulation und Beurlaubung, philosophisch-theologische Hochschule Sankt Georgen, Frankfurt am Main, dated May 9, 1942. All present in: Hans Blumenberg Nachlass, DLA Marbach.

21. According to the research of Susanne Krejsa in the archives of the Drägerwerk, Blumenberg was responsible for *Materialbeschaffung*—the sourcing and purchasing of materials. See her *Spurensuche: Der SS-Anwalt und Judenretter Helmut Pfeiffer* (Berlin: Vergangenheitsverlag, 2011), 202, fn. 530.

22. Dräger joined the NSDAP in August 1933, but his membership was backdated to May of that year; see Welf Böttcher and Martin Thoemmes, *Heinrich Dräger. Eine Biographie* (Neumünster: Wachholtz, 2011), 74, 130–3. Despite the efforts of this apologetic biography (one of its authors, Welf Böttcher, worked in corporate communications for Dräger AG), Dräger remains a deeply ambivalent figure. While Dräger was certainly responsible for protecting Blumenberg and other valuable workers in similar situations (see Böttcher and Thoemmes, *Heinrich Dräger*, 78–86), the *Drägerwerk* also profited from war production—especially the manufacturing of gasmasks. The majority of the political prisoners who worked as forced labour at the Dräger facility in Hamburg-Wandsbek were eastern European women who had been transported from the Ravensbrück concentration camp, beginning in June 1944. Dräger had apparently bought this factory from a Jewish-owned rubber-manufacturing firm (the Skara Gummiwerke) in 1937, after the firm was denied access to raw materials by the National Socialist regime (Böttcher and Thoemmes, *Heinrich Dräger*, 97–8). Hamburg-Wandsbek was used as a forced labour facility between the summer of 1944 and the end of April 1945. See Hans Ellger, "Hamburg-Wandsbek," in *Der Ort des Terrors. Geschichte der nationalsozialistischen Konzentrationslager*, ed. Wolfgang Benz and Barbara Distel, vol. 5, *Hinzert, Auschwitz, Neuengamme* (Munich: Beck, 2007), 425–7. On Dräger's party membership, his dealings with the NSDAP, the profits of the *Drägerwerk* as a result of war production, as well as his efforts to protect some workers and colleagues persecuted by the NSDAP, see Bernhard Lorentz, *Industrieelite und Wirtschaftspolitik 1928–50. Heinrich Dräger und das Drägerwerk* (Paderborn: Ferdinand Schöningh, 2001), 339–48. On the historical context concerning the employment of forced labour at Hamburg-Wandsbek, as well as the brutal conditions under which this work was carried out, see also Lorentz, *Industrieelite und Wirtschaftspolitik*, 317–35.

23. Hans Blumenberg, Fragebogen zu Inhaftierung, Stormarn Kreis, March 20, 1946, Hans Blumenberg Nachlass, DLA Marbach.

24. According to Böttcher and Thömmes, *Heinrich Dräger*, 83.

25. Wetz, *Hans Blumenberg: Zur Einführung*, 12. This is also mentioned by Eckhard Nordhofen's obituary for Blumenberg in *Die Zeit*, no. 16, April 12, 1996.

26. Blumenberg, "Der Parteibeitrag," in VP, 75–9; here: 76.

27. Hans Blumenberg to Heinrich Dräger, December 8, 1945 (Hans Blumenberg Nachlass, DLA Marbach), quoted in Böttcher and Thoemmes, *Heinrich Dräger*, 85.

28. Conversation quoted by Böttcher and Thoemmes in *Heinrich Dräger*, 81.

29. *Beiträge zum Problem der Ursprünglichkeit der mittelalterlich-scholastischen Ontologie* (Ph.D. diss., University of Kiel, 1947); see also OD.

30. One short reflection by Blumenberg on the Shoah, published from the *Nachlass*, is "Kontingent," see BG, 103.

31. Blumenberg, "Ein Leben—eine Identität?" in EMS, 39–40; here: 40.

32. This summary, along with the discussion that followed Blumenberg's lecture, is reprinted in Margarita Kranz, "Begriffsgeschichte institutionell. Die Senatskommission für Begriffsgeschichte der Deutschen Forschungsgemeinschaft (1956–66). Darstellung und Dokumente," *Archiv für Begriffsgeschichte* 53 (2011): 153–226; here: 186–93. See also the commentary in BTB, 43, 51.
33. Kranz, "Begriffsgeschichte institutionell," 167.
34. See Blumenberg, "Thesen zu einer Metaphorologie" (and accompanying discussion), in Kranz, "Begriffsgeschichte institutionell," 186–93; here: 187. For further context on this 'controversy' see Anselm Haverkamp, "The Scandal of Metaphorology," *Telos* 158 (2012): 37–58.
35. Blumenberg, "Paradigmen zu einer Metaphorologie," *Archiv für Begriffsgeschichte* 6 (1960): 7–142; later republished as PZM and PM.
36. Kranz, "Begriffsgeschichte institutionell," 165–78. See also Blumenberg's letter to Jacob Taubes dated March 22, 1965, in which he expresses some of his criticisms concerning Gadamer's running of the *Senatskommission* (BTB, 46–50). On the organisational problems associated with the group that led to Blumenberg's resignation, see the commentary in BTB, 51.
37. *Historisches Wörterbuch der Philosophie*, 13 vols., ed. Joachim Ritter and Karlfried Gründer et al. (Basel: Schwabe, 1971–2007).
38. Hans Robert Jauss, "Wissenschaftsgeschichtliche Memorabilien, K24/M06, DLA Marbach, quoted in: Julia Wagner, "Anfangen. Zur Konstitutionsphase der Forschungsgruppe Poetik und Hermeneutik," *Internationales Archiv für Sozialgeschichte der deutschen Literatur* 35, no. 1 (2010): 53–76; here: 53.
39. The research group *Poetik und Hermeneutik* held seventeen meetings between 1963 and 1994, each of which led to a volume of the papers delivered at each meeting as well as the accompanying discussions.
40. Marquard, "Entlastung vom Absoluten," 18–19.
41. Marquard, "Entlastung vom Absoluten," 26.
42. See the commentary in BTB, 118, as well as some of Blumenberg's notes on this activity, also in BTB, 221–9.
43. Taubes advised Siegfried Unseld, the Director of Suhrkamp, on new acquisitions in the fields of philosophy and theology, and was instrumental in having Blumenberg's first collection of essays published with Suhrkamp. See Taubes to Blumenberg, August 10, 1964, in BTB, 36–8. The volume in question was Hans Blumenberg, *Die Kopernikanische Wende* (Frankfurt am Main: Suhrkamp, 1965). Suhrkamp also published the *Legitimacy of the Modern Age* following Taubes's mediation, see Taubes to Blumenberg, March 25, 1965, in BTB, 53–6; here: 56.
44. Jacob Taubes to Eberhard Lämmert, June 15, 1977, quoted in BTB, 190–1.
45. Hans Blumenberg, "Kontingenz," in *Die Religion in Geschichte und Gegenwart. Handwörterbuch für Theologie und Religionswissenschaft*, 3rd ed., ed. Kurt Galling, vol. 3 (Tübingen: Mohr, 1959), 1793–4; here: 1793.
46. For background on the notion of contingency in Blumenberg, see Rüdiger Campe, "Contingencies in Blumenberg and Luhmann," *Telos* 158 (Spring, 2012): 81–99; on the sense of contingency within Blumenberg's account of anthropogenesis, see Robert Savage, "Aporias of Origin: Hans Blumenberg's Primal Scene of Hominization," in *Erinnerung an das Humane*, 62–71.
47. See Ernst Cassirer, *Subtanzbegriff und Funktionsbegriff. Untersuchungen über die Grundfrage der Erkenntniskritik* (Berlin: Cassirer, 1910). See also Müller, *Sorge um die Vernunft*, 216–23.
48. Robert A. Segal, "Hans Blumenberg as a Theorist of Myth," in *Theorizing about Myth* (Amherst, MA: University of Massachusetts Press, 1999), 142–52.
49. Hans Blumenberg, "Notiz zur Diskussion um 'Wirklichkeitsbegriff und Wirkungspotential des Mythos' (1968)," in BTB, 255–7; here: 256.

50. The translator of *Arbeit am Mythos*, Robert M. Wallace, renders *Bedeutsamkeit* as 'significance' rather than as 'meaningfulness'; both are arguably possible, since *Bedeutung* can be translated as 'meaning,' while *bedeutend* can be translated as 'significant.' For consistency with Wallace's translation I will hereafter use 'significance.'
51. Erich Rothacker, *Philosophische Anthropologie* (Bonn: Bouvier, 1964), 95–6, quoted in WOM, 69; AM, 79.
52. Erich Rothacker, *Probleme der Kulturanthropologie* in *Systematische Philosophie*, ed. Nicolai Hartmann (Stuttgart: Kohlhammer, 1942), 54–198; here: 161.
53. See Jakob von Uexküll, *Theoretische Biologie* (Berlin: Paetel, 1920); Rothacker quotes from the second edition (Berlin: Springer, 1928).
54. Rothacker, *Probleme der Kulturanthropologie*, 159.
55. Rothacker, *Probleme der Kulturanthropologie*, 161.
56. Erich Rothacker, *Geschichtsphilosophie* (Munich: Oldenbourg, 1934), 96.
57. Rothacker, *Geschichtsphilosophie*, 5.
58. Blumenberg, "Selbstverständlichkeit, Selbstaufrichtung, Selbstvergleich," in TDL, 133–48. On the uncertain dating of this text see Manfred Sommer's "Nachwort des Herausgebers," in TDL, 243–7; here: 247.
59. Blumenberg, "Lebenswelt und Technisierung unter Aspekten der Phänomenologie," *Filosofia* 14 (1963): 855–84; based on a lecture delivered to the Husserl archive in Cologne in 1959; republished in WWL, 7–54.
60. Martin Heidegger, "The Question Concerning Technology," in *Basic Writings*, ed. David Farrell Krell (London: Routledge, 1993), 311–41; here: 333; "Die Frage nach der Technik," in *Gesamtausgabe*, vol. 7, *Vorträge und Aufsätze, 1910–76*, ed. Friedrich-Wilhelm von Herrmann (Frankfurt am Main: Klostermann, 2000), 7–36; here: 29. On Blumenberg's departure from Heidegger on this question, see Heidenreich, *Mensch und Moderne*, 115–19; and Müller, *Sorge um die Vernunft*, 63–82, especially 64. See also Blumenberg's trenchant criticism of "The Question Concerning Technology" in VP, 104.
61. See Kluge's reaction to the earthquake and tsunami of March 11, 2011, and the subsequent nuclear disaster at Fukushima, in his audiobook *Die Pranke der Natur (und wir Menschen), das Erdbeben von Japan, das die Welt bewegte, und das Zeichen von Tschernobyl* [The Paw of Nature (and we Humans), the Earthquake of Japan that moved the World and the Symbol of Chernobyl] (Munich: Kunstmann, 2012).
62. See, for example, Heidenreich, *Mensch und Moderne*, 35–6; Müller, *Sorge um die Vernunft*, 29.
63. See "Lebenswelt und Technisierung unter Aspekten der Phänomenologie," first delivered as a lecture in 1959.
64. See Helmut Müller-Sievers, "Kyklophorology: Hans Blumenberg and the Intellectual History of Technics," *Telos* 158 (Spring, 2012): 155–70; here: 157–9.
65. See Blumenberg's letter to Taubes dated March 22, 1965, in BTB, 46–50; here: 48.
66. Paul Alsberg, *Das Menschheitsrätsel, Versuch einer prinzipiellen Lösung* (Dresden: Sibylle Verlag, 1922), 101.
67. Peter J. Richerson and Robert Boyd, "A Dual Inheritance Model of the Human Evolutionary Process I: Basic Postulates and a Simple Model," *Journal of Social and Biological Structures* 1, no. 2 (1978): 127–54; here: 128. This initial model is then developed in Robert Boyd and Peter J. Richerson, *Culture and the Evolutionary Process* (Chicago: University of Chicago Press, 1985), and in Peter J. Richerson and Robert Boyd, *Not by Genes Alone: How Culture Transformed Human Evolution* (Chicago: University of Chicago Press, 2005).
68. Blumenberg, "Ernst Cassirers gedenkend," in WWL, 163–73; here: 170.

69. For a comparison between some of these Anglophone approaches and the arguments of philosophical anthropology, see Christian Illies, "Biologie statt Philosophie? Evolutionäre Kulturerklärungen und ihre Grenzen," in *Evolution in Natur und Kultur*, ed. Volker Gerhardt and Julian Nida-Rümelin (Berlin: De Gruyter, 2010), 15–38.

70. Leda Cosmides and John Tooby, "The Psychological Foundations of Culture," in *The Adapted Mind: Evolutionary Psychology and the Generation of Culture*, ed. Jermome H. Barkow, Leda Cosmides, and John Tooby (New York, NY: Oxford University Press, 1992), 19–136; here: 113.

71. See Cosmides and Tooby, "The Past Explains the Present: Emotional Adaptations and the Structure of Ancestral Environments," *Ethnology and Sociobiology* 11 (1990): 375–424.

72. See E. O. Wilson, *Sociobiology: The New Synthesis* (Cambridge, MA: Harvard University Press, 1975); and *On Human Nature* (Cambridge, MA: Harvard University Press, 1979).

73. Joseph Carroll, "Human Nature and Literary Meaning," in *The Literary Animal: Evolution and the Nature of Narrative*, ed. Jonathan Gottschall and David Sloan Wilson (Evanston, IL: Northwestern University Press, 2005), 76–106; here: 98.

74. Karl Eibl, *Kultur als Zwischenwelt: Eine evolutionsbiologische Perspektive* (Frankfurt am Main: Suhrkamp, 2009), 10. Eibl applies similar arguments to literature in his *Die Entstehung der Poesie* (Frankfurt am Main: Insel, 1995), and his *Animal Poeta: Bausteine der biologischen Kultur- und Literaturtheorie* (Paderborn: Mentis, 2004).

75. Eibl, *Kultur als Zwischenwelt*, 12–15.

76. This connection has also been noted by Heidenreich in *Mensch und Moderne*, 57, footnote 108.

77. Richerson and Boyd already cite Dawkins in their paper on this subject published in 1978. See "A Dual Inheritance Model," 131–2.

78. Richard Dawkins, *The Selfish Gene*, 2nd ed. (1976; Oxford: Oxford University Press, 1989), 189, 192–3.

79. Daniel Dennett, *Darwin's Dangerous Idea: Evolution and the Meanings of Life* (London: Allen Lane, 1995), 338.

80. See Stephen Shennan, *Genes, Memes and Human History* (London: Thames and Hudson, 2002), 51.

81. See Kristian Köchy, "Natur und Kultur in der Evolution," in *Evolution in Natur und Kultur*, ed. Volker Gerhardt and Julian Nida-Rümelin (Berlin: De Gruyter, 2010), 39–58; here: 52–3.

82. Joseph Leo Koerner, "Ideas About the Thing, Not the Thing Itself: Hans Blumenberg's Style," *History of the Human Sciences* 6, no. 4 (1993): 1–10; here: 2.

83. "An Anthropological Approach to the Contemporary Significance of Rhetoric" ("Anthropologische Annäherung an die Aktualität der Rhetorik"), see AAR, republished in WWL, 104–36. Originally published in an Italian translation by Vincenzo Orlando as "Approccio antropologico all Attualitá della Retorica," in *Il Verri. Rivista di Letteratura* 35/36 (1971), 49–72.

84. See Aristotle, *Nichomachean Ethics*, 1172b, quoted in AAR, 433; WWL, 108. Blumenberg incorrectly attributes this quote to the *Metaphysics* (see WWL, 135).

85. On this subject, see Paul Fleming, "The Perfect Story: Anecdote and Exemplarity in Linnaeus and Blumenberg," *Thesis Eleven* 104, no. 1 (2011): 72–86; see especially 82 for Fleming's discussion of the role played by anecdote in *Work on Myth*.

86. Koerner, "Ideas About the Thing," 9.

87. Koerner, "Ideas About the Thing," 4.

88. Helmut Schelsky, *Die skeptische Generation. Eine Soziologie der deutschen Jugend* (Düsseldorf: Diederichs, 1957); discussed in Jens Hacke, *Philosophie der Bürgerlichkeit: Die liberalkonservative Begründung der Bundesrepublik* (Göttingen: Vandenhoeck und Ruprecht, 2006), 31.

89. Odo Marquard, *Skepsis als Philosophie der Endlichkeit*, (Bonner philosophische Vorträge und Studien), ed. Wolfram Hofgrebe (Bonn: Bouvier, 2002), 6–7, 12.

90. See LMA, WOM and GCW.

91. See SMZ, translated as SWS by Steven Rendall and PZM translated as PM by Robert Savage.

92. See SÜF, translated by Paul Fleming as CCR.

93. See ZSZ, BDM, and TDL.

94. [Meine Bücher sind ja überwiegend Nebenarbeiten und kommen nicht aus der Hauptlinie der Philosophie phänomenologischer Prägung, wie ich sie den fortgeschrittenen Studenten anbiete und unter günstigen Umständen nach meiner Emeritierung noch publizieren werde]. Blumenberg to Ulrich Thoemmes, February 3, 1984, Hans Blumenberg Nachlass, DLA Marbach.

95. See Manfred Sommer's editorial comments to all three volumes: ZSZ, 351–2; BDM, 904–5; TDL, 248–50.

96. See Blumenberg, "Ernst Cassirers gedenkend bei Entgegennahme des Kuno-Fischer-Preises der Universität Heidelberg," in WWL, 163–72; here: 170. In this connection one might also mention Blumenberg's extensive use of texts from Husserl's *Nachlass* in the first part of BDM.

97. See David Adams, "Ökonomie der Rezeption. Die Vorwegnahme des Nachlasses," trans. Michael Bischoff, in *Die Kunst des Überlebens*, 369–86; here: 381–2.

98. See, for example, Chiara Bottici, *A Philosophy of Political Myth* (Cambridge: Cambridge University Press, 2007).

2   Myth and the Human Sciences during the *Sattelzeit*

One way of viewing the relation between the notions of myth and scientific rationality in Western thought is to understand the latter as depending on the former for its identity. The Enlightenment's story about myth suggests this arrangement, in that rational thought or philosophy has, since the pre-Socratics, tended to define itself in opposition to myth, according to the well-known formula 'from *mythos* to *logos*,' which became a catch-phrase of German classical philology of the immediate post-war period, chiefly as a result of a famous study by Wilhelm Nestle.[1] Yet the relation between *mythos* and *logos* has not always been a stable one involving a progression from the former to the latter, and this was especially the case in Germany during the period (roughly 1750–1850) that Reinhart Koselleck termed the *Sattelzeit* (saddle-period).

Koselleck describes the *Sattelzeit* as an epochal threshold (*Epochen-schwelle*) that marks the transition from the early modern age to the onset of industrialised economies and the development of modern political ideas. This period, he argues, saw important changes in key concepts—such as 'the state,' 'power,' 'politics,' 'revolution,' 'society,' and 'citizen'—through which Europeans understood themselves as political and social actors.[2] These terms are said to have taken on a new anticipatory or heuristic content during the *Sattelzeit*, through a process of increased reflection on human history and progress. The growing realisation that human values are historically and culturally conditioned rather than universally ordained led to the notion that they are also open, future-directed and capable of active transformation.[3] Historical time, understood by Koselleck subjectively (in terms of how it is perceived) rather than as an objective or natural sequence, was therefore 'sped up' by this process of historical self-reflection.[4] In the *Legitimacy of the Modern Age*, Blumenberg takes up a similar position in relation to the concept of the 'epoch'—arguing that such epochs never refer to objective historical categories, but rather to the rhetorical constructions and self-understandings of an age, which arise from the "need to find a meaning in history" (LMA, 461; LDN, 536).

Koselleck's project is conceived under the rubric of the History of Concepts (*Begriffsgeschichte*), which, in opposition to the History of Ideas (roughly translated as *Geistesgeschichte*),[5] suggests that concepts do not simply develop within the rarefied realm of the history of philosophy; rather, a reciprocal relation pertains between ideas about society on the one hand and concrete social and political realities on the other. Transformations undergone by the aforementioned key political and social concepts between circa 1750 and 1850 are seen as not only *registering* social change, but also as *influencing* it too.[6] According to Koselleck's conception of it,[7] *Begriffs-geschichte* investigates not only how concepts develop diachronically, but also examines their synchronic functions in relation to other concepts, suggesting that changes in one concept can lead to reactive alterations in other contemporaneous concepts.[8]

The notion that the modern human sciences first appear during what Koselleck terms the *Sattelzeit* is also, according to Manfred Frank, to be found in Michel Foucault's so-called archaeology of the human sciences, *The Order of Things* (*Les Mots et les choses*, 1966).[9] Like Koselleck, Foucault proposes that "a number of human sciences, and a new type of philosophy," appear at "the threshold of the nineteenth century," arranged around the basic triad of psychology, sociology, and philology. At the centre of these human sciences stands the "empirico-transcendental" human being: the being that represents himself to himself.[10] The human being's empirical-transcendental status lies in the fact it plays "two roles": being at once the empirical object and the transcendental subject of the human sciences. The transcendental aspect of the human being is uncovered by the "new type of philosophy" to which Foucault refers—German idealism—which sees humans and their *a priori* cognitive faculties as the conditions of possibility for all knowledge.[11] Addressing Foucault's hypothesis concerning an epochal threshold around 1800, Manfred Frank has argued that the new level of reflexivity in historical and philological discourses that arose during this period coincided with a renewed interest in mythology to be found in German romanticism.[12]

If the human being is at once the empirical object and the transcendental subject of the human sciences, then the central problem of these sciences is whether it is possible for humans to have self-transparent and objective knowledge of their own ground: human consciousness and its origins. According to Foucault, such knowledge, which is never susceptible of complete realisation, entails an investigation of the unconscious, and for this reason the unconscious is "not simply a problem within the human sciences," but is also "coextensive with their very existence."[13] Within the purported science to which the unconscious gave rise—psychoanalysis—myth is a central subject of investigation,[14] and the prehistory of the psychoanalytic unconscious undergoes one of its most intensive phases during the *Sattelzeit*.[15] Just as Freud speculates about the origins of culture and consciousness in works such as *Totem and Taboo* (*Totem und Tabu*, 1913) and *Beyond the Pleasure Principle* (*Jenseits des Lustprinzips*, 1920)—the former text outlining a parallel between the individual unconscious and so-called primitive culture, the latter between the ontogenetic and phylogenetic origins of consciousness—so too do the human sciences of the eighteenth and nineteenth centuries propose that myth corresponds with a childhood phase in the development of the human species, in which human consciousness first conceived of gods or animistic forces. Depending upon the theory and its orientation, this primeval phase of mythic consciousness is either to be surmounted (in Enlightenment accounts) or artistically to be excavated and recreated (in accounts broadly described as romantic).

Blumenberg's theory of myth questions the Enlightenment's narrative of *mythos* to *logos*, while at the same time avoiding the romantic notion that a complete 'return' to myth is possible or desirable.[16] It is also embedded in a theory of epochs akin to that of Koselleck, arguing that mythic motifs must be adapted to new historical contexts in order to retain their meaningfulness or significance (*Bedeutsamkeit*) in a process that amounts to a kind of cultural (as opposed to natural) selection. Yet Blumenberg was sceptical about the overall project of the History of Concepts, and this scepticism gave rise to his theory of metaphor in *Paradigms for a Metaphorology* (1960), a volume that to some extent anticipates his later theory of myth (see Chapter 5 of this volume).[17]

The philosophical anthropology elaborated by Blumenberg from the 1970s, which precedes and forms the basis for his theory of myth, contains ideas about the foundations of human consciousness and the origins of myth that resemble those of Freud in their speculative character (see the final section of Chapter 8 of this volume for further discussion). Blumenberg maintains that these primeval origins are, like Freud's notion of the unconscious, not available to us as empirical objects for scientific investigation, and so must be imagined according to plausible hypotheses (BDM, 570–1).[18] In the second part of his major work on anthropology, *Description of Man*, Blumenberg offers a speculative theory of anthropogenesis in which the ontogeny of human consciousness recapitulates the geographically situated phylogeny of the species. According to this view, the individual trauma of exiting the womb and of adjusting to external reality is metaphorically akin to the change of biotope undergone by our prehistoric ancestors when they moved from the protection of the forest to the harsh realities and dangers of the open savannah (BDM, 557–67; WOM, 4–5; AM, 10–11). In *Work on Myth* and in *Cave Exits*, this move onto open ground is then succeeded by a retreat into the cave as the location of culture, the place in which, relieved from the pressures of external reality, humans project their wishes and narratives onto cave walls (WOM, 8; AM, 14; HA, 25–6; see also BDM, 144–5).

Thus, while Blumenberg is very much a twentieth-century theorist of myth—taking his bearings from key figures of early to mid-twentieth-century German thought such as Husserl, Cassirer, Freud, Rothacker, Heidegger, and Gehlen—the grandiose and deeply speculative tenor of his theories bears strong resemblances to works of the eighteenth and nineteenth centuries, resemblances of which Blumenberg is, of course, ironically aware. An account of Blumenberg as a theorist of myth demands a contextualisation of his ideas in relation to these eighteenth and nineteenth century approaches, while also requiring that these theories initially be able to speak without the intrusion of Blumenberg's voice. What follows is therefore in no way a comprehensive analysis of thinking about myth during and around the period 1750–1850,[19] but rather an investigation of key sources that will resonate with Blumenberg's theory of myth.

If Blumenberg's theory of myth would be unimaginable without the eighteenth- and nineteenth-century theories that preceded it, then what exactly happened to the Enlightenment's narrative concerning myth during the *Sattelzeit*? Keeping the synchronic-reciprocal function of concepts outlined by Koselleck in mind, it can be argued that during the *Sattelzeit* in Germany, the Enlightenment's narrative concerning the relationship between myth and scientific rationality was radically destabilised. This process of destabilisation had two causes. The first was the establishment of a new academic discipline or 'human science' that grew out of historical researches on the subject of myth, and that concerned itself with the empirical human being: namely, a philosophically informed anthropology. The second was the redefinition of the term science (*Wissenschaft*) undertaken by what Foucault refers to as the 'new philosophy' appearing at the threshold of the nineteenth century: the work of Immanuel Kant and his idealist successors. This new philosophy turned away from the empirical human being and towards the transcendental human being, and in doing so it afforded myth a place at the more speculative end of scientific rationality.

An account of this period of destabilisation, including its prelude and aftermath, stands as the centre of this chapter, and the questions that it raises are these: What is the relation between the origins of myth and the origins of culture and religion? Are myth and religion coterminous with one another? Is myth purely irrational and can it be 'left behind' or surmounted by reason? Or is there a deep continuity, even a family resemblance, between myth and reason? Does myth survive in the modern age, and if so what are its modern forms and functions? Is it possible to elaborate a 'science' of myth, in which mythic phenomena can be rendered transparent by rational analysis? Or must a 'science' of myth itself always fall back into myth?

A NEW SCIENCE OF MYTH: VICO

Implicit in the French *Encyclopaedia*'s characterisation of myth as a form of antiquated, non-rational adornment is the notion that any systematic analysis of it will be impossible. The article's author—Louis de Jaucourt (1704–79)—observes that although "mythologists" such as Euhemerus (340 BC-260 BC) may have demonstrated that many outwardly divergent myths are mere variations on the same historical material, and while Strabo may also have argued that some apparently fictional stories actually reveal ancient thinking on subjects such as physics, "it will never be possible to arrive at a sufficiently scientific unravelling of the whole to permit us to discern the origin of every myth."[20] Can mythology, this strange collection of fanciful stories, ever be an object of science? This question preoccupied the so-called mythologists of the eighteenth and nineteenth centuries, and the answer to it depends on what is meant by the term 'science.'

It is no surprise to find that the *Encyclopaedia* fails to mention a major systematic attempt to consider myth as a subject of 'scientific' study: namely, the *New Science* (*Scienza Nuova*, first ed.: 1725; second ed.: 1730; final ed.: 1744) by Giambattista Vico (1668–1744). Vico's *magnum opus* enjoyed only a limited reception during his lifetime, and was first translated into French only in 1827. The aim of the *New Science* is to develop a 'scientific' philology for understanding myths. Its theoretical core is to be found in Vico's so-called *verum-factum* principle (*New Science*, §331), according to which humans are better able to understand human history than they are the natural world, since the former is man-made while God made the latter. Isaiah Berlin offers the following useful explanation of this notion: we may be able to calculate the geometrical dimensions of a table or to analyse the anatomy of an ant, but we will never know what it is like to *be* these things in the same way that we know what it is like to be human.[21] This argument is seen as having been of central importance for the tradition of modern philosophical hermeneutics, particularly as manifested in the works of Wilhelm Dilthey and Hans-Georg Gadamer, which emphasises that the understanding (*Verstehen*) of human histories, texts and artefacts requires not scientific explanation (*Erklären*) in the manner of the Cartesian and post-Cartesian natural sciences, but rather the capacity to feel one's way or transpose oneself into (*sich einfühlen, sich hineinversetzen in*) the original historical context of a text and its creator.[22] In *The Legibility of the World*, Blumenberg would come to see Vico's argument as offering a theory of metaphor: in order to make the world into something that we can understand, we need first of all to transfer it into language, which is why metaphor must have a transcendental status, that of a "detour via the self-made" (LW, 175).

How does Vico feel his way into the myths of the ancients? These first men (Vico refers to them as "giants") were "stupid, insensate, and horrible beasts," who, despite their stupidity, possessed the gift of "poetic wisdom" (§§374–5). This wisdom was first activated when the ancients were confronted by terrifying natural phenomena (thunder, lightning) that demanded explanations. Rudimentary though they were, these explanations amounted to a "poetic metaphysics" that shaped the ancients' worldview. Since primitive human nature tends to seek human causes for non-human effects, the thunder and lightning were attributed to the sky-god Jove (Roman: Jupiter; Greek: Zeus); in this way "poetic metaphysics" provided the terrified ancients with definitive anthropomorphic agents whom they could endeavour to propitiate (§§377–9). Later, this fear of the natural elements also led the ancients to retreat into caves, a moment that for Vico constitutes the origins of civilisation (§§388–9).[23]

In what sense is this account of the origin of myth 'scientific'? Certainly not in the Cartesian sense of empirical objects being understood in terms of geometrical method and deductive logic. Such an approach is, thinks Vico, of limited use in relation to human subject matter—such as the development of laws and institutions—that are not to be explained by recourse to 'clear and distinct ideas' in the manner of Descartes. Vico replaced Descartes's notion of *a priori* deductive reasoning with a quasi-Newtonian model adapted to human subject matter, in which human (as opposed to natural) principles or laws are derived from inductive historical observation. These general principles or laws are, thought Vico, as much cultural as they are natural or physiological, and are to be found in human institutions.[24] Since human institutions emerge from a *sensus communis* based on what is probable and practical, as opposed to indubitably correct, within a given situation, they need to be understood within the historical and social contexts of their genesis (§348). Thus, writes Vico, "our Science proceeds by a severe analysis of human thoughts about the human necessities or utilities of social life [. . . and . . .] is therefore a history of human ideas" (§347).[25] From this perspective, the mythological gods conceived or made (in the sense of *poiein* or making) by the ancients constitute a primitive *sensus communis* designed to respond to the bewildering state of affairs with which they were faced when the heavens opened above them. In this sense myths are primarily public and civic as opposed to private.

Vico undertakes a rehabilitation of myth insofar as he ascribes to it a primitive yet practical cognitive content, while also seeing mythology as useful historical source material through which we can come to understand cultural truths about earlier civilisations. This is why he disputes the classical notion that myths are unreliable, by arguing that the word *mythos* actually means a 'true account' (*vera narratio*, §§808, 814) of how humans saw things in a particular cultural context.[26] Vico proposes that Homer, whom he calls the most ancient of Western poets recorded in writing (§788), is already comparatively late culture. The fables from which Homer's epics are derived were originally "true histories," most likely circulated as oral narratives by rhapsodes, in which important details about early Greek civilisation are recorded. These narratives were subsequently performed on countless occasions, and repeated performances embellished them with fantastic and scandalous elements that would have been entertaining to audiences (§§808, 814).[27] For Vico, Homer was "a purely ideal poet who never existed as a particular man." Like the rhapsodes, he was a "stitcher-together" of various oral sources, to the extent that the word 'Homer' means nothing other than "the Greek people" (§§873, 852, 875).[28] These narratives also had a definite cultural function: in an argument that reiterates Aristotle's notion that myth is the initial wonder that paves the way for philosophy, Vico sees in mythic cognition a form of childlike curiosity that he describes as "the daughter of ignorance and the mother of knowledge" (§§189, 377). For this reason he disputes the notion that *mythos* and *logos* are opposed to one another.[29]

As Max Horkheimer has argued, while Vico does subscribe to the dominant Enlightenment narrative about myth insofar as he posits a necessary
progression from mythic to philosophical thinking, he is at the same time
exceptional, within the Enlightenment context, for having seen in myth a
creative form of cognition that paves the way for philosophical abstraction
and human institutions.[30] Yet the 'scientific' element in Vico's approach to
culture is to some extent pre-modern and contingent upon faith, in that
it sees cultural development as a form of divine providence (§348). Vico
observes that although many human societies exist in isolation from each
other, they develop according to universal laws and contain common elements such as religion, marriage and burial of the dead. These "uniform
ideas, born among people unknown to each other, must have a common
ground of truth" (§333).[31] Uncovering the universal necessity of this common ground, manifested in divine providence, is the object of Vico's science, as is suggested by the subtitle of his work: "Concerning the Common
Nature of the Nations."

But there is much in Vico that points forward, too: his view of myth
as a poetic response to the physical environment anticipates Johann Gottfried Herder's (1744–1803) understanding of myth as a natural form of
poetry;[32] his notion that Homer was not a real historical individual but
rather the sum-total of an oral poetic tradition resembles a similar thesis
offered by the father of German classical philology, Friedrich August Wolf
(1759–1824);[33] his attempt to establish an independent scientific method for
philological and historical studies has been seen to anticipate Wilhelm Dilthey's lifelong endeavour to provide the *Geisteswissenschaften* (humanities
or human sciences) with a theoretical foundation distinguished from that
of the natural sciences;[34] while his appreciation of myth as a creative form
of cognition presages part two of Ernst Cassirer's *Philosophy of Symbolic
Forms* (1925).[35] In *The Legibility of the World*, Blumenberg regards Vico's
New Science as a failed attempt to usurp the primary authority of the natural sciences as *the* sciences, but an attempt that nevertheless gave rise to the
modern conception of philology as science (in the sense of *Wissenschaft*).
This science explores "the relation between writing and reading" (LW, 173),
a subject which includes both the work *of* myth and the work *on* myth. We
have not heard the last of Vico.

MYTH AND THE 'SCIENCE OF HUMAN NATURE'

If, according to Manfred Frank, the beginnings of the *Sattelzeit* coincide
with a renewed interest in myth, then the most important centre for myth
research during the early phases of this period was to be found in Göttingen. The main protagonists were Johann David Michaelis (1717–91) and
Christian Gottlob Heyne (1724–1812), who established myth research as
a sub-discipline of Biblical philology in their capacities as directors (first

Michaelis, succeeded by Heyne) of the city's University Library. According to the historical-critical hermeneutics of Michaelis and Heyne, the Bible was no longer to be seen as emerging from a supra-historical revelation; they compared biblical stories with non-biblical myths, reconstructing the influence of the latter upon the former (an example being Heyne's hypothesis that the law of Moses emerged from Egyptian sources). Heyne was particularly interested in travel literature reporting on indigenous peoples of Africa and North America, and he compared their 'primitive' myths with Greek mythology. In a similar way to Fontenelle and Vico, Heyne proposed that mythical thought belongs to the "childhood" of "human nature," emerging from "ignorance concerning what causes appearances." Myths are for Heyne *philosophemes*: pre-rational, proto-philosophical notions through which primitive human beings attempted to explain natural phenomena.[36]

Although Michaelis and Heyne did not see themselves as 'anthropologists,' their Göttingen colleagues Johann Feder (1740–1821) and Christoph Meiners (1747–1810) certainly did. Feder and Meiners promoted the research of what they called *Weltweisheit* (wisdom concerning the world), their goal being an examination of myths from various cultures of the globe, including non-European sources.[37] This research programme understood itself to be 'empirical' insofar as it took its bearings from the scientific method of Francis Bacon and from Hume's *Treatise of Human Nature* (1739–40).[38] Hume had claimed that since all of the sciences emerge from the cognitive capacities of human beings, a "science of man" would function as the foundation of a "compleat system of the sciences." This science would be based on "experience and observation" of diverse forms of human phenomena.[39] Unlike Vico's *New Science*, Hume's programme for the human sciences was definitively modern in that it did not resort to non-empirical explanatory principles such as divine providence.

Hume's arguments were crucial for the emergence of anthropology in Germany. His empiricism caused the Cartesian separation between mind and body to be questioned, bringing the "whole human being" into focus as a scientific object, particularly in the context of medical discourses.[40] The most influential interpreter of Hume was Johann Gottfried Herder, who was introduced to Hume's writings by the pre-critical Kant. As a personal acquaintance of Heyne who was familiar with developments in Göttingen, Herder also signed up for Hume's programme of developing an empirical conception of the human sciences.[41] Here, as in Göttingen, the 'empirical' element did not refer to fieldwork but rather to library work: the examination of a broad range of travel reports dealing with both European and non-European cultures. In his *Treatise on the Origin of Language* (*Abhandlung über den Ursprung der Sprache*, 1772)—a text that John H. Zammito describes as "the inaugural moment of German anthropology"[42]—Herder draws on material from far-flung parts of the globe such as Lapland, North America, Peru, and South-East Asia (Siam). And in answering the question as to whether language has a divine or human origin, Herder takes recourse to an old argument, an early version of which—as we shall see in Chapter 5 of this volume—can already to be found in Plato's *Protagoras*.

Since, according to Herder, human beings are "far inferior to animals in strength and sureness of instinct," they require a "substitute" (*Ersatz*) for these missing instincts in order successfully to interact with their environment. Animals like bees or spiders have very restricted spheres of awareness to which their instincts of hive-building or web-spinning are perfectly fitted. But the larger the sphere of awareness that an animal has, the less strictly are these drives or capacities predetermined. So, for example, a fox may learn to alter its behaviour, and perhaps even to adapt its instincts, precisely because its sphere of activity and awareness is larger than that of a bee or a spider. Since human beings are said to have the weakest of all instinctual organisations—being born "naked," "instinctless," and "miserable"— their deficiencies need to be substituted for by the capacity for language. In this Herder sees an inherent logic: human weakness is compensated by the capacity for linguistic expression because in nature "everything counterbalances." The human being "can and must invent language" in order to adapt to its environment, since without language humans would be "attached to nothing" and "secured by nothing." This is also said to explain the long periods of parental care required by human infants for their development and socialisation, since these processes of formation (*Bildung*) compensate for a lack of behavioural automatisms.[43] It is no coincidence that we are reminded here of Erich Rothacker's arguments concerning the difference between animals (like ticks) that have restricted environments (*Umwelte*) and humans who have no predetermined *Umwelt* but are open to the world (*Welt*). Herder is an absolutely cardinal precursor not only for Rothacker, but also for Helmuth Plessner's ideas concerning the 'openness' and 'eccentricity' of human beings, as well as for Arnold Gehlen's notion that the human being is a 'creature of deficiencies' (*Mängelwesen*) in need of cultural compensations.[44]

At its most rudimentary level, language is said by Herder to emerge from human responses to aural stimuli in the form of imitations and onomatopoeic expressions. The first language is therefore poetry, defined as the "imitation of resounding, acting, stirring nature." This form of primitive linguistic expression is essentially metaphorical, since language relies upon the transference of feelings onto external objects. The dawn, for example, may be associated with qualities such as "beauty," "shining," and "freshness." Myths also serve a similar function, enabling the human being to relate to aspects of its environment through naming and personifying external phenomena and endowing them with genders. The stories that then accumulate around these names are attributed to the "strayings of the imagination." Languages, metaphors and myths are always dependent on climate, environment and cultural context: so, for example, the Arab has many words for camels, swords and snakes because these objects are prominent parts of his everyday life.[45] This theory is then further developed in Herder's *Ideas*

On the Philosophy of the History of Mankind (Ideen zur Philosophie der Geschichte der Menschheit, 1784–91), where he echoes Vico and Heyne in his claim that "the mythology of every people is an expression of their own distinctive way of viewing nature."[46]

The explicitly aesthetic and literary dimensions of Herder's ideas about myth emerge in the context of his critique of French neo-classicism and his call for a renewal of German literature, both of which are to be found in his *Fragments of a Treatise on the Ode (Fragmente einer Abhandlung über die Ode*, 1765) and his *Fragments on Recent German Literature (Über die neuere deutsche Literatur. Fragmente*, 1765–7). Herder proposed that a true German-language literature should—in a similar way to the myths of Homer, to Shakespeare's dramas, and to Ossian's (i.e., James Macpherson's) dithyrambic nature lyrics in their own national contexts—be an expression of the German culture and landscape written in an appropriately rustic register. The myths of the ancients are not, in Herder's view, simply to be trotted out as a demonstration of a poet's familiarity with classical antiquity. Rather, the modern use of myth lies in its capacity to give new philosophical ideas a sensuous shape by mediating them through captivating mythic images.[47] Herder's understanding of myth as a form of cultural communication that can be still be made use of in the modern age offers, according to Manfred Frank, an early counter-argument to the Enlightenment critique of myth, as well as an anticipation of the revival of myth in German romanticism.[48]

THE 'MYTHOLOGY OF REASON'

But Herder had opponents in this new discipline of anthropology, first and foremost among them being his friend and former mentor Immanuel Kant. As early as 1758, with the inauguration of his lectures on physical geography, and especially following the commencement of his lectures on anthropology in the winter semester of 1772–3, this new research field had stood at the centre of Kant's interests.[49] Kant's initial aim had been to establish anthropology as an independent and empirically oriented academic discipline. But Kant's interest in empirical anthropology was also more or less contemporaneous with his early breakthroughs in the field of transcendental critical philosophy (roughly from 1768–9 onwards). Anthropology eventually became for Kant a mere backdrop to what were (for him) more important questions concerning the capabilities and limits of reason as a ground for human knowledge and ethics. His main publication on the subject— *Anthropology from a Pragmatic Point of View (Anthropologie in pragmatischer Hinsicht*, 1798)—demonstrates this transition by devaluing the main question of the *physiological* or empirical anthropology of the Göttingen school (essentially: how humans *are*), through favouring the project of *pragmatic* anthropology: how humans *should be*.[50] This anti-empirical move in Kant's thought is already to be found in his *Groundwork of the Metaphysics of Morals* (*Grundlegung zur Metaphysik der Sitten*, 1785), in which he calls for a "pure moral philosophy," which should be cleansed of everything empirical and belonging to anthropology.[51]

Kant's rejection of the empirical programme of the Göttingen School was related to his attempt to redefine the meaning of the term *Wissenschaft* or science in transcendental terms. While the early Enlightenment had followed Bacon, Newton and Hume in describing science or *Wissenschaft* as the systematic and objective knowledge of nature based upon hypotheses tested by empirical experiments,[52] Kant called, in his *Metaphysical Foundations of Natural Science* (*Metaphysische Anfangsgründe der Naturwissenschaft*, 1786), for a science based not only on empirical evidence but also upon the *a priori* elements of human cognition.[53] For Kant, Hume's empirical 'science of man' could never suffice, because only an account of the *a priori* and necessary laws of human cognition could deliver the certain and systematic knowledge that deserves the name of natural science. Thus, although the fourth question outlined in Kant's *Logic* of 1800—*What is the human being?*—is afforded a key importance, the question itself is to be answered more transcendentally than empirically: namely, in relation to the conditions of human knowledge, its practical use, and its limits.[54]

This focus also meant that the term *Wissenschaft* could only be used in a quite restricted sense. Since, for example, physics has a logical basis in the *a priori* categories of the understanding such as causality, it qualifies as a science in Kant's apodictic terms; however, a science like biology, which must resort to reflective teleological judgements in order to explain how an organism develops as a natural purpose or *Naturzweck*—as Kant outlines in part two of the *Critique of Judgement* (*Kritik der Urteilskraft*, 1790), see sections 61, 66, 75—is seen as being more akin to aesthetics than to science. Such judgements—that, for example, a plant develops as the expression of natural purpose—may enjoy only an heuristic and not a determinate usage, since they emerge from our reason and are not apodictically grounded in the categories of the understanding. And even more so than a plant—the branches, stems, and leaves of which might seem to interact in ways suggesting that there are teleological ideas inherent in nature—the human being exceeds the boundaries of science as Kant had defined them. Humans, in being capable of surmounting their natural tendencies in the service of the rational commands of ethics, seem to express a purpose that entirely transcends the empirical world and that leads to God as a necessary idea of reason: away from science and towards metaphysics and religion.

Kant's non-empirical redefinition of *Wissenschaft* is at once conservative and potentially radical. Its conservatism is expressed in the idea that only apodictic or logically necessary knowledge can be scientific knowledge. This essentially means that only philosophy, mathematics, and physics can be scientific (a position that can already be found in Descartes),[55] and excludes the determinate use of teleology from science. Kant's latent radicalism, which is probably unintended, lies in the notion that science must be grounded not only in the external objects of nature, but also (and perhaps primarily) in the cognitive apparatus of the subject. The key figures in German idealism—Johann Gottlieb Fichte (1762–1814), Friedrich Wilhelm Joseph Schelling (1775–1854), and George Wilhelm Friedrich Hegel (1770–1831)—effectively ignored the restrictive elements of Kant's notion of science, while literally running wild with its radical or subjective element, proposing that all manner of teleologies (of the self, of nature and of history) exist not just heuristically, but actually. If science were to be grounded in human cognition, or in what came to be known as spirit or mind (*Geist*), then its proper subject could be the way in which subjectivity makes reality per se possible (Fichte, *Science of Knowledge/Wissenschaftslehre*, 1794–5), the degree to which human subjectivity and nature are part of a greater 'I' or subject known as the world-soul (Schelling, *Ideas Towards a Philosophy of Nature / Ideen zu einer Philosophie der Natur*, 1797), or the sense in which history represents the progressive unfolding of a trans-individual *Geist* (Hegel, *Phenomenology of Spirit/Phänomenologie des Geistes*, 1807). However problematic their usages of this term may be from our present-day point of view, all three thinkers associated their respective projects with the concept of *Wissenschaft*, or science.[56]

If the early German researches on the subject of mythology carried out by the Göttingen School and by Herder had been based on Hume's empirical conception of the human sciences, what were the consequences of Kant's transcendental turn, not to mention its radicalisation by German idealism, for thinking about myth? And bearing in mind the synchronic relations between concepts outlined by Koselleck, did Kant's transcendental redefinition of science also lead to a redefinition of mythology? Kant's successors in the tradition of German idealism essentially agreed that Kant had correctly explained the conditions of human knowledge. But his notion that *a priori* elements of human cognition can only synthesise appearances (*Vorstellungen*) of the world had also served to separate the mind from external reality, now defined as the mysterious and inaccessible 'thing-in-itself.' Perhaps mythology—by dint of its origins in the distant beginnings of humanity, its primitive ability to give captivating expression to sensuous and natural forces, and its capacity to give shape to cultural institutions and local identities—might function as a kind of aesthetic bridge, which could heal the split between the mind and nature, and also between philosophical theory and political praxis?

This, at any rate, was the claim made by the authors of the "Oldest System-Programme of German Idealism" ("Das älteste Systemprogramm des deutschen Idealismus," 1796–7)—thought to have been Hegel, Schelling, and the poet Friedrich Hölderlin (1770–1843)[57]—in what amounts to a strikingly ambitious disruption of the Enlightenment's account of myth. We must, they write,

> have a new mythology, but this mythology must be in the service of the Ideas, it must become a mythology of reason [*Mythologie der Vernunft*].

Before we make the Ideas aesthetic, i.e. mythological, they are of no interest to the people and on the other hand before mythology is reasonable the philosopher must be ashamed of it.[58]

Although, for the authors of the "System-Programme," myth is not to be equated with science, it can nonetheless be put to use under the auspices of reason. It would be wrong, however, to see this use as a cynical retooling of myth as ideology or as political propaganda; rather, the authors of the "System-Programme" genuinely see myth as a central component of the philosophical project of modernity, and as a normative way of exceeding the inherent limitations of Kant's critical philosophy. Since, for Kant, ideas such as freedom as the condition of ethical behaviour are constructions of human rationality that can bear only a heuristic relation to external reality, having no sensuous referent in the real world, they are like pale abstractions that are unable to find traction within the social and political realms. In this context, the role of mythology is to offer sensuous representations of the ideas of pure reason, thereby performing a task that Kant had, in §59 of the *Critique of Judgement*, associated with the role of the symbol. Kant, who is far less optimistic than the authors of the "System-Programme" concerning the possibility of representing the ideas of pure reason sensuously, sees the symbol as an aesthetic tool which can only *indirectly* represent the idea to which it corresponds. It is in this vein, for example, that Kant claims that if a representation (*Vorstellung*) of something can be termed a kind of "cognition" (*Erkenntnis*) of it, then "all of our cognition of god is merely symbolic."[59]

Reading the "System-Programme" with the benefit hindsight provided by twentieth-century history is a sobering experience. As Andrew Bowie has argued, the "System-Programme," with its demand that theoretical ideas be rendered sensuous within the political and social contexts of the modern state, seems in retrospect to anticipate a range of phenomena spanning from the calculated use of myth by the National Socialists in Germany to the methods of advertising deployed in late capitalism.[60] The "System-Programme" demonstrated that mythology was neither antiquated nor completely irrational, but in fact central to the modern age. In this respect 'mythology' also corresponds directly with the kinds of concepts identified by Koselleck in his *Lexikon* on the *History of Concepts*: "old expressions [. . .] that were not just at the forefront of German classicism and idealism, but which also gave new contours to the terminology used in relation to the state and society."[61] Put simply: in early German idealism and romanticism myth had become modern and was not going to go away.

THE 'SCIENCE OF MYTH' AS THE HISTORY OF CONSCIOUSNESS: SCHELLING

As George S. Williamson demonstrates at some length in *The Longing for Myth in Germany* (2004), the "System-Programme" represents only the fragmentary beginning of a grander preoccupation with myth in German romanticism. Although this preoccupation emerged from the anthropological discourses that circulated in Germany during the late eighteenth century, certain variants of it took on a distinctly non-anthropological and more or less purely aesthetic dimension. Friedrich Schlegel's *Dialogue on Mythology* (*Rede über die Mythologie*, 1800) is one such case, since it tends to equate mythology with poetry, seeing mythology as an aesthetic mode that can combine sensuous natural forms with the philosophical content of German idealism. This "sensuous-intellectual" (*sinnlich geistig*) capacity of mythology is, according to Schlegel, its greatest advantage. But unlike the organic myths valorised by Herder, Schlegel's new mythology will be a distinctly modern construction, "the most artificial of all artworks."[62]

Of greater interest with specific respect to the subject of myth and the human sciences are Schelling's attempts to develop a theory, even a *Wissenschaft* or science, of mythology. Myth occupies a central position in all phases of Schelling's thought, yet its function changes depending on the overall philosophical context in which it appears. In the *System of Transcendental Idealism* (*System des transzendentalen Idealismus*, 1800) myth—which is broadly representative of all art—is a medium though which the limited and conscious 'I' of the subject can gain access to the greater and unconscious 'I' of which it is part: that of nature or the world-soul. In these terms it is the "medium" or "link" (*Mittelglied*) through which science (*Wissenschaft*) will return to poetry.[63] In the *Philosophy of Art* (*Philosophie der Kunst*, 1802–3), mythology makes possible the "presentation of the absolute within limits, without any abrogation (*Aufhebung*) of the absolute." Myths are in this sense symbolic and not allegorical. While allegory would suggest that the particular God Minerva merely *represents* or *means* the general idea of wisdom, when viewed as a mythic symbol she *is* wisdom, since the symbol absolutely fuses the real with the ideal. Unlike Kant at section 59 of the *Critique of Judgment*, Schelling—now elaborating an early version of his philosophy of identity—sees the symbol as the actual embodiment (and not as the indirect expression), of its referent. In this respect myth is "the necessary condition and primary material of all art," representing a primordial stage of unity which the art of modernity attempts to recapture.[64]

The late Schelling embeds a similar version of this notion of myth-as-symbol within a grander narrative about the origins and cultural development of all peoples (*Völker*). This narrative is to be found in the *Historical-Critical Introduction to the Philosophy of Mythology* (*Historisch-Kritische Einleitung in die Philosophie der Mythologie*, 1842),[65] which he regards as a "science of mythology" (*Wissenschaft der Mythologie*). Here the term *Wissenschaft* or science is deployed in both the Aristotelian and German idealist senses. To offer a scientific account of something means to explain its "living seed" (*lebendiger Keim*) or "essence" (*Wesen*), the source of its Being and movement. Yet the scientific object in question is not the empirical world but rather the teleological history of the 'I' or human subject. This history will uncover nothing less than a "law" (*Gesetz*) of human nature.[66] Myth, according to Schelling, is a "natural, necessary plant" which is "not made by humans," and for this reason "mankind [. . .] finds itself in a state of unfreedom" with respect to myth. Schelling holds that myth is not poetry, as this would imply that man invents myth, when in fact "the first forging place of mythology, lies beyond all poesy." Moreover, the "authentication" (*Beglaubigung*) of myth cannot be manufactured and is beyond human control. Myth is neither proto-philosophy nor proto-science, since this would imply that it corresponds with a capacity for conscious creation, and that the mythic materials were somehow at the disposal of humans. Myth is not something that a "people" (*Volk*) can adopt or create in order to found a cultural identity in the manner of Friedrich Schlegel; it is *already* their identity in advance of any process of conscious reflection.[67]

According to Schelling, myth is an "*original whole* [. . .] a body of un-pre-thinkable human knowledge." Yet here the word 'knowledge' is not strictly accurate, since the primordial ground of myth cannot be an object of cognition that is separated from the subject. This is because myth *is* consciousness, or at least the "succession of ideas, through which consciousness has actually passed"—from a mute and unconscious monotheism, via the first stirrings of a semi-conscious polytheism (the Greco-Roman pantheon), to an abstract monotheism (Christianity). Since mythology has "no reality outside of human consciousness," the Gods do not mean anything other than what they are. Myth is therefore "not allegorical [. . .] it is tautegorical."[68] Schelling's account of myth as a history of human consciousness does tell a story of progress, insofar that its stages move from natural (Greek) to revealed (Christian) religion. But in important respects Schelling offers late Romanticism's most radical critique of the Enlightenment *mythos* to *logos* narrative. If myth is literally constitutive of consciousness, then there can be no 'getting over' myth, and the on-going human need for meaning in religion and art is a necessary expression myth's foundational status. A scientific theory of myth can therefore *describe* myth as the history of human consciousness, but this does not mean that either natural or revealed religion can be resolved or overcome by science, since both exist prior to and independently of reason.[69]

Here a comparison between Schelling's approach to myth and religion and that of David Hume in the *Natural History of Religion* (1757) is instructive. Like Schelling, Hume sees polytheism as having preceded abstract theism proper; yet unlike Schelling, Hume contests the notion that a primordial monotheism underlay the emergence of polytheism. To see monotheism as having preceded polytheism would, in Hume's opinion, be akin to arguing that "men inhabited palaces before huts and cottages." The "natural progress of human thought" was one in which humans originally endeavoured to understand a variety of "unknown causes" behind misfortunes such as bad weather or pestilence. Such misfortunes caused human beings to "ask questions" concerning their causes and about how they might be averted in the future. [70]

By supposing that each natural event "is governed by some intelligent agent," polytheism endeavours "to get a determinate idea" of these agents and thereby to allay anxiety. According to Hume, the "limited influence of these agents, and their great proximity to human weakness, introduce the various distribution and division of their authority." This led to a situation in which every place became "stored with a crowd of local deities." By making an analogy between the social organisation of men and that of the gods, humans then determined that one god was likely to be more powerful than the others combined, an idea that eventually led to monotheism. The tendency of humans to slip from monotheism back into polytheism was averted, at least in some religions (namely, Judaism and Islam) through a prohibition being placed on images of God. [71]

Hume's attitude to mythic polytheism is one of ambivalence. Insofar as mythic polytheism posits a variety of causes for natural events, it displays a kind of logic that cannot simply be dismissed as absurd. Yet at the same time, the notion of a single "creator of the world"—a unified design or intention behind nature—is a rational development out of the polytheistic worldview. Hume does see the transition from polytheism to monotheism as representing a kind of progress, a movement "from rude beginnings to greater perfection." Yet unlike Schelling, he does not see monotheism as the unalloyed pinnacle in the history of religion. For Hume, monotheism is marred by its "sacred zeal and rancour," its tendency to exclude the views of other religions. By contrast, polytheism is inherently "social," in that "by limiting the powers and functions of its deities, it naturally admits the gods of other sects and nations to a share of divinity" (160). In short: "polytheism, claiming no single truth about a unique god, is more tolerant than monotheism." [72] As we shall see, this praise of polytheism reappears in *Work on Myth*.

AFTER DARWIN: LANGUAGE, MYTH, AND CULTURAL DEVELOPMENT

The death of Schelling in 1854 roughly coincides with the end of the *Sattelzeit* and also with a restoration of the old order in the relationship between myth and science. The grand, speculative and teleological *Wissenschaften* or 'sciences' of German idealism propagated by Fichte, Schelling and Hegel are subjected to a profound critique, leading to a stricter bifurcation of the natural and human sciences (*Natur- und Geisteswissenschaften*). According to an important public lecture delivered by the eminent physicist and physiologist Hermann von Helmholtz (1821–94) in 1862, while the *Geisteswissenschaften* are associated with the now discredited "Icarus-flight of speculation" that is German idealism, as well as with a form of "artistic and not strictly logical induction," only the *Naturwissenschaften* are seen as being securely based in testable hypotheses derived from non-teleological and empirical inductions.[73]

With the rise of Darwinism in the human sciences, the notion that myth represents a primitive developmental phase in human culture is given a fresh scientific currency by new ideas concerning the evolution of culture and by more systematic (yet often deeply prejudiced) research into the non-European cultures of colonised nations. In this new context, now dominated by the increasing prestige of the natural sciences, the idealist-romantic programme of the new mythology almost completely disappears, before enjoying a late and relatively isolated aesthetic resurgence in Nietzsche's *Birth of Tragedy* (*Geburt der Tragödie*, 1872/1886, to be discussed in Chapter 5 of this volume). In short: after Darwin, the Enlightenment's tale of *mythos* to *logos* is retold with conviction.

A key transitional figure between the late romanticism of Schelling and the onset of Darwinism in the study of myth is the German philologist and Sanskrit scholar Friedrich Max Müller (1823–1900), better known as Max Müller. Müller had attended Schelling's lectures on the *Philosophy of Mythology* in Berlin, but in 1846 he left Germany for Britain in order to make use of manuscripts of the *Rigveda* held by the British East India Company. Müller's many years of work on his edition of the *Rigveda* (the final volume of six appeared in 1874) were part of a long research visit to Britain that turned into a permanent stay after he was appointed as Professor of Modern Languages at Oxford in 1854.[74]

As a German scholar working in Britain, Müller was a populariser of theories about language and myth that were already dated in Germany by the middle of the nineteenth century. His breakthrough work was his essay on "Comparative Mythology" (1856), the key notions of which were further elaborated in a later lecture entitled "On the Philosophy of Mythology" (1871) and in the two-volume study *Contributions to the Science of Mythology* (1897).[75] Müller's initial argument mirrors that of the Göttingen School and of Herder, proposing that myths are primitive responses to natural phenomena. The narrative component of myth is seen by Müller to have arisen from a dearth of substantives and a surfeit of predicates in ancient languages. When, for example, the ancient 'Aryans' first encountered the sun, they described it as "the brilliant, the awakener, the runner, the ruler, the father, the giver of warmth." These originally figurative descriptions were gradually transformed into substantives, which in Sanskrit are assigned with either a masculine or a feminine gender. From there it was only a short step to the elaboration of mythic narratives involving male and female gods. [76]

Myth is therefore the "dark shadow which language throws over thought" because it emerged from the overuse of figurative predicates, with the more virulent predicates forming the basis of implausible tales that served only to obscure what had originally been simple descriptions of natural objects. Of interest is Müller's notion that if all human thought is dependent upon language, and if all language is to some extent figurative or metaphorical rather than purely conceptual, then even in the modern age myth will never disappear. "Depend upon it," writes Müller, "there is mythology now as there was in the time of Homer, only we do not perceive it, because we ourselves live in the very shadow of it." It is in this sense that the "the whole history of philosophy, from Thales down to Hegel" can be seen as "an uninterrupted protest of thought against language."[77]

For Müller, the disciplines that he refers to as 'The Science of Language,' 'The Science of Mythology,' and 'The Science of Religion' are virtually indistinguishable. This is because language roots form the basis of all myths and religions. For example, the Sanskrit root *div* (meaning to shine or sparkle) underlies the Hindu word *Dyaus* (referring to the God who lights the sky; Zeus in Greek; Jupiter in Latin) and its Indo-European derivations (*deva, deus, deity*).[78] Müller believes that etymology is the key to the 'sciences' of language, mythology and religion, but in the new context of British empiricism, he gives these old German theories a new natural scientific tenor. Drawing upon Charles Lyell's *Principles of Geology* (1830), Müller argues that just as different geological and paleontological strata point to different periods of the earth's history, so too can human history be researched through the analogous linguistic strata to be found in ancient languages and myths.[79] And with the onset of Darwinism after 1859, a number of lectures by Müller describe the language roots that underlie myths as organisms or "phonetic cells" that compete with one another in a linguistic-cultural version of the "struggle for life" discovered by "the genius of Darwin."[80]

According to Müller, "natural selection" is always "rational selection" when applied to language and myth: "out of the endless number of general notions that suggest themselves to the observing and gathering mind, those only survive and receive definite phonetic expression which are absolutely requisite for carrying on the work of life." The utility of a linguistic expression is the decisive factor in its survival: words such as 'brother' and 'sister' were, in Müller's view, essential for cultural organisation and were therefore retained, while "others disappeared when they were no longer required." Similarly, in the fields of myth and religion the more useful notions retain their currency and relevance, with the most important being "the conception of a Creator, a Ruler, a Father of man."[81] Müller argued that the most ancient idea found in the myths of the so-called Indo-European or Aryan peoples[82]—that of the sun or giver of light as the Father or God—survives in Christian monotheism,[83] and within the context of British colonialism in India, Müller understood his task to be that of rediscovering the primal monotheistic basis that allegedly underlies both Christianity and Hinduism.[84] Here the influence of Schelling becomes apparent in Müller's theories of religion and myth, and it was this notion of a primal monotheism, combined with man's alleged *a priori* capacity to give expression to the divine in language,[85] that saw Müller desperately attempting to refute Darwin's theories on human descent.[86]

But by the early 1870s Müller was fighting a losing battle against the new dominant British paradigm in the theory of myth, which took its cues from Darwin's *Descent of Man* and its essentially Humean arguments concerning the origins of language and culture.[87] While Müller had used a Kantian epistemology in his attempt to differentiate humans from animals—arguing that words always arise from concepts, and that only humans possess an *a priori* capacity for conceptual-linguistic expression—Darwin proposed, in an explicit rejection of Müller's position, that language is merely an evolved version of the "imitative cries" found among primate species. Language, for Darwin, is not originally conceptual; rather, it originates from what Hume called 'impressions,' which only later lead to 'ideas.' Indeed, Darwin even supposed that the level of abstract self-consciousness possessed by a British domestic dog might be roughly comparable with that of a "degraded Australian savage."[88]

Once Darwin had apparently confirmed an evolutionary continuum—spanning from animals, through so-called primitive humans, to advanced and complex (European) civilisations—it was self-evident that such notions, which had already been anticipated by pre-Darwinian British evolutionists such as Herbert Spencer (1820–1903),[89] would become central to the human sciences and to the theory of myth. And in the same year that Darwin published the *Descent of Man*, the first Professor of Anthropology in Britain—Edward Burnett Tylor (1832–1917)—outlined a theory of myth that was perfectly suited to the context of Empire. In *Primitive Culture* (1871), Tylor argues—also in explicit opposition to Max Müller's linguistic theory of myth—that the most primitive myths arise from physical sense impressions without the intervention of words or concepts. Animism—through which human beings invest physical objects with souls, and explain natural events by way of recourse to personified forces or gods—is therefore seen as being the most basic form of myth, while also being a key component of primitive religion. Thus, for example, the Peruvian Indians are said to explain the rain through a myth in which a princess in the sky empties her vase.[90]

In positing causal relations between personified forces and natural events, myth is for Tylor a pre-scientific form of inductive logic: primitive theories concerning cause-and-effect relations are already a cognitive achievement, it is only the relations themselves that are, in their reliance on personified forces, completely fallacious.[91] Modernity and civilisation therefore incorporate the processes through which "the growth of myth is checked by science," and myth represents the most rudimentary stage of human cultural development, preceding the more advanced stages of monotheistic religion and scientific rationality. Tylor attributes his ideas concerning the progressive "continuity of civilization" to the influence of Auguste Comte's three-stage model outlined in the *Course of Positive Philosophy* (*Cours de philosophie positive*, 1830–42), according to which human development passes through theological, metaphysical and positive (in the sense of scientific) stages. While Tylor makes the observation that in 'advanced' European societies ideas such as the soul are now only associated with human beings and with the "metaphysics of religion," many contemporary "savages" in Asia, Africa, Oceania, and Australia allegedly continue to live in "the myth-making stage of the human mind." Myth therefore relates to "the general ethnological problem of the development of civilization" and is a central theme for anthropology as a "science of culture." Culture (which for Tylor is coterminous with civilisation) is defined "in its wide ethnographic sense [. . . as . . .] that complex whole which includes knowledge, belief, art, morals, custom and any other capabilities and habits acquired by man as member of society." Different evolutionary levels of culture are to be found in contemporary civilisations, on a descending scale from the most 'advanced' (northern Europe and North America), to the purportedly most primitive (Aboriginal Australia).[92]

A similar theory of myth—and a theory influenced by Tylor, as well as by Tylor's network of researchers in the colonies—is offered by the Cambridge social anthropologist James George Frazer (1854–1941) in his epic multi-volume study *The Golden Bough* (first ed., 2 vols.: 1890; second ed., 3 vols.: 1900; third ed., 12 vols.: 1911–15).[93] Whereas Tylor's model of human progress involves the neo-Comtean stages of animism-monotheism-science, Frazer replaced these categories with those of magic-religion-science. This sequence is first explicitly developed in the second (1900) edition of *The Golden Bough*.[94] Magic is "the bastard sister of science," relying on false laws of similarity and contiguity. The law of similarity is, for example, said to suggest to Peruvian Indians that burning an effigy of one's foe will cause him real physical harm, while the law of contiguity allegedly causes some Australian Aborigines to think that following an initiation ritual in which a young boy's tooth is removed from his mouth and placed under a tree, the tooth's infestation by ants would cause the boy to suffer a disease of the mouth.[95]

The central assumption of these laws is that of a "uniformity in nature," a notion which is said to be "identical with that of modern science." As in Tylor's account, it is only the primitive laws of similarity and contiguity themselves that are incorrect. Religion then arises when more advanced cultures conceive of supernatural beings that control nature, which humans in turn endeavour to propitiate through particular rituals, while science finally represents the developmental stage at which humans realise that such acts of propitiation are useless, and instead attempt to grasp the physical laws of nature.[96] Like Tylor, Frazer assumes that some contemporary 'primitive' societies continue to function at a level which is intermediate between magic and religion, and that their practices may provide insights into the prehistory of advanced European cultures. It is within this intermediate stage that myth and ritual are most prominent.[97]

Frazer associates myth with fertility and harvest rituals. In European antiquity and among some contemporary 'primitive' peoples, he argues, nature is viewed as being subject to a cycle of birth and death. So-called kings, priests, or magicians can influence this cycle. But as these seers age and weaken, so too does their apparent power to influence nature decline, and this means that a process of renewal is necessitated, through which they are slain and replaced by younger successors who inherit the powers of their elders. By acting out these events in the form of ritual, it is hoped that nature will be influenced according to the law of similarity. The purpose of the fertility myth and its accompanying ritual is not to explain the world, as in Tylor, but to secure a bountiful harvest. Myth is therefore the primitive counterpart to applied science rather than to scientific theory in general.[98] Frazer regards these beliefs as being held in different versions by various cultures, and as underlying the totemic and sacrificial rituals found in religions all over the world.[99] It was an audacious theory that Frazer—the archetypal 'armchair' anthropologist who rarely left Cambridge—spent the majority of his career trying to substantiate. The empirical substance that allegedly undergirded the theory was to be found in an ever-widening collection of 'primitive' ethnographic data, sourced from a motley assortment of missionaries and petty colonial officials, some of whom had been primed in advance by Frazer's magic-religion-science hypothesis.[100]

Although Tylor's first book was based on his fieldwork in Mexico,[101] his ideas and those of Frazer predate the emergence of modern ethnographic method in the research of figures such as Franz Boas (1858–1942) and Bronislaw Malinowski (1884–1942). Tylor and Frazer were soon discredited for having drawn untenable relations between vastly differing peoples and historical periods in order to support their respective hypotheses concerning the evolution of culture.[102] Yet their ideas survived, not so much in professional anthropology, but in Anglophone literary criticism.[103]

As late as 1948, in his *Notes Towards the Definition of Culture*, T. S. Eliot still cites Tylor as the main authority on the concept of culture in English.[104] He also famously invokes *The Golden Bough*—and its later interpretation by Jessie Weston[105]—as source material for his epic poem *The Wasteland* (1922). When Eliot claimed that Frazer's ponderous multi-volume study is "a work of no less importance for our time that the contemporary work of Freud, throwing its light on the obscurities of the soul from a different angle," he placed Frazer at the centre of Anglo-American modernism.[106] (Freud, incidentally, had already made liberal use of *The Golden Bough* in *Totem and Taboo*). In a review of James Joyce's *Ulysses*, Eliot associates *The Golden Bough* with what he calls the "mythical method"—the practice of ordering the contents of modernity, and of comparing the 'primitive' and modern worlds, through the aesthetic use of classical myth.[107] It may therefore be the case that Tylor and particularly Frazer succeeded not in elaborating a science of myth, but rather in remythicizing myth: in making myth once again potent for art.

BLUMENBERG'S BELATEDNESS

When it comes to myth, according to Blumenberg, there is nothing new under the sun. What appears to us to be the most primeval mythic material is already the product of the work *of* myth: of the attempts of consciousness to deal with threatening aspects of the human biological situation by transforming these threats into mythic images, and to update these images by endowing them with significance in new historical contexts. Myth is therefore always already a belated phenomenon, a cultural adaptation to a now already forgotten primal scene of terror (WOM, 9; AM, 15).

The same goes for the reception of myth, the work *on* myth. This is because myth is itself always already a reception of what has gone before (WOM, 217, 270; AM, 240, 299), and in this sense the theory of myth from the pre-Socratics onwards cannot easily be separated from myth itself (WOM, 118; AM, 133). This sense of reflexivity, in which the theory of myth is itself a part of myth, is a central feature of Blumenberg's *Work on Myth*, and the belatedness of Blumenberg's theory can easily be determined when it is compared with the work on myth undertaken during the *Sattelzeit*.

Perhaps the most striking similarities of all are between Blumenberg and Vico, to whom Blumenberg does attribute a key place as the first Western thinker to have located myth at the heart of a philosophy of history (WOM, 377; AM, 412). Like Vico, Blumenberg outlines a primal scene of terror to which myth is a response, and he also embeds his theory of myth in a speculative account of the earliest human-like beings, their habitats, and (in *Cave Exits*) their eventual retreat into caves. An emphasis upon the pragmatic element of primeval culture—the sense in which it forms an institutional *sensus communis* that makes human life possible—is also something that Blumenberg takes from Vico, sharing with him a rehabilitation of rhetoric that is grounded in a critique of Cartesian method.[108] Similarly, Blumenberg shares with Herder—possibly through the mediating influences of Plessner, Rothacker, and Gehlen—the notion that myth may be a form of cultural orientation that compensates for a purported lack of strong instinctual determinants in human behaviour. Perhaps most crucially of all, Blumenberg explicitly follows Hume in attributing to myth the notion of a division of powers that alleviates anxiety. And in his critique of Carl Schmitt's political theology, he also implicitly agrees with Hume's view that mythic polytheism is more tolerant than monotheism (see Chapter 7 of this volume).

Deep continuities can also be found between Blumenberg's approach to myth and those found in German idealism and romanticism. Blumenberg's theory of metaphor, which precedes and anticipates his theory of myth, emerges from his reception of Kant's notion of the symbol (*Critique of Pure Reason*, §59), and Blumenberg's notion of "absolute metaphors," which in their orienting function serve a similar purpose to myths, display strong similarities with Kant's argument that reflective teleological judgements enable us to cognise individual phenomena within a grander, heuristic picture of the world (PM, 4–5; PZM, 11–12). The insistence of the "System-Programme" that myth is not antiquated but modern, and that a "mythology of reason" might enable sensuous representations of the ideas of reason, also resembles the role attributed to absolute metaphors in *Paradigms for a Metaphorology*.

Blumenberg does not elaborate a primal monotheism *á la* Schelling, but he does share with him the idea that if myth lies at the inaccessible origin of human consciousness, then it is not something that is simply at the disposal of the artist. In order for myths to possess significance, they must somehow resonate with the human situation as it is manifested within a particular historical context. For Blumenberg, this level of resonance owes as much to apparent 'fate' or coincidence as it does to human design, and the artist is therefore always already conditioned by myth and by historical circumstances before the work on myth even begins. For this reason, significance "has no nameable author" and "equipping something with significance is not something that we can choose to do" (WOM, 75, 68; AM, 85, 78).

Remarkable continuities also exist between the late romanticism of Max Müller and Blumenberg. Here two issues are of central interest. First, Müller's emphasis on the metaphorical content of myth and the notion that if language is irreducibly metaphorical, then myth can never be overcome, notions that can also be found in Blumenberg's *Paradigms for a Metaphorology*. And second, Müller's attempt to understand language and myth through cultural selection, by way of analogy with Darwinian natural selection. Blumenberg's elaborate critique of Darwin in part two of *Description of Man*, according to which humans, at a certain point in their history, began to evolve by cultural as opposed to natural selection, is expressed in a briefer form in *Work on Myth*: in Blumenberg's view, man learned "to subject his artefacts and instruments, instead of himself, to the process of adaptation," and these artefacts include myths (WOM, 165; AM, 183).

Unlike Tylor and Frazer, and also in contrast to important twentieth-century theorists of myth such as Freud (in *Totem and Taboo*) and Claude Levi-Strauss, Blumenberg's mature theory of myth makes barely any reference to ethnographic material from so-called primitive non-European cultures, and although Blumenberg refers to 'myth' in such a way as to suggest it is a universal cultural phenomenon, all of his examples are taken from high European culture. But Blumenberg does share with Tylor and Frazer the idea that myth is a cognitive achievement that provides the basic frame of expectation for scientific rationality: "what science repeats has already been suggested by myth" (WOM, 38; AM, 45). He differs from them, however, in maintaining that as long as there are threatening aspects of reality that cannot be controlled by human beings and their various technologies, then there will always be more work for myth to do. "Nothing surprised the promoters of the Enlightenment more," according to Blumenberg, "than the survival of the contemptible old stories—the continuation of the work on myth" (WOM, 274; AM, 303).

NOTES

1. Wilhelm Nestle, *Vom Mythos zum Logos: Die Selbstentfaltung des griechischen Denkens von Homer bis auf die Sophistik und Sokrates* (Stuttgart: Kröner, 1940). For a critical reflection on Nestle's position and its widespread influence, see Glenn W. Most, "From Logos to Mythos," in *From Myth to Reason? Studies in the Development of Greek Thought*, ed. Richard Buxton (Oxford: Oxford University Press, 1999), 25–47; here: 26–31.
2. Reinhart Koselleck, "Einleitung," in *Geschichtliche Grundbegriffe: Historisches Lexikon zur politisch-sozialen Sprache in Deutschland*, ed. Otto Brunner, Werner Conze, and Reinhart Koselleck, 8 vols in 9 (Stuttgart: Klett-Cotta, 1972–97), 1: xiii–xxvii; here: xv. See also Koselleck: "Das achtzehnte Jahrhundert als Beginn der Neuzeit," in *Poetik und Hermeneutik*, vol. 12, *Epochenschwelle und Epochenbewußtsein*, ed. Reinhart Herzog and Reinhart Koselleck (Munich: Fink, 1987), 269–82.
3. For context, see Maike Oergel, *Culture and Identity: Historicity in German Literature and Thought 1770–1815* (Berlin: De Gruyter, 2006), 4.
4. Koselleck, *The Practice of Conceptual History: Timing History, Spacing Concepts*, trans. Todd Samuel Presner (Stanford, CA: Stanford University Press, 2002), 5–7.
5. On the relation between *Begriffsgeschichte* and *Geistesgeschichte*, see Melvin Richter, *The History of Political and Social Concepts: A Critical Introduction* (New York: Oxford University Press, 1995), 3–6.
6. Koselleck, "Einleitung," in *Geschichtliche Grundbegriffe*, 1:xxiii–xxiv.
7. Here it should be noted that following the foundation of the journal *Archiv für Begriffsgeschichte* in 1955 by Erich Rothacker, two different conceptions of *Begriffsgeschichte* developed. Some participants, such as Rothacker, Joachim Ritter, and Hans-Georg Gadamer, understood *Begriffsgeschichte* to be the diachronic study of the development of Western philosophical concepts since antiquity, not unlike the history of ideas. This conception of *Begriffsgeschichte* was realised in the monumental *Historisches Wörterbuch der Philosophie*, ed. Joachim Ritter, Karlfried Gründer and Gottfried Gabriel, et al., 13 vols (Basel: Schwabe, 1971–2007). Others, like Koselleck, Otto Brunner and Werner Conze, were more interested in the synchronic relations between concepts, and the relation of these concepts in turn to concrete social and political realities during the *Sattelzeit* in Germany. This understanding of *Begriffsgeschichte* is manifested in *Geschichtliche Grundbegriffe*. See Richter, *The History of Social and Political Concepts*, 11–19.
8. Koselleck, "Einleitung," in *Geschichtliche Grundbegriffe*, 1:xx–xxi.
9. See Manfred Frank, "Ein Grundelement der historischen Analyse: Die Diskontinuität—Die Epochenwende von 1775 in Foucaults Archäologie," in *Epochenschwelle und Epochenbewußtsein*, 97–130.
10. Michel Foucault, *The Order of Things: An Archaeology of the Human Sciences* (1966; London: Routledge, 2002), xiii, 387–8, 382, 384–5.
11. Foucault, *The Order of Things*, 375, xiii.
12. See Frank, "Ein Grundelement der historischen Analyse," 99.
13. Foucault, *The Order of Things*, 397.
14. See, for example, Eric Csapo, *Theories of Mythology* (London: Blackwell, 2005), 80–131.
15. See Angus Nicholls and Martin Liebscher, eds., *Thinking the Unconscious: Nineteenth-Century German Thought* (Cambridge: Cambridge University Press, 2010).
16. See, for example, the comments of Robert M. Wallace in his "Translator's Introduction" in WOM, vii–xl; here: viii–xiv.

17. For broader context on the relation between the History of Concepts and Blumenberg's notion of 'metaphorology,' see Anselm Haverkamp, "The Scandal of Metaphorology," *Telos* 158 (2012): 37–58.

18. On Blumenberg's deployment of plausible yet unprovable arguments under the auspices of a pragmatic conception of reason, see Rüdiger Zill, "Wie die Vernuft es macht . . . Die Arbeit der Metapher im Prozeß der Zivilisation," in *Die Kunst des Überlebens: Nachdenken über Hans Blumenberg*, ed. Franz Josef Wetz and Hermann Timm (Frankfurt am Main: Suhrkamp, 1999), 164–83; here: 164.

19. For a comprehensive history of the concept of myth from early Christianity until the present, see Axel Horstmann, "Der Mythosbegriff vom frühen Christentum bis zur Gegenwart," *Archiv für Begriffsgeschichte* 23, no. 1 (1979): 7–54, 197–245. An excellent overview of primary sources on myth that covers the *Sattelzeit*, and that includes translations of key sources into English, can be found in *The Rise of Modern Mythology: 1680–1860*, ed. Burton Feldman and Robert D. Richardson Jr. (Bloomington, IN: University of Indiana Press, 1972).

20. Louis de Jaucourt, "Mythology," *The Encyclopedia of Diderot & d'Alembert Collaborative Translation Project*, trans. Nelly S. Hoyt and Thomas Cassirer (Ann Arbor, MI: MPublishing, University of Michigan Library, 2003), http://hdl.handle.net/2027/spo.did2222.0000.162 (accessed February 14, 2012). Originally published as "Mythologie," *Encyclopédie ou Dictionnaire raisonné des sciences, des arts et des métiers*, 10: 924–7 (Paris, 1765).

21. Isaiah Berlin, *Vico and Herder: Two Studies in the History of Ideas* (London: Hogarth, 1976), 23.

22. See Isaiah Berlin, "A Note on Vico's Concept of Knowledge," in *Giambattista Vico: An International Symposium*, ed. Giorgio Tagliacozzo and Hayden White (Baltimore, MD: Johns Hopkins University Press, 1969), 371–8. See also Berlin, *Vico and Herder*, 107. Dilthey's most direct adoption of the *verum-factum* principle can be found in his *Formation of the Historical World in the Human Sciences*, ed. and trans. Rudolf A. Makkreel and Frithjof Rodi (Princeton, NJ: Princeton University Press, 2002), 169–70, 297–8; *Aufbau der geschichtlichen Welt in den Geisteswissenschaften* (1910), in *Gesammelte Schriften*, 26 vols., ed. Karlfried Gründer et al. (Göttingen: Vandenhoeck und Ruprecht, 1959–2005),7: 148, 277–8. Gadamer sees Vico's *verum-factum* principle as being central to Dilthey's thought, though is more critical of its epistemological claims. See his *Truth and Method*, 2nd ed., trans. Joel Weinsheimer and Donald G. Marshall (1960; New York: Continuum, 2003), 222, 227, 276, 373; *Wahrheit und Methode, Gesammelte Werke*, vol. 1 (Tübingen: Mohr, 1986), 226, 231, 281, 379. A detailed study has recently questioned whether the *verum-factum* principle in fact forms the methodological core of Vico's *New Science*, suggesting that its importance has been overestimated within the tradition of philosophical hermeneutics. See Stefanie Woidich, *Vico und die Hermeneutik. Eine rezeptionsgeschichtliche Annäherung* (Würzburg: Königshausen and Neumann, 2007), 91–5. This does not, however, obviate the importance of the *verum-factum* principle for modern philosophical hermeneutics as espoused by Dilthey and Gadamer, even if, as Woidich argues, this importance may be based on their creative misreadings of Vico.

23. Giambattista Vico, *The New Science*, trans. Thomas Goddard Bergin and Max Harold Fisch (Ithaca, NY: Cornell University Press, 1948), 104–6, 109–10.

24. See Joseph Mali, *The Rehabilitation of Myth: Vico's New Science* (Oxford: Oxford University Press, 1992), 16–73.

25. Vico, *The New Science*, 92.

26. See Mali, *The Rehabilitation of Myth*, 3–5, 133–5, 149–51.

27. Vico, *New Science*, 277–8.
28. Vico, *New Science*, 289, 285, 290.
29. Vico, *New Science*, 64, 106. See also Mali, *The Rehabilitation of Myth*, 150.
30. Max Horkheimer, "Vico and Mythology," trans. Fred Dallmayr, *New Vico Studies* 5 (1987): 63–76; here: 70. Originally published in Horkheimer, *Anfänge der bürgerlichen Geschichtsphilosophie* (Stuttgart: Kohlhammer, 1930), 95–114.
31. Vico, *New Science*, 86.
32. See Berlin, *Vico and Herder*.
33. See Woidich, *Vico und die Hermeneutik*, 148–62.
34. See Woidich, *Vico und die Hermeneutik*, 164–5. Although Woidich discusses this thesis critically, she shows that it became a commonplace of German philosophy during the second half of the twentieth century, outlined by Hans-Georg Gadamer, Jürgen Habermas and Karl-Otto Apel, among others. On the more general importance of Vico's *New Science* for conceptualisations of the human sciences, see: Roger Smith, *Being Human: Historical Knowledge and the Creation of Human Nature* (New York: Columbia University Press, 2007), 131–5.
35. See Woidich, *Vico und die Hermeneutik*, 179–97.
36. Christian Gottlob Heyne, *Quaestio de causis fabularam seu mythorum veterum physicis* (1764), trans. Burton Feldmann and Robert D. Richardson Jr. as *Inquiry into the Causes of Fables or the Physics of Ancient Myths*, in *The Rise of Modern Mythology*, 218–20, here: 218–19. See also George S. Williamson, *The Longing for Myth in Germany* (Chicago, IL: University of Chicago Press, 2004), 30–2.
37. Michael C. Carhart, *The Science of Culture in Enlightenment Germany* (Cambridge, MA: Harvard University Press, 2007), 200, 228–9.
38. John H. Zammito, *Kant, Herder and the Birth of Anthropology* (Chicago, IL: University of Chicago Press, 2002), 237.
39. David Hume, *A Treatise of Human Nature*, ed. David Fate Norton and Mary J. Norton (1739–40; Oxford: Clarendon Press, 2000), 4.
40. Zammito, *Kant, Herder and the Birth of Anthropology*, 242–5.
41. Zammito, *Kant, Herder and the Birth and Anthropology*, 143–4, 313.
42. Zammito, *Kant, Herder and the Birth of Anthropology*, 309.
43. Johann Gottfried Herder, *Treatise on the Origin of Language*, in *Philosophical Writings*, ed. and trans. Michael N. Forster (Cambridge: Cambridge University Press, 2002), 77–8, 81, 78, 130, 127, 112, 96, 133, 139–40; *Abhandlung über den Ursprung der Sprache*, in *Werke*, ed. Günter Arnold, Martin Bollacher, et al., 10 vols. in 11 (Frankfurt am Main: Deutscher Klassiker Verlag, 1985–2000), 1: 711, 716, 712, 772, 769, 750, 732, 776, 783–4.
44. On the importance of Herder to Rothacker's conception of cultural anthropology, see Frank Tremmel, '*Menschheitswissenschaft' als Erfahrung des Ortes. Erich Rothacker und die deutsche Kulturanthropologie* (Munich: Utz, 2009), 129–32; see also Helmuth Plessner "Vorwort zur zweiten Auflage," in *Die Stufen des Organischen und der Mensch. Einleitung in die philosophische Anthropologie*, 3rd ed. (1928; Berlin: De Gruyter, 1975), vii–xxiii; here: xiv–xvi; and Arnold Gehlen, *Man: His Nature and Place in the World*, trans. Clare McMillan and Carl Pillemer (New York, NY: Columbia University Press, 1988), 25, 65–76; *Der Mensch: Seine Natur und seine Stellung in der Welt* (1940; Berlin: Junker und Dünnhaupt, 1941), 21, 60–79.
45. Herder, *Treatise on the Origin of Language*, 103, 113, 101, 117; *Abhandlung über den Ursprung der Sprache*, in *Werke*, 1:740, 751, 738, 757.
46. Johann Gottfried Herder, *Ideas on the Philosophy of the History of Mankind*, in *Herder on Social and Political Culture*, ed. and trans. F. M. Barnard

(Cambridge: Cambridge University Press, 1969), 253–326; here: 300; *Ideen zur Philosophie der Geschichte der Menschheit*, in *Werke*, 6: 301.
47. Johann Gottfried Herder, "Vom neueren Gebrauch der Mythologie," in *Sämtliche Werke*, ed. Bernhard Suphan (1877; Hildesheim: Olms, 1967), 1: 426–49; here: 429, 436, 447–8.
48. Manfred Frank, *Der kommende Gott: Vorlesungen über die neue Mythologie* (Frankfurt am Main: Suhrkamp, 1982), 143, 155.
49. Manfred Kuehn, *Kant: A Biography* (Cambridge: Cambridge University Press, 2001), 406–9; Zammito, *Kant, Herder and the Birth of Anthropology*, 284–92.
50. Kant, *Anthropology from a Pragmatic Point of View*, trans. Robert B. Louden (Cambridge: Cambridge University Press, 2006), 3; Kant, *Anthropologie in pragmatischer Hinsicht*, in *Werke in sechs Bänden*, ed. Wilhelm Weischedel, 7th ed., 6 vols. (Darmstadt: Wissenschaftliche Buchgesellschaft, 2011), 6:399. See also: Zammito, *Kant, Herder and the Birth of Anthropology*, 255–6, 301, 307.
51. Kant, *Groundwork of the Metaphysics of Morals*, ed. and trans. Mary J. Gregor, in Kant, *Practical Philosophy*, ed. Mary J. Gregor, *The Cambridge Edition of the Works of Immanuel Kant* (Cambridge: Cambridge University Press, 1997), 44; Kant, *Grundlegung zur Metaphysik der Sitten*, in *Werke in sechs Bänden*, 4:13.
52. Hans Michael Baumgartner, "Wissenschaft," in *Handbuch philosophischer Grundbegriffe*, ed. Hermann Krings, 6 vols. (Munich: Kösel, 1974), 3: 1740–64.
53. Kant, *Metaphysische Anfangsgründe der Naturwissenschaft* (1786), in *Werke in sechs Bänden*, 5: 12–13.
54. Kant, *Logik* (A25–6), in *Werke in sechs Bänden*, 3:447–8.
55. Alwin Diemer "Die Begründung des Wissenschaftscharakters der Wissenschaft im 19. Jahrhundert," in *Beiträge zur Entwicklung der Wissenschaftstheorie im 19. Jahrhundert* (Meisenheim am Glan: Anton Hain, 1968), 3–62; here: 3, 24, 61–2.
56. H. Hühn, S. Meier Oeser and H. Pulte, "Wissenschaft," in *Historisches Wörterbuch der Philosophie*, 12: 902–47; here: 915–20.
57. For the most recent research on the vexed question of authorship, see Christoph Jamme and Frank Völkel, *Hölderlin und der deutsche Idealismus* (Stuttgart: Frommann Holzboog, 2003), 3.3: 246.
58. "The Oldest System-Programme of German Idealism," trans. Andrew Bowie in *Aesthetics and Subjectivity from Kant to Nietzsche* (Manchester: Manchester University Press, 1990), 265–7; here: 266; German version in Friedrich Hölderlin, *Sämtliche Werke und Briefe in drei Bänden*, ed. Jochen Schmidt (Frankfurt am Main: Deutscher Klassiker Verlag, 1992–4), 2:577.
59. Immanuel Kant, *Critique of the Power of Judgment*, trans. Paul Guyer and Eric Matthews (Cambridge: Cambridge University Press, 2000), 227; *Kritik der Urteilskraft*, in *Werke in sechs Bänden*, 5:460–1.
60. Bowie, *Aesthetics and Subjectivity from Kant to Nietzsche*, 51–2, 57.
61. Koselleck, "Einleitung," in *Geschichtliche Grundbegriffe*, xv. There is, however, no article on "mythology" in *Geschichtliche Grundbegriffe*, though there is an extensive account of the term in the *Archiv für Begriffsgeschichte*; see Horstmann, "Der Mythosbegriff vom frühen Christentum bis zur Gegenwart."
62. Friedrich Schlegel, "Talk on Mythology," in *Dialogue on Poetry and Literary Aphorisms*, trans. Ernst Behler and Roman Struc (University Park, PA: Pennsylvania State University Press, 1968), 81–93; here: 85, 82 (translation altered); "Rede über die Mythologie," in *Kritische Ausgabe*, ed. Ernst Behler, vol. 2, *Charakteristiken und Kritiken I*, ed. Hans Eichner (Paderborn: Schöningh, 1967), 317, 312.

63. Schelling, *System des transzendentalen Idealismus* in *Sämmtliche Werke*, ed. K.F.A. Schelling, 14 vols. (1856–61), 3:629. See also Bowie, *Aesthetics and Subjectivity*, 101–2.

64. Schelling, *Philosophie der Kunst*, in *Sämmtliche Werke*, 5: 405–7. See also: Williamson, *The Longing for Myth*, 60–1; Hartmut Rosenau, "Die Mythos-Diskussion im deutschen Idealismus," in *Neue Zeitschrift für systematische Theologie und Religionsphilosophie* 34 (1992): 149–62; here: 155–6.

65. This is the first volume of Schelling's *Introduction to the Philosophy of Mythology* (*Einleitung in die Philosophie der Mythologie*); the second volume, published in 1856, will be discussed in Chapter 5 of this volume.

66. Schelling, *Historical-Critical Introduction to the Philosophy of Mythology*, trans. Mason Richey and Markus Zisselsberger (Albany, NY: State University of New York Press, 2007), 152–3; *Historisch-Kritische Einleitung in die Philosophie der Mythologie*, in *Sämmtliche Werke*, 11: 3–252; here: 219–20.

67. Schelling, *Historical-Critical Introduction*, 154, 134, 17, 43, 48–9; *Historisch-Kritische Einleitung*, in *Sämmtliche Werke*, 11: 222, 193, 18, 56–7, 63–6.

68. Schelling, *Historical-Critical Introduction*, 65, 89–90, 136; *Historisch-Kritische Einleitung*, in *Sämmtliche Werke*, 11: 89, 124–6, 195–6.

69. Schelling, *Historical-Critical Introduction*, 171; *Historisch-Kritische Einleitung*, in *Sämmtliche Werke*, 11: 246–7.

70. David Hume, *The Natural History of Religion*, in *Dialogues and Natural History of Religion*, ed. J.C.A. Gaskin (Oxford: Oxford University Press, 2008), 136, 135, 140, 143.

71. Hume, *The Natural History of Religion*, 140, 152, 143, 155, 160.

72. Hume, *The Natural History of Religion*, 155, 135, 162, 160, 195.

73. Hermann von Helmholtz, "On the Relation of the Natural Sciences to Science in General," in *Science and Culture: Popular and Philosophical Essays*, ed. and trans. David Cahan (Chicago, IL: University of Chicago Press, 1995), 76–95; here: 80, 85–6; "Über das Verhältniss der Naturwissenschaften zur Gesamtheit der Wissenschaft," in *Vorträge und Reden*, 4th ed., vol. 1 (Braunschweig: Vieweg, 1896), 159–85; here: 165, 171–2.

74. See Lourens P. van den Bosch, *Friedrich Max Müller: A Life Devoted to the Humanities* (Leiden: Brill, 2002), 21–59.

75. Friedrich Max Müller, *Comparative Mythology* (1856), in *Chips from a German Workshop*, vol. 2 *Essays on Mythology, Traditions, and Customs* (London: Longmans, Green and Co., 1867), 1–143; "On the Philosophy of Mythology: A Lecture Delivered at the Royal Institution in 1871," in *The Essential Max Müller on Language, Mythology and Religion*, ed. Jon R. Stone (New York, NY: Palgrave, 2002), 145–66; *Contributions to the Science of Mythology*, 2 vols. (London: Longmans and Co., 1897).

76. Müller, "On the Philosophy of Mythology," 155–6.

77. Müller, "On the Philosophy of Mythology," 150–1.

78. See Müller's essay on *Comparative Mythology*, 72–3, and his *Contributions to the Science of Mythology*, 1:69, also discussed in Lourens P. van den Bosch, *Friedrich Max Müller: A Life Devoted to the Humanities* (Leiden: Brill, 2002), 262–4, 271. See also Müller, *Introduction to the Science of Religion: Four Lectures Delivered at the Royal Institution in February and March 1870* (London: Spottiswoode and Co., 1870), 58–60, and Müller, *Lectures on the Origin and Growth of Religion* (London: Longmans, Green and Co., 1878), 276–8.

79. Müller, "On the Stratification of Language," in *Chips from a German Workshop*, 4:84; quoted in Bosch, *Friedrich Max Müller*, 207.

80. Müller, "Lectures on Mr. Darwin's Philosophy of Language, Third Lecture," in *Fraser's Magazine* [London] July (1873): 1–24; here: 2–3. *Lectures on the*

Science of Language, First Series (London: Longmans, Green and Co., 1861), 371–2; *Lectures on the Science of Language, Second Series* (London: Longmans, Green and Co., 1864), 305–7.

81. Müller, *Lectures on the Science of Language, Second Series*, 305–8.
82. Müller's notions concerning a so-called Indo-European or 'Aryan' race are seen to underlie later, more problematic usages of the term. See for example, Léon Poliakov, *The Aryan Myth: A History of Racist and Nationalist Ideas in Europe* (London: Chatto and Heinemann, 1974), 214; George S. Stocking, *Victorian Anthropology* (New York, NY: The Free Press, 1987), 310. Müller later ameliorated his views on the possible existence of an Aryan race, attempting to confine the term to philology by stating that "it is unscientific [. . .] to speak of an Aryan race, of Aryan blood or of Aryan skulls and then to attempt to make ethnological classifications upon linguistic foundations." See Müller, *Über die resultate der Sprachwissenschaft, Vorlesung gehalten in der kaiserlichen Universität zu Strassburg am 23. Mai 1872* (Strasbourg, Trübner, 1872), 17.
83. Müller, *Introduction to the Science of Religion* (London: Longmans, Green and Co., 1873), 102–4.
84. See Müller, "Westminster Lecture, On Missions," in *Chips from a German Workshop*, 4: 251–90.
85. Müller, *Introduction to the Science of Religion*, 17–20.
86. See Müller's three "Lectures on Mr Darwin's Philosophy of Language," in *Fraser's Magazine* (1873): May, 525–41; June, 659–79; July, 1–24.
87. For an account of Müller's position within the landscape of nineteenth-century British anthropology, see Stocking, *Victorian Anthropology*, 56–62.
88. Charles Darwin, *The Descent of Man, and Selection in Relation to Sex*, 2 vols. (London: John Murray, 1871), 1:48–9, 56–7, 62.
89. See Herbert Spencer, "Progress: Its Law and Cause" (1857), in *Essays Scientific, Political and Speculative*, 3 vols. (London: Longman, Brown, Green, Longmans and Roberts, 1858), 1: 1–54. For broader context on British theories of evolution prior to Darwin, see J.W. Burrow, *Evolution and Society: A Study in Victorian Social Theory* (Cambridge: Cambridge University Press, 1966), 114; Stocking, *Victorian Anthropology*, 128–42.
90. Edward Burnett Tylor, *Primitive Culture: Researches into the Development of Mythology, Philosophy, Religion, Art and Custom*, 2 vols. (London: John Murray, 1871), 1:271–2, 258–60, 269.
91. See Robert A. Segal, "Tylor's Theory of Myth as Primitive Science," in *Theorizing About Myth* (Amherst, MA: University of Massachusetts Press, 1999), 7–18; here: 14–15.
92. Tylor, *Primitive Culture*, 1:17–18, 268–9, 286, 452–3, 256–7, 1, 23–4.
93. On Tylor's importance for Frazer, see: Robert Ackerman, *J.G. Frazer: His Life and Work* (Cambridge: Cambridge University Press, 1987), 82–3. One supplier of questionable ethnographic evidence to Frazer was the Oxford-cum-Australian biologist and would-be anthropologist, Baldwin Spencer (1860–1929), who had worked with Tylor in Oxford before relocating to Melbourne. See Angus Nicholls, "Anglo-German Mythologics: The Australian Aborigines and Modern Theories of Myth in the Work of Baldwin Spencer and Carl Strehlow," *History of the Human Sciences* 20, no. 1 (2007): 83–114.
94. See Frazer's "Preface to the Second Edition" in *The Golden Bough: A Study in Magic and Religion*, 3rd ed., 8 vols. in 12 (New York, NY: Macmillan, 1935), 1:xx. See also Ackermann, *J.G. Frazer*, 164–79.
95. Frazer, *The Golden Bough*, 1:222, 56, 176.

96. Frazer, *The Golden Bough*, 1:220–2.
97. See Robert A. Segal, "The Myth and Ritual Theory," in *Theorizing About Myth*, 37–46; here: 39.
98. Segal, "The Myth and Ritual Theory," 41.
99. Frazer, *The Golden Bough*, 1:8–10.
100. A case in point was Baldwin Spencer, whose correspondence with Frazer led him to conclude that Aboriginal totemism is magical and not religious. Frazer then subsequently used Spencer's findings in the second (1900) edition of *The Golden Bough*. See Nicholls, "Anglo-German Mythologics," 99–102.
101. Edward Burnett Tylor, *Anahuac: or, Mexico and the Mexicans Ancient and Modern* (London: Longmans, Green and Co, 1861).
102. See: Frederik Barth, "Britain and the Commonwealth," in *One Discipline, Four Ways: British, German, French, and American Anthropology*, ed. Frederik Barth, Andre Gingrich, Robert Parkin and Sydel Silverman (Chicago, IL: University of Chicago Press, 2005), 3–53; here: 9–10; Robert Ackerman, *The Myth and Ritual School: J.G. Frazer and the Cambridge Ritualists* (New York, NY: Garland, 1991), 47.
103. On the importance of Frazer in particular for Anglophone modernism and literary criticism, see: John B. Vickery, *The Literary Impact of the Golden Bough* (Princeton, NJ: Princeton University Press, 1973); Marc Manganaro, *Myth, Rhetoric and the Voice of Authority: A Critique of Frazer, Eliot, Frye and Campbell* (New Haven, CT: Yale University Press, 1992).
104. T.S. Eliot, *Notes Towards the Definition of Culture* (London: Faber and Faber, 1948), 22.
105. See Jessie L. Weston, *From Ritual to Romance* (Cambridge: Cambridge University Press, 1920).
106. Eliot discussing Frazer in *Nouvelle Revue française* (1923), quoted in Vickery, *The Literary Impact of the Golden Bough*, 235.
107. T.S. Eliot, "*Ulysses*, Order and Myth," *The Dial* 75 (November 1923): 480–3.
108. Similarities between Vico's and Blumenberg's accounts of myth have been noted by Mali in *The Rehabilitation of Myth*, 10, 107.

3 German Philosophy and the 'Will to Science'

Hans Blumenberg is the inheritor of a question that has preoccupied European and particularly German thought since at least the middle of eighteenth century: is a science of myth possible? Since myth is a product of human consciousness, this question also presupposes another, even more fundamental line of inquiry: is an objective and non-ideological science of human nature a realistic possibility for the human species? The answers to these questions provided during the eighteenth and nineteenth centuries depended in part upon what one understood by the term 'science.' If a science of human nature were to base itself solely upon "experience and observation" of human beings, as Hume's *Treatise of Human Nature* had suggested, then a science of myth would find its foundation in the ethnographic recording of different myths found in various cultures. Any 'scientific' conclusions concerning myth would therefore need to be based on a suitably broad and culturally diverse range of inductions, and collecting this empirical material would be a key feature of any science of myth. This was the approach, not only of Hume and his early German followers in Göttingen, but also of Herder and later so-called armchair anthropologists, such as Tylor and Frazer. According to this research model, the human science of 'anthropology' is broadly understood to consist of hypotheses that have been proven on the basis of rigorous inductive inquiries into different cultures. In its later nineteenth-century manifestations—and especially in Tylor and Frazer—it would also be informed by wildly teleological, colonial, and quasi-Darwinian ideas about cultural development which, however problematic they may appear to be from our contemporary perspective, were taken by their proponents to have a secure 'scientific' basis in empirical observations.

Another approach to the science of myth was to suggest that it emerges from transcendental structures of human consciousness that can philosophically be demonstrated without any necessary recourse to empirical inductions. This was the path opened up by the critical philosophy of Kant—a path subsequently taken by the authors of the "Oldest System-Programme of German Idealism," by the later Schelling in his *Historical-Critical Introduction to the Philosophy of Mythology* and, more distantly, by Max Müller's attempts to outline a 'Science of Mythology.' Seen from this perspective, myths are not empirical or ethnographic 'objects' that can be collected and analysed inductively. Rather, they emerge from the relationship between the human mind and the Being in which it is situated. Any anthropology that might be seen to underlie this approach to myth would therefore need to be established *a priori*: it would be nothing less than a philosophical unveiling of the essence of human consciousness. Such an unveiling was precisely Schelling's aim in the *Historical-Critical Introduction to the Philosophy of Mythology*.

The genesis of Blumenberg's theory of myth can only adequately be understood when it is set against the backdrop of these nineteenth-century debates in the theory of myth, which turn on the opposition between empiricism and idealism. By the end of the nineteenth century, scientific empiricism had enjoyed a decisive victory in these debates within philosophy, as a consequence of what Hans Vaihinger referred to in 1876 as the "great crash" (*großer Krach*) or discrediting of German idealism—in particular, the thought-systems of Fichte, Schelling, and Hegel.[1] This 'collapse,' according to Herbert Schnädelbach in his authoritative history of philosophy in Germany between 1831 and 1933, "plunged philosophy into a profound identity crisis," [2] and this crisis was accompanied by a shift in the meaning of the term 'science' (*Wissenschaft*).

While Fichte, Schelling and Hegel had broadly taken *Wissenschaft* to mean a system of knowledge that related to an overall conception of the Absolute—whether conceived as subjectivity, as nature, or as the unfolding of reason in history—these teleological conceptions of *Wissenschaft* came to be discredited by empiricist and materialist conceptions of science favoured by the experimental natural sciences.[3] The scientific ideal of objectivity—which came to find its expression in the complete avoidance of teleology, ideology or 'values'—is expressed in Max Weber's famous lecture of 1919: "Science as a Vocation" ("Wissenschaft als Beruf"). For Weber, a "great tool of scientific work" is the experiment, "the medium of reliably controlled experience," which enables the subjective presuppositions of the researcher to be surmounted. And even in the "historical-cultural sciences" (*historische Kulturwissenschaften*), while one might be able to "interpret political, artistic, literary, and social phenomena in terms of their origins," one cannot hope scientifically to answer the value-question as to whether such phenomena are "worthwhile" in themselves.[4] If, as Schnädelbach suggests, the project of a scientific philosophy came to be equated with "the liberation from German Idealism" and the teleology associated with it,[5] then this meant conceiving of radically new senses in which philosophy could be considered as scientific. In this chapter, we will explore three different but interrelated attempts, undertaken variously during the late nineteenth and early twentieth centuries, to rehabilitate the scientific status of philosophy in Germany: Edmund Husserl's early phenomenology, Wilhelm Dilthey's hermeneutics as conceived within the broader context of what he called the human sciences (*die Geisteswissenschaften*), and philosophical anthropology. All three of these developments in German thought are of central importance to Blumenberg's theory of myth.

HUSSERL, DILTHEY, AND THE 'WILL TO SCIENCE'

In the opening section of part two of *Description of Man*, entitled "Contingency and Visibility," Blumenberg outlines the extent to which Edmund Husserl's phenomenology arose under the pressures exerted by the successes enjoyed by the natural sciences in the late nineteenth century. The outright refusal of phenomenology to include the findings of psychology and evolutionary biology into its own research programme found its methodological expression, according to Blumenberg, in what Husserl called the phenomenological reduction:

> Phenomenology came into being under the conditions of the outgoing nineteenth century and against its results. The phenomenological reduction was the process of separating off a theoretical research field, which could be disconnected from the results of nineteenth-century science and all conceivable subsequent science, and made autonomous.
>
> (BDM, 474)

For precisely this reason, phenomenology, insofar as it deployed a transcendental method, ran the risk, in Blumenberg's view, of merely repeating the results that had been achieved by Kant's critical philosophy at the end of the eighteenth century. It was Kant's transcendental turn, argues Blumenberg, which eventually led to the speculative excesses of German idealism, against which the positive natural sciences so decisively reacted during the second half of the nineteenth century (BDM, 474). Husserl recognised this danger in his programmatic essay entitled "Philosophy as Rigorous Science" ("Philosophie als strenge Wissenschaft," 1910–11), arguing that while philosophy has, at least since the Socratic-Platonic era, displayed a "fully conscious will for rigorous science," Hegel's thought served only to "weaken or to adulterate" this will by failing to provide a critique of reason akin to that outlined by Kant.[6] The false path taken by German idealism, according to Husserl, then led to what he regards as the historical relativism of the philosophy of worldviews, or *Weltanschauungen*, a form of "historical scepticism" that he associates with the thought of Wilhelm Dilthey. Rather than establishing a logically necessary and apodictic science characterised by "supratemporal" (*überzeitlich*) validity and "absolute, timeless values," historicism makes the "epistemological mistake" of seeing philosophical truths as being contingent upon the historical conditions that give rise to them. This means that philosophy can achieve "no unqualified validity or validity-in-itself," which in Husserl's terms means that philosophy must be regarded as being radically unscientific.[7]

The other 'epistemological mistake' made by historicism in general and by Dilthey in particular was, opines Husserl, the attempt to combine the findings of the empirical natural sciences, and especially the new discoveries of psychology, with the aims of philosophy. Husserl understands psychology to be a form of "naturalism," according to which psychological states are to be understood as always being accompanied and determined by physiological states—the so-called psychophysical parallelism associated with Gustav Theodor Fechner that was, according to Michael Heidelberger, later taken up as an "empirical postulate" by Wilhelm Wundt.[8] In Husserl's view, such naturalism is subject to the essential naivety that characterises all of the natural sciences, in that it assumes that consciousness is simply present as a natural object without at the same time inquiring as to *how* it presents itself to the scientific observer in the first place.[9] In the face of the threats posed to philosophy by historicism on the one hand and by naïve psychologism on the other, Husserl proclaims that "the highest interests of human culture demand the development of a rigorously scientific philosophy."[10]

Before we examine precisely what Husserl means by 'rigorously scientific,' it is important to note that his perception of a crisis in the *Geisteswissenschaften* in general and in philosophy in particular was a common feature of German thought leading up to and around 1900. And the fact that Dilthey failed to arrive at a solution acceptable to Husserl did not prevent Dilthey himself from being anxious about the perceived relativism of the human sciences. In fact, Dilthey had attempted to develop a new and independent philosophical justification for them in his *Introduction to the Human Sciences* (*Einleitung in die Geisteswissenschaften*, 1883). Here Dilthey calls not for the application of natural scientific methods to the human sciences, but rather for the complete methodological separation of the human sciences from the natural sciences. This demarcation of the human sciences was to be undertaken though an analysis of the concept of experience (*Erfahrung, Erlebnis*). It was precisely the internal, psychological, cultural, and non-empirical character of human experiences that helped Dilthey to define the unique subject matter of the *Geisteswissenschaften* as outlined in *Introduction to the Human Sciences*:

> Thus there arises a special realm of experiences (*Erfahrungen*) which has its independent origin and its own material in inner experience (*im inneren Erlebnis*) and which is, accordingly, the subject matter of a special science of experience (*Erfahrungswissenschaft*). And so long as no one can claim to make Goethe's life more intelligible by deriving his passions, poetic productivity, and intellectual reflection from the structure of his brain or the properties of his body, the independent position of such a discipline cannot be contested.[11]

In this passage it is Goethe's supposedly preternatural creativity, expressed in the apparently life-like force of his poetic expression, which demonstrated the very limits of the positivist natural sciences and demanded an alternative scientific methodology that could do justice to inner experience.

Explaining the precise nature of this 'special science of experience' remained the central task of Dilthey's career, and it is especially the later Dilthey, the allegedly historicist philosopher of *Weltanschauungen*, who is Husserl's target in "Philosophy as Rigorous Science." In his *Formation of the Historical World in the Human Sciences* (*Der Aufbau der geschichtlichen Welt in den Geisteswissenschaften* 1910), Dilthey refers to the fundamental phenomena of research in the *Geisteswissenschaften* as "life-expressions" (*Lebensäußerungen*).[12] Any particular life-expression—whether it be a poem by Goethe or an historical document of some other kind—will in some sense reflect the historically contingent culture and values from which it emerged. These values are characterised as the objective mind or spirit (*objektiver Geist*) of a particular culture or historical period, and they find their embodiment in cultural artefacts such as customs, laws and religious ideas.[13]

The researcher in the *Geisteswissenschaften*, especially when concerned with historical documents or with literary texts from earlier periods, will necessarily be confronted by a temporal gulf between the "objective mind" of his or her own age and the values expressed in the objects of research, and "the greater the inherent distance between a given life-expression and the one who seeks to understand it, the more frequently uncertainties will arise."[14] This gulf is to be overcome through a combination of historical contextualisation and imaginative empathy, entering-into (*Hineinversetzen*) or transposition (*Transposition*). By carefully reconstructing the historical context of the document in question, and by empathetically entering into the state of mind or its author and his or her age, the researcher in the *Geisteswissenschaften* re-experiences (*nacherlebt*) the original *Erlebnis* that underlies the text. This procedure, Dilthey points out, requires both philological skill and what he calls a "personal kind of genius" (*persönliche Genialität*). The fundamental task of the *Geisteswissenschaften*, which is precisely this "development of historical consciousness," is a kind of technique that can be handed down over generations of scholarship and is therefore in a very broad sense 'scientific.'[15] Yet the task of empathetic and imaginative self-transposition into another age is also suggestive of a kind of non-rational or artistic gift associated with the term *Genialität*. It was, in short, very far indeed from what Husserl regarded as being 'rigorous science,' while also being redolent of the backhanded compliment given to the *Geisteswissenschaften* by Herman von Helmholtz in 1862, according to which they are comprised only of "judgements according to psychological tact."[16]

In an earlier essay, entitled "The Rise of Hermeneutics" (1900), Dilthey gives these themes a more explicit methodological treatment. Echoing Vico's *verum-factum* principle, Dilthey argues that one advantage enjoyed by the *Geisteswissenschaften* over the *Naturwissenschaften* is the fact that they deal with the 'unmediated' internal understanding of one human consciousness by another, as opposed to the grasping of external objects in nature.

Yet it is precisely here where the difficulties begin, since Dilthey claims that it is virtually impossible to gain an objective understanding of our own consciousness, precisely because we are situated *within* our own particular historical and cultural contexts rather than standing objectively outside of them. A reflexive awareness of our own cultural situation and the ways in which it shapes our view of research objects in the *Geisteswissenschaften* is first revealed to us by way of comparison—that is, by comparing our own historical position with that of others. The theoretical possibility of universally valid interpretation lies precisely within this realm of inter-subjective understanding across different historical epochs, and is made possible by the fact that both the individualities of the interpreter and the interpreted have been formed "upon the substratum of a general human nature" (*auf der Grundlage der allgemeinen Menschennatur*).[17]

When Dilthey once again gestures toward a 'universal human nature' in the *Formation of the Historical World in the Human Sciences*, he also moves decisively in the direction of a philosophical anthropology, which for him means to step outside of the "pure and rarefied air of the Kantian critique of reason" in order to do justice to the historical realities of human life. "If there were a science of the human being," writes Dilthey, "it would be anthropology, which aims at understanding the totality of lived experiences according to their structural nexus."[18] In *Work on Myth*, Blumenberg casually remarks that the concept of *Bedeutsamkeit* (significance)—perhaps *the* central concept in his theory of myth—can be attributed to Dilthey, without troubling the reader with any further philological details (WOM, 67; AM, 77). Dilthey's emphasis on the importance of historically and culturally determined *Weltanschauungen* can of course be located in Erich Rothacker's notion that significance is always related to specific human interests, which in turn are contingent upon particular historical and cultural contexts. Rothacker would, however, attempt to 'naturalise' Dilthey by relating the idea of *Bedeutsamkeit* to the notion of human cultural environments, by way of contrast to Jakob von Uexküll's theories concerning the catalysts or signals to which animals respond in their natural environments.[19] As we shall see, it is arguably via Rothacker that Dilthey's ideas enter *Work on Myth*.

THE PROBLEM OF 'VALUES' IN THE HUMAN SCIENCES

Apart from Dilthey's attempts to ground the *Geisteswissenschaften* in either naturalistic psychology or the theory of *Weltanschauungen* and self-reflexive historical consciousness, there were also other contemporary models of the human sciences that the radicalism of Husserl's phenomenological reduction needed to reject out of hand. These were elaborated by the so-called Baden-School of neo-Kantianism associated with Wilhelm Windelband and Heinrich Rickert. The key issue at stake for both thinkers was that of understanding human values scientifically. Both were dissatisfied with Dilthey's attempt to differentiate the *Geisteswissenschaften* from the *Naturwissenschaften* in *Introduction to the Human Sciences* and both thought that the two scientific cultures could more logically be separated in relation to their formal use of concepts as opposed to their actual subject matter.

The most important distinction for both thinkers is that first made by Windelband in his Strasbourg rectorial address of 1894 between the so-called nomothetic and idiographic research methods. Windelband argues that the new research field of psychology rendered Dilthey's distinction between the natural and human sciences obsolete, in that psychology dealt with both the external (physiological) and internal (psychical) dimensions of the human being, effectively applying the materialist methods of the natural sciences to the subject matter of mind, or *Geist*. In seeking to arrive at general laws of human mental functioning, psychology was, in Windelband's view, in fact closer to the natural sciences than to the human sciences.[20] This is because the natural sciences function on the nomothetic level, seeking to uncover general laws or principles such as those found in physics, whereas the human sciences are idiographic, seeking to understand unique events or individuals in history.[21] Whereas natural science selects its objects of research neutrally or objectively, in terms of how they conform to or depart from general laws, the selection of facts in the human sciences is never neutral: rather, it is always teleological and motivated by human interests. The fact, for example, that Goethe had a doorbell and a key made in 1780 is for Windelband not an historical fact, since it is of no significance within the broader picture of German or indeed European history. An historical fact becomes worthy of research only when it forms a "significant component" (*bedeutsamer Bestandteil*) within a "total organic conception."[22] This distinction made by Windelband is a Kantian one, since he is aware of Kant's warnings about the uses of teleological judgements in science. Such uses may only ever be heuristic and regulative, which means that in Kant's terms a science that relies exclusively on teleological judgements is unscientific. This, indeed, was the speculative trap that had snared German idealism.

Rickert in turn attempted a solution to this problem in his conception of the cultural sciences (*Kulturwissenschaften*), as outlined in his *Cultural Science and Natural Science* (*Kulturwissenschaft und Naturwissenschaft*, 1898).[23] Rickert prefers this term to *Geisteswissenschaften* on the basis of Windelband's earlier critique, arguing that disciplinary boundaries are not to be drawn substantially—in terms of an erroneous distinction between *Natur* and *Geist* that had in any case been rendered problematic by the psycho-physical psychology of Fechner and Wundt—but rather functionally or formally, according to the respective goals which the various sciences set out to achieve. Following Windelband, Rickert makes a thoroughgoing distinction between nature and culture. Nature is the world of physical events, laws and processes that are free from human intervention. Culture exists where humans have either intervened in nature (through, for example, farming) or have set up institutions (religions, the state, social manners) that are connected with values. Natural objects are objects of pure value-free perception (*Wahrnehmung*), whereas cultural objects are objects of understanding (*Verstehen*) that are selected according to their meaning or significance (*Bedeutung*). Natural science, in being concerned purely with *Wahrnehmung*, or perception, is value-free (*wertfrei*), whereas the cultural sciences are value-laden (*wertbehaftet*), dealing exclusively with significances that are selected according to values.[24]

The value-laden processes of selection that characterise the cultural sciences raise the possibility that they may turn out to be completely arbitrary and subject to mere convention or what Rickert refers to as "individual wishes and opinions."[25] When one strives, however, to arrive at trans-individual values, where should this striving cease? Any set of values that are either historically or geographically limited would, according to Rickert, fall short of the required standards of scientific objectivity. If the laws of nature have unconditional validity, then the values of the cultural sciences must also be universal.[26] This situation demands that the science of history (*Geschichts-wissenschaft*) be made subject to a philosophy of history (*Geschichts-philosophie*) that would be capable of arriving at universal values, according to which research in the cultural sciences could be conducted.[27] Rickert is of course not in a position to outline precisely what these values would be, but the whole direction of his argument clearly leads to Kant's notion of *a priori* values associated with the exercise of reason alone. Rickert's solution to the crisis of historicism was therefore, as Charles R. Bambach and Herbert Schnädelbach have argued, a return to Kantian metaphysics in all but name.[28]

Husserl's notion of philosophy as rigorous science was conceived against the backdrop of precisely these debates concerning historicism, the relativism of worldviews, the competition between philosophy and a natural scientific psychology, and the question as to how the presence of normative values in philosophy could find an objective scientific justification. His solution to these problems, outlined in the first book of his *General Introduction to a Pure Phenomenology* (*Allgemeine Einführung in die reine Phänomenologie* 1913), is well known and requires no detailed exposition here: phenomenology would resolve these problems by simply setting them out of play through the phenomenological reduction.

Phenomenology, too, would be a "new science," but certainly not a science of the *human* being; rather, it would be a science of "Essential Being [. . .] an *a priori*, or, as we also say, eidetic science."[29] This science would suspend, or 'bracket-out,' the everyday intuitive assumptions that make life possible—such as the notion of an object-world that exists, before me, as I write at this desk, or even that my body belongs to me—in order to explore and scientifically to describe the pure and objective content of consciousness as such. In doing so, we neither lose touch with reality, nor descend into a spiral of Cartesian doubt about whether the world exists. Rather, we continue to exist in the "fact world"—the world that we all agree exists—but simply suspend all of our natural and theoretical assumptions about it. This procedure, Husserl points out, is not to be confused with the value-free or non-metaphysical world of the positivist natural sciences.[30] These natural sciences remain characterised by the natural attitude insofar as the everyday object-world forms the unspoken basis of their analyses. It is precisely this assumption—namely, that objects exist and belong to our world of human intentions and projects—which we suspend, along with all of the sciences that have erected themselves upon it. "*All the sciences*," writes Husserl,

> *which relate to this natural world [. . .] I disconnect them all, I make absolutely no use of their standards, I do not appropriate a single one of the propositions that enter into their systems, even though their evidential value is perfect, I take none of them, no one of them serves for me as a foundation.*[31]

It is a paradox that the very strength of early phenomenology's 'will to science' led it to suspend all of the natural sciences—including sciences of the human being such as psychology and anthropology—so that the way could be cleared for a new beginning. As Blumenberg observes in *Description of Man*, the idea "that the lived-body (*Leib*) as a piece of nature could make the I into a piece of nature" was to be "forfeited through the transcendental reflection and the transmundane ego discovered within it" (BDM, 475). And even as late as his Freiburg inaugural address in 1917, Husserl still made it perfectly clear that through the phenomenological reduction " the actuality of all material Nature is [. . .] kept out of action and that of all corporeality along with it, including the actuality of my body, the body of the cognizing subject."[32] The 'I' of phenomenology was in this way initially to be a pure, transcendental consciousness, disconnected from the lived-body (*Leib*) and its surroundings. Only in the second part of his *Ideas* (initially written between 1912 and 1915, but compiled and published from the *Nachlass* as late as 1952), did Husserl begin explicitly to investigate the role played by the lived-body or *Leib* in human perception and orientation.[33] But even this *Leib* was definitely not to be understood only as a natural object or *Leibkörper* in the terms outlined by the natural sciences.[34] The task of integrating the biological sciences into philosophy, and especially of taking up philosophical positions in relation to Darwin, was left to philosophical anthropology.

WHAT IS PHILOSOPHICAL ANTHROPOLOGY?

If the respective efforts made by Dilthey, Windelband, Rickert, and Husserl to develop a new 'scientific' method either for the humanities in general or for philosophy in particular can be seen as anxiously competitive responses to the rising exactitude and prestige of the natural sciences, then philosophical anthropology can also be viewed, according to Herbert Schnädelbach, as yet another example of the attempted "rehabilitation of philosophy as science."[35] But to Anglophone readers not familiar with the history of German philosophy, the title 'philosophical anthropology' might seem odd. *Philosophische Anthropologie* has little to do with Anglophone anthropology—with the academic discipline that arose during the second half of the nineteenth century through the work of largely 'armchair' anthropologists such as Edward Burnett Tylor, and which was later refined into an ethnographic method by fieldwork anthropologists such as Franz Boas and Bronislaw Malinowski. In fact, philosophical anthropology does not directly engage in fieldwork or in encounters with 'exotic' non-European cultures at all, even if it may at times draw on such data. Insofar as it is seen as a sub-discipline of philosophy, it is simply the reposing—within the context of the early twentieth century and its scientific advancements—of Kant's fourth question: *What is the human being?* It is for this reason that Schnädelbach describes philosophical anthropology as a "German peculiarity."[36]

Philosophical anthropology undertakes an exploration of how human beings *in general* can be distinguished from other forms of life, especially from animals. And as its main historian, Joachim Fischer, has demonstrated, philosophical anthropology came to express its 'will to science' through its fascination with the contemporary biological sciences.[37] In this it endeavoured to overcome the problems associated with the legacy of German idealism. Kant's answer to his fourth question, outlined in his *Anthropology from a Pragmatic Point of View*, was to divide the human being into two: the human being is subject to a series of natural drives, but also has the ability to overcome these drives through the exercise of reason. German idealism would later inherit this division between the human-as-nature and the human-as-reason or spirit, attempting to overcome it through philosophical argument or aesthetics. Schelling, for example, would argue that it is precisely myth that enables human consciousness to reunite itself with nature or the Absolute. Certainly by the beginning of the twentieth century, and in the wake of Darwinian biology, such arguments were seen as being unacceptably speculative, and it is for this reason that philosophical anthropology undertook to re-establish the prestige of philosophy by connecting it with the biological sciences.

It is possible, however, to speak of philosophical anthropology in both a broad and a narrow sense. One could suggest, as Max Scheler has done, that philosophical anthropology has existed at least since Aristotle if one understands it merely to be the activity of defining in philosophical terms the essence of the human being.[38] But the philosophical anthropology associated with twentieth-century German philosophy, to which Blumenberg can be seen to have made late contributions in *Description of Man* and *Work on Myth*, arguably has its inaugural moment in 1915, with the publication of Max Scheler's short essay, "On the Idea of the Human." Here we already see the extent to which this new direction in German philosophy would take its bearings from what might be called the anti-Darwinian tendency in the German biological sciences.

Scheler makes explicit reference to the writings of the comparative anatomist Hermann Klaatsch (1863–1916) in order to argue that human beings are defined precisely by their lack of biological specialisation.[39] Klaatsch proposed that both human beings and anthropoid apes (*Menschenaffen*) evolved from common ancestors. But whereas anthropoid apes are said to have developed particular adaptations suited to their biological niches, such as smaller thumbs or larger incisors, the human being failed to adapt in this way and allegedly remained in a "primordial state" (*Urzustand*) in its organic development. The key to what Klaatsch calls the "puzzle of human development" is thus the idea that humans avoided the "struggle for life" and *did not* evolve through natural selection: "precisely that our ancestors luckily escaped the blessings of the struggle principal (*Kampfprinzip*) must be described as a main point of human development," writes Klaatsch.[40] Scheler uses the research of Klaatsch to arrive at more general philosophical conclusions concerning the place of human beings in what he calls the cosmos. The human being, now defined by Scheler as the "sick animal" (*krankes Tier*), began to use its reason and to develop tools only because of its failure to adapt in bodily terms, and Scheler accordingly describes reason itself as a "surrogate for instincts that are absent or have become uncertain." Thus, whereas other animals became increasingly specialised, the human being is a poorly adapted dilettante with no definable function or essence.[41] Rather, therefore, than adapting *organically*, humans are said to have adapted *culturally*, through their use of culture and technology.

In his later, more detailed contribution to philosophical anthropology, *The Position of Man in the Cosmos* (*Die Stellung des Menschen im Kosmos*, 1928), Scheler sharpened this argument into an explicitly anti-Darwinian programme with even more speculative dimensions. Taking into account a range of debates on the relation between animals and human beings, Scheler rejects both the Darwinian idea that there are only gradual differences in intelligence between animals and humans, and the diametrically opposed notion that animals possess no intelligence or freedom of choice at all. Instead he proposes that the essence of the human being, and the reason for its "special position" (*Sonderstellung*) in the cosmos, must be attributed to something which is separate from everything associated with life and evolution: namely the notion of *Geist*, which corresponds with an "existential separation from the organic." While an animal is bound to its specific environment (*Umwelt*) and develops adaptations only in relation to it, the human being has only world (*Welt*), and is therefore radically open, undetermined, and flexible in its orientation.[42]

The initial directions outlined by Scheler are then systematically developed by Helmuth Plessner in what is the most detailed account of philosophical anthropology to have appeared during the 1920s: *The Stages of the Organic and Man (Die Stufen des Organischen und der Mensch*, 1928). More so than Scheler, Plessner is concerned with situating philosophical anthropology in relation to both Dilthey's conception of the human sciences and Husserl's phenomenology. His starting point is the notion that both the "materialist-empirical" and the "idealist-*a priori*" approaches to the human being have failed to provide clear answers to questions concerning the relation between "nature" (*Natur*) and "mind" or "spirit" (*Geist*). The naturalistic approach failed because it could not account for psychological phenomena that were not reducible to identifiable causes in the "physical world," whereas the mental or psychical approach foundered due its having neglected scientific findings concerning "corporeal nature." While the Baden school of Windelband and Rickert reduced philosophy to a mere "theory of method" (*Methodenlehre*) that demarcated separate fields of research for the human and natural sciences, it was Dilthey who promised to bring these two fields into a productive synthesis.

Hermeneutics, which Plessner sees as inquiring into "the self-understanding of life in the medium of experience through history," endeavoured to unite the concrete details of empirical experience (*Erfahrung*) with a more general theory of the human sciences. This theory displayed two advantages according to Plessner: its conception of experience (*Erfahrung*) was empirical and not excessively speculative in the manner of Henri Bergson or Oswald Spengler; and it was not embedded within a grander teleological system *à la* the philosophy of Hegel. But it nevertheless failed to provide objective results concerning human life-expressions because it always viewed these from a particular historical and cultural perspective that distorted them. What was therefore required of hermeneutics was something akin to the "phenomenological reduction," through which all distorting prejudices are allegedly suspended, but even this approach simply ignored the place of the human being within the natural world.[43]

Against this historical backdrop, the central claim of Plessner's philosophical anthropology comes into view:

> Without a philosophy of the human being [there can be] no theory of human life-experience in the human sciences. Without a philosophy of nature [there can be] no philosophy of the human being.[44]

As in the case of Scheler, the philosophy of nature upon which philosophical anthropology would be based was to be found in the purported objectivity of the contemporary biological sciences, particularly in the ideas of Jakob Johann von Uexküll and Hermann Klaatsch.[45] From Chapter 1 of this volume, we are already familiar with Uexküll's theory concerning animals and their environments. A primitive animal, like a tick, for example, simply reacts by way of reflex to specific sensory triggers in such a way as to ensure its survival. In the case of higher animals with consciousness, such as dogs, the situation is slightly more complicated. Whereas the relation between environmental trigger and reaction in the case of a tick is automatic, a dog is capable of inserting a hiatus in between the stimulus and the reaction that follows. In such cases, the chances of reacting in a disadvantageous way (from the perspective of survival) may be increased, but a securing network of possible reactions is provided by both instinct and experience.[46]

This is not, however, the case with human beings. Human beings, according to Plessner, are "exzentrisch" (eccentric)—not in the sense of having strange hobbies, but rather in their lack of adaptive specialisation and in their capacity for reflexive self-awareness. Not only are their reactions not automatic in the manner of a tick; the range of their possible behaviours in a given situation is also not narrowed by instinct to the same extent as that of a dog. Here the ideas of Klaatsch again become relevant. The purported lack of human organic specialisation in comparison with other primates— and especially the flexibility of the human hand—allowed culture to arise: "out of the continual improvement in tools, culture then gradually came into being." Thus the level, or *Stufe*, of life attained by humans is at once the highest (by virtue of their possession of self-reflexive consciousness), but also the most precarious and uncertain (in that human action is only weakly predetermined). Seen in these terms, our distant pre-human ancestor (*Urmensch*) is a being "dominated by fear and trembling, that sees itself as defenceless and therefore naturally strives to gain means of self-defence." The human being—described by Plessner as "existentially poor, incomplete, naked"— thus finds the essential expression of its nature in helplessness and fear, which in turn give rise to inventiveness and artificiality (*Künstlichkeit*). "Artificiality in acting, thinking, dreaming," writes Plessner, "is the internal means through which the human being [. . .] comes to stand in harmony with itself."[47]

The human being's relation to nature is therefore not direct—as in the case of the tick with its automatic reactions or the dog with its instincts— but rather indirect, delayed and mediated by culture. From this perspective, the "historical dynamic of human life" is nothing other than the series of human attempts to come to terms with this homelessness and eccentricity through the creation of various compensatory life-expressions, technologies, and institutions. The capacity for "expressivity" (*Expressivität*) through language, and all the cultural forms to which this capacity gives rise, provide what Plessner refers to as the "existential proof" for the human being's special and contradictory place in nature: that of the being which is *naturally artificial*.[48] In this way Plessner's version of philosophical anthropology undertakes to reinforce and objectivise the historicist hermeneutics of Dilthey by underpinning it with a basis in the biological sciences.

'SIGNIFICANCE' AND 'DEFICIENCY' IN ROTHACKER AND GEHLEN

This was the state of the art of philosophical anthropology in 1928. Erich Rothacker and Arnold Gehlen then deepened the scientific rhetoric already apparent in Scheler and Plessner. An important example, which also points forward to a central concept in Blumenberg's theory of myth, is Rothacker's notion, outlined in his *Philosophy of History* (*Geschichtsphilosophie*, 1934), that a definitive difference between human beings and animals lies in the human ability to take up a position of "distance towards things" by transforming them into mental objects endowed with different degrees of "significance" (*Bedeutsamkeit*). It is this capacity that enables the human being to categorise its world into "separated forms" and then to select which of these forms are meaningful for its purposes. "Only that which concerns me," writes Rothacker,

> that which 'is something' to me, that which means something, that awakens my interest, that touches upon my being, that appears to me as noteworthy, then as memorable, and finally as worthy of the further steps of linguistic and conceptual acquisition [. . .] only that will find an entry point into my world over this first and most elementary threshold.[49]

This is Rothacker's "principle of significance" (WOM, 67; AM, 77) that would become so central to Blumenberg's theory of myth, and which again—and in a similar way to Plessner—combines the historicist hermeneutics of Dilthey with the anthropological theorising of Uexküll and Scheler concerning the 'special place' of the human being within the natural world.

As reinterpreted by Blumenberg, significance is "related to finitude" and can be positive or negative, attractive or threatening. The human being cannot be indifferent and pay equal attention to everything upon its horizon. Rather, some things—on account of their perceived danger, or perhaps their usefulness for the purposes of survival—will inevitably stand out and awaken human interests more than others, and their ability to do so will depend on the surrounding historical and cultural contexts in which they appear. One should also not be misled by Rothacker's mode of expression into thinking that the 'principle of significance' is purely subjective in the sense of 'that which concerns me.' In Rothacker's context, 'me' means the individual as the member of cultural group, just as, in Uexküll's account, different species respond to different catalysts or signals in their respective environments. This is why Blumenberg maintains that significance in myth, like other forms of aesthetic judgment, involves "the exclusion of dispute that accompanies the claim to objectivity." Significance is certainly not a scientific category associated with "empirical demonstrability," but it must contain at least some element of objectivity in order to speak to the collective human interests of an epoch (WOM, 67–8, AM, 77–8). In short: significance will mean that, for Blumenberg, there is no such thing as 'private' or 'individual' myth.

Gehlen's attempts to further 'scientise' philosophical anthropology in *Man: His Nature and Place in the World* (*Der Mensch: Seine Natur und seine Stellung in der Welt*, 1940) are also relevant to Blumenberg's theory of myth. His main methodological contribution, which was heuristically adopted by Blumenberg during the 1970s, is completely to undermine the Cartesian distinction between mind and body and thereby to question the tendency of earlier philosophical anthropology—especially that of Scheler—to invoke the category of *Geist* as the feature which distinguishes human beings from the rest of nature. Such an approach, according to Gehlen, makes the mistake of using *ontological* as opposed to *functional* concepts in order to describe the special human situation. Here Gehlen endeavours to 'biologise' the way in which the central question of philosophical anthropology is asked, and he does so by invoking not only Uexküll but also the contemporary Dutch biologist Frederik Buytendijk, who had collaborated with Plessner on research during the 1930s.[50]

"If any approach can be called biological," writes Gehlen, "then it is the following one: to ask by what means a given being is able to exist."[51] This approach was already suggested by Buytendijk, who questioned Darwin's notion of there being an ascending evolutionary scale between the behaviour of higher animals and humans. If, according to Buytendijk, one follows Uexküll's suggestion that non-human species live within and respond to different environmental niches and have entirely different needs, then human inventiveness is not, as Darwin had thought, the evolutionary "culmination" of lower animal intelligence; rather it is a special human feature that corresponds with the human being's lack of a specific biological niche and accordingly its lack of pre-given adaptations.[52] The answer to Gehlen's functional question about human beings is therefore not that they possess a mysterious capacity associated with *Geist* or intellect, but rather that the only way in which these "hopelessly unadapted" beings could possibly survive is through compensatory action (*Handlung*): through the use of inventiveness, technology, and institutions.[53] Reason is therefore not a higher metaphysical faculty, but simply a survival mechanism that responded to the human being's special biological needs.

For Gehlen, the human being is a *Mängelwesen* or 'creature of deficiencies' that lacks the biological adaptations and instinctive responses found in animal species.[54] Because of this lack of biological specialisation, man must "by relying on his own means and efforts [. . .] find *relief* from the burden of overwhelming stimulation; he must transform his deficiencies into opportunities for survival."[55] Here a central concept for Gehlen is that of *Handlung* (action), since "man is an acting being" (*das handelnde Wesen*). Through their interventions, humans create a second order nature—the world of culture, including language, houses, tools, weapons, and so forth—in order to survive.[56]

In *Primal Man and Late Culture* (*Urmensch und Spätkultur*, 1956), Gehlen's account of culture then becomes a "philosophy of institutions" that endeavours to explain how institutions developed in order to compensate for human deficiencies. At their primordial origins, all institutions have a "direct fulfilment-value for primary human needs" and arise from the repetition and selection of certain habits that are conducive to the prospering of a group.[57] In part one of *Primal Man and Late Culture*, Gehlen's favoured example is the creation of stone tools. The early production of these simple cutting devices was a habit (*Gewohnheit*) that increased a group's chances of survival, and institutions are nothing more than "systems of shared habits."[58] When particular individuals in the group revealed themselves to be especially gifted at making tools, this work was designated to them alone. The toolmaker was then relieved (*entlastet*) from performing certain tasks (hunting, gathering food), and he in turn relieved others from having to make their own tools. This division of labour is institutional, and enables not only increased survival but also helps to foster group identity.[59] At a certain point, the elaborate decoration of these stone tools meant they partially became separated from their original purpose, in that they also came to serve the function of artworks or status symbols. This separation of an institution from its original purpose demonstrates that the function of institutions can change over time, and that as human societies become more advanced and efficient, their creative energies are freed up and find expression in habits that do not serve the immediate purposes of survival alone.[60]

Gehlen argues that precisely because humans are 'deficient' insofar as they lack pre-determined instinctive behavioural patterns, institutions provide human drives or "impulses" (*Antriebe*) with pre-given structures that provide relief from the effort of continually having to improvise actions and make decisions.[61] At their most archaic level, institutions are pre-reflective, being founded in rituals, totems, and taboos. The abstract notion of the "blood-relationship" (*Blutsverwandtschaft*)—which inscribes the institution of the family and related practices such as the incest-taboo and exogamic marriages—is in this sense a primordial institution, and a prehistoric group's identification with a particular animal or totem was "the only possibility to create and retain the consciousness of a sharply defined [. . .] sense of group belonging."[62] Institutions are therefore inherited historical practices and "command systems" (*Führungssysteme*)—a term that appears frequently in the National Socialist historical context of *Man*[63]—that make human life possible, and a culture without institutions would, according to Gehlen, be completely "chaotic" and unstable.[64]

The writings of Scheler, Plessner, Rothacker, and Gehlen—and their extensive reliance on biological research by Klaatsch, Uexküll, and Buytendijk, among others—might suggest that the rise of philosophical anthropology led philosophy to become a discipline that simply summarised the insights of the biological sciences without contributing anything new to them. According to this scenario, biology would be the foundation, upon which philosophical anthropology would elaborate. But this was explicitly *not* the original self-understanding of philosophical anthropology. Writing in 1928, Scheler saw philosophical anthropology as a "foundational science" (*Grundwissenschaft*), which would provide all of the empirical sciences that deal with the human being with a "final philosophical underpinning." This philosophical foundation would, in Scheler's opinion, give these sciences a secure research direction going forward.[65] But only one year later, one of the new rising stars of German philosophy—Martin Heidegger—would throw the very idea of philosophical anthropology as a *Grundwissenschaft* into question, and the way in which he did so has important implications for Blumenberg's theory of myth.

NOTES

1. Hans Vaihinger, *Hartmann, Dühring und Lange. Zur Geschichte der deutschen Philosophie im XIX. Jahrhundert. Ein kritischer Essay* (Iserlohn: Baedecker, 1876), 1.
2. Herbert Schnädelbach, *Philosophy in Germany, 1831–1933*, trans. Eric Matthews (Cambridge: Cambridge University Press, 1984), 5.
3. H. Hühn, S. Meier Oeser and H. Pulte, "Wissenschaft," in *Historisches Wörterbuch der Philosophie*, ed. Joachim Ritter et al., 13 vols. (Basel: Schwabe, 1971–2007), 12: 902–47; here: 928–31.
4. Max Weber, "Science as Vocation," in *From Max Weber: Essays in Sociology* (New York: Oxford University Press, 1946), 129–56; here: 141, 145 (translation altered); "Wissenschaft als Beruf," in *Gesammelte Aufsätze zur Wissenschaftslehre* (Tübingen: Mohr, 1922), 524–55: here: 538, 542.
5. Schnädelbach, *Philosophy in Germany*, 66.
6. Edmund Husserl, "Philosophy as Rigorous Science," trans. Quentin Lauer, in *Phenomenology and the Crisis of Philosophy* (New York: Harper and Row, 1965), 71–147; here 76–7; "Philosophie als strenge Wissenschaft," in *Gesammelte Werke (Husserliana)*, vol. 25, *Aufsätze und Vorträge (1911–1921)*, ed. Thomas Nenon and Hans Rainer Sepp (Dodrecht: Martinus Nijhoff, 1987), 3–62; here: 6–7.
7. Husserl, "Philosophy as Rigorous Science," 122, 136, 129, 125; "Philosophie als strenge Wissenschaft," in *Gesammelte Werke*, 25: 41, 52, 46, 43.
8. Husserl, "Philosophy as Rigorous Science," 169, 171; "Philosophie als strenge Wissenschaft," in *Gesammelte Werke*, 25: 8, 12–13. On the notion of psychophysics as an "empirical postulate," see Gustav Theodor Fechner, *Elemente der Psychophysik*, 2 vols. (Leipzig: Breitkopf und Härtel, 1860), discussed here by Michael Heidelberger in his essay "Gustav Theodor Fechner and the Unconscious," in *Thinking the Unconscious: Nineteenth-Century German Thought*, ed. Angus Nicholls and Martin Liebscher (Cambridge: Cambridge University Press, 2010), 200–40; here: 212. See also Wilhelm Wundt, *Grundzüge der physiologischen Psychologie*, 6th ed., 3 vols. (Leipzig: Wilhelm Engelmann, 1911) 3: 769–70. Wundt writes that "there are, in the strictest sense of the word, no purely psychical, but rather only psychophysical laws of development," 770.
9. Husserl, "Philosophy as Rigorous Science," 85–9; "Philosophie als strenge Wissenschaft," in *Gesammelte Werke*, 25: 13–15.
10. Husserl, "Philosophy as Rigorous Science," 78; "Philosophie als strenge Wissenschaft," in *Gesammelte Werke*, 25:7.
11. Wilhelm Dilthey, *Introduction to the Human Sciences*, ed. and trans. Rudolf A. Makkreel and Frithjof Rodi (Princeton, NJ: Princeton University Press, 1989), 61 (translation altered); *Einleitung in die Geisteswissenschaften* (1883), in *Gesammelte Schriften*, 26 vols., ed. Karlfried Gründer et al. (Göttingen: Vandenhoeck und Ruprecht, 1959–2005), 1:8–9.
12. Wilhelm Dilthey, *The Formation of the Historical World in the Human Sciences*, ed. and trans. Rudolf A. Makkreel and Frithjof Rodi (Princeton, NJ:

Princeton University Press, 2002), 226; *Der Aufbau der geschichtlichen Welt in den Geisteswissenschaften*, in *Gesammelte Schriften*, 7:205. Makkreel and Rodi translate *Lebensäußerungen* as "life manifestations." Here I favour the rendering of Kurt Mueller-Vollmer (i.e., "life-expressions"), in Dilthey, "The Understanding of Other Persons and Their Life Expressions," in *The Hermeneutics Reader: Texts of the German Tradition from the Enlightenment to the Present*, ed. and trans. Kurt Mueller-Vollmer (New York: Continuum, 1985), 152–64; here: 152.

13. Dilthey, *The Formation of the Historical World*, 226–9; *Der Aufbau der geschichtlichen Welt* in *Gesammelte Schriften*, 7:205–8.
14. Wilhelm Dilthey, *The Formation of the Historical World*, 231 (translation altered); *Der Aufbau der geschichtlichen Welt* in *Gesammelte Schriften*, 7:210.
15. Dilthey, *The Formation of the Historical World*, 233–7; *Der Aufbau der geschichtlichen Welt* in *Gesammelte Schriften*, 7:213–17.
16. Hermann von Helmholtz, "On the Relation of the Natural Sciences to Science in General," in *Science and Culture: Popular and Philosophical Essays*, ed. and trans. David Cahan (Chicago, IL: University of Chicago Press, 1995), 76–95; here: 85–6; "Über das Verhältniss der Naturwissenschaften zur Gesamtheit der Wissenschaft," in *Vorträge und Reden*, 4th ed., vol. 1 (Braunschweig: Vieweg, 1896), 159–85; here: 171–2.
17. Dilthey, "The Rise of Hermeneutics," trans. Frederic Jameson, *New Literary History* 3, no. 2 (1972): 229–44; here: 231, 243; "Die Entstehung der Hermeneutik," in *Gesammelte Schriften*, 5:317–31; here: 317–18, 329.
18. Dilthey, *The Formation of the Historical* World, 298; Dilthey, *Der Aufbau der geschichtlichen Welt*, in *Gesammelte Schriften*, 7:279.
19. Dilthey's attempts to outline a method for the *Geisteswissenschaften* play a central role in Rothacker's *Logik und Systematik der Geisteswissenschaften* (1927; Munich: Oldenbourg, 1965). See also Frank Tremmel's consideration of Dilthey's influence upon Rothacker in *Menschheitswissenschaft als Erfahrung des Ortes. Erich Rothacker und die deutsche Kulturanthropologie* (Munich: Herbert Utz, 2009), 55–88, as well as Joachim Fischer's discussion in *Philosophische Anthropologie. Eine Denkrichtung des 20. Jahrhunderts* (Freiburg: Alber, 2008), 136–9.
20. Wilhelm Windelband, "History and Natural Science," trans. Guy Oakes, *History and Theory* 19, no. 2 (1980): 165–84; here: 173–4; "Geschichte und Naturwissenschaft (Staßburger Rektoratsrede 1894)," in *Präludien. Aufsätze und Reden zur Einleitung in die Philosophie*, 3rd ed. (Tübingen: Mohr, 1907), 355–79; here: 361–2.
21. Windelband, "Natural History and Science," 175; "Geschichte und Naturwissenschaft," 364.
22. Windelband, "Natural History and Science," 181; "Geschichte und Naturwissenschaft," 372–3.
23. See Heinrich Rickert, *Kulturwissenschaft und Naturwissenschaft*, 6th ed. (1898; Tübingen: Mohr, 1926).
24. Rickert, *Kulturwissenschaft und Naturwissenschaft*, 18–19.
25. Rickert, *Kulturwissenschaft und Naturwissenschaft*, 132, 137.
26. Rickert, *Kulturwissenschaft und Naturwissenschaft*, 132–4.
27. Rickert, *Kulturwissenschaft und Naturwissenschaft*, 139.
28. Charles R. Bambach, *Heidegger, Dilthey and the Crisis of Historicism* (Ithaca, NY: Cornell University Press, 1995), 116–17; Schnädelbach, *Philosophy in Germany*, 58.
29. Edmund Husserl, *Ideas: General Introduction to Pure Phenomenology*, trans. W. R. Boyce Gibson (1931; Abingdon: Routledge, 2012), 1, 5; *Allgemeine Einführung in die reine Phänomenologie*, in *Gesammelte Werke*, vol. 3/1,

Ideen zu einer reinen Phänomenologie und phänomenologischen Philosophie, ed. Karl Schuhmann (The Hague: Martinus Nijhoff, 1976) 3, 8.

30. Husserl, *Ideas*, §§30–2, (on pages 55–9); *Allgemeine Einführung*, in *Gesammelte Werke*, 3/1:60–6.

31. Husserl, *Ideas*, §32, (page 59), emphasis in the English version; *Allgemeine Einführung*, in *Gesammelte Werke*, 3/1:65.

32. Husserl, "Inaugural Lecture at Freiburg im Breisgau," trans. Robert Welsh Jordan, in *Husserl: Shorter Works*, ed. Peter McCormick and Frederick A. Elliston (Notre Dame, IN: University of Notre Dame Press, 1981), 10–17; here: 15; "Die reine Phänomenologie, ihr Forschungsgebiet und ihre Methode (Freiburger Antrittsrede)," in *Gesammelte Werke*, vol. 25, 68–81; here: 76.

33. See Husserl, *Ideas Pertaining to a Pure Phenomenology and to a Phenomenological Philosophy*, Second Book, *Studies in the Phenomenology of Constitution*, trans. Richard Rojcewicz and André Schuwer (Dodrecht: Kluwer, 1989), see §§ 18a-b, 35–42 (on pages 60–70, 151–70); *Ideen zu einer reinen Phänomenologie und phänomenologischen Philosophie, zweites Buch, phänomenologische Untersuchungen zur Konstitution*, ed. Marly Biemel, *Gesammelte Werke*, vol. 4 (The Hague: Martinus Nijhoff, 1952), 55–65, 143–62. See also Elizabeth A. Behnke, "Edmund Husserl's Contribution to Phenomenology of the Body in *Ideas II*," in *Issues in Husserl's Ideas II*, ed. Thomas Nenon and Lester Embree (Dordrecht: Kluwer, 1996), 135–60.

34. See Husserl, *Studies in the Phenomenology of Constitution*, §52 (especially pages 214–15); *Phänomenologische Untersuchungen zur Konstitution*, in *Gesammelte Werke*, vol. 4, 203–4.

35. Schnädelbach, *Philosophy in Germany*, 220.

36. Schnädelbach, *Philosophy in Germany*, 219.

37. Fischer, *Philosophische Anthropologie*, 43, 515, 521.

38. Max Scheler, *Philosophische Weltanschauung*, in *Gesammelte Werke*, ed. Maria Scheler and Manfred S. Frings, 15 vols. (Basel: Francke; Bonn: Bouvier, 1971–97), 9:73–182; here: 126.

39. Max Scheler, "Zur Idee des Menschen," in *Gesammelte Werke*, 3:170–95; here: 191–2.

40. Hermann Klaatsch, "Die Stellung des Menschen im Naturganzen," in *Die Abstammunglehre. Zwölf gemeinverständliche Vorträge über die Deszendenztheorie im Licht der neueren Forschung*, ed. O. Abel et al. (Jena: Gustav Fischer, 1911), 321–483; here: 325–6, 363, 349.

41. Scheler, "Zur Idee des Menschen," in *Gesammelte Werke* 3:192, 185.

42. Scheler, *Die Stellung des Menschen im Kosmos*, in *Gesammelte Werke*, 9:7–72; here: 31–3.

43. Helmuth Plessner, *Die Stufen des Organischen und der Mensch*, 3rd ed. (1928; Berlin: Walter De Gruyter, 1975), 5, 18, 21–4.

44. Plessner, *Die Stufen des Organischen*, 26.

45. The main text by Uexküll that is cited by Plessner is *Umwelt und Innenwelt der Tiere*, 2nd ed. (1909; Berlin: Springer, 1921); as in the case of Scheler, Plessner appears to rely on Klaatsch's "Stellung des Menschen im Naturganzen." See, in particular, Plessner, *Die Stufen des Organischen*, 312–13.

46. Plessner, *Die Stufen des Organischen*, 247–51.

47. Plessner, *Die Stufen des Organischen*, 309–10, 312–13, 316.

48. Plessner, *Die Stufen des Organischen*, 324, 339–40, 309.

49. Erich Rothacker, *Geschichtsphilosophie* (Munich: Oldenbourg, 1934), 99.

50. Arnold Gehlen, *Man: His Nature and Place in the World*, trans. Clare McMillan and Carl Pillemer (New York, NY: Columbia University Press, 1988), 13–23; *Der Mensch: Seine Natur und seine Stellung in der Welt* (1940; Berlin: Junker und Dünnhaupt, 1941), 10–17; (German citations are from the second edition of 1941, which Blumenberg owned and annotated; Blumenberg's

heavily annotated copy can be consulted at the *Deutsches Literaturarchiv* Marbach). On Buydentijk's work with Plessner, see Carola Dietze, *Nachgeholtes Leben. Helmuth Plessner, 1892–1985*, 2nd ed. (2006; Göttingen: Wallstein, 2007), 123–9. In 1933, Buytendijk arranged a new academic home for Plessner in Groningen following Plessner's departure from Germany on account of his father's Jewish background. See Dietze, 97–9.

51. Gehlen, *Man*, 10; *Der Mensch*, 10.
52. F.J.J. Buytendijk, "Tier und Mensch," *Die Neue Rundschau* 49 (1938): 313–37; here: 330–1.
53. Gehlen, *Man*, 25–6, 20–1; *Der Mensch*, 22, 17.
54. Gehlen, *Man*, 26–31; *Der Mensch*, 22–9.
55. Gehlen, *Man*, 28; *Der Mensch*, 25.
56. Gehlen, *Man*, 24, 29–30; *Der Mensch*, 20, 26–7.
57. Arnold Gehlen, *Urmensch und Spätkultur: Philosophische Ergebnisse und Aussagen* (Bonn: Athenäum, 1956), 9, 20.
58. Gehlen, *Urmensch und Spätkultur*, 25.
59. Gehlen, *Urmensch und Spätkultur*, 37–41.
60. Gehlen, *Urmensch und Spätkultur*, 33–5.
61. Gehlen, *Urmensch und Spätkultur*, 25–7.
62. Gehlen, *Urmensch und Spätkultur*, 221, 224, 229.
63. See, in particular, Gehlen, *Der Mensch*, 448. This section of *Der Mensch*, entitled "Oberste Führungssysteme" (the highest command systems), was removed from post-war editions, and therefore does not appear in the English translation, which is based on the third edition (published in 1950). In a fragment published from the *Nachlass*, Blumenberg himself refers to Gehlen's wish carefully to 'select' the writings that would appear in the complete edition of his works, ostensibly in the spirit of 'self-criticism.' See "Dürchlässe: Enges Sieb, Weites Netz," in BG, 36–7.
64. Gehlen, *Urmensch und Spätkultur*, 23.
65. Max Scheler, *Philosophische Weltanschauung*, in *Gesammelte Werke*, 9:120.

4 Davos and After, or the Function of Anthropology

Hans Blumenberg's theory of myth is based on a hypothesis that emerges from the tradition of philosophical anthropology. This hypothesis has implications for two questions that have traditionally been posed by palaeoanthropology. First: the question of *anthropogenesis* or *hominisation*—how did humans become human? And second, the question concerning the function of culture, which necessarily also touches upon the function of myth. Before we examine this hypothesis and its broader intellectual context later in this chapter, it is worth dwelling upon the manner in which Blumenberg approaches it in an essay of 1971:

> What man is has been formulated as a thesis in countless, more or less formal, attempted definitions. The varieties of what we now call philosophical anthropology can be reduced to one pair of alternatives: Man can be viewed either as a poor or as a rich creature. The fact that man is not fixed, biologically, to a specific environment can be understood either as a fundamental lack of proper equipment for self-preservation or as openness to the fullness of a world that is no longer accentuated only in terms of vital necessities. Man is made creative either by the urgency of his needs *or* by playful dealings with his surplus talents.
>
> (AAR, 429; WWL, 104)

If one were to hazard a reflexive interpretation of this opening gamut—in line with the suggestion of Joseph Leo Koerner that Blumenberg's writings can be read as *metatexts* that demonstrate stylistically what is also being argued at the conceptual level (see Chapter 1 of this volume)—then one would need to keep in mind that this essay has as its subject the relation between philosophical anthropology and rhetoric.

If, as Blumenberg will go on to suggest later in this essay, human beings are barred from access to "eternal truths and definitive certainties" about key questions relating to their existence, and if even "the history of science showed in detail how verification, too, represents the pattern of agreement subject to later revocation," then the rhetorical solution for philosophical anthropology might well be to choose one of the two alternatives outlined above as a provisional model for understanding the human situation (AAR, 436; WWL, 112). In order for philosophical anthropology even to exist as a research programme, one of these alternatives would need to be chosen, even if the evidence in its favour may be less than conclusive. Indeed, according to one recent interpreter of Blumenberg, "no matter how one decides, the decision will have to lack any further justification or legitimation."[1] It is precisely in this sense that rhetoric would be a means of "putting into effect and defending, both with oneself and before others, a self-conception that is in the process of formation" (AAR, 442; WWL, 119) and that is therefore always contingent and less than definitive. At the conclusion of this apparently programmatic essay, Blumenberg then emphasises the Kantian approach to human subjectivity, thereby underlining the epistemological impossibility of ever arriving at a definitive human self-identity:

> Man has no immediate, no purely "internal" relation to himself. His self-understanding has the structure of "self-externality." Kant was the first to deny that inner experience has any precedence over outer experience; we are appearance to ourselves, the secondary synthesis of a primary multiplicity, not the reverse. The substantialism of identity is destroyed; identity must be realized, it becomes a kind of accomplishment, and accordingly there is a pathology of identity. What remains as the subject matter of anthropology is a "human nature" that has never been "nature" and never will be. The fact that it makes its appearance in metaphorical disguise—as animal and as machine, as sedimentary layers and as stream of consciousness, in contrast to and in competition with a god—does not warrant our expecting that at the end of all creeds and all moralizing it will lie before us revealed.
>
> (AAR, 456; WWL, 134)

As a very late contribution to philosophical anthropology—a mere 'direction of thought' (*Denkrichtung*) in German philosophy which, according to its chief historian, struggled even to establish itself as a recognisable school,[2] and which has more recently still been likened to a "field of ruins" requiring a thorough-going revision and reconstruction[3]—Blumenberg's essay might be seen as a kind of obituary, announcing that the self-consciously scientific efforts of Scheler, Plessner, Rothacker, and Gehlen have now been subsumed under the rather less prestigious and eminently non-scientific heading of rhetoric.

Yet this heavily reflexive reading of Blumenberg's essay would fail to ask the question as to why he would then go on to devote a good part of the 1970s to work on philosophical anthropology, including quite detailed researches into palaeoanthropology. Thus, although one might indeed argue that for Blumenberg in 1971 there may have been "no sufficient reason for deciding upon the alternative between rhetoric and anthropology,"[4] one would nevertheless need to investigate the outcome of these later anthropological researches in the second part of *Description of Man* and in *Work on Myth*. The former text, in particular, is a key focus of this chapter, since it demonstrates the extent to which Blumenberg sought systematically to work through and to come to terms with the attempts, first made by phenomenology and later by philosophical anthropology, to deliver a science of human nature. As is the case with respect to the nineteenth-century theories of myth, reviewed in Chapter 2 of this volume, so too in *Description of Man* do we find Blumenberg grappling with what the term 'science' actually means when applied to the human being. Does it mean an *a priori* 'rigorous science' of human consciousness, as Husserl had suggested? Or must a philosophical anthropology also be based upon empirical knowledge about the human being taken from disciplines such as palaeoanthropology and evolutionary biology?

These questions were also very much on the agenda of German philosophy in the spring of 1929, when Martin Heidegger and Ernst Cassirer met for a public philosophical debate in the Swiss town of Davos. Both thinkers, according to a recent and authoritative study of the Davos encounter by Peter E. Gordon, were explicitly concerned with philosophical anthropology and especially with the ideas of Max Scheler, not to mention with the subject of myth.[5] Since the thought of Blumenberg has been said to lie somewhere not only *after* but also *between* the ideas of Heidegger and Cassirer,[6] an examination of this debate and its undeniable importance for Blumenberg's theory of myth will form part of this chapter. The legacy of Davos and more specifically the presence of Heidegger are also key determining factors in the late works of Husserl, particularly the so-called *Krisis-Schrift*, the *Crisis of the European Sciences and Transcendental Phenomenology* (*Die Krisis der europäischen Wissenschaften und die transzendentale Phänomenologie*, 1936). It is this work and one of its central concepts—that of the *Lebenswelt* or life-world—that will be seen to have played a decisive role in shaping Blumenberg's theory of myth. Furthermore, Husserl's notion of the life-world is also a crucial influence upon Blumenberg's reception of what is perhaps *the* decisive source on palaeoanthropology to have found its quiet way onto the pages of *Work on Myth*: the writings of Paul Alsberg.

MYTH AT DAVOS: HEIDEGGER CONTRA CASSIRER

The importance of the Davos meeting in relation to Blumenberg's theory of myth lies in two interrelated areas. The first is the question as to how philosophical anthropology, and in particular Scheler's *The Position of Man in the Cosmos*, was received by Cassirer and Heidegger at Davos. The second lies in Heidegger's claim, first outlined in his 1928 review of Cassirer's *Philosophy of Symbolic Forms, Volume Two: Mythical Thought* (*Das mythische Denken*) and then implicitly repeated at Davos, that myth corresponds with a key feature of *Dasein* outlined in *Being and Time* (1927): that of "thrownness" (*Geworfenheit*).[7]

Cassirer's take on Scheler was outlined in his Davos lecture on "Spirit and Life in Contemporary Philosophy" ("Geist und Leben in der Philosophie der Gegenwart"), first published in 1930.[8] Here he regards the central problem of philosophical anthropology—the relation between mind or spirit (*Geist*) and nature—as a legacy of German idealism. Whereas Schelling's speculative solution to this problem had been his philosophy of identity—according to which the categories of the mind mirror those of nature because both have a common source in the Absolute—philosophical anthropology, at least in Scheler's version, is seen by Cassirer to posit a fundamental opposition between *Geist* and the natural world. The problem here, as Cassirer sees it, is that Scheler arrives at this position only by way of *negation*: it is the human being's lack of instinctual coordination with its environment that gives rise to *Geist* as a survival function that is defined by its "existential separation" from nature. For Cassirer, this negative definition of *Geist* is deficient. By seeing *Geist* only as the negation of instinct, as a form of asceticism, Scheler neglects to account for the inherent creative "power" (*Kraft*) of the human mind, which it is able to "draw out of its own depths." Here Cassirer means the entire in-between or mediating realm (*Zwischenreich*) of symbolic forms, comprised by "language and art, by myth, and by theoretical knowledge," which actively shapes the human being's "spiritual horizon."[9] This activity inheres in the faculties of the human mind as originally outlined by Kant's critical philosophy, which Cassirer extends into a philosophy of culture in his three-volume opus, the *Philosophy of Symbolic Forms* (1923–9).

The way in which Heidegger would respond at Davos to both Cassirer and Scheler was already suggested by his 1928 review of Cassirer's *Mythical Thought* (1925), the second volume of the *Philosophy of Symbolic Forms*. In that volume Cassirer attempts an ambitious new theory of myth that is designed to chart a middle course between the deductive or *a priori* approach to myth found in German idealism (e.g. in Schelling), and the inductive or empirical consideration of myth (e.g. in Tylor or Frazer). Schelling's speculative inquiry into myth as the "self-revelation of the absolute," as the product of the "unity of human consciousness," is seen by Cassirer to result in a theory that merely absorbs "all concrete, particular differentiations," rendering them "unrecognisable." By contrast, the allegedly inductive or ethnographic method of investigation favoured by Tylor and Frazer tends to see myth only as a "natural form" of the human spirit, which "could be understood simply by the methods of empirical natural science and empirical psychology." In Cassirer's view both of these theories of myth are inadequate, and so he proposes a new mode of inquiry, which "neither seeks to explain the mythical world through the essence of the absolute nor merely reduces it to a play of empirical-psychological forces."[10]

Cassirer's approach belongs to what he calls "modern critical episte-mology," by which he means Hermann Cohen's updated version of Kant's critical philosophy used for scientific purposes. Although this scientific approach to human cultures takes into account the benefits of inductive method and what Cassirer refers to as "psychologism," it also holds that the "unity of culture" cannot simply be demonstrated "empirically through the phenomena." Rather, "we must explain it through the unity of a specific 'structural form' of the spirit."[11] This explanation involves widening the scope of Kant's intuitions of sensibility and his categories of the understand-ing to include a more diverse range of pre-rational cognitive structures, one of which is myth.

Cassirer's description of myth resembles the 'tautegorical' theory of Schelling insofar as he suggests that primitive myth does not posit a *relation* between the image and the object: rather, in myth the image *is* the object, or in a ritual "the dancer *is* the god, he *becomes* the god." Here Cassirer's analysis of myth is also similar to those of Tylor and Frazer (both of whom he cites extensively), since for Cassirer myth is not only pre-scientific but also pre-monotheistic. Mythic causality is subject to a pre-scientific arbi-trariness, since in myth "anything can come from anything"; but insofar as it raises "the question of origins" (*Ursprungsfrage*) at all, myth does repre-sent the beginnings of what will later become scientific causality. Similarly, while myth and religion can be said to be indistinguishable in the earliest phases of cultural development, religion takes a decisive step beyond myth when it begins to recognise the image *as an image* rather than as something that is indistinguishable from what it represents. This is said to explain the later "prohibition of idolatry" in the Old Testament, which arises from a conception of God that must always be beyond sensuous representation. Most importantly, for Cassirer myth cannot be substantialised: it is neither an emanation of the absolute, nor is it merely an empirical or ethnographic phenomenon that can be observed by way of its effects. It is much more a universal and *a priori* activity of human thought that can only be under-stood in *functional* rather than *ontological* terms.[12]

An important issue in both Heidegger's and Blumenberg's receptions of Cassirer is the question as to whether, and if so to what extent, Cassirer is seen to repeat the Enlightenment's narrative of *mythos* to *logos*. Cassirer himself addresses this question in the closing section of *Mythical Thought*, where he takes up a critical attitude toward Auguste Comte's "hierarchy of cultural development," which passes through the earlier 'theological' and 'metaphysical' stages, to arrive at the final 'positive' stage of empirical sci-ence. Cassirer refers to this progressive model as a "positivist cult," accord-ing to which the primitive stage of myth must be seen to "die away" once scientific rationality has superseded it. This strict teleology, according to Cassirer, "does not permit a purely immanent evaluation of the achieve-ment of the mythical-religious consciousness," and makes the mistake of seeking "the goal of myth and religion outside themselves." When viewed as legitimate forms of thought in their own right, myth and religion are shown "to have within them their own source of motion." Myth in particular displays a "continuous drive" to "surpass" itself, but in such a way that the "negation and rejection of certain mythical figures [. . .] does not mean that they are simply relegated to nothingness."[13] And in 1946, in his *Myth of the State*, Cassirer would claim that even in the twentieth century "myth has not been really vanquished and subjugated"; rather "it is always there, lurking in the dark."[14] This final comment was of course made by Cassirer in the context of National Socialism, and will be considered in more detail in Chapter 7 of this volume.

Heidegger's review of *Mythical Thought* proposes that Cassirer's theory of myth can be placed within the context of neo-Kantianism. Cassirer's main neo-Kantian precursor, Hermann Cohen, had argued that Kant's critical philosophy can be reinterpreted as a critical scientific method, according to which *a priori* mathematical and logical categories generate (*konstruieren*) scientific experience. Within this context, Kant's notion of the 'thing in itself' came to be seen as a mere limit-concept, as a theoretical realm of objectivity toward which scientific knowledge might strive, rather than as the definitive grounding of a metaphysical conception of truth.[15] In Cohen's words, the 'thing in itself' represents nothing less than the endless "task" (*Aufgabe*) of scientific cognition.[16] Cassirer, according to Heidegger, expands this neo-Kantian approach to myth. "The consciousness of the objects of mathematical physics as it is conceived in Herman Cohen's Kant interpretation," writes Heidegger, "serves to guide" Cassirer's characterisation of myth.[17]

Yet following this preamble concerning neo-Kantianism, Heidegger uses the vocabulary of *Being and Time* in order simultaneously to describe and to usurp Cassirer's account of mythical thought. Whereas Cassirer maintains that mythical consciousness provides orientation by "introducing certain differentiations" (such as, for example, the sacred and the profane) into the indistinctness of pre-existing reality,[18] Heidegger rephrases this claim as follows: "mythical *Dasein* procures for itself in this way a uniform overall orientation." Heidegger's clever use of the term *Dasein* presages what will become his main critique of Cassirer's approach to myth, since he doubts whether a "neo-Kantian epistemology"—with its emphasis on categories such as "consciousness," "spirit," and "reason"—can penetrate to what Heidegger calls "the kernel of the transcendental problematic." In fact, it is precisely Cassirer's "preoccupation with the neo-Kantian problem of consciousness" that is said to prevent him from "gaining a grasp on the central problem."[19]

"The interpretation of the essence of myth as a possibility of human *Dasein*," according to Heidegger, must be "grounded in a radical ontology of *Dasein* in light of the problem of Being in general." The neo-Kantian distinction between subject and object, and the related notion that *a priori* (and in that sense transcendental) categories make certain kinds of experience possible, represents for Heidegger only a superficial and belated approach to the consideration of myth. This is because prior to any differentiation between a discrete subject and the objects of its consciousness, and prior to the existence of any stable *a priori* categories according to which experience may be ordered, *Dasein* (which means Being-in-the world) is always already confronted by its own "thrownness" (*Geworfenheit*), by a sense of "being-delivered-over [. . .] to the world, so that this Being-in-the-world is overwhelmed by that to which it is delivered over." Myth, for Heidegger, is the primary means through which this sense of being overwhelmed is expressed, and this leads him to conclude that "mythical *Dasein* is primarily determined through thrownness."[20]

In *Being and Time*, Heidegger claims that thrownness is neither a "fact that is finished" (*fertige Tatsache*), nor a "fact that is settled" (*ein abgeschlossenes Faktum*). Instead, thrownness is an irreducible aspect of *Dasein's* facticity, of the concrete conditions of human historical existence. Human beings are always already situated within and confronted by these concrete conditions before they have developed any clearly defined cognitive categories (such as subject and object, then and now, here and there) through which to order them. This is why Heidegger refers to thrownness as "Being-already-in" (*Schon-sein-in*), and as having already been "thrown *into a world*" in such a way that it is subject to "anxiety" (*Angst*). This anxiety, according to Heidegger, "brings *Dasein* face to face with its ownmost Being-thrown," and is characterised by a thorough-going indistinctness: "that in the face of which one has anxiety is not encountered as something definite (*ein bestimmtes Besorgbares*) with which one can concern oneself."[21]

In this way, *Angst* or anxiety is explicitly juxtaposed with fear (*Furcht*). Whereas anxiety is totally indeterminate, fear is associated with a sense of "detrimentality" (*Abträglichkeit*) which has a "definite range of what can be affected by it" and which is "made definite, and comes from a definite region." Thus "in fearing, fear can look at the fearsome explicitly, and 'make it clear' to itself" in a way that is simply not possible with respect to anxiety.[22] Heidegger therefore sees myth as expressing the sense of "over-poweringness" that arises from the thrownness and anxiety peculiar to *Dasein*. And insofar as Cassirer's *Mythical Thought* merely confines itself to a consideration of myth as a "functional form of creative consciousness," Heidegger claims that it does not penetrate to the "fundamental philosophical problem of myth," which exists prior to the differentiation between consciousness and its objects, and lies at the very heart of *Dasein* itself.[23]

The problems outlined in Heidegger's critique of *Mythical Thought* then take on a specifically temporal dimension one year later at Davos, and it is especially this temporal dimension that becomes central to Blumenberg's critique of Cassirer in *Work on Myth*. In *Being and Time*, Heidegger proposes that *Dasein's* having been thrown into a world means that it is always already delivered over to a historicity, to a *position* in history, over which it can have no complete awareness or control. Any view of the world taken up by *Dasein* is necessarily infiltrated by its historicity, which Heidegger sees *Dasein* as "handing down" to itself, and which he describes as the "average" or "public" way of "interpreting" *Dasein* "today" or at any given point in history.[24] Heidegger then applies this notion of historicity to Kant's critical philosophy at Davos, and later (in a much more detailed treatment), in *Kant and the Problem of Metaphysics* (*Kant und das Problem der Metaphysik*, 1930).

The aim of Kant's first *Critique* was, according to Heidegger, not one of providing an objective metaphysical foundation for the natural sciences that would apodictically be true for all time. Rather, it was the task of "laying the ground" for metaphysics from a position of radical human finitude and historicity.[25] This ground laying is for Heidegger always temporally situated, precisely because time is "the ground for the possibility of selfhood" and therefore "already lies within pure apperception," being that which "first makes the mind into a mind."[26] But for Cassirer this first 'ground laying' level of Kant's architectonic, represented by the basic intuitions of space and time and the synthetic "power of imagination," was seen from the perspective of what he called the *terminus ad quem*—the objective goal or point of arrival that the critical philosophy reached when it established the necessary and *a priori* truths of mathematics or, for that matter, ethics, both of which are "no longer relative to the finitude of the knowing creature." This "breakthrough" (*Durchbruch*) to universal or apodictic knowledge is, for Cassirer, the central achievement of Kant's system. In this way, the initial *terminus a quo* (the point of departure), which is only historically relative and therefore limited in its validity, is finally justified when seen from the end-stage of a teleological process (the *terminus ad quem*), at which apodictic knowledge has been achieved.[27]

In the discussion at Davos, Heidegger questioned Cassirer's account as follows:

> One could say that for Cassirer the *terminus ad quem* is the whole of a philosophy of culture in the sense of an elucidation of the wholeness of the forms of the shaping consciousness. For Cassirer, the *terminus a quo* is utterly problematical. My position is the reverse: The *terminus a quo* is my central problematic, the one I develop [. . .] If Kant says: The three basic questions are allowed to lead back to the fourth: What is man?, then this question in its character as question has become questionable. I attempted to show that it is not at all self-evident to start from the concept of *logos*, but instead that the question of the possibility of metaphysics demands a metaphysics of *Dasein*.[28]

Heidegger's abiding interest in investigating the origins of metaphysics—rather than its ends or concepts (*logoi*)—then leads him to Scheler's proposed foundational science (*Grundwissenschaft*) of philosophical anthropology. If

Kant's first three questions (*What can I know? What should I do? What may I hope for?*), should indeed be answered in relation to the fourth question (*What is the human being?*) then perhaps Scheler might have provided an informative answer.

Heidegger had, in *Being and Time*, certainly praised Scheler's emphasis upon the world-openness of the human being, the sense in which the human being cannot be defined according to pre-existing features or instincts in the way that animals can.[29] But at Davos, as well as in *Kant and the Problem of Metaphysics*, Heidegger rejected philosophical anthropology on the grounds that its mode of inquiry is insufficiently fundamental. The question concerning man's essence, according to Heidegger at Davos, lies in the "nothingness of his *Dasein*." This question is not to be answered through studying humans "empirically as given objects," and nor can it "be understood in such a way that I project an anthropology of man."[30] In Heidegger's view, Kant himself had already realised that anthropology, in being merely empirical and not metaphysical, could not penetrate to the "center of philosophy." At best it could offer what Heidegger calls a "regional ontology of human beings,"[31] which in being merely 'regional' does not ask the most primary of philosophical questions: not *What is the human being?* but rather *How is experience given to me?* or in Heidegger's own terminology, *What is the Being of beings?*[32]

When Blumenberg came to write his theory of myth during the 1970s, the reputations of Cassirer and Heidegger could have presented him with a contrast laden with historical pathos. With the benefit of hindsight, Cassirer could have been seen as the defender of the orthodox interpretation of Kant's critical philosophy and by extension of the humanist values of the Enlightenment, whereas Heidegger might have appeared as the philosopher who had subjected the critical philosophy to a "violent" interpretation or appropriation,[33] and who later succumbed to the seductions of National Socialism. That Blumenberg had carefully studied the Davos disputation, including Heidegger's review of Cassirer's *Mythical Thought*, is revealed in a late text that was written well after *Work on Myth* and published from the *Nachlass* in 1997.[34] There Blumenberg explains the apparent 'victory' of Heidegger with deep irony, suggesting that the question of the "meaning of Being" (*Sinn von Sein*) was able to awaken greater expectations than Cassirer's apparently more quotidian attempt to broaden the table of *a priori* symbolic forms, even if Heidegger could not fulfil these expectations.[35] The opposition between Heidegger and Cassirer at Davos was, according to Blumenberg, that of "substance *or* function": while Heidegger saw in myth a fundamental mode of *Dasein*'s existential situation, Cassirer was primarily interested in how myth made certain cultural achievements possible (EMS, 164–5).[36]

In this late *Nachlass* text there is also a sense in which Blumenberg interprets Davos as one of Heidegger's first propaganda coups—a kind of forerunner to the Freiburg Rectorial Address of 1933. The main legacy of Davos, according to Blumenberg, was that it demonstrated, already in 1929, the extent to which favouring the category of *Being* can lead one to lose sight of *meaning* (EMS, 166). Blumenberg's trenchant and at times public criticisms of Heidegger in his late writings can at least partially be explained by facts that came to light during the 1980s.[37] Writing in 1986, and in answer to the perennial question as to whether Heidegger's public support for National Socialism in 1933 expressed his inner philosophical affinity with fascism or a mere psychological aberration that was quickly overcome, Blumenberg cites an anecdote from Karl Löwith's *My Life in Germany Before and After 1933 (Mein Leben in Deutschland vor und nach 1933)*, which had also appeared in 1986. Löwith reports on his meeting with Heidegger in Italy in 1936, during which Heidegger is said openly to have worn the NSDAP insignia and to have confirmed that his "political engagement" on behalf of National Socialism emerged from his own concept of historicity.[38] At least for Blumenberg, this credible account put the inner relation of Heidegger's philosophy to his politics beyond question.

But during the 1970s, Blumenberg took Heidegger very seriously as a theorist of myth. Indeed, *Work on Myth* shows that Blumenberg did not initially see the outcome of Davos as being one of either/or, one of substance *or* function, since its pages reveal the influences of *both* Heidegger and Cassirer.[39] Evidence for this can also be found outside of *Work on Myth*. The key text is Blumenberg's address of 1974, "In Memory of Ernst Cassirer" ("Ernst Cassirers gendenkend"), delivered upon his having received the Kuno Fischer Prize of the University of Heidelberg, which Cassirer had also been awarded in 1914. While its ostensible purpose is a consideration of Cassirer's philosophical legacy, its actual content amounts to Blumenberg defining his own approach to philosophy in explicit opposition to that of Cassirer.

Blumenberg begins his address with the proposition that the Davos disputation represented the decline in prominence of neo-Kantianism. In a world in which every "technological press of a button" confirms the reliability of science, it was no longer necessary to outline a philosophy that secured the epistemological foundations of scientific knowledge in the manner of Hermann Cohen. Yet Cassirer's *Philosophy of Symbolic Forms*, which was still incomplete in 1929, is said to have continued in the spirit of neo-Kantianism, creating a "table of categories" through which cultural objects were to be understood. The problem with this approach, according to Blumenberg, is that its "neo-Kantian teleology" tended to view its objects according to a standardised model of the scientific. This approach led to a "dissonance" between the actual material dealt with by the *Philosophy of Symbolic Forms*—myth, language, religion and art—and its overarching trajectory towards the purportedly "unsurpassable definitiveness" of scientific knowledge. Thus, despite Cassirer's prominent opposition to Auguste Comte's three-stage model of progress, the "overall conception" (*Gesamtkonzeption*) of his work is said to be the idea that the scientific present offers a superior point of view from which to consider the intellectual achievements of the past, a past that includes "the background of myth." The chief lesson that is therefore to be drawn from the case of Cassirer is precisely to strive for what he *did not succeed* in achieving: namely, to outline a history of culture that *does not* undertake a "functionalization of history according to the contemporary needs of the present," and that *does not* see the present as the "goal of history."[40]

In *Work on Myth*, this critique is then repeated, but with the important difference that Blumenberg now invokes the actual language used by Cassirer and Heidegger at Davos. Here Cassirer is said to have considered myth only from "the point of view of the *terminus ad quem.*" Despite Cassirer's anti-Comtean "affirmations of the autonomous quality of this symbolic system of forms," writes Blumenberg, myth "remains, for Cassirer, something that has been overcome." Writing against Cassirer's alleged reinforcement of the *mythos* to *logos* narrative, Blumenberg then observes that

> My opinion, in contrast to this, is that in order to perceive myth's genuine quality as an accomplishment one would have to describe it from the point of view of its *terminus a quo*. Removal away from, not approach toward, then becomes the criterion employed in the analysis of its function [. . .] Once he has emerged from the regularity of a condition in which his behavior was determined by his environment, the hominid creature has to deal with the failure of the indicators and determinants of his behaviour, with the indeterminacy of what the constituent parts of reality 'mean' for him. He begins to set up 'significances' [*Bedeutsamkeiten*] over against the disappearance of strict meanings [*Bedeutungen*] (WOM, 168–9; AM, 186–7).

This passage—one of the most important theoretical statements in *Work on Myth*—is noteworthy for three reasons. First, and despite the fact that the Cassirer-Heidegger confrontation is never explicitly mentioned in its pages, it demonstrates that *Work on Myth* undertakes a settling of accounts with Davos, and that this settling at least initially seems to favour Heidegger. Second, this 'settling' is far from being a passive 'settling down' into Heidegger's pre-existing position, since the above quotation shows how Blumenberg actively reinserted the claims of philosophical anthropology into his theory of myth, despite Heidegger's outright rejection of philosophical anthropology. The "hominid creature" mentioned above can only be understood in relation to the entire theoretical background of Uexküll, Scheler, Plessner, Rothacker and Gehlen. Third: Blumenberg's critique of Cassirer's theory of myth is by and large confined to the *Philosophy of Symbolic Forms* and not to the *Myth of the State*. In the latter text, to be examined in Chapter 7 of this volume, Cassirer regards myth precisely as that which has *not* been overcome, and which has indeed *returned* in the modern form of political propaganda under National Socialism.

Can one speak, then, of a 'Heideggerian' Blumenberg in *Work on Myth*? Only with some very important reservations. The extent to which Blumenberg's conception of *Bedeutsamkeit* or significance emerges not only from the contexts of Dilthey and Rothacker, but also from Heidegger's analysis of *Dasein*, is revealed in an earlier section of *Work on Myth*. Blumenberg invokes §18 of *Being and Time*, in which Heidegger argues that significance corresponds to the capacity of *Dasein* to "assign" or "refer" (*verweisen*) valences to certain things so that they stand out from others. This capacity, Heidegger argues, implies the "involvement" of *Dasein* in these things,[41] with their potential "serviceability" (*Dienlichkeit*) or their "detrimentality" (*Abträglichkeit*). But even prior to this setting up of individual significances there must also be a more general context in which they can appear, a context of primordial familiarity that is pre-theoretical. This context is what Heidegger refers to as the "worldhood of the world," and as the "relational totality" (*Bezugsganze*) that functions as the frame for significance.[42]

It is this setting up of a context for significances that Blumenberg describes as the work of myth: "Significance is the form in which the background of nothing, as that which produces anxiety, has been put at a distance" (WOM, 110; AM, 125). Through the work of myth, anxiety, which corresponds to an empty and indeterminate horizon full of non-specific threats, can become fear, which is more controllable precisely because it can be directed toward a certain something. In this way Blumenberg takes over Heidegger's differentiation between objectless anxiety and object-directed fear and inserts the 'work of myth' between them. He thereby acknowledges that Heidegger's "fundamental ontology" provides an "orientation" that helps one to "gain access to the 'work of myth'" (WOM, 110; AM, 125). But as Vida Pavesich and Oliver Müller have persuasively argued, it precisely here, where the 'work of myth' is inserted, that we might also locate a correction of Heidegger that displays the influence of Cassirer. The fact that mythic significance is "wrung from a situation that produced anxiety" (WOM, 110; AM, 125) shows the orienting capacity of what Cassirer would call symbolic forms. In Blumenberg's recasting of Cassirer, such symbolic forms develop through long and slow processes of cultural selection rather than being the result of a primordial 'decision' or 'attitude' taken up by *Dasein*. And while Heidegger's conception of anxiety might seem to be ahistorical precisely because he sees it as an irreducible aspect of *Dasein*, Blumenberg ends up taking quite a different path. As we shall shortly see, he associates anxiety and lack of orientation with a hypothetical scenario taken from palaeoanthropology, a scenario that has already been put at a distance by the work of myth.[43]

The two most comprehensive overviews of Blumenberg's thought that currently exist, those of Felix Heidenreich and Oliver Müller, have both shown the extent to which the early Blumenberg in fact struggled to define his own approach to philosophy against that of Heidegger.[44] Blumenberg's unpublished *Habilitation* thesis, *The Ontological Distance. An*

Investigation into the Crisis of Husserl's Phenomenology (*Die ontologische Distanz. Eine Untersuchung über die Krisis der Phänomenologie Husserls* 1950)[45] took its main concept—that of *Geschichtlichkeit*, or historicity—from Heidegger's *Being and Time* and applied it to the phenomenological reduction of Husserl. The torturous opening premise of this study runs as follows: "the historicity of the history of thought could [. . .] not be conceptualised as an object among the objects of thought" (OD, 3). When this phrase is unpacked, it simply means that philosophy can never take up a purely objective or unprejudiced position because it always sets out from an historical perspective that cannot be overcome. Any attempt to neutralise the distorting effects exerted by history upon thought would need to make historicity into a discrete object so that it could be analysed and assimilated into the philosophical system. But the sheer fact, so heavily emphasised by Heidegger, that humans are always already *in* history means that their historicity can never become an external object for them in this way. Blumenberg accordingly sees Husserl's phenomenological reduction as a failed attempt to evacuate historicity from philosophy so that a 'pure' or unprejudiced method can be secured. "The crisis of phenomenology," writes Blumenberg, "is rooted in this failure to recognise the extension of history into Being" (OD, 189). This insight would become a commonplace of post-war German philosophy, and is most prominently seen in Hans-Georg Gadamer's claim that "history does not belong to us; we belong to it," and that "the self-awareness of the individual is only a flickering in the closed circuits of historical life."[46] The *Ontological Distance* represents only the early stages of Blumenberg's reception of Husserl. He would return to the late Husserl, and to the crisis of phenomenology, in the 1960s and 1970s, and the way in which he did so prepared the way for his theory of myth.

CRISIS AND THE LIFE-WORLD

In the index to *Work on Myth*, only one page number appears next to the name Edmund Husserl. One might therefore think that Husserl's phenomenology played little role in the genesis of Blumenberg's theory of myth. But those who knew Blumenberg's position in the history of German philosophy, and who were aware of his earlier work with Ludwig Landgrebe in Kiel, would of course have seen Husserl's influence on virtually every page of *Work on Myth*. Those who did not (including, perhaps, many Anglophone readers) would have been none the wiser. Already in the *Ontological Distance*, myth is seen from the perspective of phenomenology. In this text Blumenberg deploys the idea of the "ontological distance" in two different, though related, senses. The first sense refers to the way in which consciousness creates a distance between itself and its objects, so that objects can be understood. Myth represents the pre-conceptual stage in this process, in which the act of naming renders a preliminary object-world possible: "the name, not the concept, is the form of mythical thought," writes Blumenberg, a proposition that he seems to have taken from Cassirer (OD, 38).

The second sense of the ontological distance has to do with Heidegger's conception of historicity. A key feature of the modern age was that of Cartesian doubting or *zweifeln*. Doubts about the reality of the object-world led to the foundation of the Cartesian *cogito* and the separation of *res cogitans* (thinking substance) from *res extensa* (extended substance). Truth about the world is then secured by the *a priori* deductions of *res cogitans* and ultimately by Descartes's arguments to prove the existence of God. In Kant's critical philosophy, and in its later reception in German idealism, this sense of stability is disrupted by Kant's finding that the *a priori* cognitive faculties create a world of representations for us, which may or may not correspond with the 'things in themselves.' And Descartes's God, which had previously underpinned the ultimate truth of *res extensa*, has in Kant become only a necessary idea of reason rather than an objectively valid truth. Dilthey's 'critique of historical reason' then shows that the *a priori* aspects of subjectivity highlighted by Kant are in fact infiltrated by history, leading to different historical worldviews that change over time (OD, 4). As we have seen, for Husserl this situation demanded a new beginning similar to that achieved by Descartes. Now Cartesian doubting (*zweifeln*) is replaced by what Blumenberg sees as phenomenology's "desperation" (*Verzweiflung*), by its attempt to overcome the historicity of the subject through the phenomenological reduction. This reduction is interpreted by Blumenberg as the phenomenological subject's attempt to distance itself from, and thereby to overcome, its own historicity (OD, 25–9). The failure of this second version of the "ontological distance" then leads to a situation of crisis, and to Hussserl's *Crisis of the European Sciences*. The role played by this so-called *Krisis-Schrift* in the works of Hans Blumenberg cannot be overestimated.

The clearest example of Husserl's influence on Blumenberg can be found in Husserl's ideas concerning the life-world (*Lebenswelt*). Through this notion, Husserl attempted to accommodate historicity within phenomenology rather than trying to overcome it by way of the phenomenological reduction. The 'crisis' of which Husserl speaks in this text is at once scientific, existential and at least latently political. The scientific situation is similar to that which Husserl outlined in "Philosophy as Rigorous Science." The positivism of the natural sciences is seen as that which "decapitates" (*enthauptet*) philosophy by declaring the questions of metaphysics to be unacceptably speculative and therefore unanswerable in scientific terms. The "natural-scientific mathematization" of the world becomes the "endless scientific task" of European humanity performed by technocratic experts, and science is akin to a "machine everyone can learn to operate correctly without in the least understanding the inner possibility and necessity of this sort of accomplishment." This consequence represents nothing less than a "crisis of European humanity itself," since the retreat of metaphysics means that technological progress no longer has an overarching and normative goal. And the political dimensions of this crisis were of course to be found in the tragedy of the First World War, in which one of Husserl's sons died, and the looming threat (in 1936) of another war that would be fought with even more lethal technology. Added to this was the fact that Husserl was, also in 1936, stripped of his right to teach on account of his Jewish background.[47]

Remarkably, given Husserl's earlier critique of Dilthey's historicism, the task of philosophy within this context becomes that of historical and critical reflection upon the current plight of European humanity in order to achieve a new and "radical self-understanding." This can only be carried out by penetrating to the largely unexpressed "presuppositions" (*Voraussetzungen*) that underlie the logic of modern science. These pre-understandings belong to what Husserl calls the "life-world"—a "realm of original self-evidences," which exists prior to scientific logic and which is "always already there." Precisely because the life-world shapes in advance the horizon of all scientific questions, it remains "completely closed off" to the objective sciences, even to human sciences such as psychology and anthropology. Redefining the task of philosophy once again in response to this crisis, Husserl claims that it will be a "science of the universal *how* of the pregivenness of the world."[48]

In earlier versions of this argument, especially that delivered in the "Vienna Lecture" of 1935, but also elsewhere, Husserl characterises this science of the life-world as providing nothing less than a new justification for the human sciences. While psychology and anthropology are summarily dismissed because they belong to "natural-scientific psychological and humanistic inquiry," which makes the mistake of thinking that the human sciences need to be underpinned by the methods of natural science, Husserl's new version of phenomenology seeks to understand "historical man insofar as he acts and holds sway subjectively in his surrounding world."[49] It is "absurd and circular," writes Husserl, to expect that the overall trajectory of natural science and therefore of European humanity can be understood in natural scientific terms.[50] Only a philosophical science of the life-world would be up to such a task.

One of Blumenberg's main responses to Husserl's proposed science of the life-world was to draw attention to the extreme difficulties involved in theorising something that is by definition radically pre-reflective and therefore pre-theoretical.[51] The method by which Husserl proposed to undertake such a task was a revised version of the phenomenological reduction. This new model of the reduction would no longer penetrate to an objective mentality free of all prejudices, to an ego "empty of content." Instead, it would set aside the results of the "objective sciences" so that a deeper realm, that of "the life-world which is valid for us prescientifically," could be explored. Husserl himself recognised the almost mythical dimensions of such an enterprise, comparing it with Faust's descent into the mysterious realm of "the mothers of knowledge" in Part Two of Goethe's drama.[52] Blumenberg's preoccupation with Husserl's notion of the life-world dates back at least to the early 1960s, and takes on an increasing intensity during the second half of the 1970s, with a number of important essays on this topic being collected in the *Nachlass* volume *Theory of the Life-World*.[53] This work on the life-world can be seen to prepare the way for *Work on Myth*.

Blumenberg regards the life-world as "Husserl's most successful invention" (TDL, 37), and the sense in which he interprets it in relation to philosophical anthropology is seen in his claim that the life-world is a "post-biological environment-surrogate," which represents the success of "adaptive accomplishments and amenities" that arise from culture as opposed to nature (TDL, 15). The life-world is at once "pre-logical," "pre-predicative," and comprised of "prejudices" and "institutions" that have proven themselves resistant to the Enlightenment (TDL, 120, 123–4). Husserl's first version of the phenomenological reduction, which had attempted to set aside all pre-understandings in the name of rigorous science, is seen by Blumenberg to have run up against the "obstinacy of resistance" provided by the life-world (TDL, 128). This is because the life-world tends, precisely by virtue of it being characterised by self-evidences, to withdraw itself from being considered as an *object* of analysis. It is "the world in which philosophy is *not yet* possible, and also the utopian final world [. . .] in which philosophy is *no longer* necessary" (TDL, 33). The utopian character of the life-world inheres in a sense of "happiness," which arises from the "freedom from pain and fear, worry and disquiet, and also from doubt concerning the constancy of the positively valued circumstances of everyday normality" (TDL, 48–9). In this situation, theory or thought is to be regarded as an "exceptional state" or "state of emergency" (*Ausnahmezustand*, TDL, 61), which swings into action only when the life-world is disrupted.

Since, in Blumenberg's view, human beings are capable of compensatory cultural adaptions, "cultural systems tend toward the production of life-worlds and, when they are lost, toward their restoration" (TDL, 59). The processes through which this activity takes place, and their direct relevance to the phenomenon of myth, are outlined by Blumenberg in an essay published from the *Nachlass* that can in many ways be regarded as *Work on Myth* in embryonic form: "Self-Evidentness, Self-Erection, Self-Comparison" ("Selbstverständlichkeit, Selbstaufrichtung, Selbstvergleich," TDL, 133–48). Here Blumenberg points out that "the life-world is not everything, that is the case." Rather, any given life-world is a contingent and fragile construction that is created in order to compensate for a lack of pre-determined or automatic responses to environmental conditions. Because the life-world represents only a selection of "everything, that is the case," its boundaries are always "occupied by occurrences of alienation, terror, horror and of fear." In the most extreme cases, these potential threats of invasion will be dealt with by endowing them with identities and names, and by ascribing to them certain spheres of accountability, or ways in which they can be influenced (TDL, 135).

Blumenberg explicitly compares this situation with Heidegger's existential analysis of anxiety in *Being and Time* (TDL, 136). To deal with this anxiety, human beings are said to possess a "preventative constitution," which enables them to anticipate possible threats on the horizon by naming and supplicating them:

> Magic and myth are such attempts, made at the periphery of the life-world, to reverse the direction of any intrusions. Above all, to take control of and to reassure oneself concerning the powers which stand behind the unknown, to fragment them, and to reduce their strength through the procedure of the division of powers, in that one has them become entangled within their own zone in rivalries and power struggles, of which myth is full and in which the human being can at least occasionally expect to intervene through cult and magic.
>
> (TDL, 136)

The main *Technik* (both technique and technology) of this mythical "border-traffic" (*Grenzverkehr*) is provided by metaphor (*Metaphorik*, TDL, 137). It is metaphor that allows the unknown elements that lie beyond the boundaries of the life-world to be integrated within it, by way of metaphorical substitution. These stories begin *within* the life-world but end *beyond* it, allowing that which is out of view to be integrated. An example mentioned by Blumemberg is an ancient Egyptian myth concerning the tidal changes in the Nile (see TDL, 138). These variations are explained by a myth according to which an unknown 'someone' stands at the source of the river and periodically empties a jug into it. The person with the jug, although unknown and unknowable in empirical terms, is a cultural construction that marks the edges of the life-world. And crucially, the myth ends without any questions concerning the person's identity, the size of the jug, or the origin of the water that flows out of it. Unlike science, myths provide simple explanations and then end. In Blumenberg's words: "they are allowed to be finite" (TDL, 138).

The Nile example is what Blumenberg refers to as an aetiological myth—a myth of causes. Questions concerning aetiology represent a stage in cultural development in which the most primordial fears have already been surmounted by earlier myths. A more elemental example is the terror produced by a natural phenomenon such as lightning. When such terrors intrude upon the life-world they are endowed with numinous qualities: the lightning becomes an *Augenblicksgott* or "momentary god." Over time such natural phenomena can in turn be used metaphorically not just to explain natural events but also to characterise the gods themselves: "the lightning is not a god, rather God is, in his actions, as unexpected and deadly as lightning" (TDL, 138).

Similarly, a myth can change or lose its power depending upon its surrounding cultural setting, and especially the role played by technology within that setting. In an earlier essay, Blumenberg points out that technological advances are gradually absorbed into the more or less unconscious horizon of expectations that constitutes the life-world, thereby changing that which is perceived to be life threatening and therefore significant. This is the historical process that Blumenberg refers to as *Technisierung*,[54] through which technological advances are simply taken for granted and no longer generally reflected upon or understood. Instead, they sink back into the "universe of self-evidences" which is the life-world (TDL, 211). Accordingly, Blumenberg observes that the invention of the lightning rod served to reduce the mythic potential of lightning, since "every enlightenment depletes the potential of names and the metaphors." The Enlightenment is therefore defined as "the depletion (*Aufbrauch*) of that which could lie beyond the life-world" (TDL, 138). But this does not necessarily mean that myth will be brought to an end by the Enlightenment: the capacity of science to explain threatening aspects of the world is accompanied by an ever-increasing specialisation and complexity in science itself, which means that it is no longer transparent to the everyday observer. This knowledge is delegated to a collection of scientific experts or even to non-human agents such as computers, but if this system of delegation were to break down, then fears of the unknown and uncontrollable could be just as powerful as they were in the most primordial cultures (TDL, 138–9). The image of 'science out of control'—perhaps expressed most powerfully in Stanley Kubrick's *2001: A Space Odyssey* (1968, to be discussed in Chapter 6 of this volume), is also potentially fecund ground for myth.

THE 'ANTHROPOLOGICAL REDUCTION': ALSBERG

Another important feature of the essay "Self-Evidentness, Self-Erection, Self-Comparison" is the way in which Blumenberg begins to conjoin his theory of myth with notions taken from philosophical anthropology and from palaeoanthropology. In this short essay these ideas remain underdeveloped, but they are given a more detailed treatment in part two of *Description of Man*, also written in the second half of the 1970s. In the "Self-Evidentness" essay there are three ideas that have important implications for Blumenberg's understanding of the relations among human evolution, culture, and myth. First, the developmental transition to upright gait is said to have increased the human being's perceptual horizon and therefore its capacity to assess and to integrate potential threats to the life-world (TDL, 143). Second, human perception itself is, along the lines originally suggested by Uexküll, said to be fundamentally different from the stimulus-reaction model of animal environments, in that humans do not just react to stimuli according to pre-determined instincts; rather they self-reflexively compare and measure themselves up against potential threats on the horizon, including gods (TDL, 143–4). Third, human beings are said to have effectively "deactivated" (*ausgeschaltet*) the "Darwin-Mechanism" of natural selection through their use of technology, which represents a fundamental evolutionary switchover to *cultural* selection. Seen in this way, human creativity is in fact the "final intensification of selection" (TDL, 141, 143).

When one reads *Work on Myth*, and especially its opening section— "After the Absolutism of Reality"—it often seems as though these important and controversial theses taken from palaeoanthropology, which effectively amount to the working hypothesis upon which the entirety of *Work on Myth* is built, have already been decided upon and are more or less self-evident. Readers are expected simply to accept, for example, that primeval man "came close to not having control of the conditions of his existence and, what is more important, believed that he simply lacked control of them." This lack of control is said to have emerged from "leaving the shrinking rain forest for the savanna," which was accompanied by the transition to "bipedal posture." These radical geographical and physiological changes led to a widening of the human being's perceptual horizon, but also to an increase in its exposure to predators. Intense anxiety was triggered by this new condition of seeing and being seen, which was nothing less than a "situational leap" that demanded "super-accomplishment in consequence of a sudden lack of adaptation." Confronted by its predators, this poorly adapted being had to survive either by means of anticipating dangers before they arose or by using technology in order culturally to escape from its hopeless biological predicament (WOM, 3–5; AM, 9–10).

The "absolutism of reality" is described by Blumenberg as a "limit concept" (*Grenzbegriff*) that is based upon the "common core of all currently respected theories on the subject of anthropogenesis" (WOM, 4; AM, 9). This notion of a "limit concept," or *Grenzbegriff*, seems to have been derived from Blumenberg's earlier description of the life-world as a *Grenzvorstellung* or "limit representation" that is bound up with the revised phenomenological reduction of Husserl's *Krisis-Schrift*. Husserl, according to Blumenberg, saw the life-world not as an *object* of science but as a "limit representation" (*Grenzvorstellung*), as the "construction of an ahistorical beginning of history, of an atheoretical prehistory" (TDL, 200). The philosopher, in exposing the life-world to conscious analysis, is always already outside of the life-world. The life-world is thus posited as a "limit representation" that embodies what is irretrievable to thought precisely because, in being self-evident, it is also by and large unconscious. Against this background, the "limit concept" of the "absolutism of reality" can be seen to function in a similar way, to the extent that it might emerge not from the *phenomenological* but rather from what might be dubbed the *anthropological* reduction (my coinage, not Blumenberg's).

What is the 'anthropological reduction'? The anthropological reduction would have to be something quite different to its phenomenological counterpart, since as Blumenberg himself notes, both Husserl and Heidegger had rejected philosophical anthropology: Husserl because it seemed to rely upon the empirical sciences and was therefore insufficiently transcendental; Heidegger because it could offer only a 'regional' rather than a fundamental ontology (BDM, 496). The first version of the anthropological reduction can be found in the essay "An Anthropological Approach to the Contemporary Significance of Rhetoric" (1971). As we have seen, Blumenberg considers in this essay two mutually exclusive options concerning the human being: it is either 'poor' by virtue of its lack of biological adaptations, or 'rich' by virtue of its rhetoric and its symbol-producing gifts. The first position is associated by Blumenberg with philosophical anthropology (explicitly with Gehlen but also implicitly with Scheler and Plessner), the second with Cassirer's *Philosophy of Symbolic Forms*. Faced with this apparent *aporia*, Blumenberg thinks that it can be sidestepped by stripping away or "destroying" (*destruieren*) all ideological claims about what the human being 'naturally' *is*, in order to replace them with an answer to the *functional* question as to how the human being *is possible* (AAR, 438–9; WWL, 115).

This approach is then elaborated upon at length in *Description of Man*, where it is described—again echoing Husserl—as a "minimisation" (*Minimalisierung*) of the question concerning the human being (BDM, 522). This 'minimisation' follows Blumenberg's discussion of a number of "definition essays"—that is, attempts, or *Versuche*—to define what the human being is (see BDM, 512–16). Blumenberg is aware that any essential or essentialist definition of the human being will have political consequences. The most common objection to such definitions is attributed to Adorno in *Negative Dialectics* (*Negative Dialektik*, 1966), a text that Blumenberg had studied in 1967–8:[55] that any statement concerning what the human being is today would serve to sabotage what the human being *could be* in the future (BDM, 487–8).[56] The 'decisionist' alternative associated with Thomas Hobbes, according to which the question concerning the human being is simply delegated to the state or sovereign when difficult moral issues (such as abortion) arise, would also be unacceptably absolutist for Blumenberg. This question is, he thinks, so crucial to the lives of human beings that it cannot be delegated to the state (BDM, 507–9). And Aristotle's answer to the human question—according to which the human being is a 'rational animal'—is also seen to be problematic because Aristotle simply *adds* reason to the human organism as a kind of supplement that differentiates it from animals. The problem with such an approach, in Blumenberg's view, is that reason is thereby not explained as a feature of the human organism and its existential conditions. Aristotle's account fails, in other words, to explain why reason was necessary for human beings to *survive* in the first place (BDM, 509–10).

The anthropological reduction (or perhaps: minimisation) thus attempts a non-ideological or value-free description of the human being, on the basis that "philosophy is a process of dismantling things that are taken for granted" (AAR, 438; WWL, 114).[57] When one 'dismantles' or 'reduces' the human being in this way, one is left with the brute question not of what it can do, but of how it was able to survive. In *Description of Man*, Blumenberg then reconsiders the 'poor or rich' *aporia* from this perspective, suggesting that the 'poor' alternative—represented under the guises of Scheler's notion of the human as a maladapted dilettante, and of Gehlen's 'creature of deficiencies'—may be the superior path from a *functionalist* point of view. This approach is, thinks Blumenberg, to be seen not as a "value-judgement" (*Wertungsentscheid*), but rather as a "rationalisation of the anthropological question," in that it frees philosophical anthropology from its "substantialist presuppositions" (BDM, 523). The main consequence of this "minimisation" is that it gives rise to a critical rephrasing of Kant's fourth question: not "What is the human being? Rather: "How did the human being become what it is?" and "How is the human being possible?" (BDM, 523, 535).

At this point we need to recall that in the opening pages of *Work on Myth*, Blumenberg claims that his description of the human primal scene under the title of the "absolutism of reality" emerges from "currently respected theories on the subject of anthropogenesis" (4). Here it is germane briefly to investigate precisely *which* theories of anthropogenesis actually influenced Blumenberg's answer to the question "How is the human being possible?" This investigation soon reveals that Blumenberg's main source from palaeo-anthropology was scarcely a contemporary one. In the anthropology essay of 1971, Blumenberg credits Paul Alsberg's study *Das Menschheitsrätsel* (*The Puzzle of Humanity*, 1922) with having embarked upon the only possible "scientific course for an anthropology," precisely because it offers an explanation of "the functional system" of human life (AAR, 438–9; WWL, 115). Alsberg's study then goes on to play a central role in *Description of Man* (see, for example, BDM, 571, 575–9, 581–90). How could it be that an obscure book published in 1922 was seen by Blumenberg in the 1970s as "currently respected," and what did this book have to say about anthropogenesis?

Paul Alsberg (1883–1965) studied medicine and was a bacteriologist and later a practising doctor in Berlin. The *Puzzle of Humanity*—a version which was also published in English translation as *In Quest of Man* (1970)—was his only book, and its German reception was muted by the fact that it was subjected to the book burnings of 1933, on account of Alsberg's Jewish descent.[58] Alsberg was interned in the Oranienburg concentration camp during 1933–4, but was released (through American assistance) in 1934, upon which he immigrated to England. This minimal information concerning Alsberg is provided by the Berlin sociologist and anthropologist Dieter Claessens, who republished *The Puzzle of Humanity* under the even more dramatic title of *The Prison Breakout* (*Der Ausbruch aus dem Gefängnis*) in 1975.[59] Blumenberg may well have been made aware of Alsberg's book through the work of Claessens, who had afforded Alsberg a prominent place in his own sociological take on philosophical anthropology, initially outlined in *Instinct, Psyche, Validity* (*Instinkt, Psyche, Geltung*, 1968) and then elaborated in *The Concrete and the Abstract* (*Das Konkrete und das Abstrakte*, 1980).[60] But it is equally possible that Blumenberg first encountered the ideas of Alsberg in the classical texts of philosophical anthropology: Scheler discusses Alsberg prominently in *The Position of Man in the Cosmos*,[61] while Helmuth Plessner—writing in the Foreword to the second (1965) edition of *The Stages of the Organic and Man*—sees Alsberg as having exerted an influence on Gehlen's functional approach to philosophical anthropology in *Man*.[62] The fact that Alsberg is never once cited by Gehlen in that work, which was first published in 1940, can probably be attributed to Gehlen's ideological orientation during that period rather than to any lack of theoretical affinity, since Gehlen later refers to Alsberg as a "genius outsider" in an essay on philosophical anthropology originally published in 1971.[63]

Alsberg's solution to the so-called puzzle of humanity is the concept of *Körperausschaltung* (deactivation of the body), which he opposes to *Körperanpassung* or bodily adaptation. The former concept is associated with hominisation or the process of becoming human, whereas the latter is used to describe evolution by natural selection. Alsberg agrees with Darwin's finding that the human being initially evolved from non-human origins, but he does question the view—which he attributes to Darwin, to Ernst Haeckel and to Wilhelm Wundt—that the difference between animal and human mentality is one only of degree and not of fundamental type. Alsberg also rejects the classical view that humans can be differentiated from animals by virtue of intellect or *Geist*, seeing this as a speculative claim that cannot be proven. Criticising both biological materialism and philosophical idealism, Alsberg attributes hominisation to what he calls a "change of principle" (*Prinzipienwechsel*) that occurred in our pre-human ancestors. "If the essential difference of the human being from the animal is to be maintained," he writes, "we cannot get by without the acceptance of a change of principle."[64] This move is at once theoretical and rhetorical, in that Alsberg is proposing to respond to the most famous and influential publication on Darwinian natural selection in German—Ernst Haeckel's *Welträthsel* (*The Puzzle of the World*, 1899)[65]—with his own special solution to the *Menschheitsrätsel* or puzzle of humanity. The implicit claim is that the human 'puzzle' demanded a particular solution that Haeckel was unable to provide.

A remarkable feature of Alsberg's hominisation story is the extent to which he himself views it as being hypothetical, perhaps even borderline fictional. It is, according to Alsberg, a story for which physical evidence is radically lacking, and which therefore requires a "the strongest usage of fantasy," but it is a story that nonetheless enables the puzzle of humanity to be solved theoretically, if not empirically.[66] This story begins shortly after our pre-human ancestor left the trees to live upon more open ground, and its hero is named *Pithekanthropogoneus*, or "man-engendering ape."[67] In Alsberg's view, this species lived long before the specimen then known

as *Pithecanthropus erectus* (also known as 'Java Man'), which was discovered by Eugene Dubois in East Java in 1891.[68] While the 'Java Man'
specimens are now thought to be 1.8 million years old, a paper by Alsberg
published shortly after *The Puzzle of Humanity* argues that this specimen
already showed proto-human features such as upright gait and reduced
incisors. These features demonstrated, according to Alsberg, that in 'Java
Man' the process of *Körperausschaltung* was already well underway and
that he should therefore be known as *Homo Trinilis*.[69] The purported ini-
tiator of this process—*Pithekanthropogoneus*—is accordingly situated by
Alsberg well before 'Java Man,' at some undefined point in the *middle*
of the long Tertiary period (65 million to 2.6 million years ago).[70] From
today's point of view this chronology is extremely problematic. The climatic changes that Alsberg implicitly associates with the emergence of
Pithekanthropogoneus—aridification, which caused the shrinking of the
rainforests and the emergence of open grasslands—are thought to have
begun in East Africa around 6–8 million years ago, well after the middle
of the Tertiary period but well before the appearance of the first species
of *Homo*,[71] with a further intensification of these changes between circa
1.8–2.8 million years ago being viewed by many as having led directly to
hominin evolution.[72]

What happened at Alsberg's primal scene of hominisation? In being gradually forced from a life in the trees and onto the open savannah, *Pithekanthropogoneus* was faced with a situation in which he could no longer
always flee from his predators by hiding in vegetation or climbing trees.
Thus, while *Pithekanthropogoneus* had originally been a "fleeing creature"
(*Fluchttier*) that took refuge in the trees, a gradual increase in the time that
it spent on the ground forced it to develop a new means of survival: it was
compelled to become a *Kampftier*: a "fighting creature." Drawing upon
Hermann Klaatsch's arguments concerning the non-specialised flexibility of
the hand, Alsberg argues that *Pithekanthropogoneus* lacked bodily weapons with which to fight off its predators. That helplessness led it to resort
to non-bodily means of survival. The ability of *Pithekanthropogoneus* to
use its hands allowed it initially to roll, and subsequently to throw, stones
in the direction of its predators, and over time it also began to hoard these
projectiles in anticipation of future battles. The need to carry these weapons around gradually led to upright gait, because the hands were no longer
available to assist with walking or crawling. This "non-bodily method of
defence" is described by Alsberg as *the* turning point in hominisation: the
hand, and its ability to use projectile weapons, is what made us human, and
the human being literally threw itself into existence. Once the success of this
method of defence was proven, human development was forever switched to
an exclusively "human track" (*Menschenbahn*) that departed from natural
selection. It is therefore *cultural selection*, or non-bodily adaptation through
technology, that defines the human principle for Alsberg. This also means
that as technology played a progressively greater role in human survival,

bodily adaptations and instincts waned due to the reduction in physical selective pressures placed upon humans.[73]

As has recently been argued by Kasper Lysemose, Alsberg's account of hominisation could also be interpreted not as a choice in favour of fighting *over* fleeing, but rather as both fighting *and* fleeing.[74] This is because the key cultural achievement of *Pithekanthropogoneus* is to be able to fight from a position of *distance* by using its weapons as intermediaries. Seen in this way, the use of weapons is merely the beginning of other, more abstract, modes of mediation, and the "human principle" (*Menschheitsprinzip*) becomes indistinguishable from what Alsberg terms the "cultural principle" (*Kultur- prinzip*). For Alsberg there is a continuum between the use of stone tools and other primitive technologies on the one hand and the use of language and concepts on the other. The concept, like the weapon, is a technology of distance, allowing us to refer to things that are not immediately at hand. The human being is thus a cultural being that relies on non-bodily means in order to survive, and these means are "tools" (*Werkzeuge*)—namely, "tech- nology, language, and reason."[75]

This argument is also decisive for Blumenberg. The idea that civilisation is associated with the gaining of distance through the interposition of sym- bolic forms can already be found in Cassirer's notion of symbolic forms.[76] But the key difference between Blumenberg and Cassirer, according to Rüdi- ger Zill, is that for Blumenberg this notion of distance not only explains the contingent origins human civilisation; it also tells us how the human being could even have *come to be* in the first place. Blumenberg derived this notion from his reading of Paul Alsberg.[77]

What are the political implications of Alsberg's story of hominisation? For those who would suspect that any anthropology based upon a primor- dial encounter with a predator might be suggestive of Carl Schmitt's concept of the political (to be discussed in Chapter 7 of this volume),[78] Blumenberg has an answer that appears in the late collection *The Completeness of the Stars* (*Die Vollzähligkeit der Sterne*, 1997). Here Blumenberg does concede that the "primordial scene" (*Urszene*) is "absolutely political" because a being under threat from potential predators must quickly decide whether that which approaches over the horizon is a friend or an enemy, and in cases of doubt the latter assumption will be safer. But once technology is able to insert sufficient distance between the subject and its potential predators, at least in theory there will be more time to make decisions about friendship, precisely because the process of becoming friends—that of getting to know someone—takes time, the accumulation of a shared history. The downside to this aspect of technological modernity lies in the fact that technology, while creating a deliberative space between friend and enemy, also escalates their capacity to destroy one another from positions of great distance.[79]

Was Alsberg's account of hominisation "currently respected" in the 1970s? That of course depends upon whom you are asking, and here differ- ent national traditions of anthropology seem to have played a decisive role in the reception of Alsberg's *Puzzle of Humanity*. Upon its publication in English as *In Quest of Man* in 1970, it was met with perplexity. Writing in *Man*, the Irish anatomist M.A. MacConaill described Alsberg's approach as "Aristotelean and even medieval," arguing that *Körperausschaltung* is akin to a formal cause that distinguishes humans from animals. The tone of this review is not entirely unsympathetic, but suggests that the book combines a "neo-Darwinian" approach with a humanist value system that is radically unscientific.[80] In *The Quarterly Review of Biology*, no less a figure than the evolutionary biologist Theodosius Dobzhanksy, one of the main contributors to the modern evolutionary synthesis,[81] wrote that although Alsberg is not an "anti-evolutionist," he holds that there is an "abyss" between human and animals. The difference lies in what Dobzhanksky terms "cultural transmission," the sense in which human cultural practices are passed down through generations, which is distinguished from "biological heredity transmitted via the genes in the sex cells." Rather than even bothering to assess Alsberg's argument, Dobzhanksy merely declares it to be "very puzzling," presumably based upon the fact that, now seen in the context of the 1970s, it completely ignores the long established role played by genetics in human evolution.[82]

In Germany, and outside of the field of orthodox evolutionary biology, matters were rather different. Dieter Claessens admits that Alsberg's theory of descent, and especially the extremely vague timescale of his palaeoanthropology, are antiquated and can safely be ignored.[83] The earliest stone chopping tools—not projectiles, which would in any case be difficult to identify in the fossil record—were in the 1960s thought to have been used by *Homo habilis* ('handy man'), which is dated to between 1.4–2.3 million years ago; that is, certainly not in the middle of the Tertiary period.[84] (More recent findings, published in 2003, suggest 2.6 million years ago as a likely onset date for basic chopping tools).[85] At the same time, however, Claessens argues that Alsberg's theory of *Körperausschaltung* manages to avoid the metaphysical pitfalls of philosophical anthropology and to illuminate key aspects of what it is to be human. Even though Gehlen had himself accused Scheler of resorting to the metaphysical category of *Geist* (intellect or spirit) in order to explain the special place of human beings in the cosmos, Plessner and Gehlen had, in the view of Claessens, both propagated metaphysics in everything but name. The idea that human beings are biologically 'eccentric,' and the notion that they are 'creatures of deficiency,' both place the human being at odds with nature—seeing it as an incomplete body that is compensated by the achievements of mind. Alsberg had shown, according to Claessens, that human development could be attributed neither to *Geist* or mind, nor to an *a priori* assumption that it is a 'creature of deficiencies.' Instead it *became* a 'creature of deficiencies' by virtue of its own principle of development, that of *Körperausschaltung*, and it developed its mental capacities not because it possessed reason in advance, but merely because it sought to survive. In the words of Claessens: "Alsberg explains [. . .] more through less, a sign for a better theory." And this theory, opines Claessens, helps not just to clarify how the human being came to be, but also what human nature is today and what it might become in the future. The achievement of distance from nature through technology can be used to explain everything from telecommunications to the use of machines in industry.[86]

Although there is, to the best of my knowledge, no evidence that Blumenberg read Claessens's rehabilitation of Alsberg during the early 1970s, it is certainly possible that he did. Like Claessens, Blumenberg is taken with Alsberg's vision of the human being as a creature of distance. The advantage of Alsberg's theory is that it identifies "the capability of *actio per distans*" as *the* specific feature of human functionality (BDM, 570, 575). And also like Claessens, Blumenberg finds Alsberg's account of hominisation to have more explanatory power than that of Gehlen. While Gehlen fails to provide an explanation for upright gait, Alsberg shows that walking upright and being a creature of distance belong together, in that carrying weapons became the main function of the hands (BDM, 575). The fact that *Pithekanthropogoneus* does not resemble any pre-human ancestor identified by contemporary palaeoanthropology also does not trouble Blumenberg. Although *Pithekanthropogoneus* is a "fictional ancestor" (BDM, 577), and although Blumenberg describes this account of anthropogenesis as a "cryptogenesis"—as a story of the origin, the details of which cannot be proven or disproven by scientific means (BDM, 581–2)—he favours Alsberg's hominisation story on account of its theoretical productivity and functional effectiveness (*Leistungsfähigkeit*). "In a field in which we know almost nothing and in which we will perhaps also know almost nothing in the future," argues Blumenberg, "it must be permitted to choose the most functionally effective (*leistungsfähigste*) model" (BDM, 575). The implication of this statement is that no single story about hominisation will be able to provide an absolute foundation upon which a theory of the human could be erected. The anthropological reduction therefore involves selecting a story of anthropogenesis that has functional explanatory power and at least *plausible* elements, even if it cannot be empirically *demonstrable*.[87]

HYPOTHESES AND THEIR USES

Hans Blumenberg's theory of myth can only be understood when it is considered in relation to the story of philosophy in Germany from the mid nineteenth century up until the first half of the twentieth century. In the words of Herbert Schnädelbach: "the history of philosophy in the century of science is in essence a history of philosophical reactions to what was happening in science and in connexion with science in a changed culture."[88] It is the story of a discipline that tried and ultimately failed to offer a 'scientific'—in the sense of objectively valid, value-free, and foundational—theory of the human being. These attempts at laying scientific foundations proceeded along two paths, which at times intersected with one another. The first option was to underpin a theory of the human being with empirical scientific knowledge. This tendency was initially to be found in the early Dilthey's recourse to empirical psychology, and later in the attempts of philosophical anthropology to construct a theory of the human being in line with evidence taken from the biological sciences such as that provided by Klaatsch and Uexküll. The second option was that of Husserl's phenomenological reduction: to avoid the findings of the empirical sciences altogether by undertaking a supposedly value-free analysis of 'pure' consciousness as such. Both options ultimately failed precisely because the human being can never be a self-transparent object of scientific analysis. Any view of what the human being is will inevitably be infiltrated by the human being's pre-understandings and self-orientations concerning its position in the world—by what the late Husserl dubbed the life-world—and these pre-understandings and self-orientations are always already marked by historicity. This conclusion was reached, in different ways, by Dilthey's "The Rise of Hermeneutics" and his *Formation of the Historical World in the Human Sciences*, by Windelband's and Rickert's conclusions concerning the unavoidable importance of values in the human sciences, by Heidegger in *Being and Time*, and by Husserl in his *Krisis-Schrift*.

Blumenberg's theory of myth incorporates the notion that historicity and the prejudices to which it gives rise cannot be overcome by philosophy. Yet it also retains, albeit in a radically scaled-down and perhaps even ironic form, the 'will to science' found in both phenomenology and philosophical anthropology. It is from this perspective than we can begin to understand what I have called the 'anthropological reduction,' or what Blumenberg might have termed the 'anthropological minimisation.' This position can be outlined as follows: no story of anthropogenesis can be accepted as final and definitive, because any such story will always be told from a specific point in history, and the origin of which such stories speak is in any case so far behind us that no empirical evidence could ever possibly prove or disprove their truth. The finitude and historicity of human consciousness mean that the *terminus ad quem*, the 'correct' and final position according to which earlier theories are assessed and toward which they are seen to progress, will never be reached. This was the essence of Blumenberg's critique of Cassirer's theory of myth.

But this limitation does not mean that any old story about the origins of the human being will do.[89] In an age characterised by rapid increases in scientific knowledge about the human being, the story of anthropogenesis must at least be scientifically plausible, and it should also be captivating or significant, since these aspects of a story lie at the heart of its functional effectiveness (*Leistungsfähigkeit*). There is no question that the hero of Paul Alsberg's primal scene is—from the standpoint of present-day palaeoanthropology—entirely speculative, and Alsberg himself attributes his imagining of this scene to what he calls *Phantasie*. But the idea that technology can place a buffer between the human being and the selective pressures of its environment, thereby having a conservative effect on human bodily development, was already present in Alfred Russel Wallace and in Darwin's *Descent of Man*, and it remains on the agenda of contemporary evolutionary theory. As Wallace wrote in 1864:

> Man, by the mere capacity of clothing himself, and making weapons and tools, has taken away from nature that power of changing the external form and structure which she exercises over all other animals [. . .] man does this by means of intellect alone; which enables him with an unchanged body still to keep in harmony with the changing universe [. . .] from the time, therefore, when [. . .] the intellectual and moral faculties became fairly developed, man would cease to be influenced by "natural selection" in his physical form and structure.[90]

Darwin would go on to cite this passage with approval in the *Descent of Man*, proposing that humans, through their "weapons, tools, and various stratagems," are less exposed to the selective pressures of nature than are animal species and therefore require fewer changes in "bodily structure" in order to survive "greatly changed conditions."[91] The crucial difference between Darwin and Alsberg lies in the extent to which natural selection is ameliorated or deactivated by the buffer of technology. In Darwin there is no sense of a total changeover from bodily to technological adaptation as there is in Alsberg. And even more crucially, the mental capacities which give rise to technology and culture are themselves seen by Darwin to have been gradually "perfected or advanced through natural selection" and not through the contingent outcome of a primordial confrontation like that staged by Alsberg.[92]

What positions on these questions are to be found in the contemporary literature? Today the process that was hominisation is still seen as something that can only be inferred due to the lack of an adequate fossil record, and just how early in the Pliocene *Homo* may have begun remains "a matter of conjecture."[93] When it comes to the specific theories of Alsberg, the question as to whether tool use had a conservative or regressive effect on phylogenetic bodily development is certainly still live, but the idea that tools necessarily led to anatomical change and to speciation is seen as painting an overly simplistic picture that neglects other possible speciation causes such as isolated populations and genetic drift.[94] The notion that tool use led directly to bipedalism is also regarded as inherently speculative, since there is no empirical evidence that the earliest bipedal hominins used tools or stone weapons, and it is equally likely that tool use was in fact first made possible by bipedalism.[95] The theory that some hominin species prior to *Homo habilis* may have thrown stones at predators in order to protect itself on the open savannah is, however, still seen as being "quite plausible" without being provable.[96] And while the importance of technology for human evolution is beyond dispute, no contemporary paleoanthropologist would be likely see the throwing of stone projectiles as a contingent event that led to a change of evolutionary principle in the manner of Alsberg. Tool use is more commonly regarded as having gradually arisen from mental capacities that evolved through natural selection.[97]

Likewise, while some contemporary research suggests, in a similar way to Alsberg, that human technology (such as medicine, housing, agriculture) has been successful in buffering humans from the forces of natural selection to the extent that genetic human evolution has been radically reduced, this success is never total and is always dependent on the availability of the natural resources that make these technologies possible. The fact that these resources, and the technologies that depend upon them, are neither limitless nor evenly distributed throughout the world means that some human populations (especially those in the developing world) are more exposed to selective pressures—exerted, for example, by infectious diseases—than others. And the extent to which technology itself can give rise to new environmental problems such as global warming means that new selective pressures may arise as a direct result of human intervention into nature.[98] There is thus no sense in which human natural selection could ever be 'deactivated' in the way imagined by Alsberg, whose apparently unbounded optimism concerning technology seems out of step with our own age. Indeed, Blumenberg seems to have recognised that while human beings can protect themselves from natural selective pressures through technology, this selfsame technology could be their undoing. "If we affirm the end of biological evolution in man and through man," writes Blumenberg, "then we must accept that there is no stopping instrumental evolution [. . .] it is possible, that man may finally go under as a consequence of his instrumental evolution" (BDM, 552).

In his last long work—*Cave Exits* (1989)—Blumenberg offers the following definition of philosophy:

> Philosophy is essentially constituted by claims that can neither be proven nor refuted, and which are selected from the point of view of their functional effectiveness. These are then nothing other than hypotheses, with the difference that they contain no directions for possible experiments or observations, but only allow something to be understood, which would otherwise have to confront us as completely unknown and uncanny.
>
> (HA, 22)

It its pragmatic admission of the provisional and uncertain character of all philosophy, this statement could not be further from Husserl's notion of philosophy as rigorous science. But this is not an admission concerning the irrelevance or dispensability of philosophy. It is much more a statement to the effect that philosophy is *indispensable* as a means of providing plausible, if ultimately unprovable, answers to the most profound human questions. If human self-understanding necessitates telling a story about the origin of the human being without being able scientifically to prove this story, then it is philosophy that must speculatively explore these further reaches to which scientific rationality cannot penetrate. Seen in these terms, philosophy would then have to be the "discipline, which speaks of that which man can no longer achieve" (HA, 810). The fact that the hypotheses of philosophy are not testable does not mean that they are without use as a means of providing human orientation. And in this respect the orienting work done by philosophy is akin to what Blumenberg calls the work of myth (see HA, 810).

Hans Blumenberg's theory of myth is ultimately self-reflexive. Myth can never be a completely externalised 'object' which 'theory' then undertakes to describe, since this would imply that theory had overcome myth once and for all. Instead, any theory of myth must itself do work similar to that originally done by myth. It must tell a tale about the original conditions that gave rise to myth, about the *terminus a quo*, even if that origin is so far behind us that the story itself cannot be verified. And as is the case for myth in general, the story told by the theory of myth should also be a good one, loaded with significance. The title that Blumenberg gave to his drama of the origin was the 'absolutism of reality,' and Paul Alsberg's *Puzzle of Humanity* certainly influenced its plot.

There is in fact nothing unusual about Alsberg's recourse to narrative. By applying Vladimir Propp's work on the *Morphology of the Folktale* (1925) to key texts in twentieth-century Anglophone palaeoanthropology, Misia Landau has shown the extent to which they in fact rely on narrative structures also found in myth. These narratives tend to involve an initial state of equilibrium (our pre-human ancestor's life in the trees), followed by a disruption of this state (the change of climate from rainforest to savannah), which forces the protagonist into a journey in which challenges and predators are encountered. The tests of this journey then "bring out the human in the hero," and in meeting these tests the hero is often aided by a special agency, often seen to be intelligence, plasticity, or technology. The fact that these narratives are very difficult to test and falsify does not necessarily mean that they are completely unscientific.[99] In fact, Landau wonders whether there is "any way to present an evolutionary or historical account that does not involve storytelling."[100]

Similarly in their *Myths of Human Evolution*, the paleoanthropologists Nils Eldredge and Ian Tattersall refer to the opening sequence of Stanley Kubrick's *2001: A Space Odyssey*, in which a territorial battle between two groups of primates is finally won by the group that first learns to use animal bones as weapons. This "absorbing scenario," they write, "may or may not have happened," but it "may also present us with an accurate view of the basic patterns of change in human evolution."[101] It is this realm of the 'may or may not'—of mythic plausibility—that is occupied by the opening sections of *Work on Myth*, and when Blumenberg claims that palaeoanthropology specialises in developing these primordial scenarios (BDM, 575), he shows a similar awareness of the mythic components in stories of anthropogenesis. One can only speculate about why Paul Alsberg's name did not make it onto the pages of *Work on Myth*. But if significance arises from "the resistance that reality opposes to life and the summoning up of energy that enables one to measure up to it" (WOM, 75; AM, 86), then Alsberg's stone-thrower, who begins to put the 'absolutism of reality' at a distance through technology, thereby setting in motion the process of cultural selection to which myth belongs, surely meets this criterion. And Blumenberg heightens the drama of this evolutionary occasion by underscoring its contingency, suggesting that if the first stone had not been thrown, then the human being might not have come to be at all (BDM, 576). The long process through which hominin species gradually came to use tools—described in the recent literature as a series of "incremental steps" that unfolded over millennia[102]— is concentrated by Blumenberg into a single mythic moment with maximum dramatic effect, since in it literally everything is at stake. Like any proper hero, Alsberg's fictive protagonist rises to the occasion and brings the human being into existence "with a throw" (BDM, 575, 582).[103] *Pithekanthropogoneus* finds an escape clause in the physical conditions of his existence by taking recourse to technology. This tale of triumph is Promethean.

NOTES

1. Eva Geulen, "Passion in Prose," *Telos* 158 (Spring, 2012): 9–20.
2. Joachim Fischer, *Philosophische Anthropologie. Eine Denkrichtung des 20. Jahrhunderts* (Freiburg: Alber, 2008), 14.
3. Chistian Thies, *Einführung in die philosophische Anthropologie* (Darmstadt: Wissenschaftliche Buchgesellschaft, 2004), 7.
4. Geulen, "Passion in Prose," 14.
5. See Peter E. Gordon, *Continental Divide: Heidegger, Cassirer, Davos* (Cambridge, MA: Harvard University Press, 2010), in particular: 69–77.
6. See Vida Pavesich, "Hans Blumenberg's Philosophical Anthropology: After Heidegger and Cassirer," *Journal of the History of Philosophy* 46, no. 2 (2008): 421–48; here: 423.
7. See Martin Heidegger, "Ernst Cassirer, *Philosophy of Symbolic Forms*," trans. Peter Warnek, in Heidegger, *Kant and the Problem of Metaphysics*, 5th ed., trans. Richard Taft (Bloomington: Indiana University Press, 1997), 180–90; here: 188; "Ernst Cassirer, *Philosophie der symbolischen Formen. 2. Teil: Das mythische Denken*," *Deutsche Literaturzeitung* 5, no. 21 (1928): 1000–12; reprinted in Heidegger, *Gesamtausgabe*, vol. 3, *Kant und das Problem der Metaphysik*, ed. Friedrich-Wilhelm von Herrmann (Frankfurt am Main: Klostermann, 1991), 255–70; here: 267.
8. Ernst Cassirer, "Geist und Leben in der Philosophie der Gegenwart," *Die neue Rundschau* 41 (1930): 244–64.
9. Cassirer, "Geist und Leben," 255, 259.
10. Ernst Cassirer, *The Philosophy of Symbolic Forms*, vol. 2, *Mythical Thought*, trans. Ralph Manheim (New Haven, CT: Yale University Press, 1955), 9–10 (hereafter: *Mythical Thought*); *Philosophie der symbolischen Formen. Zweiter*

Teil: Das mythische Denken, ed. Klaus Rosenkranz (1925; Hamburg: Felix Meiner, 2002), 11–12 (hereafter: *Das mythische Denken*).

11. Cassirer, *Mythical Thought*, 11; *Das mythische Denken*, 13.
12. Cassirer, *Mythical Thought*, 39, 46, 239–40, 14; *Das mythische Denken*, 48, 58, 279–81, 16.
13. Cassirer, *Mythical Thought*, 236–7, 243; *Das mythische Denken*, 276–7, 285.
14. Ernst Cassirer, *The Myth of the State* (New Haven, CT: Yale University Press, 1946), 280.
15. On Cohen's reinterpretation of Kant in relation to scientific method, see Hermann Cohen, *Kants Theorie der Erfahrung* (Berlin: Dümmler, 1871); see also: Klaus Christian Köhnke, *Entstehung und Aufstieg des Neukantianismus* (Frankfurt am Main: Suhrkamp, 1986), 273–301, especially 288; and Gordon, *Continental Divide*, 52–6.
16. Hermann Cohen, *Kants Theorie der Erfahrung*, 2nd ed. (1871; Berlin: Dümmler, 1885), 518–19.
17. Heidegger, "Ernst Cassirer, *Philosophy of Symbolic Forms*," 181; "Ernst Cassirer, *Philosophie der symbolischen Formen*," in *Gesamtausgabe*, 3:256.
18. Cassirer, *Mythical Thought*, 75; *Das mythische Denken*, 89.
19. Heidegger, "Ernst Cassirer, *Philosophy of Symbolic Forms*," 182, 186–7; "Ernst Cassirer, *Philosophie der symbolischen Formen*," in *Gesamtausgabe*, 3:259, 265–6.
20. Heidegger, "Ernst Cassirer, *Philosophy of Symbolic Forms*," 187–8 (translation altered); "Ernst Cassirer, *Philosophie der symbolischen Formen*," in *Gesamtausgabe*, 3:265–7.
21. Heidegger, *Being and Time*, trans. John Macquarrie and Edward Robinson (Malden, MA: Blackwell, 1962), 223, 322, 236, 393; *Sein und Zeit*, in *Gesamtausgabe*, vol. 2, *Veröffentlichte Schriften 1914–70*, ed. Friedrich-Wilhlem von Herrmann (Frankfurt am Main: Klostermann, 1977), 237, 368–9, 255, 453.
22. Heidegger, *Being and Time*, 179–80; *Sein und Zeit*, in *Gesamtausgabe*, 2:187.
23. Heidegger, "Ernst Cassirer, *Philosophy of Symbolic Forms*," 188, 186, 190; "Ernst Cassirer, *Philosophie der symbolischen Formen*," in *Gesamtausgabe*, 3: 267; 264; 269.
24. Heidegger, *Being and Time*, 435; *Sein und Zeit*, in *Gesamtausgabe*, 2:507.
25. Heidegger, *Kant and the Problem of Metaphysics*, §3 (9–12); *Kant und das Problem der Metaphysik*, in *Gesamtausgabe*, 3:13–18. See also Heidegger's comments to this effect in the "Davos Disputation between Ernst Cassirer and Martin Heidegger," in *Kant and the Problem of Metaphysics*, 193–207; here: 193–4; "Davoser Disputation zwischen Ernst Cassirer und Martin Heidegger" in *Gesamtausgabe*, 3:274–96; here: 274–5.
26. Heidegger, *Kant and the Problem of Metaphysics*, §34 (132–6); here: 134; *Kant und das Problem der Metaphysik*, in *Gesamtausgabe*, 3:188–95; here: 191.
27. Cassirer, "Davos Disputation," 194–6; "Davoser Disputation," in Heidegger, *Gesamtausgabe*, 3:275–7.
28. Heidegger, "Davos Disputation," 202; "Davoser Disputation," in *Gesamtausgabe*, 3:288.
29. Heidegger, *Being and Time*, 73; *Sein und Zeit*, in *Gesamtausgabe*, 2:63–4.
30. Heidegger, "Davos Disputation," 204; "Davoser Disputation," in *Gesamtausgabe*, 3:291.
31. Heidegger, *Kant and the Problem of Metaphysics*, §§37–8 (146–53); here: 148; *Kant und das Problem der Metaphysik*, in *Gesamtausgabe*, 3:208–9; here: 211.

32. See Heidegger, *Kant and the Problem of Metaphysics*, §40 (155–58); here: 156; *Kant und das Problem der Metaphysik*, in *Gesamtausgabe*, 3:222–6; here: 223.

33. This is Heidegger's own formulation in *Kant and the Problem of Metaphysics*, where he writes that "in order to wring from what the words say, what it is they want to say, every interpretation must necessarily use violence [*Gewalt*]" (141); *Kant und das Problem der Metaphysik*, in *Gesamtausgabe*, 3:202.

34. Blumenberg, "Affinitäten und Dominanzen," in EMS, 161–8.

35. On Heidegger's skill at raising philosophical expectations that he was unable to fulfil, see also Blumenberg, "Das Sein—ein MacGuffin," in EMS, 157–60.

36. In another essay published from the *Nachlass* and probably written in the late 1970s—"Die Lebenswelt als Thema der Phänomenologie" (TDL, 111–32)—Blumenberg also suggests that the Davos disputation ended with Heidegger winning "at least on points," a victory that led to the decline of neo-Kantianism, see 113.

37. See also, for example, "Was wäre, würde Heidegger verstanden?" in EMS, 34–6; "Das Sein—ein MacGuffin," in EMS, 157–60 (the latter originally published in the *Frankfurter Allgemeine Zeitung*, May 27, 1987).

38. Blumenberg, "Die Veführbarkeit des Philosophen," in VP, 100–6; here: 102–3. Here the substantive *Verführbarkeit* is derived from *verführen*: to lead astray or seduce. Löwith uses this word playfully in relation to Heidegger's acceptance of the position of *Rektor* at Freiburg University in 1933: "der Verführung zur Führung der eigenen Universität gab er nach," (he gave in to the seduction of leading his own university). See Karl Löwith, *Mein Leben in Deutschland vor und nach 1933. Ein Bericht* (Stuttgart: Metzler, 1986), 32. For the passages from Löwith's account quoted by Blumenberg, see 55–6.

39. On this subject, see Oliver Müller, *Sorge um die Vernunft. Hans Blumenbergs phänomenologische Anthropologie* (Paderborn: Mentis, 2005), 241–50.

40. Blumenberg, "Ernst Cassirers gedenkend," in WWL, 163–73; here: 164–5, 167–8.

41. "Involvement" is the rather inexact rendering of *Bewandtnis* used by Macquarrie and Robinson, and they correctly point out (see *Being and Time*, 115, fn. 2) that there is no English equivalent for this term, which refers to the meaning, distinguishing characteristic or relevance that something may have within a particular setting. When Heidegger writes that "der Seinscharakter des Zuhandenen ist die Bewandtnis" (*Gesamtausgabe*, 2:112), he means that the "ready-to-hand" *matters* to or is *important* for *Dasein* because of its particular existential context. This is why *Dasein* can be described as being "involved" with that which is ready-to-hand. From this it is easy to see that the ready-to-hand would also have a certain meaning (*Bedeutung*) and significance (*Bedeutsamkeit*) for *Dasein*.

42. See Heidegger, *Being and Time*, § 18 (114–23); here: 114–15, 118–22; *Sein und Zeit*, in *Gesamtausgabe*, 2:111–20; here: 111–12; 114–19.

43. Pavesich, "Hans Blumenberg's Philosophical Anthropology," 434–5; Müller, *Sorge um die Vernunft*, 246–50.

44. Felix Heidenreich, *Mensch und Moderne bei Hans Blumenberg* (Munich: Fink, 2005), 25–30; Müller, *Sorge um die Vernunft*, 47–59.

45. References are to the second manuscript version of this work, which is available at the *Deutsches Literaturarchiv* Marbach under the following title: *Die ontologische Distanz. Eine Untersuchung zur Krisis der philosophischen Grundlagen der Neuzeit.*

46. Hans Georg Gadamer, *Truth and Method*, trans. Joel Weinsheimer and Donald G. Marshall (1960; New York: Continuum, 2003), 276–7; *Wahrheit und*

Methode, in *Gesammelte Werke*, 10 vols. (1960; Tübingen: Mohr Siebeck, 1999), 1:281.

47. Edmund Husserl, *The Crisis of European Sciences and Transcendental Phenomenology*, trans. David Carr (Evanston, IL: Northwestern University Press, 1970), 9, 51–2, 12; Husserl, *Gesammelte Werke (Husserliana)*, vol. 6, *Die Krisis der europäischen Wissenschaften und die transzendentale Phänomenologie*, ed. Walter Biemel (The Hague: Martinus Nijhoff, 1954), 7, 51–2, 10.

48. Husserl, *The Crisis of European Sciences*, 17, 103, 127, 142, 112, 146; *Die Krisis*, in *Gesammelte Werke*, 6: 16, 105, 130, 145, 114, 149. For context see Verena Mayer, *Edmund Husserl* (Munich: Beck, 2009), 17–36.

49. Husserl, "The Attitude of Natural Science and the Attitude of Humanistic Science. Naturalism, Dualism and Psychophysical Psychology (1930?)," in *The Crisis of European Sciences*, 315–34; here: 323; "Naturwissenschaftliche und geisteswissenschaftliche Einstellung. Naturalismus, Dualismus und psychophysische Psychologie," in *Gesammelte Werke*, 6:294–313; here: 302.

50. Husserl, "Philosophy and the Crisis of European Humanity (The Vienna Lecture)," in *The Crisis of European Sciences*, 269–99; here: 273; "Die Krisis des europäischen Menschentums und die Philosophie," in *Gesammelte Werke*, 6:314–48; here: 318.

51. See Manfred Sommer's "Nachwort des Herausgebers," in TDL, 243–7.

52. Husserl, *The Crisis of European Sciences*, 155, 147, 153; *Die Krisis*, in *Gesammelte Werke*, 6:158, 150, 156.

53. Three of the four essays focused on here—"Theorie der Lebenswelt," "Die Lebenswelt als Thema der Phänomenologie," and "Selbstverständlichkeit, Selbstaufrichtung, Selbstvergleich"—were published from the *Nachlass* in 2010, but were written, according to Manfred Sommer, in the second half of the 1970s (see TDL, 247). The fourth essay, "Lebenswelt und Technisierung unter Aspekten der Phänomenologie," was first delivered as a lecture in 1959 and then subsequently published in *Filosofia* 14 (1963): 855–84, as well as in WWL, 7–54.

54. See Blumenberg, "Lebenswelt und Technisierung unter Aspekten der Phänomenologie," in TDL, 181–224.

55. See Blumenberg to Taubes, September 20, 1967, in BTB, 134–6.

56. "We cannot say what man is [. . .] To decipher the human essence by the way it is now would sabotage its possibility." Theodor W. Adorno, *Negative Dialectics*, trans. E. B. Ashton (London: Routledge, 2004), 124; *Negative Dialektik* (Frankfurt am Main: Suhrkamp, 1966), 128.

57. In the German version, Blumenberg uses the substantive *der Abbau*, meaning that philosophy is the dismantling or reduction of those things that are taken for granted (WWL, 114).

58. Paul Alsberg, *Das Menschheitsrätsel, Versuch einer prinzipiellen Lösung* (Dresden: Sibyllen-Verlag, 1922); translated as *In Quest of Man: A Biological Approach to the Problem of Man's Place in Nature* (Oxford: Pergamon Press, 1970).

59. See Dieter Claessens, "Vorwort zur Neuauflage," in Paul Alsberg, *Der Ausbruch aus dem Gefängnis. Zu den Entstehungsbedingungen des Menschen*, ed. Dieter Claessens, commentary by Hartmut and Ingrid Rötting (Gießen: Focus, 1975), 5–7. A second revised edition of *Das Menschheitsrätsel* also appeared in 1937 (Vienna: Sensen-Verlag).

60. See Dieter Claessens, *Instinkt, Psyche, Geltung. Bestimmungsfaktoren menschlichen Verhaltens* (Cologne: Westdeutscher Verlag, 1968), 81–94; *Das Konkrete und das Abstrakte. Soziologische Skizzen zur Anthropologie*

(Frankfurt am Main: Suhrkamp, 1980). See also Fischer, *Philosophische Anthropologie*, 419–24.

61. See Max Scheler, *Die Stellung des Menschen im Kosmos*, in *Gesammelte Werke*, ed. Maria Scheler and Manfred S. Frings, 15 vols. (Basel: Francke; Bonn: Bouvier, 1971–97), 9:7–72; here: 46–7.

62. See Helmuth Plessner, "Vorwort zur zweiten Auflage," *Die Stufen des Organischen und der Mensch*, 3rd ed. (1928; Berlin: Walter De Gruyter, 1975) vii–xxiii; here: xvi.

63. Gehlen bestows this honour on Alsberg in his essay "Philosophische Anthropologie," in *Gesamtausgabe*, vol. 4, *Philosophische Anthropologie und Handlungslehre*, ed. Karl-Siegbert Rehberg (Frankfurt am Main: Vittorio Klostermann, 1983), 236–46; here: 238. On the broader importance of Alsberg's book for philosophical anthropology in general as well as for Gehlen in particular, see Joachim Fischer, *Philosophische Anthropologie*, 47–8, 271.

64. Alsberg, *Das Menschheitsrätsel*, 23, 25–8, 83–4, 80.

65. Ernst Haeckel, *Die Welträthsel. Gemeinverständliche Studien über monistische Philosophie* (Bonn: Emil Strauß, 1899).

66. Alsberg, *Das Menschheitsrätsel*, 277, 363.

67. Alsberg, *Das Menschheitsrätsel*, 309, 402; the English rendering is the coinage of Robert Savage in "Aporias of Origin: Hans Blumenberg's Primal Scene of Hominization," in *Erinnerung an das Humane. Beiträge zur phänomenologischen Anthropologie Hans Blumenbergs*, ed. Michael Moxter (Tübingen: Mohr Siebeck, 2011), 62–71; here: 67.

68. Alsberg, *Das Menschheitsrätsel*, 343.

69. Paul Alsberg, "Pithecanthropous Erectus—Homo Trinilis," *Zeitschrift für Morphologie und Anthropologie* 25, no. 2 (1925): 165–70. Alsberg also repeated this claim in "The Taungs Puzzle. A Biological Essay," *Man* 34 (1934): 154–9. This specimen is today classified as *Homo erectus*.

70. Alsberg, *Das Menschheitsrätsel*, 374–6.

71. Pierre Sepulchre et al., "Tectonic Uplift and Eastern Africa Aridification," *Science* 313, no. 5792 (September 2006): 1419–23.

72. The rainforest to savannah hypothesis emerged in the early twentieth century, has been elaborated in numerous versions, and has periodically been disputed, revised and resurrected. For an overview of its history see Richard Potts, "Environmental Hypotheses of Hominin Evolution," *Yearbook of Physical Anthropology* 41 (1998): 93–136; here: 106–9. For a summary of current opinion in this area see the volume *Understanding Climate's Influence on Human Evolution* published by the Committee of the Earth System Context for Hominin Evolution (Washington, DC: The National Academies Press, 2010), 16–43. The generally accepted conclusion reached by this volume is that "African savannah grasslands became an increasingly prominent component of the landscape after the mid-late Pliocene," and especially from 1.8–2.8 million years ago (26, 35). On the relation between these climatic changes and hominin evolution, see E. S. Vrba et al., *Paleoclimate and Evolution* (New Haven, CT: Yale University Press, 1995).

73. Alsberg, *Das Menschheitsrätsel*, 309–12, 356, 350, 361–2, 377–7, 431.

74. Kasper Lysemose, "The Being, the Origin and the Becoming of Man: A Presentation of Philosophical Anthropogenealogy and Some Ensuing Methodological Considerations," *Human Studies* 35, no. 1 (2012): 115–30; here: 119.

75. Alsberg, *Das Menschheitsrätsel*, 448–9.

76. See, for example Cassirer's notion of culture as a form of *Distanzsetzung* (placing or inserting of distance) in "Geist und Leben," 259.

77. See Rüdiger Zill, "Überlebensthemen. Vom Umgang mit der Sterblichkeit des Menschen bei Hans Blumenberg," in *Überleben. Historische und aktuelle Konstellationen*, ed. Falko Schmieder (Munich: Fink, 2011), 265–80; here: 274–8.
78. See Carl Schmitt, *The Concept of the Political*, trans. and introd. George Schwab (Chicago, IL: University of Chicago Press, 1996), 25–7; *Der Begriff des Politischen*, (1927; Berlin: Duncker and Humblot, 1979), 26–8.
79. See Blumenberg, "Die Heterogonie von 'Feind' und 'Freund,'" in VS, 345–8; also reprinted in BSB, 222–6.
80. M. A. MacConaill, "In *Quest of Man: A Biological Approach to the Problem of Man's Place in Nature*, by Paul Alsberg," *Man* 5, no. 4 (1970): 705.
81. See his *Genetics and the Origin of Species* (New York: Columbia University Press, 1937).
82. Theodosius Dobzhansky, "In *Quest of Man: A Biological Approach to the Problem of Man's Place in Nature*, by Paul Alsberg," *The Quarterly Review of Biology* 46, no. 1 (1971): 100–1.
83. Claessens, *Instinkt, Psyche, Geltung*, 80.
84. This was already established during the early 1960s by the discoveries of Mary and Louis Leakey in East Africa. See L.S.B. Leakey, P. V. Tobias and J. R. Napier, "A New Species of the Genus *Homo* from Olduvai Gorge," *Nature* 202 (April 4, 1964): 7–9. See also Kathy D. Schick and Nicholas Toth, *Making Silent Stones Speak: Human Evolution and the Dawn of Technology* (New York: Simon and Schuster, 1994), 126–8.
85. Sileshi Semaw et al., "2.6-million-year-old stone tools and associated bones from OGS-6 and OGS-7, Gona, Afar, Ethiopia," *Journal of Human Evolution* 45 (2003): 169–77. The hominid species that used these tools is yet to be identified.
86. Claessens, *Instinkt, Psyche, Geltung*, 80, 91–2, 84.
87. On Blumenberg's hypothetical scenario of anthropogenesis, see Barbara Merker, "Geschichte(n) der Paläoanthropologie," in *Hans Blumenberg beobachtet. Wissenschaft, Technik und Philosophie*, ed. Cornelius Borck (Freiburg: Alber, 2013), 111–25.
88. See Herbert Schnädelbach, *Philosophy in Germany, 1831–1933*, trans. Eric Matthews (Cambridge: Cambridge University Press, 1984); Chapter 3, especially 92.
89. On these methodological considerations, see also Lysemose, "The Being, the Origin," 125–8.
90. Alfred Russel Wallace, "The Origin of Human Races and the Antiquity of Man Deduced from the Theory of Natural Selection," *Anthropological Review* 2 (1864): clvii–clxxxvii; here: clxiii.
91. Charles Darwin, *The Descent of Man, and Selection in Relation to Sex*, 2 vols. (London: John Murray, 1871), 1:158–9.
92. Darwin, *Descent of Man*, 1:159. See also Schick and Toth, *Making Silent Stones Speak*, 18.
93. William H. Kimble, "The Origin of *Homo*," in *The First Humans—Origin and Early Evolution of the Genus* Homo, ed. Frederick E. Grine, John G. Fleagle, and Richard E. Leakey (Dodrecht: Springer, 2009), 31–7; here: 32, 36.
94. Robert Foley and Marta Mirazón Lahr, "On Stony Ground: Lithic Technology, Human Evolution, and the Emergence of Culture," *Evolutionary Anthropology* 12 (2003): 109–22; here: 117, 120. See also Ian Tattersall, *Becoming Human: Evolution and Human Uniqueness* (Oxford: Oxford University Press, 1988), 139.

95. Schick and Toth, *Making Silent Stones Speak*, 45–7.
96. Tattersall, *Becoming Human*, 130.
97. Schick and Toth, *Making Silent Stones Speak*, 18; Tattersall, *Becoming Human*, 128–9.
98. Jay T. Stock, "Are Humans Still Evolving?" *European Molecular Biology Organization Reports* 9 (2008): 51–4. This article, along with other contemporary sources on human evolution, is discussed in relation to Blumenberg's position by Rebekka A. Klein in "Das Ende der Humanevolution? Blumenbergs Argumente gegen einen Erklärungsprimat in Darwins Evolutionstheorie," in *Auf Distanz zur Natur: Philosophische und theologische Perspektive in Hans Blumenbergs Anthropologie*, ed. Rebekka A. Klein (Würzburg: Königshausen und Neumann, 2009), 165–82.
99. See for example, the speculative scenario that opens the study by Kathy D. Schick and Nicholas Toth, *Making Silent Stones Speak*, 15–16.
100. Misia Landau, "Human Evolution as Narrative," *American Scientist* 72 (1984): 262–8. Landau develops this argument at greater length in *Narratives of Human Evolution* (New Haven, CT: Yale University Press, 1994).
101. Nils Eldredge and Ian Tattersall, *The Myths of Human Evolution* (New York: Columbia University Press, 1982), 5–6.
102. Foley and Lahr, "On Stony Ground," 120.
103. See also Lysemose, "The Being, The Origin," 20.

5   Promethean Anthropologies

Hans Blumenberg's use of the title *Work on Myth* promises a study that will outline the central characteristics of myth in general rather than inquiring into the dynamics of one particular myth. Yet the reality with which the reader of *Work on Myth* is confronted is rather more complicated. We have already seen the extent to which Blumenberg's anthropology arises from a story of hominisation in which our pre-human ancestor comes to be human by resisting, through foresight and the use of technology, the threatening biological situation with which it is confronted. The 'absolutism of reality' is Blumenberg's imaginative reconstruction of this primordial situation along generally plausible scientific lines that are overlain with dramatic affect. Since the precise details of this original situation are not knowable, the person who reconstructs them is, in Blumenberg's view, also allowed a certain degree of imaginative license. The way in which this licence is put to use will in turn reveal the storyteller's prejudices or pre-understandings concerning the essential nature of the human being. Blumenberg makes use of this licence through his preference for an anthropology in which the human being must find artificial or cultural ways to compensate for an absence of biological or instinctive automatisms within a given situation. This anthropology is simultaneously anti-Platonic and anti-Cartesian, while also being 'Promethean.'

That these terms—anti-Platonic, anti-Cartesian, and Promethean—are in a certain sense synonymous will be revealed here through an overview of what I will call 'Promethean anthropologies.' It is Plato's *Protagoras* which first outlines in philosophical terms, and from the disreputable perspective of Sophism, what a 'Promethean anthropology' might be. Reactions to this basic model can then be found in the writings of Vico, Herder, Schelling, and Nietzsche. All of these writers belong to the background of Prometheus reception that is elaborated upon in *Work on Myth*. But perhaps the most explicit 'Promethean anthropologist' of all—insofar as he directly translates the Platonic version of the Prometheus myth into a modern philosophical anthropology—is Arnold Gehlen.

In the second (1941) edition of Gehlen's *Man* that can be viewed, complete with Blumenberg's handwritten annotations, at the German Literary

Archive in Marbach, the phrase *like Prometheus* has, within the following passage, been underlined by its former owner:

> Man is ultimately an *anticipatory* being. Like Prometheus, he must direct his energies toward what is removed, what is not present in time and space. Unlike animals, he lives for the future and not in the present. This disposition is one of the preconditions for an acting existence, and human consciousness must be understood from this point of view.[1]

In writings that prepare the way for *Work on Myth*—in particular *Paradigms for a Metaphorology* (1960) and *Theory of Non-Conceptuality* (1975)— Blumenberg also underlines the sense in which the human being deals with its existential situation by being a creature of distance in both temporal and spatial terms. These texts, when read alongside *Work on Myth*, reveal the full degree to which, in Blumenberg's theory of myth, there is never a total separation between the 'theory' being propounded and the 'object' that it analyses. Both the metaphor and the concept—and, as we shall see, in Blumenberg's account the boundary separating the two is often unclear—can help to divide up and order reality by enabling one to refer to objects that are not immediately present. And if "myth allows man to live, by depleting superior power," then it is Prometheus, the great cultural compensator, who "represents the archaic division of powers in its pure form" (WOM, 31, 301; AM, 38, 331). There is a distinct possibility, in other words, that Blumenberg focuses on the Prometheus myth at the expense of other myths precisely because his own account of the 'absolutism of reality' is a Promethean one.

READING THE *PROTAGORAS*

In *Protagoras*, Hippocrates awakens Socrates in the early hours of the morning to inform him that Protagoras of Abdera is visiting Athens. It is Hippocrates's aim to have Socrates introduce him to Protagoras, whom he regards as a wise man and the "the cleverest of speakers" (311a).[2] The fact that Protagoras is a sophist is soon established by the ensuing conversation between Socrates and Hippocrates, and this conversation also reveals the low esteem in which Protagoras's profession is held. While Hippocrates would feel no shame in learning to be a sculptor from Polycleitus or Pheidias, there is something shameful in paying Protagoras for lessons in the art of sophistry (311c–312a). Socrates accordingly warns Hippocrates about putting his soul in the care of Protagoras. While a sophist may teach the art of speaking eloquently, it is the content of this speech that must be assessed according to the harms or benefits that it may cause the soul, and it turns out that the purported knowledge communicated by sophists is not at all easy to define in comparison with that of a painter or a carpenter (312–14).

Socrates and Hippocrates then proceed to the venue at which Protagoras is speaking, and a discussion between Socrates and Protagoras ensues. When Protagoras claims that he teaches what Socrates refers to as the art of political virtue (*arête*) and of making men into good citizens (319a), Socrates expresses a general doubt as to whether virtue or *arête* can in fact be taught at all, since all humans inherently possess it (320b). Upon hearing this objection, Protagoras responds by providing both a *mythos* (outlined from 320c–322d) and a *logos*, or logical account, in which the contents of the myth are supplemented (at 322d–324d), in order to persuade Socrates of his case.³

When, explains Protagoras, the gods decided to create mortal creatures, they charged the brothers Epimetheus ('afterthought') and Prometheus ('forethought') with the task of equipping them with the qualities that they would need for survival. The dim-witted Epimetheus was to be the distributor of these gifts, and Prometheus would carry out an inspection following the initial distribution. But while various qualities such as wings, thick fur, or hard hooves were given to animals, Prometheus's inspection revealed that Epimetheus had forgotten about the human beings, who were left naked, shoeless, and without means of flight or defence. In order to assist the human beings, Prometheus stole fire and crafts from Hephaestus and Athene, a theft for which he was later punished. While the possession of fire and of crafts did initially enable humans to survive, they soon discovered that they were still weak in comparison with the animals, and so needed to band together in settlements for the sake of self-preservation. But this new form of social organisation brought with it new problems, since living in close proximity to one another led the humans to treat their neighbours unjustly. When Zeus saw this life-threatening state of political disarray, he sent Hermes to impart justice and virtue (*arête*) to the human beings. When Hermes asked Zeus to whom these abilities should be allotted, Zeus answered that all humans must have them. Thus, while only carpenters may talk meaningfully about carpentry or painters about painting, all humans have the ability to know *arête* and have a right to speak about affairs of the state. This ability to know *arête* is not an inherent natural possession like the wings, fur or hooves belonging to certain animals or the various crafts allotted to particular human beings *before* they came to be; because it was given by Zeus *after* human beings were created, it is much more a general capability that must be taught and practised, and this mode of instruction— that is, teaching the art of political virtue or *arête*—is what constitutes the profession of Protagoras.⁴

The ontological status of *arête* is the key question in the *Protagoras*. Do all human beings have *arête* by nature? Do all human beings have an equal capacity for *arête*? Or can *arête* be developed in some human beings more than in others? Obviously Protagoras does not want all human beings to have an equal and inherent capacity for *arête* and he says so at 323c-d. In other words, having *arête* is not like having hands or feet. If this were the case, it would mean that the sophist would have no job to do, since all humans would, by nature, already have *arête*. This effectively means that *arête* both is and is not nature. It is nature in that Zeus has given all human beings a capacity for *arête*. But it is not entirely nature because that capacity is only a kind of latency that must be brought out by culture and education. Protagoras's position concerning *arête* must remain a relatively weak one precisely so that he can claim an essential role for sophism: it is never a substantial thing but only a latent potential that must be brought out by culture. It exists, in other words, on the boundary between nature and culture, without ever falling completely onto either side of that boundary. As we shall see, it is this aspect of the *Protagoras* that interests Blumenberg in *Work on Myth*.

The debate between Protagoras and Socrates has, broadly speaking, received two interpretations. On the one hand it has been seen, especially by prominent German classicists of the early twentieth century with whom Blumenberg would have been familiar, as one of Plato's standard critiques of sophism akin to those found in other contemporary dialogues such as the *Meno* and in later dialogues such as the *Sophist*. According to this view, Protagoras's understanding of *arête* is characterised by an inferior relativism that Socrates (and implicitly Plato) reject.[5] On the other hand, some interpret the dialogue more as a rapprochement between philosophy and sophistry in that Socrates and Protagoras end up essentially agreeing that *arête* is teachable, a position that in turn underscores the benefits of a liberal or non-technical education.[6] But even if one accepts the claim that Protagoras and Socrates agree that *arête* can be taught, their pedagogic practices do seem to be different: whereas Protagoras arrives at this position by way of an introductory *mythos* that is later supplemented by a rhetorical *logos*, Socrates prefers dialectic. The key question relating to the differences between Socrates and Protagoras—and therefore also between philosophy and sophistry—thus becomes whether there are objective or non-rhetorical grounds upon which to distinguish philosophy from sophistry.

In recent scholarship this issue is highly contested. Some argue that Socrates is not depicted as being superior to Protagoras in that the two interlocutors deploy different methods that complement one another and have an "equal stature" in the dialogue.[7] Others maintain that the key distinguishing feature is not one of method but rather one of purpose: Protagoras's use of *eristic* (rhetorical argumentation) implies that his goal is simply to win the argument at hand, whereas Socratic elenchus or dialectic holds that winning the argument must always coincide with uncovering the truth.[8] Yet as Alexander Nehamas points out, even this distinction is not clear in the *Protagoras*, since this early dialogue offers no objective or non-rhetorical criteria for distinguishing truth from appearance. These criteria are introduced not by the historical Socrates of the early dialogues, but by Plato in the middle period dialogues, in his theory of forms, and this theory is in turn deployed as the chief means of making a decisive distinction between philosophy and sophistry in late dialogues such as the *Sophist* (see, for example, 268c), where sophists merely *appear* to be like philosophers. As this argument is extremely important for Blumenberg's take on the Platonic tradition in *Work on Myth*, Nehamas is worth quoting here at length:

> Sophistic influence can be securely avoided, Plato argues in the *Phaedo*, the *Republic* and the *Sophist*, only by supplementing the elenchus with the study of the unchanging nature of the world [. . .] But distinguishing philosophy from sophistry in this manner is no longer neutral. It presupposes accepting a specific and deeply controversial philosophical theory and, even more radically, a family of distinctions between appearance and reality which is itself equally partisan.[9]

Blumenberg's interpretation of Protagoras's great speech is close to that of Nehamas, while at the same time undertaking a far more explicit rehabilitation of sophism. Whereas Nehamas reads the *Protagoras* in his role as a learned commentator on classical philosophy, for Blumenberg there is much more at stake, since Plato's text and its reception have major implications for Blumenberg's theory of myth.

It is, of course, not difficult to see the parallels between Protagoras's tale of anthropogenesis and the tradition of German philosophical anthropology, according to which culture compensates for the human being's lack of biological equipment in relation to its environmental situation. And this is precisely the spirit in which Blumenberg reads Plato's text: for him the *Protagoras* represents "the potential antagonism between Sophism and all philosophy of the Platonic kind." Prometheus as presented by Protagoras offers nothing less than an "anthropological framework" for sophism, which characterises rhetoric—and its capacity to cultivate *arête*—as an emergency solution to an existential problem. This anthropology holds that "man is referred to means because he is not equipped with knowledge of ends and, for existential reasons, cannot wait for such knowledge to be found" (WOM, 330; AM, 360–1). This formulation repeats Blumenberg's rehabilitation of rhetoric in the anthropology essay of 1971, where rhetoric corresponds with what he calls the "principle of insufficient reason": the need to find a provisional justification for action when no final or absolute justification is available, since human beings are irrevocably situated "outside the realm of Ideas" (AAR, 447–8, 432; WWL, 124–5, 107).

The Platonic doctrine of ideas is antagonistic to this anthropology because it assumes that human beings *are* at least latently in possession of *arête*, of the ideas or of absolute ends, which can be arrived through philosophical dialectic. As Plato will argue in later dialogues—see for example, *Meno* 86a–b and *Phaedrus* 249b–c—philosophy enables us to recollect the divine knowledge that our souls once possessed before they descended to the corporeal realm. For Blumenberg, the theory of the ideas and the related notion of *anamnesis* thus dispense altogether with the Promethean anthropology of the sophists:

> If man is the appearance of an Idea or the realization of a form that is firmly established in the cosmos of the Ideas or of the forms, the myth of Prometheus loses its importance [. . .] In the reflected splendour of the Ideas, one can no longer even ask whether man belongs in reality. In or after this metaphysics, the idea that a creature that is present in the world could be worthless, that it could be better for it not to exist, can no longer be conceived by any god, and no Titan needs to refute it.
>
> (WOM, 331; AM, 362)

Like Nehamas, Blumenberg also regards this doctrine of ideas as partisan, controversial and therefore rhetorical. The theory of ideas was, in Blumenberg's opinion, much more comforting than logically demonstrable or practically useful, since it "prevailed by affirming, reassuringly, that there remained nothing essential to be accomplished in the world," because "the decisions had already been made in the realm of the Ideas" (WOM, 331; AM, 362).

But rhetorical victories like this one are never final. As a sophist, Protagoras must have realised that "the main thing must be to make it plausible that man is a creature who is fundamentally left in the lurch by nature" (WOM, 329; AM, 360). This argument was never completely killed off by Plato, and Blumenberg—with the help of Alsberg and other contributors to philosophical anthropology—revives it in *Work on Myth*, which can in this sense be regarded as an updated and extended version of Protagoras's great speech.

Blumenberg's readings of pre-Platonic sources on Prometheus—Hesiod's *Theogony* and *Works and Days*, Aeschylus's *Prometheus Bound*—are by and large standard and unremarkable. He treats these texts as primary sources that are worthy of interpretation and integration into an anthropological narrative concerning the fate of Prometheus in Western culture. Only Protagoras's great speech—which, compared with Hesiod and Aeschylus, must be regarded as a decidedly late and meagre text on Prometheus—is treated by Blumenberg not only as source material but also as a point of methodological departure. And when Blumenberg states that from the perspective of sophism—and as a consequence of Epimetheus having overlooked man when natural gifts were being distributed—"culture is a necessity of nature itself," he could just as well be referring to his own theory of myth (WOM, 329, 332; AM, 360, 363–4). This theory of myth must, like Protagoras's tale, tell a story about the origin that is plausible without being final for three reasons. First, only a plausible story about the origin can gain purchase on our attention and be captivating. Second, plausibility is all that we can have because a definitive account of the origin will never be available to us. And third, even if definitive stories of the origin are not at our disposal, we still need to tell them in order to understand, at least provisionally, who we are.

HESIOD, AESCHYLUS, AND LUCIAN

How, then, does Blumenberg treat the earlier written versions of the Prometheus story—those of Hesiod and Aeschylus—as anthropological source material? Both texts are interpreted within the speculative framework of palaeoanthropology. We can only guess, according to Blumenberg, "at the borderline situation in which the accidental acquisition of fire had passed over into its permanent possession." The possession of fire corresponds with "one of the lowerings of the level of the absolutism of reality," and this threshold situation—represented by the transition to a stage of culture in which fire had become a readily available technology—is mythically expressed in "the idea that fire had to be stolen from the gods and brought to men" (WOM, 299; AM, 329). This requires Blumenberg to interpret Hesiod and Aeschylus in ways that will allow the texts to conform to his anthropological narrative.

The accounts in Hesiod's *Theogony* (lines 562–4) and *Works and Days* (line 50), present Blumenberg with an ostensible problem, since in those texts the theft of fire is merely the restoration of something that humans had already possessed before Zeus took it away from them. In the *Theogony*, Prometheus—a second generation Titan who is the son of Iapetus and Clymene—seeks to deceive Zeus by offering the bones of a sacrificial animal that are attractively glazed with fat, rather than granting him a real share of the most delectable meats that are given by Prometheus to humans (*Theogony*, lines 538–42). Zeus takes revenge for this trickery by withdrawing fire from the human realm. The fact that Zeus "recognized the trick" when he was offered bones instead of meat (line 550),[10] is for Blumenberg seen to be a late adjustment to oral narratives that predated Hesiod's text. The *Theogony* is thus "the reformed version, which no longer wants to believe the highest god capable of succumbing to the cunning of the patron of men" (WOM, 303; AM, 333). That humans already possessed fire before Zeus took it away from them is also interpreted by Blumenberg through his speculative palaeoanthropology concerning the transition from the occasional to the permanent possession of fire. According to this reading, what is stolen by Prometheus is not fire itself but rather "the provision of the technique by which to produce fire." Prometheus's ability to hide an ember within a fennel stalk (see *Theogony*, lines 565–6) represents the technological means of preserving and transporting fire for future use. The 'absolutism of reality' can only be lowered in a decisive way when the means of doing so are controllable and reproducible rather than fortuitous and opportunistic. The Prometheus myth therefore represents the "irreversibility" of the theft of fire (WOM, 301; AM, 331).

Zeus's method of coping with this irreversibility is depicted in his treatment of men in *Works and Days*: "to set against the fire I shall give them an affliction in which they will all delight as they embrace their misfortune" (lines 57–9).[11] Whereas formerly men did not need to struggle in order to survive, Zeus now hides from them the means of their subsistence (line 43), while also introducing woman (in the form of Pandora, the source of delight) and all the troubles that she is said to bring. Zeus's need for revenge demonstrates that—unlike in the case of the deceptive sacrificial offering—he was actually deceived by Prometheus's technique of hiding the ember in the fennel stalk (line 49). This is despite the fact that Zeus purportedly "sees everything and notices everything" (lines 267–8).[12] The question for Blumenberg therefore becomes whether the Prometheus story as presented by Hesiod actually represents a reduction in the 'absolutism of reality,' or whether all of Prometheus's tricks are ultimately cancelled out by counter-tricks introduced by an omniscient Zeus.

For Blumenberg the ledger ends up decisively in Prometheus's favour. Pandora is "a trifle, an annoyance, not a threat, in comparison to the secure possession of fire," which represents nothing less than "the definitive practicability of existence." Thus, although it appears to have been Hesiod's intention to represent Zeus as being close to all-powerful—as responding to deceptions with equally powerful counter-deceptions—Blumenberg sees Hesiod as having been overcome by "the insuperable resistance of his mythical material." From the human perspective, 'winning' does not mean being happy and carefree. It means being able to survive under hostile conditions. Despite the fact that Prometheus's tricks bring with them a host of miseries, only the technology provided by Prometheus ensures human survival. The myth is therefore to be read by way of analogy with palaeoanthropology. In Hesiod Prometheus is "not first the potter who makes men" from earth and water, since this version of the myth appears much later, most famously in Ovid's *Metamorphoses* (Book 1, lines 68–88); rather he creates men by making their lives possible through giving them fire as technology, which is "their *differentia specifica*, as it will be again in anthropological paleontology" (WOM, 308; AM, 338).

The biological deficiency of human beings and their consequent need for technological compensation also stand at the heart of Blumenberg's interpretation of Aeschylus. For Blumenberg, the central message of Aeschylus's versions of the Prometheus myth is that "it would be better for man not to exist" (WOM, 309; AM, 339). Prometheus is now described as the son of Themis or Earth, who has given him the gift of prophecy (line 209). We also learn that Prometheus was a loyal advisor to Zeus in his war against Zeus's father, Cronos (lines 216–25). Presumably because human beings were first created during the reign of Cronos (see *Works and Days*, lines 108–12), Zeus sees in them an inferior species that he expressly wishes to destroy: "Of wretched humans he took no account, resolved / To annihilate them and create another race" (lines 233–4).[13] No clearer instance of the 'absolutism of reality' can be imagined that Zeus's outright opposition to human beings, an opposition that Prometheus in turn opposes for no apparent reason (lines 235–7). The notion that fire is not just fire, but also a series of related methods and technologies, receives a much fuller treatment in Aeschylus. From Prometheus, human beings received reason, carpentry, knowledge of the seasons, mathematics, writing, and prophecy, along with other gifts (lines, 443–539).

For Blumenberg, this amounts to nothing less than the creation of human beings, in that Prometheus "pulled them out of complete worthlessness." Before Prometheus's intervention humans were insentient beasts; after Prometheus's intervention, it has become "impossible for Zeus to implement his verdict that they were not worthy of existence" (WOM, 309–10; AM, 340). Keeping in mind Blumenberg's earlier reliance on Paul Alsberg's story of anthropogenesis, one could easily substitute 'Nature' for 'Zeus' in Aeschylus's narrative. In both accounts, human inventiveness and self-assertion are presented as unnatural contingencies that *might not* have stepped in to assist a species that was apparently deficient. The fact that this sense of contingency is reemphasised in Plato's version of the Prometheus story is another reason for its centrality in *Work on Myth*: who knows what would have happened had Prometheus not been present to correct his foolish and negligent brother? The fact that Zeus appears to be friendlier in the *Protagoras* than in Hesiod or Aeschylus, granting to human beings their means of political organisation in the capacities for virtue and justice, is also not a problem for Blumenberg. In Blumenberg's account of myth it is only the presence of absolutism (in the form of threats to human existence, autonomy, and wishes) and the human response to it that matters. The names that are given to this absolutism are readily changeable according to cultural context.

In Blumenberg's readings of the classical Prometheus reception that follows Plato's *Protagoras*, emphasis is placed upon the idea that Prometheus himself is a "master of rhetoric" (WOM, 345; AM, 377–8). The key source is the *Prometheus* of Lucian of Samosata, in which Prometheus defends himself before Zeus's servants Hermes and Hephaestus, in what amounts to a kind of satirical courtroom drama. Hermes introduces levity to the proceedings by blithely informing Prometheus that "the eagle will soon fly down to eat away your liver, so that you may have full return for your handiwork in clay." In setting out his defence, Prometheus represents his deception in dividing up the sacrificial animal as an entertaining dinner party joke that was taken in the wrong spirit by Zeus: "how childish it is to be angry and enraged unless he gets the lion's share himself," exclaims Prometheus. The creation of mankind from clay—a notion that does not appear in Hesiod or Aeschylus, but that will be crucial to Goethe's reception of Prometheus—is then characterised as a service to the gods rather than a betrayal of them, since "divinity was not quite complete in the absence of its counterpart."[14] Who else would have erected temples to the gods and made offerings to them if humans had not been created? Here, according to Blumenberg,

Myth appears as a comprehensive process of the entanglement of gods and men, and in the rhetoric of this Prometheus, that is men's opportunity to pass from their former worthlessness into a state in which their existence is necessary for the gods themselves.

(WOM, 346; AM, 378)

The existence of humans is rhetorically justified only because they can show "divinity to be the happier state."[15]

Blumenberg finds the roots of this notion of Prometheus-as-rhetorician already in Aeschlyus. In *Prometheus Bound*, Prometheus displays a strategic patience in waiting until the most advantageous moment at which to reveal the prophecy handed down by his mother concerning Zeus's coupling with Thetis, who would bear a son capable of overthrowing him. Prometheus's rhetorical brinksmanship in withholding this secret "until it would have its most favourable degree of effect" (WOM, 330; AM, 361, see also *Prometheus Bound*, lines 990–2) is a mark of his cunning. Although this final deal is not actually made in *Prometheus Bound*—and was presumably reserved for the *Prometheus Unbound* that followed it, of which only fragments have survived—it is presented laconically enough in Lucian's *Dialogues of the Gods* (see WOM, 347–8; AM, 379–80), where Zeus grants Prometheus his liberty after the latter has warned him about Thetis.[16] (As Blumenberg notes, in earlier versions of the myth depicted on Attic vases of the seventh century BC, Heracles is the liberator of Prometheus, a role already suggested by his slaying of the eagle in the *Theogony*, see WOM, 304; AM, 334).[17] If, as Blumenberg emphasises time and again, "Prometheus is a key figure for anthropology" and "not for theology," then his significance lies precisely in this ability to overcome a situation that is comparable with the "needy and pitiful" state of human beings before he stepped in to assist them. It is in this sense that Prometheus is "author of the human species," allegorically represented in the potter who makes humans from clay (see WOM, 330, 325; AM, 361, 356).

In terms of classical philology, there is nothing particularly original in Blumenberg's readings of Hesiod, Aeschlyus, and Lucian, and many of the philological claims that he makes concerning historical additions made to the Prometheus story were already well established prior to *Work on Myth*. All three of Blumenberg's important philological claims—the idea that sources prior to the *Theogony* probably depicted Zeus as having been successfully deceived by Prometheus's sleight of hand in dividing up the sacrificial animal; the point regarding representations of Heracles as Prometheus's liberator on Attic vases; and the claim that the first depictions of Prometheus creating humans from clay appear in the works of Philemon and Menander (see WOM, 328; AM, 359)—can be found in earlier German encyclopaedias of mythology.[18] Blumenberg's innovations with respect to the Prometheus story are much more philosophical than philological, and as we shall see, these innovations stand in a tradition of anthropological myth interpretation that already existed in the eighteenth and nineteenth centuries.

VICO, HERDER, SCHELLING, AND NIETZSCHE

According to Blumenberg, Giambattista Vico regards Prometheus as being "suspect" because of his defiance of Zeus (WOM, 378; AM, 413). For Vico the Prometheus myth is first and foremost an example of the "philosophy of authority" which leads to "poetic morals" and the origins of civilisation.[19] Thus, it is no surprise when Vico emphasises Prometheus having been "chained to a high rock," while at the same time failing to mention his success in stealing fire from Zeus. Instead, Prometheus is said simply to have taken fire from the sun.[20] But even if Vico's take on Prometheus does not accord with the story of self-assertion favoured by Blumenberg in *Work on Myth*, Blumenberg still regards Vico as the first thinker to have lent systematic plausibility to the idea that myth was originally an "exercise of reason" (WOM, 377; AM, 412). Although their interpretations of the Prometheus tale are certainly not the same, their respective philosophical anthropologies are still broadly Promethean and anti-Cartesian. Both see culture as a repertoire of compensations that first made human beings out of creatures that were originally, in Vico's words, "stupid, insensate, and horrible beasts."[21] And as Blumenberg himself suggests, both also reject "the Cartesian program of an absolute beginning" to reason, which was purportedly preceded by a morass of mythic irrationality (WOM, 380; AM, 415). The view that myth was always already rational is shared by Vico and Blumenberg.

In Herder's *Treatise on the Origin of Language*, linguistic expression is described as "Prometheus's heavenly spark," which is said to have caught "fire in the human soul."[22] Herder's use of this metaphor is interesting precisely because the question being addressed in his essay is whether the ultimate cause of language was divine or human. This is at once a question concerning origins and a teleological question, and Herder answers it in a way that was no longer available to Blumenberg in the post-teleological human sciences of the twentieth century. Herder's answer remains ambiguous. Language is characterised as an endogenous human invention that arose as a substitute for instincts; but this initial position is nevertheless framed within a broader theological context, since the human soul that created language is ultimately regarded as being the work of God. In trying to find an immanent logic that led to the compensation that is language, Herder is also unable to avoid teleology, since he locates it within a system of natural substitutions and counterbalances in which everything is "disposed and distributed intentionally"—though by whom or what this distribution is made we are not told.[23] As we saw in Chapter 4 of this volume, Blumenberg finds a way of making a similar argument about compensations through what I have called the 'anthropological reduction'—a move that is rather less teleological than Herder's position but still very far indeed from being empirically demonstrable.

The preoccupation with beginnings, and the impossibility of knowing anything definitive or conceptual about them, is something that unites Blumenberg's and Schelling's theories of myth. Understanding Blumenberg's relation to Schelling requires one to distinguish what Blumenberg refers to as absolutism from what the later Schelling understands to be the Absolute. For Blumenberg, the Prometheus story is just one paradigmatic instance of humans being forced to deal with the 'absolutism of reality,' in this case embodied by Zeus. Blumenberg refuses to grant the Prometheus story a foundational status, because his phenomenological method holds that our access to the mythic tradition is shaped by the belated perspective of the historically situated observer. The Prometheus story is paradigmatic not because of any purported foundational quality, but only because it has survived, thereby enabling us still to have access to its contents.

This is not the case in Schelling's attitude toward Prometheus, outlined in the Berlin lectures delivered during the 1840s and published as the *Philosophical Introduction to the Philosophy of Mythology* (*Philosophische Einleitung in die Philosophie der Mythologie*, 1856).[24] The account of Prometheus in this text seems exclusively to have been shaped by Schelling's reading of Aeschylus, and it assumes a central importance in Schelling's understanding of myth. As Blumenberg correctly points out, for Schelling Prometheus is "the one myth of the end of all myths" (WOM, 584; AM, 632). In Schelling, human beings were not originally confronted by threatening environmental conditions subsumed under the title of the 'absolutism of reality'; rather, they are conditioned by the Absolute. The Prometheus myth is *the* myth, and the *end* of myth, because it portrays the movement of negation that is the origin of human self-consciousness. The central category of German idealism—that of *Geist* (mind or spirit)—was originally, according to Schelling, not something theoretical; it was much more a pre-conceptual desire or "will" (*Wollen*), the "desire of the soul" (*Wollen der Seele*) for freedom and self-realisation. *Geist* is therefore to be equated with what Schelling refers to as "the anti-divine" (*das Gegengöttliche*)—that which opposes the primordial Absolute. Yet since the Absolute is literally everything, this movement of negation must originally have occurred within the Absolute itself. This is why Schelling claims that Prometheus is "only the principle of Zeus himself." He is the principle of internal negation that Zeus mistakenly experiences as an external opposition. From this perspective, it is becomes understandable that Schelling emphasises the fact that Prometheus originally advised Zeus in his battle against the Titans and only subsequently turned against him.[25]

In Schelling's account, human beings also experience Prometheus as something external—as more than human and therefore God-like—because he pushes them from the rudimentary stage of un-reflected pure will into that of self-consciousness. As Prometheus claims in Aeschylus's version of the tale, human beings certainly had eyes before he came to their assistance, but their "sight was meaningless."[26] Schelling takes his cue from this line. "The bare will of the human being is blind," he writes, "and must be transformed into understanding." Since the Prometheus story represents this coming-to-be of self-consciousness, it is not a "thought" (*Gedanke*) that was autonomously conceived by human beings. It is much more a "primordial thought" (*Urgedanke*) in which the human race first became conscious of itself. Prometheus is therefore nothing less than the "principle of humanity that we have referred to as *Geist*."[27] It is thus no exaggeration when Blumenberg claims that for Schelling Prometheus is "the prototype of Idealism's roundabout route [*Umweg*]" thereby being "not *a* story that is told but *the* story of history [*die Geschichte der Geschichte*]" (WOM, 581–2, AM, 629, 631).

Is this also a 'Promethean anthropology' akin to Blumenberg's? The answer to this question must be both yes and no. For the methodological reasons already mentioned, Blumenberg does not afford the Prometheus story a foundational significance in the manner of Schelling. What the two thinkers share, however, is an insistence upon the primordial claims of myth upon human consciousness. There is no historical moment in which myth was autonomously 'thought up' by human beings. Rather, to be human, for both Blumenberg and Schelling, means to require the Promethean compensation of myth. According to Blumenberg, myth allowed us psychologically to survive the pressures of absolutism, while in Schelling's view, it established our very identities as self-conscious beings defined both within and in opposition to the Absolute.

The final 'Promethean anthropologist' of the nineteenth century to whom Blumenberg turns in *Work on Myth* is the early Friedrich Nietzsche, and especially Nietzsche's treatment of the Prometheus myth in *The Birth of Tragedy* (*Die Geburt der Tragödie*, 1872/1886). In Blumenberg's view, it is in Nietzsche's interest that Prometheus should remain in chains for as long as possible.[28] This is so for two reasons. First, if Prometheus refuses to set himself free by telling Zeus of the prophecy concerning the son who will overthrow him, then Zeus's decline will be assured. This represents an early version of what Nietzsche will later call the death of God, since "the god's fall is the condition of the possibility of man's ascent" (WOM, 605; AM 656). Second, for the myth to retain its original barbaric force, there can be no suggestion of Prometheus's making a 'bourgeois' deal with Zeus in order to secure his freedom. Prometheus's love for human beings must remain completely irrational and in that sense Dionysian, a total violation of "Apollonian measure" (WOM, 615; AM, 667–8). This is why, in Blumenberg's account, Nietzsche decides at one point to have Prometheus "ripped apart" (*zerissen*) not by an eagle, but by a vulture (WOM, 612; AM, 664).[29] As Blumenberg states:

In Nietzsche's view of myth the decisive thing is that the surmounting or at least coming to terms with the underlying stratum of terror and suffering both is necessary, in order to be able to exist at all, and must never be definitive, so that man can still be capable of feeling the power of life.

(WOM, 615; AM, 667)

Blumenberg opposes Nietzsche's position by suggesting that one of the main achievements of myth is precisely to forget or at least trivialise the 'absolutism of reality', not to remember or preserve its full terror. This also means ushering in a state of affairs that Nietzsche attributes to Euripides's purported destruction of tragedy: "cowardly self-satisfaction with comfortable consumption."[30] While Nietzsche's Prometheus must be the archetypal anti-bourgeois, "the barbarian who loves men without rhyme or reason," he nonetheless "produces the bourgeois mode of life" by giving fire and technology to humans (WOM, 617; AM, 669).

The idea that human beings were inherently deficient and needed this Promethean assistance is suggested by Nietzsche in his *Nachlass* fragment of 1873, "On Truth and Lie in an Extra-Moral Sense" ("Über Wahrheit und Lüge im aussermoralischen Sinne"), which seems to be a reckoning with Plato's *Protagoras*. There we are informed of the total contingency and fragility of human existence—of the idea that in the cosmic scheme of things, the human intellect may turn out to have existed "only for a minute." That the intellect was necessary at all is merely attributed to the fact that humans were "weaker" and "less robust" than animals, for they have been "denied the chance of waging the struggle for existence with horns or the fangs of beasts of prey." Instead, they preserved themselves with sophistry and rhetoric, with "deception, flattery, lying, and cheating." Seen in this way, language was not originally designed to gain access to Platonic forms, or what Kant called the 'thing in itself.' Its function was only to describe "the relations of things to man" through the "boldest metaphors." For Nietzsche, "everything that sets the human being apart from the animal depends upon this capability." The requirement that these metaphors set themselves up as truths rather than mere appearances is attributed by Nietzsche to the social organisation of human beings, to their tendency to gather together in "herd-like" fashion and their concomitant need to settle disputes by making binding truth claims.[31] As we shall see, the notion that metaphors and myths might have made human life possible, perhaps even preceding and conditioning concepts, is one that Blumenberg shares with Nietzsche. Thus, when Blumenberg observes that "Nietzsche has learned from Plato what Sophism is, but does not go along with the negative evaluation of it," we sense his approval of Nietzsche's position (WOM, 608; AM, 658).

FROM METAPHOR TO MYTH

In *Paradigms for a Metaphorology* (1960), Blumenberg claims that there is a close relation between what he calls "absolute metaphors" on the one hand and myths on the other:

> myth bears the sanction of its primordial, unfathomable origin [. . .] whereas metaphor can present itself as a figment of the imagination, needing only to disclose a possibility of understanding in order for it to establish its credentials.
>
> (PM, 78; PZM, 112)

This distinction, according to Blumenberg, is "purely genetic," suggesting differences in processes of legitimation but a similarity of function between metaphor and myth (see PM, 78–9; PZM, 112–13).[32] The context to this claim is provided by Kant's critical philosophy, which in turn suggests a common heritage behind Blumenberg's theory of myth and that of German idealism (exemplified, as we have seen in Chapter 2 of this volume, by the so-called "Oldest System-Programme"). As Blumenberg himself points out (see PM, 4; PZM, 11), the basis for his theory of metaphor can be found in §59 of Kant's *Critique of Judgement*, where Kant provides a definition of what he calls symbol.[33] Here Kant claims that "intuitions are always required" to "demonstrate the reality of our concepts."[34] The role of what Kant refers to as symbol, and of what Blumenberg will call absolute metaphor, is established in relation to Kant's understanding of reflective judgements. A reflective judgement corresponds to the regulative use of the ideas of pure reason in situations where the observer posits a relation between individual objects and an overall design, purpose or order of things. So, for example, the synergy between the wings and tail of a bird may suggest that it is an organised being designed according to an overall purpose (§§61, 65). Such speculative ideas of reason may, in Kant's view, enjoy only a heuristic use in the natural sciences in order to organise an overall research programme. They may also extend to theological ideas such as the notion of an intelligent design or God (§75).

In such cases of speculative abstraction, no sensuous intuition will be capable of matching the complexity of the ideas of reason. Instead, we are forced to make do by transposing our reflections concerning sensuous objects of intuition onto these more complex ideas. These images of sensuous objects in turn provide us with intuitions of the abstract ideas of reason, since the symbolical is a "species of the intuitive" (§59). Thus, Kant claims, "a monarchical state is represented by a body with a soul if it is ruled in accordance with laws internal to the people, but by a mere machine (like a hand mill) if it is ruled by a single absolute will, but in both cases it is represented only symbolically" (§59). In this analogy, the things being conjoined—a monarchical state on the one hand, and the living body or machine on the other—are different, but there is a similarity "between the rule for reflecting on both and their causality."[35] Potential attributes of a total abstraction—the state—are thereby represented through a mode which is admittedly inexact and non-conceptual or pre-conceptual, but which provides a rough sensuous representation of the ideas being expounded. In this we hear echoes of the "System-Programme's" call for a "mythology of reason" that would be "in the service of the Ideas," by rendering them sensuous and "aesthetic."[36] Blumenberg maintains that such symbols "correspond fairly exactly to metaphors." Such metaphors are absolute in that they "prove resistant to terminological claims and cannot be dissolved into conceptuality" (PM, 4–5; PZM, 11–12).

The clearest example of this point is provided by what Blumenberg calls "background metaphorics" concerning the overall structure and organisation of the world (PM, 62–76, PZM, 91–110). Obviously, 'the world' as a totality can never be an object of empirical experience and is more akin to what Kant would call an idea of reason. Yet in order for the human being to have some kind of orientation in relation to existence, he or she needs to have a guiding image of the world, even if this image is resistant to conceptual clarification. As Blumenberg writes:

> What the world really is—this least decidable of all questions is at the same time the never undecidable, and therefore always already decided, question. That it is 'cosmos' was one of the constitutive decisions of our intellectual history.
>
> (PM, 15; PZM, 26)

While in *Paradigms for a Metaphorology* Blumenberg does not undertake a systematic attempt to relate these background metaphorics to Husserl's notion of the life-world, the similarities between these notions are unmistakable. These metaphorics constitute "the guiding idea" from which the "terminological propositions" of a thought system can be *abgelesen* or "read off" (PM, 62; PZM, 91). Here background metaphorics may precede and condition philosophical concepts. Thus, when Descartes compares nature with a machine, or a natural organism such as a tree with a clock, he suggests that the inner workings of nature are mechanistic, even if—and in contrast to the case of clock—we are unable (or in his view *not yet* able) to take nature to pieces and perceive all of its intricate cause-and-effect relations (see PM, 68–9; PZM, 99–100). In other words, the metaphor provides one with a basic frame of theoretical expectations. This orientation is pre-conceptual because a complex idea (that of a minutely intricate and complex organism) is merely being transposed onto a sensuous intuition (a machine or clock that can be dismantled and reassembled) so that it can be represented. In this way, absolute metaphors are "pragmatic," giving "structure to a world," by "representing the nonexperiencable, nonapprehensible totality of the real" (PM, 14; PZM, 25).

That Blumenberg ascribes a similar orienting function to myth is already apparent prior to *Paradigms for a Metaphorology*. One of his key absolute metaphors, as outlined at length in an essay published in 1957,[37] is the notion that light offers a sensuous representation of what it means to unveil the truth. Here Blumenberg invokes Plato's allegory of the cave (*Republic* 514a-520a) to demonstrate that what light means within philosophical metaphorics is always related to darkness (ÄMS, 143). Those chained in the cave take the shadows projected onto its walls to be real things rather than mere appearances. They are ignorant of the world of light outside—the world of forms that is directly illuminated by the sun—to which only philosophers can ascend (ÄMS, 149). Here darkness is depicted as potentially more comfortable than light because the eyes are shielded from the full force of the sun's rays, but darkness is also a state of pitiable ignorance and limitation. Within the broader context of Plato's oeuvre—and when the *Protagoras* is seen to predate the *Republic*—the original giver of light is Prometheus, as Blumenberg goes on to note in *Paradigms for a Metaphorology* (PM, 79; PZM, 113–14). That these metaphorical modes of argumentation are indebted to and embedded within the context of myth was, already in 1957, not lost on Blumenberg. "The idea that philosophical logos overcame prephilosophical mythos has narrowed our view of the scope of philosophical terminology," he observes (ÄMS, 139). And while ancient Greek thought, and especially Plato, tended to privilege seeing over hearing—hearing being heavily associated with language and rhetoric and therefore with opinion (ÄMS, 161)—this hierarchy is for Blumenberg undermined by the fact that the primary medium of Platonic thought came to be the dialogue. It is thus of no small significance to Blumenberg that the main criterion used by Plato to distinguish philosophy from sophistry—his theory of forms—is outlined in the *Republic* precisely through deploying the metaphorics of light.

Both Anselm Haverkamp and Robert Savage have outlined the extent to which *Paradigms for a Metaphorology* was a subversive contribution to *Begriffsgeschichte* or 'the history of concepts.'[38] Blumenberg explicitly questioned the view that metaphors are merely *Restbestände* or "*leftover elements* [. . .] on the path *from mythos to logos*" by showing that absolute metaphors and myths may form the horizon of expectations for concepts or what he broadly terms 'theory' (PM, 3, PZM, 10). For this reason, "metaphorology seeks to burrow down to the substructure of thought" (PM, 5; PZM, 13), thereby suggesting that a 'history of concepts' would remain superficial in the absence of what Blumenberg rather diplomatically referred to—in an article published in Joachim Ritter's *Archive for the History of Concepts*—as the "auxiliary service" (*Hilfsdienst*) of metaphorology.[39] But was the explicitly outlined research programme of metaphorology abandoned and left in "an experimental state" by Blumenberg, as Anselm Haverkamp suggests?[40] Or did *Work on Myth* continue it by other means? Haverkamp has elsewhere referred to *Work on Myth* as a "monumental new beginning" in Blumenberg's thought,[41] but it can also be seen as a continuation and expansion of directions already present in the metaphorology.

In this context, a key document is Blumenberg's long essay on myth written for the Poetics and Hermeneutics meeting of 1968: "The Concept of Reality and the Effective Potential of Myth" ("Wirklichkeitsbegriff und Wirkungspotential des Mythos", see WWM).[42] According to Manfred Fuhrmann, the editor of the volume that arose from the colloquium, its purpose was to establish the "function" of myth in a "no-longer-mythical" age—presumably the present.[43] The Blumenberg-Taubes correspondence now reveals the extent to which Blumenberg and Taubes in fact conceptualised this conference themselves. In a letter to Taubes, Blumenberg suggested that the conference should address the "transformations, late forms, and anamnestic formalisations of myth" under the working title of "the reality of mythical late horizons."[44] Taubes later responded with an ambitious list of invitees, which included Jean Bollack, Paul Ricoeur, Herbert Marcuse, Michel Foucault, Karl Kerényi, Pierre Bordieu, and E. M. Cioran, among others (from this list only Bollack attended).[45] The title of the volume in which the papers appeared—*Terror und Spiel* (*Terror and Play*)—demonstrated Blumenberg's key influence on the entire proceedings, since these are also the two categories—albeit slightly renamed as "terror" and "poetry"—through which he attempts to understand myth.

"Terror" is Blumenberg's early term for what will later be called the 'absolutism of reality': the function of myth is to reduce the "original horrors of the superior power" by naming them (WWM, 57). The truth of these original horrors is not addressed by Blumenberg, since "absolute beginnings render us speechless in the precise sense of the word" (WWM, 28). In the earliest written documents of Western antiquity "the terrible" (*das Schreckliche*) has already been transformed into "the bearable" (*das Erträgliche*, WWM, 23). Here Blumenberg takes recourse to ethnographic theories about non-Western cultures in order to explain the function of myth, a move which did not end up featuring in *Work on Myth*. In particular he uses the ideas of Bronislaw Malinowski on myth and ritual, based on Malinowski's fieldwork in the Trobriand Islands. Myth, writes Malinowski in *Myth in Primitive Psychology* (1926), "comes into play when rite, ceremony, or a social or moral rule demands justification, warrant of antiquity, reality, and sanctity."[46] Blumenberg takes this argument to mean that myths served the secondary function of explaining the rituals through which the original terrors were ameliorated. At the same time, however, Blumenberg concedes that he is not competent to assess this theory and intends to use it only as a working hypothesis (WWM, 33–4). Indeed, in the discussion that followed this paper, one of Blumenberg's interlocutors (the classical philologist Jean Bollack) complained that Blumenberg had used ethnography dealing with non-Western cultures in order to examine European sources—something that Blumenberg would refrain from doing again.[47]

In other respects, however, Blumenberg's Poetics and Hermeneutics essay of 1968 contains many of the arguments that would reappear in *Work on Myth*: creating a distance from the original terrors is said to be the decisive cultural accomplishment of myth (WWM, 17); myth is characterised as being always already in the process of its own reception (WWM, 28); Prometheus is highlighted as a *Leitfossil* (guiding fossil) within the Western tradition of myth (WWM, 26); tradition is said to exercise a selective effect on myth according to the criterion of significance (WWM, 35); while the capacity for variation and for reducing absolutism are said to be the key features that differentiate myth from dogma (WWM, 21, 42–3). The variation inherent in myth is made possible by the fact that myths—as belated explanations of rituals—are released from the law of strict repetition associated with ritual and therefore become autonomous aesthetic complexes (WWM, 34). A number of these arguments were hotly contested at the Poetics and Hermeneutics meeting (especially by Jacob Taubes),[48] and since many of them remained in *Work on Myth*, the nature of these debates will be considered in Chapters 7 and 8 of this volume.

The other innovation of this essay was that of bringing its two leading concepts—terror and poetry—into a productive relation that would open the way for the literary analyses that appear in *Work on Myth*. As Odo Marquard points out in the commentary that followed Blumenberg's lecture, Blumenberg initially presents this relation as an antinomy, only subsequently to resolve it. In Blumenberg's words, myth is either the "pure expression of the passivity of demonic stupefaction" (that is: terror); or "the imaginative excess of anthropomorphic appropriations of the world" (in other words: poetry or play, WWM, 13). Blumenberg's resolution of this apparent antinomy, according to Marquard, runs as follows: the initial overcoming and distancing (*Distanzierung*) of these terrors means that they can later be rendered into aesthetic objects. What was once a question of survival is transformed into a matter of play in which the materials are still captivating—precisely because the terrors that they have surmounted continue to remain latently present.[49]

If there *is* a new beginning undertaken by Blumenberg in the 1970s, then it consists in replacing this emphasis on the relation between ritual and myth—derived from his reading of non-Western ethnographic sources like Malinowski's work on the Trobriand Islanders—with more universal theories concerning the cultural evolution of human beings in general. As one of the commentators at the Poetics and Hermeneutics meeting suggested, if Blumenberg's theory that myth represents the overcoming of terror could not be rendered plausible by written sources from classical antiquity, then he would need to develop a hypothesis concerning the "pre-Homeric period."[50] A radical and indeed *prehistoric* solution was provided by German philosophical anthropology, which tended to make universal pronouncements about *der Mensch* (the human being) as such, rather than about particular cultures or periods.

Evidence of its deployment can be found in a text written by Blumenberg in the mid-1970s—*Theory of Non-Conceptuality* (*Theorie der Unbe-
griflichkeit*).[51] Here we find very explicit references to a theme that would
become central to *Work on Myth*: that of *actio per distans*. In Blumenberg's account, the key function of the concept (*Begriff*) is to allow human
beings to refer to objects that are not immediately present, but that need
to be anticipated for the purposes of survival (TDU, 11–12). Addressing
Descartes's philosophical criteria of clarity and distinctness, Blumenberg
maintains that the concept must possess a certain lack of clarity and lack of
definitiveness in order to be flexible enough to anticipate a range of possible
situations or phenomena (TDU, 12). Referring to things that are not—or
not yet—present offered an evolutionary advantage to a species that had
traditionally relied on fleeing to survive and was not suited to body on body
combat. The concept is therefore seen to be a more developed form of distance technology that was originally presaged by the throwing of projectiles as a means of self-defence (TDU, 13). Thus, although Paul Alsberg is
not cited in the *Theory of Non-Conceptuality*, it is clear that his *Puzzle of
Humanity* is one of its key anthropological sources.

The other key source relied upon by Blumenberg was Arnold Gehlen,
and particularly Gehlen's notion of the relief (*Entlastung*) provided by language and symbols. Language, in Gehlen's view, makes an efficient ordering of the sensory world possible by erecting a second nature in the form
of a symbolic world.[52] Instead of having to experience individual objects
directly, the human being that is endowed with language can make these
objects "retrievable" (*abrufbar*) when they are part of a pre-existing linguistic schema (TDU, 28). Once possible threats are rendered conceptually
or metaphorically retrievable from a position of distance, they become less
threatening, and can even become objects of aesthetic pleasure. This is why,
for Blumenberg, "*the success of the concept is simultaneously the reversal
of its function*": what was once "unknown and terrible" is later allowed
to return as a "pleasurable object" (TDU, 27–8, emphasis in the original).
The "prime example" of this conversion of sources of terror into aesthetic
objects is myth, which "according to its function [. . .] originally belongs
completely within the purposive context of the liberation from dread," but
ultimately becomes "an inexhaustible reservoir of basic figures" that can
safely be enjoyed in poetry and tragedy (TDU, 27). Myth draws upon these
original terrors from a position of distance, which means that it is also freed
from the "negative qualities of fear and dread." That which was originally
both unforeseeable and unpredictable (*das Unhervorsehbare*) reappears as
the tame and domesticated, while fear has transformed itself into nothing
more than a "pleasurable frisson" (TDU, 28).

This connection between metaphor and myth is again expressed in relation to what Blumenberg refers to as absolute metaphors (TDU, 65). A key
example used by Blumenberg is a phrase such as *it is raining*. Here the
'it' has the function of providing a background metaphorics according to

which the 'it' is the undetermined 'something' of which the rain is predicated. It is this lack of determination in the absolute metaphor that leads to the "mythic giving of names." If, according to Blumenberg, "the rain was a reality that was decisive for life," then it could not merely be allocated to a "cryptic it"; rather, the source of rain had to be given a name and a history, as well as the "capability of being influenced" (*Beeinflußbarkeit*). It is thus precisely *"the lack of determination,"* that *"leads [. . .] straight into myth,"* and myths are in this sense extended and elaborated absolute metaphors (TDU, 66–7, emphasis in the original).

Metaphors and myths display less exactitude than concepts because the objects to which they refer are less precisely known and determined. This is similar to, but not quite the same, as Nietzsche's notion, outlined in "On Truth and Lie in an Extra-Moral Sense," that concepts are mere "residues" of "perceptual metaphors" (*Anschauungsmetaphern*). For Nietzsche, all human perception is originally metaphorical in that it involves the carrying-over (*Übertragung*) of "nerve-stimuli" onto mental "images," a process which is then followed by a second transposition of the mental image onto a linguistic sound. Once these designated sounds become stable conventions for referring to objects, they gain a conceptual status. For Nietzsche, the question whether these concepts actually correspond to their objects is unanswerable, since we have no access to the truth 'in itself.' What is called 'truth' exists not through a correspondence between concept and object, but through the extent to which a metaphor or concept proves itself over time to be a useful—in the sense of power enhancing—convention for life. For Nietzsche, metaphor thus persists at the root of all conceptual thought.[53] Similarly, for Blumenberg concepts are metaphors that have been formalised in such a way that their "room for play" (*Spielraum*) has been reduced: the concept must remain generic and open, but only to the extent that it may refer to future examples belonging to a general class. The concept is an "instrument" that is tested out in the real world, and successful concepts prevail precisely by dint of their proven usefulness in the interests of survival (TDU, 12–14). The difference here is only one of nuance: what Nietzsche sees as a process of rationalist decline, as the triumph of a pale abstraction over an originally vivid intuition,[54] is regarded by Blumenberg as a mark of human progress through self-assertion.

Blumenberg's analysis might also be compared with Max Müller's notion that myth arose from an overabundance of predicates and a lack of substantives in ancient languages.[55] In Blumenberg's view, absolute metaphors—such as the 'it' in *it is raining*—become myths "as soon as we ask questions" about them (TDU, 73). But at the same time, Blumenberg does not share Müller's penchant for intricate philological argumentation concerning language roots in ancient Greek and Sanskrit, and he would not pejoratively describe myth as the "dark shadow which language throws over thought."[56] For Blumenberg, metaphor and myth are positive *achievements* of language and human consciousness. Both of them pave the way for concepts and rationality, and as long as there are aspects of human experience that remain resistant to conceptual reduction, they will remain as key components of culture.

The key 'Promethean anthropologists' treated here—Plato's Protagoras, Vico, Herder, Schelling, and Nietzsche—combine philosophical argumentation with storytelling. Each of them tells a story about the origin of something. For Protagoras the Prometheus story explains the origin and status of the human being and of rhetoric; for Vico it recounts the origin of civilisation; for Herder it helps us to understand the origin of language; for Schelling it unveils the origin of consciousness; and in Nietzsche's loose adaptation in "On Truth and Lie in an Extra-Moral Sense," it explains the origin and function of language, of metaphors, and eventually of concepts. Blumenberg stands squarely in this tradition insofar as his own tale of the origin—that concerning the 'absolutism of reality'—is also a Promethean one that explains how metaphor and myth provided the human being with orientation in a situation of crisis. When it comes to explaining the origins of myth, Blumenberg implies, even 'theory' must revert to stories.

NOTES

1. Arnold Gehlen, *Man: His Nature and Place in the World*, trans. Clare McMillan and Carl Pillemer (New York, NY: Columbia University Press, 1988), 25; *Der Mensch: Seine Natur und seine Stellung in der Welt* (1940; Berlin: Junker und Dünnhaupt, 1941), 20–1; in the original German version, the phrasing is: "Er ist—ein Prometheus—angewiesen auf das Entfernte."
2. Plato, *Protagoras*, trans. W.K.C. Guthrie, in *The Collected Dialogues*, ed. Edith Hamilton and Huntington Cairns (Princeton, NJ: Princeton University Press, 1961), 310.
3. See G.B. Kerferd, "The Doctrine of Justice and Virtue in the *Protagoras* of Plato," *The Journal of Hellenic Studies* 73 (1953): 42–5; here: 42; see also Kerferd, *The Sophistic Movement* (Cambridge: Cambridge University Press, 1981), 131–5.
4. Kerferd, "The Doctrine of Justice and Virtue," 43–4; Kerferd, *The Sophistic Movement*, 140–3.
5. See, for example, Paul Friedländer, *Platon*, 3 vols. (Berlin: De Gruyter, 1928), 2:1–36; in particular: 14–15; see also the commentary in Wilhelm Nestle's edition of the *Protagoras* (Leipzig: Teubner, 1931), 1–57, especially 43–50.
6. See Michael Gagarin, "The Purpose of Plato's *Protagoras*," *Transactions and Proceedings of the American Philological Association* 100 (1969): 133–64; here: 144.
7. Gagarin, "The Purpose of Plato's *Protagoras*," 133, 144–5, 150, 161–4.
8. See Gregory Vlastos, "The Socratic Elenchus," *Oxford Studies in Ancient Philosophy* 1 (1983): 27–58; here: 31. Kerferd, *The Sophistic Movement*, 62–3.
9. Alexander Nehamas, "Eristic, Antilogic, Dialectic: Plato's Demarcation of Philosophy from Sophistry," *History of Philosophy Quarterly* 7, no. 1 (1990): 3–16; here: 13.
10. Hesiod, *Theogony and Works and Days*, trans. M.L. West (Oxford: Oxford University Press, 1988), 19.
11. Hesiod, *Theogony and Works and Days*, 38.
12. Hesiod, *Theogony and Works and Days*, 45.

13. Aeschylus, *Prometheus Bound and Other Plays*, trans. Philip Vellacott (Harmonsworth: Penguin, 1961), 27.

14. Lucian, *Prometheus*, in *Lucian*, vol. 2 (Loeb Classical Library, No. 54), trans. A.R. Harmon (Cambridge, MA: Harvard University Press, 1915), 245, 251, 255.

15. Lucian, *Prometheus*, 256.

16. Lucian, *Dialogues of the Gods*, in *Lucian*, vol. 7 (Loeb Classical Library No. 431), trans. M.D. MacLeod (Cambridge, MA: Harvard University Press, 1961), 257–61.

17. See *Theogony*, lines 527–9.

18. The claims concerning Prometheus's successful deception of Zeus and the depiction of Heracles in Attic works of art appear in Walther Kraus's article on Prometheus in *Paulys Realencyclopädie der classischen Altertumswissenschaft*, vol. 45 (Stuttgart: Druckenmüller, 1957), 653–702; here: 660, 700. An annotated copy of Kraus's article can be found in Blumenberg's *Nachlass*. The information on Philemon and Menander is already attested in the article on Prometheus found in W.H. Roscher's monumental *Ausführliches Lexikon der griechischen und römischen Mythologie*, 6 vols. (Leipzig: Teubner, 1896–1937), see in particular, vol. 3, section 2, 3032–110; here: 3044–5. This claim also reappears in Kraus's account (see 682).

19. Giambattista Vico, *The New Science*, trans. Thomas Goddard Bergin and Max Harold Fisch (Ithaca, NY: Cornell University Press, 1948), §§386–7, 502–3 (pp. 109, 152).

20. Vico, *New Science*, §§387, 549, 713 (pp.109, 173, 241).

21. Vico, *New Science*, §374 (p. 104).

22. Herder, *Treatise on the Origin of Language*, in *Philosophical Writings*, ed. and trans. Michael N. Forster (Cambridge: Cambridge University Press, 2002), 65–166; here: 97; *Abhandlung über den Ursprung der Sprache*, in *Werke*, ed. Günter Arnold et al., 10 vols. in 11 (Frankfurt am Main: Deutscher Klassiker Verlag, 1985–2000), 1:733.

23. Herder, *Treatise on the Origin of Language*, 81–2, 163, 112; *Abhandlung über den Ursprung der Sprache*, in *Werke*, 1:715–16, 809, 750.

24. This is the second volume of the *Introduction to the Philosophy of Mythology* (*Einleitung in die Philosophie der Mythologie*). The first volume is discussed in Chapter 2 of this study.

25. Friedrich Schelling, *Philosophische Einleitung in die Philosophie der Mythologie*, in *Sämmtliche Werke*, ed. K.F.A. Schelling, 14 vols. (1856–61), 11: 461, 460, 481, 484.

26. Aeschylus, *Prometheus Bound and Other Plays*, 34 (line 447).

27. Schelling, *Philosophische Einleitung in die Philosophie der Mythologie*, in *Sämmtliche Werke*, 11: 484, 482.

28. In a later Prometheus fragment of 1874, discussed by Blumenberg in *Work on Myth* (see WOM, 618–19; AM, 670–2), Nietzsche rewrites the tale by claiming that Prometheus and his vulture (not eagle!) are still on the rock and have been forgotten. This is because Prometheus refused to tell Zeus of his prophecy and so was not set free. Zeus only releases Prometheus after he (Prometheus) agrees to create a new version of the human race. See Nietzsche, *Kritische Studienausgabe*, ed. Giorgio Colli and Mazzino Montinari, 15 vols. (Berlin: De Gruyter, 1967–77), 7:835–7 (hereafter cited as *KSA* followed by volume and page numbers).

29. See Nietzsche, *The Birth of Tragedy*, §4, in *KSA*, 1:40.

30. See Nietzsche, *The Birth of Tragedy*, §11, in *KSA*, 1:78.

31. Nietzsche, "Über Wahrheit und Lüge im aussermoralischen Sinne," in *KSA*, 1:873–90; here: 875–6, 879, 881, 877; "On Truth and Lie in an Extra-Moral

Sense," trans. Walter Kaufmann, in *The Portable Nietzsche*, ed. Walter Kaufmann (New York: Penguin, 1976), 42–6; here: 42, 43, 45–6, 44 (the quote from page 881 of the German edition is my translation, since Kaufmann translates only part of Nietzsche's text).

32. For a more detailed analysis of this distinction see Rüdiger Zill, "Wie die Vernuft es macht . . . Die Arbeit der Metapher im Prozeß der Zivilisation," in *Die Kunst des Überlebens: Nachdenken über Hans Blumenberg*, ed. Franz Josef Wetz and Hermann Timm (Frankfurt am Main: Suhrkamp, 1999), 164–83; here: 180–1.

33. On the importance of §59 of Kant's third *Critique* for Blumenberg's theory of metaphor, see Rüdiger Zill, "Der Vetrakt des Zeichners. Wittgensteins Denken im Kontext der Metapherntheorie," in *Wittgenstein und die Metapher*, ed. Ulrich Arnswald, Jens Kertscher, and Matthias Kroß (Berlin: Parerga, 2004), 137–64; here: 151–3.

34. Immanuel Kant, *Critique of the Power of Judgment*, ed. and trans. Paul Guyer and Eric Matthews (Cambridge: Cambridge University Press, 2000), 225; *Kritik der Urteilskraft* in *Werke in sechs Bänden*, ed. Wilhelm Weischedel, 7th ed., 6 vols. (Darmstadt: Wissenschaftliche Buchgesellschaft, 2011), 5:458.

35. Kant, *Critique of the Power of Judgment*, 226; *Kritik der Urteilskraft* in *Werke in sechs Bänden*, 5:459–60.

36. "The Oldest System-Programme of German Idealism," trans. Andrew Bowie in *Aesthetics and Subjectivity from Kant to Nietzsche* (Manchester: Manchester University Press, 1990), 265–7; here: 266; German version in Friedrich Hölderlin, *Sämtliche Werke und Briefe in drei Bänden*, ed. Jochen Schmidt (Frankfurt am Main: Deutscher Klassiker Verlag, 1992–4), 2:577.

37. Hans Blumenberg, "Licht als Metapher der Wahrheit im Vorfeld der philosophischen Begriffsbildung," in *Studium Generale* 10 (1957): 432–47. Reprinted in ÄMS, 139–71.

38. Anselm Haverkamp, "The Scandal of Metaphrology," in *Telos* 158 (2012): 37–58; here: 41–2. Robert Savage, "Translator's Afterword" in PM, 133–46, here: 138.

39. Hans Blumenberg, "Beobachtungen an Metaphern," *Archiv für Begriffsgeschichte* 15 (1971): 161–214; here:163. Also quoted by Savage in PM, 137.

40. Haverkamp, "The Scandal of Metaphrology," 40.

41. See Haverkamp's "Editorisches Nachwort," in TDU, 115–19; here: 115.

42. Blumenberg did not attend this meeting due to illness. See the commentary in BTB, 156.

43. Manfred Fuhrmann, "Vorbemerkung des Herausgebers," in *Terror und Spiel. Probleme der Mythenrezeption* (Poetik und Hermeneutik 4), ed. Manfred Fuhrmann (Munich: Fink, 1971), 9–10; here: 9.

44. Blumenberg to Taubes March 22, 1965, in BTB, 46–50; here: 49.

45. Taubes to Blumenberg, September 20, 1966, in BTB, 100–3.

46. Bronislaw Malinowski, *Myth in Primitive Psychology* (New York: Norton, 1926), 28.

47. See the discussion that followed Blumenberg's paper in "Mythos und Dogma," in *Terror und Spiel*, 527–47; here: 534.

48. See "Mythos und Dogma," in *Terror und Spiel*, 527–47, especially 538–47.

49. See Marquard's comments in "Mythos und Dogma," 527–30.

50. See "Mythos und Dogma," 546; the commentator in question is the Romanist Harald Weinrich.

51. Blumenberg delivered lectures on the "Theorie der Unbegrifflichkeit" during 1975. See Anselm Haverkamp's commentary in TDU, 115–19; here: 116.

52. See Gehlen, *Man*, 38–42; *Der Mensch*, 34–40.

53. Nietzsche, "Über Wahrheit und Lüge," in *KSA* 1: 882, 879, 880–1, 883, my translation. See also Lawrence M. Hinman, "Nietzsche, Metaphor, and Truth," *Philosophy and Phenomenological Research* 43, no. 2 (1982): 179–99.
54. Nietzsche, "Über Wahrheit und Lüge," in *KSA* 1: 889.
55. Friedrich Max Müller, "On the Philosophy of Mythology: A Lecture Delivered at the Royal Institution in 1871," in *The Essential Max Müller on Language, Mythology and Religion*, ed. Jon R. Stone (New York, NY: Palgrave, 2002), 145–66; here:155–6.
56. Müller, "On the Philosophy of Mythology," 150–1.

6   Goethe's 'Prometheus,' or on Cultural Selection

If Hans Blumenberg's theory of myth had remained solely preoccupied with the *terminus a quo*—with the hypothetical origin or point of departure that produced myth as a form of cultural or non-biological adaptation—then his subject matter would probably have remained confined to speculations concerning ancient pre-literate cultures and classical antiquity. That this did not end up being the case can be attributed to Blumenberg's initial argument of 1968 concerning the relation between terror and play, which was later transformed into the notion that in the modern age of science, myths can be aestheticised once the terrors to which they originally referred have been surmounted. The central category of myth—that of *Bedeutsamkeit* or significance—can in this way no longer exclusively be tied to questions of bare survival or withstanding the 'absolutism of reality,' but must also be determined in relation to the surrounding historical contexts in which the myth appears. The more a myth—such as that of Prometheus—offers material that can be adapted to varying cultural conditions and contexts, the higher are its chances of survival across different epochs. In short: Blumenberg's theory of myth amounts to a historicist version of philosophical anthropology insofar as the human being's cultural adaptations and compensations are increasingly determined by its historical circumstances, and especially by the technologies at its disposal. In this way, Blumenberg avoided one of the chief pitfalls that the young Jürgen Habermas attributed to Gehlen's version of philosophical anthropology: seeing an "early stage of human development"—namely, a lack of biological adaptations for which strong institutions must provide compensation—as being generally applicable to all of human history.[1] Even if Blumenberg strategically favours the hypothesis that human beings were biologically 'poor' because it displays functional efficacy in explaining the origins of culture, he is equally preoccupied with the 'richness' that later emerges from this situation: the aesthetic play that becomes possible once the initial terrors have been left behind.

It is perhaps because of the underlying Promethean debt in his theory of myth, explored in the previous chapter, that Blumenberg expressly wishes to avoid creating the impression that the Prometheus story is a "fundamental myth" (*Grundmythos*), in relation to which all other myths are variations that merely incorporate later "foreign bodies" (WOM, 174; AM, 192). Because the theorist of myth stands in the phenomenological position of the historically situated observer, Blumenberg argues, he or she could never know enough about the origin of myth to be able to justify such a founda-tional claim. It is on the basis of *belated* observation—rather than through access to any definitive origin—that Blumenberg claims a central impor-tance for Prometheus. "The radical myth," he writes,

> does not have to be the initial myth [. . .] On the contrary, the myth that is varied and transformed by its receptions, in the forms in which it is related to (and has the power of being related to) history, deserves to be made a subject of study if only because such a study also takes in the historical situations and needs that were affected by the myth and were disposed to 'work' on it.
>
> (WOM, 174; AM, 192)

More than any other myth, claims Blumenberg, the Prometheus myth has been 'worked on' during the modern age in such a way that it was been able to retain its significance. The reason why this is the case is not difficult to identify: Prometheus's defiance of Zeus and his association with technology and higher knowledge could easily be rendered meaningful within the mod-ern age's "existential programme" of "self-assertion" set against the histori-cal backdrop of a prior theological absolutism (LMA, 138; LDN, 151). Seen in this way, a myth that has the 'power of being related' to history is more likely to survive successive rounds of cultural selection because it can be adapted to meet human interests across various epochs. Even *before* enter-ing the modern age, the Prometheus story had already survived for over two millennia, and its ability to do so must have depended upon a "high degree of constancy" in its narrative core, accompanied by an "equally pronounced capacity for marginal variation" (WOM, 34; AM, 40).

It would be impossible to elucidate here all of the modern literary varia-tions on the Prometheus myth—those for example, of André Gide and Franz Kafka (see WOM, 627–36; AM, 679–89)—that are tracked by Blumenberg in *Work on Myth*. Here our main task will be to examine the *dynamics* of cultural selection with respect to myth by posing two questions. First, how and through what factors is a myth adapted to a new cultural context and are these factors ever at the disposal of an individual author? Second, pre-cisely what level of narrative stability does a myth need to retain in order for it to be identifiable as part of a tradition, and are there cases in which the variations to which a myth is subjected actually serve to obliterate the myth's core content—that is, to fundamentally change the myth, to destroy it, or to bring the myth to an end? Our analysis will reveal that because Blumenberg bases his understanding of myth reception on the situation of rhapsodes who performed already well-known epic poems in ancient Greece, he also challenges the modern notion of authorship—associated with the aesthetics of genius—according to which an individual author is in complete control of his or her materials (WOM, 156; AM, 173). The clearest example of this phenomenon will be found in Blumenberg's reading of Goethe's poem and drama-fragment dealing with the Prometheus story, and the turbulent reception of these texts in Germany during the late eighteenth century.

THE GOETHE COMPLEX

Odo Marquard has described *Work on Myth* as Blumenberg's "Goethe book," presumably on the basis that over one hundred of its pages deal with this most canonical of German writers.[2] Indeed, in the opening pages of the Goethe section of *Work on Myth* (Part IV), Goethe receives a rather grandiose introduction: "Everything up to this point in this book," writes Blumenberg, "has a gradient; all the lines converge on a hidden vital point at which the work expended on myth could prove to be something that was not fruitless." In Goethe's life, the work on myth may in fact have been *fruitful* insofar as it endowed this life with "the contours of its self-comprehension, its self-formulation, indeed its self-formation" (WOM, 399; AM, 435). But just as this begins to sound like typical German Goethe idolatry, Blumenberg's tone changes: on the same page we are told of Goethe's "rigidity" and "ungenerosity," and of the "egotism of this minister to a petty prince." Goethe's life, according to Blumenberg, was not "exemplary" in moral terms. It is much more a paradigm case of a life spent working on myth—and especially on the story of Prometheus—in order to create a sustainable myth of the self. The other respect in which Goethe is exemplary is that his work on myth has been meticulously preserved for us by Goethe philology—by a seemingly endless series of critical editions, handbooks, and biographies. It is this sense in which Goethe's life is "open for our access" (*zugänglich*) not as an empirical fact but as a textual construction in which "reality" and "illusion" are intricately interwoven (WOM, 399–400; AM, 435).

Of course, Blumenberg is not the first German philosopher to have placed Goethe at the centre of a theory. If suffering from a literary 'Goethe complex' coincides with what Harold Bloom refers to as the *Anxiety of Influence*[3]— the experience of being overshadowed by a dominant precursor—then a philosopher's Goethe complex might involve testing out one's theory of human nature on the man who is allegedly the most fully realised instance of what a certain class of Germans used to call *Bildung*: the full development and unfolding of a cultured personality. "To determine one's own standpoint in relation to Goethe," wrote Hans-Georg Gadamer in 1947, "has always been an authentic concern of philosophical consciousness."[4] This was particularly so during the first half of the twentieth century, which saw the publication of numerous studies by philosophers who preoccupied themselves with Goethe, among them Wilhelm Dilthey, Georg Simmel, and Georg Lukács.[5]

If a philosopher's Goethe complex is expressed through the activity of making Goethe into the paradigmatic research-object for a theory—in Dilthey's case, the notion that poetry is the expression of lived experience; in that of Simmel, the idea of an organic unity between nature and human productivity within the dissonant context of industrialised modernity; and in that of Lukács, the contention that bourgeois society places limitations on the free development of the individual—then Blumenberg can also be seen to have made an ironic contribution to this tradition in *Work on Myth*.

Why is Blumenberg's contribution to this tradition ironic? Blumenberg deliberately undermines, through scepticism, the approach to Goethe's life and works, which can be traced back to the origins of Goethe philology. This approach was informed by the notion that Goethe's literary works amount to literary transfigurations of his real lived experiences. The meaning of the works could, according to this model, only be uncovered through an intimate knowledge of the life that gave rise to them. That Goethe himself installed this biographical conception of literary criticism during the late stages of his life is suggested by a text entitled "A Word for Young Poets" ("Ein Wort für junge Dichter"). In this pithy public relations campaign, probably written sometime in 1832, Goethe claims that in the history of German literature he was not the master but rather the liberator of young German poets, in that he taught them that a writer must work "from the internal outwards," since "poetic content [. . .] is the content of one's own life." To the generation of German poets that will follow in his wake, Goethe exclaims, "only ask yourselves in relation to every poem: whether it contains a lived experience and whether you have conveyed this lived experience."[6]

From this it becomes easy to see that the model of poetic subjectivity elaborated by Goethe in the final years of his life was of foundational significance for the positivist origins of professional German studies (*Germanistik*) in the early works of Wilhelm Dilthey and in the writings of Wilhelm Scherer.[7] The contents of the archive at Weimar—having been touched by the hand of Goethe himself and soon to be available as scientific objects conducive to what the early Dilthey, writing in 1878, calls "inductive treatment"—would make a "general theory of poetic fantasy" into a real scientific possibility.[8] According to the model elaborated by Scherer in his role as adviser to the Weimar Edition of Goethe's works, the biographical facts of Goethe's life were to be seen as the empirical causes that underlie the works.[9] This of course meant that the ultimate arbiter of the meanings contained in the works could only be the person who underwent the original experiences that gave rise to them: namely, Goethe himself. This is why Goethe's autobiography, *Poetry and Truth* (*Dichtung und Wahrheit*, 1811–33) is seen by Scherer to have fathered Goethe philology through its foundational acts of self-explication. Goethe, he writes, "carved out for us the paths that we now attempt to trace in miniature."[10]

Blumenberg is aware that this approach to literary criticism placed an inordinate amount of power in the hands of Goethe as the allegedly most authoritative interpreter of his own works. This point demonstrates Blumenberg's ironic awareness, not so much of *a* Goethe complex, but of *the* Goethe complex: of the intricate web of biographical anecdotes—provided by the letters, diaries, and reported conversations of Goethe and his contemporaries—in relation to which the literary works have been interpreted. This Goethe complex resembles the structure of myth for the following reason: the purported 'origin'—that is, the 'real' experiences that are seen to underlie the works—have always already been 'worked on' or 'worked up' into literary anecdotes. There is thus no sense in which any knowledge of the 'life' could underpin authoritative readings of the works, precisely because the life is always already 'work.' Although Blumenberg never really spells this position out in explicit terms, it certainly explains his approach to Goethe in *Work on Myth*: that of closely interweaving interpretations of the literary works with reflections on their accompanying biographical anecdotes and asides, the veracity of which is almost always left open to question. The point of these readings is to see Goethe's self-interpretations as a rhetorical performance that is at the same time a defence of his own identity.

Blumenberg deploys this reading method in his account of Goethe's "Prometheus" poem of 1773. In what is the most detailed and authoritative recent interpretation of this poem in English—that offered by David Wellbery in the *Specular Moment*—the following observation concerning Blumenberg's take on the poem is made. Blumenberg, in Wellbery's view,

> discusses the text as a kind of immanent product of the poet's individuality [. . .] However intriguing Blumenberg's commentary might be as a biographical construction or speculative fiction, it contributes little to an understanding of the poetic specificity of the text.[11]

This assessment is in certain respects correct: anyone who reads *Work on Myth* with the expectation of finding close textual interpretations of Goethe's individual poems will be disappointed. Yet what Wellbery refers to as "the poet's individuality" is never afforded an exemplary interpretative status by Blumenberg. In other words, he does not interpret the works, in a positivist fashion, according to the life. Blumenberg's aim is much more to demonstrate that the entire Goethe complex—the intricate system of meaning comprised both of poetic texts *and* of autobiographical anecdotes about them—is a grand literary conglomerate that can *in its entirety* be seen as coherently related to the Prometheus myth. Goethe's reception of Prometheus is therefore not confined simply to one poem and the related two act drama fragment of 1773.[12] It is nothing less than a "central configuration" of Goethe's "understanding of himself and the world" (WOM, 430; AM, 467). And in this scenario, 'Goethe' is never precisely the same as the real historical individual who lived between 1749 and 1832; rather, in phenomenological terms he is always already an after-effect, a culturally constructed "massif" that rises up before the reader out of the works (WOM, 399; AM, 435).

In order to investigate how Blumenberg elaborates this claim, let us first examine the full text of Goethe's "Prometheus":

Cover over your heaven, Zeus,
With cloudy murk,
And exercise yourself, like a boy
Beheading thistles,
On oaks and mountain peaks;
You must let my earth
Stand anyway,
And my hut, which you didn't build,
And my hearth,
For the glow of which
You envy me.

I know nothing more impoverished
Beneath the sun than you, gods!
You feed miserably
On sacrificial taxes
And the breath of prayers
Your majesty,
And would starve, were
Not children and beggars
Hopeful fools.

When I was a child,
Didn't know where in or out,
I turned my confused eye
Toward the sun, as if above it were
An ear to hear my lament,
A heart like mine,
To take pity on one so distressed.

Who helped me
Against the Titans' excess?
Who saved me from death,
From slavery?
Didn't you accomplish everything yourself,
Sacredly glowing heart?
And you glowed young and good,
Deceived, thanked for your salvation
The sleeping one up there?

I should honor you? Why?
Did you ever lighten the pain
Of the one so burdened?
Did you ever still the tears
Of the one so afraid?
Wasn't what forged me into a man
All-powerful time
And eternal destiny,
My lords and yours?

Did you perhaps imagine,
I would hate life,
Flee into deserts,
Because not all the
Blossom-dreams of youth bore fruit?

Here I sit, form human beings
After my image,
A race that will be equal to me,
To suffer, to weep,
To take pleasure and feel joy,
And not to respect you,
Like me![13]

Bedecke deinen Himmel Zeus
Mit Wolkendunst!
Und übe Knabengleich
Der Disteln köpft
An Eichen dich und Bergeshöhn!
Mußt mir meine Erde
Doch lassen stehn,
Und meine Hütte
Die du nicht gebaut,
Und meinen Herd
Um dessen Glut
Du mich beneidest.

Ich kenne nichts ärmers
Unter der Sonn als euch Götter.
Ihr nähret kümmerlich
Von Opfersteuern
Und Gebetshauch
Eure Majestät
Und darbtet wären
Nicht Kinder und Bettler
Hoffnungsvolle Toren.

Da ich ein Kind war
Nicht wußt wo aus wo ein
Kehrt mein verirrtes Aug
Zur Sonne als wenn drüber wär
Ein Ohr zu hören meine Klage
Ein Herz wie meins
Sich des Bedrängten zu erbarmen.

Wer half mir wider
Der Titanen Übermut
Wer rettete vom Tode mich
Von Sklaverei?
Hast du's nicht alles selbst vollendet
Heilig glühend Herz
Und glühtest jung und gut
Betrogen, Rettungsdank
Dem Schlafenden dadroben

Ich dich ehren? Wofür?
Hast du die Schmerzen gelindert
Je des Beladenen
Hast du die Tränen gestillet
Je des Geängsteten?
Hat nicht mich zum Manne geschmiedet
Die allmächtige Zeit
Und das ewige Schicksal
Meine Herrn und deine.

Wähntest etwa
Ich sollt das Leben hassen
In Wüsten fliehn,
Weil nicht alle Knabenmorgen
Blütenträume reiften.

Hier sitz ich, forme Menschen
Nach meinem Bilde
Ein Geschlecht das mir gleich sei
Zu leiden, weinen
Genießen und zu freuen sich
Und dein nicht zu achten
Wie ich![14]

Of immediate interest are those aspects of the Prometheus story that Goethe has ignored or dispensed with: there is no mention here of Prometheus having deceived Zeus through his division of the sacrificial animal or the theft of fire; there is no ostensible punishment of Prometheus, he is not situated on the Caucasus, and no eagle nibbles at his liver; Prometheus has no secret concerning Zeus to withhold and bargain with; and no one is required to come and set him free. Admittedly some of these events are potentially alluded to: the sacrifice in the "sacrificial taxes" on which the gods are said to feed; the fire in the glow of the hearth; and the punishment in the "all-powerful time" that has "forged" Prometheus into the man that he is. But this is all more or less back-story or assumed cultural knowledge.

As Blumenberg and other commentators have noted,[15] it is likely that Goethe used the 1770 edition of Benjamin Hederich's *Complete Mythological Lexicon* (*Gründliches mythologisches Lexikon*) as his main source for the Prometheus story (WOM, 403; AM, 438). This would explain Goethe's emphasis—most readily observable in the final stanza of the poem—on the image of Prometheus as he who models human beings after the example of the gods. Hederich's account of Prometheus's deeds does not follow the usual chronology by beginning with Hesiod, but rather with Ovid's *Metamorphoses* (Book 1, lines 80–2), where Prometheus combines earth with rainwater, moulding this mass into "into the likeness of gods who govern the universe."[16] Later in his entry, Hederich also refers to a pictorial image of Prometheus in which he is seated in his workshop next to a bucket containing clay, which he uses to form human beings.[17] This use of clay does not appear in the Prometheus poem of 1773, but it is present in Goethe's drama fragment of the same year, which is normally held to predate the poem.[18] Here Zeus's servant, Merkur, refers to the world that Prometheus has made of clay and which—in another feature that Goethe seems to have taken from Hederich—is endowed with life by Minerva. The drama fragment also contains a plot element that is not found in the poem, but that will be absolutely crucial to Blumenberg's interpretation: Zeus is described in the drama fragment as Prometheus's father, and Prometheus lays down the following challenge to Merkur in his role as the representative of Zeus: "Your will! Against mine!/One against one!"[19]

Blumenberg reads this key element of the Prometheus fragment into Goethe's poem, noting that it is not present in Hederich's account and so must intentionally have been added by Goethe himself. Goethe, Blumenberg argues, must have been impressed by Hederich's openness to different versions of the myth, which led Hederich to conclude his entry with the observation that "everyone can produce more such interpretations himself."[20] This Goethe did by introducing the father-son scenario, which Blumenberg regards as the "weightiest possible infringement" (WOM, 404; AM, 439). While this may be correct, there is also other classical material on which Goethe could have drawn in his representation of a completely defiant Prometheus. One source is Lucian's dialogue *Zeus Catechized*,[21] in which Cyniscus poses the following question to Zeus: if it is true that life is controlled in advance by Destiny and the Fates, as Homer and Hesiod suggest, then what is possibly to be gained in offering sacrifices to you, Zeus? Upon hearing this, Zeus does concede that the Fates decide everything, including what happens to the gods, and that the gods have no influence over them. His rather feeble justification for sacrifices is that they are tributes to the gods' superiority, and he also expresses resentment towards Cyniscus for asking him "clever questions" in the manner of a "sophist." Cyniscus responds that a sophist may well want to know on precisely what basis this claim to superiority is made, while also suggesting that the gods' immortality is in any case not something to be wished for if the gods are, like humans, at the mercy of the Fates.[22]

Similar 'sophistical' arguments are made by Prometheus in stanza five of Goethe's poem—"I should honor you? Why?"—though in this case we are dealing with a monologue, which raises the question of whether Zeus actually exists independently of Prometheus's consciousness. While Blumenberg does not explicitly consider this question, this interpretation accords with what I have referred to as Promethean anthropology—the anthropology of cultural compensation. David Wellbery takes a similar line in the *Specular Moment* by suggesting that Prometheus's opening command to Zeus in the first stanza can be seen as a rhetorical act that neutralises the threat of Zeus's whipping up a storm. If the possibility of such a storm can be named and anticipated to the extent that Prometheus purports to order it into existence, then this command can be seen as his rhetorical way of dealing with an 'absolutism of reality' that is no longer absolute. In Wellbery's formulation, the content of Prometheus's opening argument is as follows: "so little does the action you threaten endanger me that I order you to do it."[23] Seen from this perspective, the remainder of the poem consists of Prometheus literally talking Zeus out of existence: Zeus is described as being impoverished and reliant upon his supplicants (stanza two); offering sacrifices to him is said to secure no tangible benefits (stanzas four and five); and he is seen to be subject to the vagaries of destiny in the same way that humans are (stanza five).

All of this raises the possibility, entertained in stanza three, that when the helpless and disoriented young Prometheus looked up to the sun in order to find solace there—"as *if* [*als wenn*] above it were/An ear to hear my lament,/A heart like mine" (emphasis mine)—he was engaging in nothing more than anthropomorphic projection or what Blumenberg would call the orienting work of myth. If giving up useless prayer and building your own hut and hearth is the way to self-reliance through the deployment of technology, then it is easy to see why this poem so appealed to the author of the *Legitimacy of the Modern Age*. Here, in Goethe's modern historical context, the compensatory possession of fire no longer refers to a technology that enables bare survival. Rather the glow (*glühen*) of Prometheus's hearth (stanza one), and of his heart (stanza four), represent poetic self-assertion as the ability rhetorically to counter one myth—that of an all-powerful Zeus—with another: that of the self as an autonomous creative entity that is not subject to any prior law.

Blumenberg's treatment of the poem is a standard one insofar as he situates it within the broader discourse on genius that belongs to the period in German literature known as the Storm and Stress (*Sturm und Drang*, roughly the late 1760s until the end of the 1770s).[24] "The point of Goethe's early reception of Prometheus," he writes, "lies in the icon of the workshop, which could be related to the aesthetic genius" (WOM, 406; AM, 440-1). The modeller of human beings in his workshop is akin to the mimetic poet who creates a second world in language. This connection between Prometheus and poetry is already made by Shaftesbury at the beginning of the eighteenth century when he writes that "such a poet is indeed a second maker; a just Prometheus under Jove."[25] Blumenberg's main concern is not to offer an internal analysis of the poem, but rather to consider its reception as a case study in both the work *on* and the work *of* myth. The work *on* myth can be found in Goethe's decision, seen in the Prometheus dramafragment, to transform the relation between Zeus and Prometheus into one of father to son instead of god to titan. The work *of* myth flowed from this transformation, since it turned out to be decisive in endowing the Prometheus story with a new significance in the context of theological debates in late eighteenth-century Germany, exemplified in the so-called pantheism controversy.

As can be seen in Karl Eibl's commentary on the poem in the recent Frankfurt Edition of Goethe's works,[26] the pantheism controversy came to dominate its reception.[27] The basic story is as follows: Goethe sent the Prometheus drama fragment, as well as the poem, to the philosopher Friedrich Heinrich Jacobi some time in 1774. Six years later, in 1780, Jacobi showed this poem, the original copy of which he seems to have retained, to the eminent writer and dramatist Gotthold Ephraim Lessing and asked for his reaction. Lessing is said to have reacted positively to its contents and to have interpreted Goethe's text theologically: "the point of view from which the poem is taken, that is my own point of view [. . .] the orthodox conceptions of God are no longer for me; I cannot take pleasure in them." When Jacobi inquired of Lessing whether this reaction meant that he was in agreement with the philosophy of Spinoza, Lessing is said to have responded affirmatively: "if I should name myself after someone, I would know of no other."[28] This admission was controversial because Spinoza's philosophy—commonly described as pantheism—was held by Jacobi to amount to atheism.[29] If, according to Spinoza's famous formulation in the *Ethics—Deus sive Natura* (God or Nature)—God is held to be indistinguishable from nature, being the "immanent, and not the transitive cause of all things,"[30] then the orthodox image of an external creator-God is effectively eliminated. Although, as Eibl notes, the interpretative leap from Goethe's "Prometheus" to the *en kai pan* (one and all) of pantheism is rather a large one,[31] it was nonetheless plausible within the context of the genius discourse of the period. If God is nature, and if the poet is also part of the natural world, then the poet or genius can harness godlike qualities. And although this position hardly amounts to atheism, and could simply be described as another way of viewing the divine, the mere allegation of atheism was enough to cause a controversy.

Indeed, whether or not it was Goethe's intention to write a 'pantheist' or an 'atheist' poem is beside the point, since within German intellectual circles of the period, it was Lessing's alleged admission of pantheism in relation to Goethe's text that was of significance. Jacobi, who was ill disposed towards the Enlightenment and its positive reception of Spinoza, saw an opportunity to cause a scandal by publishing Lessing's admission alongside a copy of Goethe's poem. This he did with another dramatic flourish: the poem was printed without the author's name and without pagination so that it could easily be torn out of the book, lest it upset censors on the lookout for atheists.[32] This gesture appeared to suggest that if Spinozism offers the most systematic expression of pantheism, and if pantheism—through its elimination of an external creator-God—amounts to atheism, then Lessing's commitment to Spinoza's philosophy was at the same time a declaration of atheism. All of this material appeared in Jacobi's *On the Teachings of Spinoza in Letters to Moses Mendelssohn* (*Über die Lehre des Spinoza in Briefen an den Herrn Moses Mendelssohn*, 1785), which contains Jacobi's correspondence with the German-Jewish Enlightenment thinker Moses Mendelssohn concerning both Spinozism and Lessing. For his part, Mendelssohn took a more balanced view of matters, regarding his friend Lessing as a "defender of theism and rational religion," and he urgently wished to make this clear in his *To the Friends of Lessing* (*An die Freunde Lessings*), published in 1786.[33] Mendelssohn is said to have been so preoccupied with this scandal that he hand-delivered the manuscript of this volume to his publisher, forgetting to put on his overcoat before going out. As a consequence Mendelssohn fell ill and died on January 4, 1786, giving rise to the tale—or myth?—that he literally died of the pantheism controversy that had been triggered by Goethe's poem.

It is when Goethe comes to write a retrospective account of this controversy and of the role that "Prometheus" is said to have played in it, that we see the 'Goethe complex' swing into action. In part three (book 15) of *Poetry and Truth*, written in 1812–13 and published in 1814,[34] Goethe describes what the Prometheus myth meant to him as a young man. In a discussion concerning the sense of helplessness that humans can feel when confronted by fate, Goethe says that he always took refuge in his "natural gift" (*Naturgabe*) of poetic inspiration, which he thought was his "very own possession," and which "no outside influence could either facilitate or hinder." This gift was so reassuring that Goethe decided to base his "entire existence" (*ganzes Dasein*) upon it. This reminded him of "the old mythological figure of Prometheus," who, "separated from the gods" in his "workshop," was able to people his own world. In this way the "fable of Prometheus," writes Goethe, "came to life in me." Tailoring the "old titanic garments" to suit his own figure, Goethe accordingly composed his poem, probably without realising that it would become "priming powder for an explosion" in the pantheism controversy. This controversy brought to light "the most secret concerns of worthy men," concerns of which they themselves were unconscious and which had "slumbered in an otherwise very enlightened society." The ramifications of this emergence from latency were so violent that Mendelssohn, "one of our worthiest men," is said to have died of them.[35]

This section of *Poetry and Truth* is important for Blumenberg on a number of levels. Goethe's tailoring of the Prometheus figure to suit his own personal and aesthetic purposes is said to describe how a mythical narrative can be fitted to a life outline. After having expressed to a friend his view that "God seems not to want me to become an author,"[36] the young Goethe came to see writing as an act of autonomous creation in spite of God. That is why, according to Blumenberg, Goethe saw himself as an aesthetic polytheist who tended to use the name 'god' with an "indefinite article," since to be a writer in a Christian culture meant to be *a* god in opposition to God (WOM, 406; AM, 441). The effect that Goethe's Prometheus had on the surrounding intellectual culture demonstrates for Blumenberg the "disproportions of intention and effect" that occur within myth reception (WOM, 407; AM, 442–3). The versions of the Prometheus myth to which Goethe had ready access were a consequence of the contingencies of his age, perhaps exemplified by the mundane fact that Hederich's volume was the most commonly used source at the time. Hederich's dominant image of Prometheus as the potter in his workshop in turn shaped Goethe's approach to Prometheus as an artistic genius or 'second maker'—a conception that of course carried significant theological implications.

The fact that Goethe could scarcely have foreseen how forcefully this initially private poem would come to resonate among his contemporaries demonstrates that when it comes to myth, the author is neither completely in control of his materials—precisely because they precede and to a certain extent condition him—nor of their reception. How and why a culture 'selects' a myth and finds it to be significant is an historical process that is beyond the total control of any individual author, even of the so-called Olympian, Goethe. But what the author *can* control—or at least attempt to influence after the event—is his or her own reception. In Blumenberg's view, Goethe uses the pantheism controversy rhetorically to underline his capacity to influence a culture. The expression "priming powder for an explosion" is a case of retrospective work on myth in which "the reception of myth gives itself mythical features" (WOM, 414; AM, 451). Goethe willingly exaggerated the effect that the pantheism controversy had upon Mendelssohn so that the poem and its reception could be "done up (*getrimmt*) in terms of significance" (WOM, 416, 426; AM, 452, 465). Again, there is a sense of identification with Prometheus here, in that the latent explosive energy of the poem resembles the glowing fire of Prometheus's hearth. Finally, and most significantly in terms of the history of German literature, from this analysis there emerges a rather different portrait of Goethe to that of the great classical author: Goethe is now depicted as a wily rhetorician or sophist who specialises in endowing himself with mythic significance by dressing up in the old titanic garb.

THE DAEMONIC AND ITS DANGERS

Goethe's biographical 'working through' of the Prometheus mythologem is something that Blumenberg also locates in much later texts, even those that do not explicitly invoke the name Prometheus. The clearest case is Goethe's notion of the daemonic (*das Dämonische*), which has a long and complicated reception history in Goethe studies,[37] and which receives its most extended treatments in Part Four (Book Twenty) of *Poetry and Truth* (written in early to mid-1813), and in Johann Peter Eckermann's *Conversations with Goethe in the Last Years of His Life* (*Gespräche mit Goethe in den letzten Jahren seines Lebens*, 1835). The latter text in particular involves Goethe's most explicit reckonings with Napoleon, whom he met in October 1808, and whom he later came to describe as a "daemonic" (*dämonisch*) individual. In Blumenberg's view, "the continuity of the relation to Napoleon extends further than anything else in Goethe's life, with the exception of that of the two figures, Prometheus and Faust, a continuity that for its part includes the complex involving Napoleon" (WOM, 466; AM, 505).

The term 'daemonic' comes from the ancient Greek root *daíw* (*daio*)— meaning to distribute or divide.[38] In this respect it refers to the processes, most readily referred to in Orphic beliefs, through which the gods endow humans with divine gifts and determine their fates.[39] Heraclitus also uses the term daemon (or *daimon*) in this sense when he observes that a man's daemon is his fate.[40] In the Platonic tradition, daemons are intermediaries between the divine and human worlds (see, for example, *Phaedrus* 246e), and the term is at times used figuratively to describe abstract concepts, such as erotic love or *eros*. The most famous instance of this usage occurs in the speech of Diotima in the *Symposium* (202e), where she describes *eros* as a *daimon* because it helps to bring human minds closer to the divinity of the forms. A specific instance of this type of divine illumination is also to be found in Socrates's *daimonion* or divine sign, which has the negative function of dissuading Socrates from reaching hasty conclusions on matters that require deeper philosophical analysis (see, for example, *Phaedrus*, 242b-c).[41]

In *Poetry and Truth*, Goethe draws upon the richness and suggestiveness of this term in order to describe the mysterious and fateful force that seemed to have shaped the course of his life:

> It was not divine, for it seemed irrational; not human, for it had no intelligence; not diabolical, for it was beneficent; and not angelic, for it often betrayed malice. It was like chance, for it lacked continuity, and like Providence, for it suggested context. Everything that limits us

seemed penetrable by it, and it appeared to dispose at will over the elements necessary to our existence [. . .] This essence, which appeared to infiltrate all the others, separating and combining them, I called daemonic, after the example of the ancients and others who had perceived something similar. I tried to save myself from this fearful thing by taking refuge, as usual, behind an image.[42]

Blumenberg interprets this passage as a paradigmatic case of the work *of* myth. Whereas Socrates, presumably after being dissuaded from letting matters rest by his *daimonion*, continues with elaborating a philosophy that allows him finally to take refuge in concepts or *logoi*, "Goethe is not a philosopher [. . .] because it is behind an image that he takes refuge" (WOM, 401; AM, 437). If Goethe's taking refuge behind an image is a modern expression of the function of myth—that of coping with forces beyond the control and comprehension of the subject—then Goethe is an exceptional case because "no one has ever articulated more precisely why reason admits needs, which it arouses itself, without being able, in its regular discipline, to satisfy them." The term daemonic is therefore said only to perform the auxiliary function of giving a name to "the unresolved remainder" of Goethe's experience (WOM, 401; AM, 437).

Here the functionalism of Blumenberg's theory of myth is revealed in the fact that he is not at all interested in the actual term 'daemonic' and its rich and complicated conceptual history, especially among contemporaries of Goethe such as Hamann and Herder,[43] but only in the rhetorical work that it is able to do in Goethe's texts: "What matters is not this title and the interpretative eagerness to which it has given rise; what matters is the 'remainder'" (WOM, 401; AM, 437). This act of naming this 'remainder' shows how myth can still be resorted to by reason, "not in order to acquire secretly, after all, the excess that is denied to it, but in order not to let unreason gain power over the unoccupied space" (WOM, 401; AM, 437). In this way, Blumenberg wants to make it perfectly clear that he is not accusing Goethe of mysticism or irrationalism. Rather, Goethe only takes refuge behind an image as a result of his rational apprehension of the limits of reason. The daemonic therefore "belongs to the category of the mythical" because it "circumscribes—does not explain, perhaps only gives a name to—a potency that has not been fully analyzed historically" (WOM, 515; AM, 559)

But the daemonic also has its dangers. The elderly Goethe tended at times to associate it with the fates of individuals—like Napoleon—who he thought to be divinely illuminated. This sense of the term can be found in Goethe's explanation of the poem "Primal Words. Orphic" ("Urworte. Orphisch," 1817), that appeared in the volume *On Morphology* (*Zur Morphologie*) in 1820. Here we are told that the daemon is the "necessary, limited individuality of the person that is immediately announced at birth [. . .] from here the future fate of the person should also now emerge."[44] And it is this

notion that extraordinary individuals are illuminated by an indwelling daemon that enjoys a more or less hyperbolic use in Johann Peter Eckermann's
Conversations with Goethe.[45] In the remarks by Goethe that are recorded
(and in all likelihood embellished) by Eckermann, daemons are associated
with the "hereditary elements of nature." Here Goethe invokes Aristotle's
notion of *entelechy*: the inborn potentiality of the individual that will unfold
during its development.[46] The main problem here is that in Goethe's often
freewheeling remarks to Eckermann, the aesthetic and political senses of
the term become almost interchangeable: whereas the daemonic natures of
Raphael, Mozart, and Shakespeare produced great works of art,[47] it was
Napoleon's daemonic illumination that made his life into "the striding of a
demigod from battle to battle and from victory to victory."[48]

It is through the example of Napoleon that Goethe begins to recognise
the dangers of the daemonic. During their meeting in October 1808, and in
the context of a discussion of Voltaire's drama *Oedipus*, a play described as
a "drama of fate" (*Schicksalsstück*), Napoleon is reported to have said to
Goethe: "what does one want now with fate [*Schicksal*], politics is fate."[49]
Blumenberg reads this statement as Napoleon reoccupying the position
of classical fate with a modern notion of secular political destiny, even if
Napoleon originally meant political fate not in the active sense of *making*
history, but in the passive sense of being *affected* by it (WOM, 487; AM,
529). This, indeed, had been Goethe's experience in October 1806, when
Napoleon's army invaded Weimar. Goethe, however, reinterpreted Napoleon's statement in the *active* sense, meaning that to determine fate through
politics is to presume to have the power of a God, and to take on a role with
Promethean pretensions.

Here the dangers of the daemonic are revealed, since to be daemonic in the
sense of being driven by an internal "energy" or *Tatkraft*—as Goethe puts
it in his conversation with Eckermann on March 2, 1831[50]—may also mean
to invite other daemonic powers to oppose one. Goethe already reaches
this conclusion in his conversation with Eckermann on March 11, 1828,
when he states that it is external daemonic forces that ultimately "tripped
up" Napoleon and brought him undone, presumably during the failed Russian campaign of 1812.[51] The decidedly negative Promethean lesson to be
learned from the case of Napoleon is that to presume to be a god is to invite
the opposition of other would-be gods, or as Goethe stated in a remark to
Eckermann on February 10, 1830: "Napoleon gives us an example of how
dangerous it is to raise oneself into an absolute and to sacrifice everything in
the execution of an idea."[52]

It is for this reason that the elderly Goethe then wishes dispel the notion
that he, like Napoleon, is a daemonic individual, and he does so through the
following comment to Eckermann on March 28, 1831: the daemonic, Goethe
claims, "does not lie in my nature, but I am subject to it."[53] Here Goethe
shifts the active sense of the daemonic—that of the energetic and overween-
ing creative individual of the "Prometheus" poem—onto Napoleon. At the

same time he also reserves the passive position—that of he who is subjected to the political whims and projects of such daemonic individuals—for himself. For the elderly Goethe who appears in Eckermann's *Conversations*, the example of Napoleon is used to defend what Blumenberg calls Goethe's "life concept" (WOM, 466; AM, 505), which is to be the person who can both look into and evade the abyss, and who can experience but then also renounce and survive dangerous Promethean adventures. Or as Blumenberg puts it: "Whenever Goethe turns to the daemonic he gains the advantage of being able to extricate himself again from comparisons with himself [. . .] He uses the name of the 'daemon' [. . .] in, as it were, a displaced location: for the other person's fate, when he had just related it to himself" (WOM, 468, 477; AM, 508, 518).[54] In short: the perceived dangers of 'political Prometheanism' meant that the great poet who had once modeled himself on Prometheus did not wish to do so anymore.

ON CULTURAL SELECTION

Our survey of the Prometheus material in this and the previous chapter is instructive for the purposes of understanding Blumenberg's arguments concerning the role played by cultural selection in myth. Blumenberg's working hypothesis can be found in Paul Alsberg's idea that the decisive factor in human development was that of gradually ameliorating the role played by natural selection through the insertion of technological buffers—weapons, housing, medicine, language, concepts, and so on—between the human being and the natural selective pressures of its environment. If this is the case, then it must also be assumed that new processes of selection displaced the natural processes that had been reduced. In order to apply this argument to myth, Blumenberg introduces a phenomenon referred to as the "distortion of temporal perspective." By this he means the fact that "what appears on the basis of written evidence [. . .] as something very early and old must be regarded from the point of view of the history of man as something very late" (WOM, 149, 151; AM, 165, 167–8).

The earliest authors in the Western classical tradition—Homer and Hesiod—are viewed by Blumenberg as *late* culture in that their texts are merely the written versions of oral narratives that may already have been tested and honed for millennia. Because this age of oral communication represented a "phase of continual and direct feedback" about literary contents, it must have "enforced a more fine-textured and intensive testing [*Erprobung*]" of these materials than that which applies to written sources (WOM, 152; AM, 168). This is explained by the fact that "transmission by word of mouth favours the 'pregnance' of what is transmitted"—its memorable character and its capacity to captivate—over all other aesthetic criteria (WOM, 153; AM, 170). Here Blumenberg is referring to the ancient Greek literary festivals at which rhapsodes (reciters of epic poetry) performed for prizes (see WOM, 155; AM, 172)—a phenomenon alluded to by Hesiod in *Works and Days* (lines 655–8), where he claims to have won such a contest.[55] Blumenberg accordingly imagines the rhapsode as "one who adapts himself with precision and flexibility to his audience and its desires" (WOM, 155; AM, 172)—that is: as something akin to Vico's "stitcher-together" of narratives.[56] These processes of high-pressure cultural selection meant that when the basic figurations of classical myth were first written down, they were already "so sharply defined [*prägnant*], so valid, so binding, so gripping in every sense" that their chances of surviving over the epochs were very high (WOM, 150–1; AM, 166).

The idea that these contests were always judged according to the tastes of audiences alone is not entirely correct. Certainly, as Andrew Ford points out, such performances "always occurred in a social space" and their audiences are thought to have "vociferously showed their preferences," but in many cases prizes were awarded by prominent citizens or elected judges (*kritai*) rather than directly by audiences.[57] Blumenberg's preference for the aesthetic criterion of significance (determined by audiences) can be seen as a continuation of his favouring of rhetoric over Platonic dialectic. As Ford shows, it was Plato, particularly in the *Laws*, who militated against popular judgements concerning poetry by introducing a philosophically informed criticism.[58] And there is also another way in which Blumenberg's theory of selection via audience reception is broadly anti-Platonic. When seen from Blumenberg's perspective of cultural selection, the theory of the archetype associated with the depth psychology of Carl Gustav Jung misunderstands the key components of myth as "innate ideas" in the collective unconscious. Blumenberg argues that these ideas only *appear* to us to be innate because the processes of testing that they have withstood and to which they have been adapted have ensured their survival over long periods of time, conferring upon them an air of timelessness (WOM, 151; AM, 167). Once again, Blumenberg's emphasis on the adaptive and persuasive powers of rhetoric is at the same time a critique of the 'Platonic' reliance on eternal forms in the theory of myth.

Here the question arises as to whether Blumenberg wishes to endow this argument concerning myth with a 'scientific' character. In Blumenberg's view, those who have applied the Darwinian notion of selection to human cultures have been mistaken in their use of a "narrow interpretation of the concept of selection that restricts it to its performance in biological explanation" (WOM, 165; AM, 182). Apparently paraphrasing Alsberg, Blumenberg proposes that "the organic system resulting from the mechanism of evolution becomes 'man' by evading the pressure of that mechanism by setting against it something like a phantom body" (WOM, 165; AM, 182). The phantom body or prosthesis to which Blumenberg refers is culture in the form of *actio per distans*, which ranges from stone projectiles to metaphors, myths, concepts, and eventually the science of the modern age.

Seen in these terms, "the world we live in is a less Darwinistic world the more theory and technology *are* (objectively transposed) Darwinistic worlds" (WOM, 165; AM, 183). This cryptic formulation merely suggests that natural selection is displaced by cultural and especially technological selection once the pressures exerted by nature have been put at an adequate distance. While technological selection would then consist in favouring those procedures that optimise human survival or save human labour,[59] other aspects of cultural selection may become increasingly aesthetic. In fact, as Blumenberg suggests in *Description of Man*, there is a direct relation between technological and aesthetic selection. The more that technology reduces the dangers to which we are exposed and the labours that we must undertake in order to survive, the more time that we have to spend on aesthetic pleasures: "gaining time in order to kill time, that seems to me to be the fundamental structure of the entire modern age," observes Blumenberg (BDM, 616). Thus, after myths have cast off (*vertreiben*) the fear associated with the 'absolutism of reality,' part of their function becomes that of simply killing time (WOM, 34; AM, 40).

But while Blumenberg certainly suggests that an *analogical* relation may hold between natural and cultural selection, he does not pursue this argument systematically in *Work on Myth*. If Blumenberg's theory of myth *were* to pursue this analogy in a similar way to the theory of memes proposed by Richard Dawkins and others, it would need to demonstrate at least four hypotheses. First, that myths or mythologems are cultural replicators that have been copied and transmitted with a high degree of accuracy over the ages, in a similar way to genes being biological replicators. Second, that literary texts or similar cultural products are akin to what Dawkins refers to as organisms, "survival machines" or gene "vehicles" within the realm of biology[60]—that is, the larger bodies or structures that house the gene (or in this case the mythologem or meme) in question. Here, for example, Goethe's "Prometheus" poem would be seen as the 'vehicle' for the Prometheus mythologem or meme. Third, that one can cogently draw an analogy between thematic variations in mythologems and variation in genes. And fourth, that the different historical contexts to which a mythologem is exposed are akin to the different environments in which genetic variations in organisms prove to be either conducive or inimical to survival. While these premises might initially seem to be roughly plausible, there are significant problems with all of them.

As mentioned in Chapter 1 of this volume, some contemporary theorists of evolutionary biology—namely Richard Dawkins and Daniel Dennett—have made apparently similar attempts to find processes akin to natural selection in the realm of culture, through positing the existence of 'memes' as units of cultural replication, variation, and selection. Yet both Dawkins and Dennett have recently expressed doubts as to whether the analogy between natural selection with respect to genes, and cultural selection in relation to memes, can have anything more than a heuristic or even metaphorical status. One problem concerns the *function* of memes. In *The Selfish Gene*, Dawkins is at times unclear as to whether the function of memes is that of benefiting human survival or simply of sheer self-replication. In the case of memes relating to technology, for example, one could easily claim that the transmission of cultural practices such as stone tool manufacture or the use of fire provided our ancestors with clear biological advantages that were in turn favoured by natural selection—enabling, for example, the cutting and cooking of meat. But this may not hold for non-physical memes, such as myths or even religious ideas. In *The God Delusion*, Dawkins certainly regards the idea of God as one of the most successful memes or cultural replicators in human history, which he sees as having succeeded through its psychological appeal, thereby enhancing the purposes of the religion 'memeplex' alone rather than the genetic interests of the human species.[61] In this way, he suggests that biological and cultural evolution are analogous, though entirely separate, processes which both involve replicators: in some cases memes may be units of culture that occupy human brains with the sole 'aim' of replicating themselves.

A similar position is taken up by Daniel Dennett in *Darwin's Dangerous Idea*, where he describes memes as "distinct memorable units," such as, for example, parts of Homer's *Odyssey* or a piece of music by Mozart. The competition between memes is described as "the major selective force in the infosphere," just as competition between genes dominates the biosphere. Memes either expire or survive depending on their ability to replicate and to exercise appeal in cultural environments—with 'environment' meaning "minds and other memes."[62] But a common reservation expressed by both Dawkins and Dennett is whether units of culture can replicate themselves with the same level of accuracy as genes do and therefore whether the mutation rate of memes may simply be too high to speak meaningfully of cultural evolution or selection.[63]

In a recent work on the theory of cultural selection, the sociologist W.G. Runciman also underlines important differences between cultural and biological transmission. While the biological transmission of genes consists of passive copying, memes can be actively reinterpreted by their recipients, which can lead to much higher rates of distortion and to changes that can occur even within the lifespan of one generation.[64] Another important question is whether such a particulate theory—in which memes function as independently transmissible 'units'—can actually describe the enmeshed complexes of ideas that are human cultures.[65] Regardless of the accuracy of the gene-meme analogy, an issue than cannot be resolved here,[66] what Blumenberg *does* appear to share with Dawkins and Dennett is precisely this analogical approach to understanding cultural selection. This approach points to possible similarities between natural and cultural selection on the one hand, yet sees cultural selection as having its own independent dynamic on the other.

How might these ideas be applied to the example of Prometheus? While the Prometheus story *has* successfully replicated itself to the extent that it has retained a general thematic core, or 'mythologem,' for more than two millennia—namely the struggle between Prometheus and Zeus and the idea that Prometheus favours human beings against Zeus's wishes—the copying of this mythologem is far more inexact, and visible changes appear within it over a much shorter period of time, than is generally the case with mutations in biological organisms. Precisely because, in Blumenberg's account, myths originated as oral narratives, they were from the beginning subject to sharp variations that were limited only by the criterion of significance. It is this tendency for variation that differentiates myth from dogma, in which the prohibition of narrative variations enforced by writing and the book is akin to the prohibition of images (WOM, 216; AM, 240).

Thus, while Blumenberg does maintain that variation in myth is always accompanied by a certain level of stability in the basic narrative than can to some extent be replicated (WOM, 34; AM, 40), these processes of variation peculiar to myth must be seen as being subject to wholly different conditions—such as historical contingency and individual whim—than those found in genetic variation. Here Goethe's use of the Prometheus material is a case in point: had he not consulted Hederich's *Complete Mythological Lexicon*, Goethe might not have placed the same level of emphasis upon the image of Prometheus in his workshop, and so might have written a completely different poem. Likewise, when we consider how an individual author 'works on myth,' he or she is not simply the generic representative of a society or of an historical epoch in the way than an animal belongs to an environment. We must also afford an importance to the individual author's subjective and perhaps also *purposive* reaction to the mythic materials. This subjective and at times *conscious* mode of variation within myth reception—the capacity of a particular individual or group to shape a myth in a certain way—would seem to cause stronger alterations in the mythologem than the minute differences between organisms associated with random genetic variation. Thus, to maintain anything like a strict analogy between memetic and genetic variation would be going much too far. At best, this analogy might function as a heuristic device—a guiding metaphor—to aid understanding.

The real explanatory power of *Work on Myth* lies in its capacity to offer a coherent theory of myth reception grounded in a historicist account of human nature, elements of which still remain plausible within the biological sciences. As we have seen in Chapter 4 of this volume, while the time-scale of Alsberg's palaeoanthropology is contradicted by more recent research findings, and while his primal scene concerning the emergence of culture is inherently speculative and neglects to consider that it was gradual cognitive adaptations that in all likelihood gave rise to tool use and technology, the key idea that technology and culture created a buffer between humans and the pressures of natural selection is still credible. If this is so, then human environments are not only natural but also cultural, and significance—the key factor in Blumenberg's account of myth—cannot be reduced to biological factors and must change according to historical context.

Here the difference between Blumenberg's position and the theories of evolutionist literary critics such as Joseph Carroll and Karl Eibl is not a trivial one. Blumenberg may be inclined to accept that some myths may be significant because they contain themes that relate to biological survival and reproductive success—for example, Carroll's argument concerning "mate selection" as the central biological theme in Jane Austen's *Pride and Prejudice*[67]—but his historicist orientation would not allow him simply to *reduce* the significance of myths to a substrate of biological instincts and interests. Similarly, Blumenberg might be likely to agree with Eibl's notion that narrative might have begun as an "in-between-world" (*Zwischenwelt*) that enhanced survival chances by providing fictional realms in which to test out or 'prefigure' possible courses of action, or by offering a source of pleasure that reduced stress.[68] But Blumenberg's account goes well beyond such a position by suggesting that in technologically advanced cultures that are less exposed to the pressures of natural selection, narratives or myths may take on significances that have *absolutely nothing* to do with orientation in the interests of biological survival, and much more to do with their specific historical and cultural contexts.

In Goethe's age, for example, the possession and control of fire had been taken for granted for millennia, and so it had to symbolise something other than bare survival if it was going to retain its significance in the late eighteenth century. It did so because it came to represent artistic creativity within a culture that valorised the notion of aesthetic genius. Admittedly, cultural memory relating to the original survival function of fire may persist in Goethe's "Prometheus," thereby contributing to its overall significance. But this primordial sense of significance is at the same time overlain with aesthetic and theological content specific to late eighteenth-century Germany. In being able to harness and speak to this content, the Prometheus mythologem proved itself to be adaptable to a new historical situation.

There are, therefore, some good reasons for arguing that historical contexts are akin to cultural 'environments' that do work on myths in a way that is *roughly* analogous to the selective work done on organisms by natural selection: drawing out and reinterpreting those components of the mythologem that suit the age. But here an important distinguishing feature of cultural variation and selection must be underlined. It is true that some variations in myths may occur due to inexact copying or because of other capricious factors in processes of cultural inheritance. Yet other variations might—to use the expressions of Robert Boyd and Peter J. Richerson—be consciously improved upon or "guided" by human agents, while also being selected via a "biased" form of transmission, due to their utility, appeal, or cultural prestige within a given cultural setting.[69] Although the theories of Boyd and Richerson relate primarily to the acquisition, modification, and transmission of learned cultural behaviours, they may nonetheless be roughly applicable to our present (aesthetic) example. After learning about the Prometheus mythologem via Hederich's *Lexicon*, Goethe may have altered it precisely because he was aware of what would be significant and appealing within his own particular cultural context. The fact that human agents can, at least to some extent, exert a conscious influence upon *both* cultural variation *and* cultural selection means that their dynamics must be fundamentally different from those of genetic variation and natural selection.

In short: the analogy between natural and cultural selection in *Work on Myth* is by and large metaphorical in its function. But when this metaphor is considered *as a metaphor*—with all of the critical questions and reservations that this approach entails—then it can enable historically nuanced accounts of myth reception that are grounded in a generally plausible account of human nature, while also avoiding evolutionist biological reductionism. For a theory of myth, this is no small achievement.

THE ABSOLUTISM OF TECHNOLOGY

One possible criticism of *Work on Myth* could be that because Blumenberg by and large confines himself to the Prometheus myth at the expense of other myths, he is not able to show why—in comparison with *other* myths—the Prometheus story proved itself to be more adaptable and durable. Nor does he undertake systematic comparisons between contemporaneous versions of the Prometheus story in order decisively to demonstrate why one version triumphed over another in the struggle for significance within a particular historical context. The fact that Blumenberg does use the phrase "survival of the fittest" with respect to the operation of selective forces upon technology and culture certainly creates the expectation that such arguments could also be made with respect to myth (WOM, 165; AM, 183). In the realm of technology, the survival of the fittest associated with cultural selection might seem, at least with respect to archaic *Homo sapiens*, to be more or less self-explanatory: those technologies that furthered biological survival also ended up surviving themselves. This is less transparently the case for culture and myth: first, because they also carry out non-biological functions; and second, because the criterion according to which they are selected—that of significance—does not always correspond with strictly biological interests.

In this context, a comparison with the quasi-Darwinian arguments of Max Müller is illuminating. As we saw in Chapter 2 of this volume, Müller explicitly argues that in languages there is a form of "*Natural Selection*" or "*Natural Elimination*" "between "phonetic cells" or language roots, in which those language roots that demonstrate superior efficiency and utility end up surviving.[70] Blumenberg does not make precisely this argument, since especially within the modern age, significance does not always relate to efficiency and utility, but seems closer to what Richard Dawkins refers to as the "psychological appeal" of successfully replicating memes. Here it is useful to recall one of Blumenberg's clearest definitions of significance: "significance [. . .] arises as a result of the representation of the relationship between the resistance that reality opposes to life and the summoning up of energy that enables one to measure up to it" (WOM, 75; AM, 86). In *Work on Myth*, Blumenberg certainly entertains the possibility that a myth can appear to 'die out' or be 'brought to an end' when the original 'resistance of reality' invoked by earlier versions of the myth has been overcome within the surrounding culture, often as the result of advances in technology. When this happens, the myth must be capable of being reinvented in such a way that it can convincingly present new absolutisms that must in turn be measured up to.

One of the most useful examples of attempting to bring a myth to its end can be found in Blumenberg's discussion of Aristophanes's comedy, *Birds* (see WOM, 322–4; AM, 353–5). In this absurd narrative, the normal relations between gods and humans have been disrupted by the fact that Peisetairos, a disgruntled former resident of Athens, has advised a group of birds to erect a walled kingdom in the clouds in order to block the communication of sacrifices between humans and the gods (lines 180–93). After the detrimental effects of this blockade begin to be felt by the gods, Prometheus arrives on the scene in order to advise Peisetairos on how to bargain with a now depleted and famished Zeus (lines 1496–555). But Aristophanes's Prometheus is certainly not the dauntless rebel of *Prometheus Bound*. He is in fact a rather timid fellow—in Blumenberg's words, a "fainthearted sissy" (*furchtsamer Zimperling*, WOM, 322; AM, 354)—who walks under a parasol so that Zeus will not see him speaking to the enemy. Not much is said of Prometheus's former heroic deeds, though Peisetairos does pay him one compliment: "thanks to you we cook our food!"[71] Here the former absolutism of Zeus has been so radically reduced that a comedic Athenian and a group of birds persuade him to give up not only his sceptre, but also Princess, the woman who oversees all of Zeus's powers. All of this is done with ridiculous ease, after Prometheus provides them with a handy tip-off regarding the powers of Princess (lines 1531–546). It was resistance to the absolutism of Zeus on behalf of humans that had formerly endowed Prometheus with significance, but now all of this has been forgotten, and even Prometheus's most symbolic gift—that of fire—is so taken for granted that it has sunk bank in the self-evidence of the life-world, becoming just another form of everyday technology. Here the Prometheus myth's "loss of identity" is said by Blumenberg to belong to the category of bringing myth to an end (WOM, 323; AM, 355).

When interpreted in relation to phenomenology—which is to say, from the position of the historically situated observer—the category of 'bringing to an end' is similar to the limit-concept (*Grenzbegriff*) of the 'absolutism of reality.' It is a theoretical possibility that can be used to outline a theory, but it is not something that can ever be an object of experience. Just as one would need to have experienced the origin of culture in order to make the claim that Prometheus is *the* definitive myth of myths, so too would one have to stand at the end of time in order to know, definitively, whether or not *a* myth—or myth in general—has been brought to an end:

> the limit concept of work on myth would be to bring myth to an end, to venture the most extreme deformation, which only just allows or almost no longer allows the original figure to be recognized. For the theory of reception this would be the fiction of a final myth, that is, of a myth that fully exploits, and exhausts, the form.
>
> (WOM, 266; AM, 295)

'Bringing to an end' therefore refers to a process through which a former level of significance is reduced by a new cultural context. Here, the theft of fire has ceased to mean what it used to mean, because it has already been in the possession of human beings for so long.

But this does not mean that the significance of a myth cannot be revivified by new potential sources of absolutism. Only if human consciousness experienced no resistance at all to its projects and wishes, and no disruptions at all to its life-worlds, could there be an end to myth. And here Blumenberg introduces Freudian terminology—to be further explored in Chapter 8 of this volume—in order to explain such a purely theoretical state of paradise: "one could describe this point as the absolute dominion of the wish, of the pleasure principle, at the opposite end of a history that must have begun with the absolute dominion of reality, of the reality principle" (WOM, 269; AM, 298). It is the fate of human consciousness always to be situated *between* these two purely theoretical points, which is where the work on myth is carried out.

Even at technologically advanced stages in human history, there is still space for myth to do its work, and perhaps also for captivating Promethean tales to be told. One such narrative can be found in *2001: A Space Odyssey* (1968), the joint creation of Arthur C. Clarke and Stanley Kubrick.[72] Although the film is certainly not a retelling of the Prometheus story, its opening tale of anthropogenesis—appropriately entitled "The Dawn of Man"—definitely displays something resembling Promethean or even 'Alsbergian' elements: when two warring tribes of primates confront one another in episodic battles, the tribe that eventually wins does so by being the first to use animal bones as weapons. This decisive cognitive advantage is depicted as having been communicated to the victorious primates through their encounter with a smooth black monolith that has been placed on earth by a superior alien intelligence.

From this neo-Promethean dawn of technology we are suddenly transported to the year 2001, in which the TMA-1 space mission is investigating a similar monolith found buried on the moon, which appears to be transmitting signals in the direction of Jupiter. Eighteen months later, another mission is despatched in the direction of Jupiter in order to investigate to whom or what this indecipherable information is being sent. The mission's spaceship, the *Discovery*, is under the control of a HAL9000 computer, which appears to have emotions similar to those of human beings, but which is thought to be intellectually superior to the ship's crew and incapable of error. Within the confines of the ship, the HAL9000 is close to omniscient, seeing and hearing everything and even lip-reading private conversations among the crew. But when the HAL9000 undergoes an episode of paranoia, it uses the ship's machinery in order to kill Frank Poole—one of only two conscious crew on the ship—while he is outside the ship repairing its antenna. The HAL9000 then proceeds to murder three more of the crew by switching off their life-support systems while they are in cryogenic hibernation. The only remaining member of the crew, David Bowman, is then locked out of the ship by the HAL9000 while trying to rescue the hapless Poole. Bowman is eventually able, through sheer human cunning, to re-enter the ship and shut the HAL9000 down. In the advanced technological age, the absolutism of the gods has been replaced by the absolutism of technology, embodied by the HAL9000, and the 'significance' of the tale lies in one man's ability to overcome an absolutist threat to human life that has been created by science itself. That this essentially art-house film—with extended set pieces containing very little dialogue—could be such a box-office and critical success can be attributed to its ability to generate a high level of significance within a specific historical context: just one year before the Apollo 11 mission landed the first men on the moon.[73] It is not known whether Hans Blumenberg ever saw this film.

NOTES

1. Jürgen Habermas, "Anthropologie," in *Das Fischer Lexikon Philosophie*, ed. Alwin Diemer and Ivo Frenzel (Frankfurt am Main: Fischer, 1958), 18–35; here: 31.
2. Odo Marquard, "Entlastung vom Absoluten," in *Die Kunst des Überlebens: Nachdenken über Hans Blumenberg*, ed. Franz Josef Wetz and Hermann Timm (Frankfurt am Main: Suhrkamp, 1999), 17–27; here: 21. Blumenberg's other 'Goethe book' is *Goethe zum Beispiel* (Frankfurt am Main: Insel, 1999), a series of shorter texts published from the *Nachlass*.
3. Harold Bloom, *The Anxiety of Influence: A Theory of Poetry* (London: Oxford University Press, 1975).
4. Hans-Georg Gadamer, "Goethe und die Philosophie," in *Gesammelte Werke*, 10 vols. (Tübingen: Mohr, 1985–95), 9:56–71; here: 57.
5. See, for example, Wilhelm Dilthey, *Das Erlebnis und die Dichtung. Lessing, Goethe, Novalis, Hölderlin* (Leipzig: Teubner, 1906); Georg Simmel, *Goethe* (Leipzig: Klinkhardt und Biermann, 1913); Georg Lukács, *Goethe und seine Zeit* (Bern: A. Francke, 1947).

6. Goethe, "Ein Wort für junge Dichter," in *Sämtliche Werke nach Epochen seines Schaffens* (Münchner Ausgabe), ed. Karl Richter, Herbert G. Göpfert, Norbert Miller, and Gerhard Sauder, 21 vols. in 31 (Munich, 1985–98), 18/2:219–20 (hereafter cited as MA followed by volume and page numbers).

7. For further context, see Karl Robert Mandelkow, *Goethe in Deutschland. Rezeptionsgeschichte eines Klassikers*, 2 vols. (Munich: Beck, 1980–9), 1:211–24, in particular: 216–17.

8. Wilhelm Dilthey, "Über die Einbildungskraft der Dichter," in *Zeitschrift für Völkerpsychologie und Sprachwissenschaft* 10 (1878): 42–104, here: 42–3.

9. See Peter Salm, "Wilhelm Scherer," in *Three Modes of Criticism: The Literary Theories of Scherer, Walzel and Staiger* (Cleveland, OH: The Press of Case Western Reserve University, 1968), 5–37; here: 9, 13–18. See also Hans-Harald Müller "Wilhelm Scherer," in *Wissenschaftsgeschichte der Germanistik in Porträts*, ed. Christoph König, Hans-Harald Müller, and Werner Röcker (Berlin: de Gruyter, 2000), 80–94.

10. Wilhelm Scherer, "Goethe Philologie" (1877), in *Aufsätze über Goethe*, ed. Erich Schmidt (Berlin: Weidmann, 1886), 1–27; here: 12, 14.

11. David E. Wellbery, *The Specular Moment: Goethe's Early Lyric and the Beginnings of Romanticism* (Stanford, CA: Stanford University Press, 1996), 445.

12. See Goethe, "Prometheus" (drama fragment), in MA, 1/1: 669–80.

13. This translation is David E. Wellbery's rendering in *The Specular Moment*, 288–90.

14. The original German text is taken from Johann Wolfgang von Goethe, *Sämtliche Werke, Briefe, Tagebücher und Gespräche* (Frankfurter Ausgabe), 2 parts, 40 vols., ed. Hendrik Birus, Dieter Borchmeyer, Karl Eibl, and Wilhelm Voßkamp, et al. (Frankfurt am Main: Deutscher Klassiker Verlag, 1985–2003), 1/1: 203–4 (hereafter cited as FA followed by part, volume and page numbers).

15. See Gerhard Sauder's commentary in MA, 1/1:868-69.

16. Ovid, *Metamorphoses*, trans. David Raeburn (London: Penguin, 2004), 9.

17. Benjamin Hederich, *Gründliches mythologisches Lexikon* (Leipzig: Gleiditsch, 1770), 2090–8; here: 2091–2.

18. See Gehard Sauder's commentary on both pieces in MA, 1/1: 868–72; 983–7. For a more detailed consideration of the relation between the drama fragment and the poem and the reasons why the former is seen to predate the latter, see Christian Zimmermann, *Das Weltbild des jungen Goethe*, vol. 2: *Interpretationen* (Munich: Wilhelm Fink, 1979), 119–26.

19. Goethe, "Prometheus" (drama fragment), in MA, 1/1: 669.

20. Hederich, *Gründliches mythologisches Lexikon*, 2098, also quoted in WOM, 404; AM, 439.

21. See Gerhard Sauder's commentary (MA, 1/1: 869) for the suggestion of Lucian as an influence.

22. Lucian, *Zeus Cathechized*, in *Lucian*, vol. 2, (Loeb Classical Library, No. 54), trans. A. R. Harmon (Cambridge, MA: Harvard University Press, 1915), 59–87.

23. Wellbery, *The Specular Moment*, 295.

24. For an interpretation of this poem in the context of this genius discourse, see Jochen Schmidt, *Geschichte des Genie-Gedankens in der deutschen Literatur, Philosophie und Politik, 1750–1945*, 2 vols. (Darmstadt: Wissenschaftliche Buchgesellschaft, 1985), 1:254–69.

25. Shaftesbury, *Soliloquy: Or, Advice to an Author* (London: John Morphew, 1710), 55.

26. See Karl Eibl's commentary in FA, 1/1: 922–8.

27. For a brief overview of the controversy, see Frederick Beiser, "The Limits of Enlightenment," in *A New History of German Literature*, ed. David E. Wellbery, Judith Ryan, et al. (Cambridge, MA: Harvard University Press, 2004), 418–24.

28. Friedrich Heinrich Jacobi, *Über die Lehre des Spinoza in Briefen an den Herrn Moses Mendelssohn* (Breslau: Löwe, 1785), reprinted in *Die Hauptschriften zum Pantheismusstreit zwischen Jacobi und Mendelssohn*, ed. Heinrich Scholz (Berlin: Reuther and Reichard, 1916); references are to the newer reprinted edition of Scholz's edition, ed. Wolfgang Erich Müller (Waltrop: Hartmut Spenner, 2004), 45–282; here: 77.

29. In Jacobi's words: "the correctly understood teachings of Spinoza do not permit any kind of religion," in *Über die Lehre des Spinoza*, 173.

30. Benedict de Spinoza, *Ethics*, ed. and trans. Edwin Curley (Harmondsworth, UK: Penguin, 1996), 16.

31. Eibl in FA, 1/1:923.

32. See Eibl's commentary in FA, 1/1:923; see also Blumenberg's discussion in WOM, 418; AM, 455.

33. Moses Mendelssohn, *An die Freunde Lessings, Ein Anhang zu Herrn Jacobi, Briefwechsel über die Lehre des Spinoza* (Berlin: Voß, 1786), reprinted in *Die Hauptschriften zum Pantheismusstreit*, 283–325; here: 293.

34. See the commentary in FA, 1/14: 1002–3.

35. Goethe, *From My Life, Poetry and Truth, Parts One to Three*, trans. Robert R. Heitner, notes by Thomas P. Saine, *Goethe's Collected Works*, vol. 4 (New York: Suhrkamp, 1987), 469 (translation altered); Goethe, *Dichtung und Wahrheit*, in FA, 1/14: 694–6.

36. Goethe to Ernst Theodor Langer, January 17, 1769, in FA, 2/1: 148–50; here: 150; also quoted by Blumenberg in WOM, 406; AM, 441.

37. For an overview, see Angus Nicholls, *Goethe's Concept of the Daemonic: After the Ancients* (Rochester, NY: Camden House, 2006), 4–10.

38. H. G. Liddell and R. Scott, *A Greek-English Lexicon*, 9th ed., ed. Sir Henry Stuart Jones and Roderick McKenzie (Oxford: Oxford University Press, 1996), 365–6.

39. See Jane Ellen Harrison, *Prolegomena to the Study of Greek Religion* (Cambridge: Cambridge University Press, 1908), 587.

40. See Heraclitus, *Fragments*, trans. T. M. Robinson (Toronto: University of Toronto Press, 1987), fragment 119, p. 69.

41. The function of the *daimonion* has a long reception history, which is summarised in Nicholls, *Goethe's Concept of the Daemonic*, 57–64.

42. Goethe, *From My Life, Poetry and Truth, Part Four*, trans. Robert R. Heitner, notes by Thomas P. Saine, *Goethe's Collected Works*, vol. 5 (New York: Suhrkamp, 1987), 597; Goethe, *Dichtung und Wahrheit*, in FA, 1/14: 839–40.

43. See the discussion in Nicholls, *Goethe's Concept of the Daemonic*, 77–105. For a broader interpretation and critique of Blumenberg on the daemonic in Goethe, see also Angus Nicholls, "The Goethe Complex: Hans Blumenberg on *das Dämonische*," in *Das Dämonische: Schicksale einer Kategorie der Zweideutigkeit nach Goethe*, ed. Lars Friedrich, Eva Geulen, and Kirk Wetters (Munich: Fink, 2014), 97–119.

44. Goethe "Urworte. Orphisch," in FA, 1/20: 491–7; here: 492.

45. From Blumenberg's perspective, whether Goethe in fact made such statements, or whether they are embellished in Eckermann's recollection, is beside the point: either way we are dealing with 'Goethe,' the author as a borderline 'mythical' figure.

46. See Goethe to Eckermann, December 6, 1829, in FA, 2/12:364; and Goethe to Eckermann, March 11, 1828, in FA, 2/12:656. On this notion of *entelechy* and Goethe's reception of it, see Nicholls, *Goethe's Concept of the Daemonic*, 66–8, 93–4, 139, 241–2, 250–1.

47. Goethe to Eckermann, December 6, 1829, in FA, 2/12:364.
48. Goethe to Eckermann, March 11, 1828, in FA, 2/12: 651.
49. Goethe, "Unterredung mit Napoleon," in *Werke* (Hamburger Ausgabe), ed. Erich Trunz, 14 vols. (Munich: Deutscher Taschenbuch Verlag, 2000), 10:543–7; here: 546.
50. Goethe to Eckermann, March 2, 1831, in FA, 2/12:455.
51. Goethe to Eckermann, March 11, 1823, in FA, 2/12: 660
52. Goethe to Eckermann, February 10, 1830, in FA, 2/12:382.
53. Goethe to Eckermann, March 11, 1828, in FA, 2/12:455.
54. Here I have altered Robert Wallace's translation of the terms *das Dämonische* and *Dämon*, to 'the daemonic' and 'daemon' (as opposed to 'the demonic' and 'demon'). On the question of translating these terms from German into English, see Nicholls, *Goethe's Concept of the Daemonic*, 12–15.
55. On the role of rhapsodes see Andrew Ford, "The Classical Definition of ΡΑΨΩΙΔΙΑ," *Classical Philology* 83, no. 4 (1988): 300–7.
56. Giambattista Vico, *The New Science*, trans. Thomas Goddard Bergin and Max Harold Fisch (Ithaca, NY: Cornell University Press, 1948), §854 (p. 285); "stitcher-together" is taken to be the earliest meaning of the term rhapsode, and suggests a culture in which there was not a clear distinction between creative authorship and retelling of earlier tales; see Ford, "The Classical Definition of ΡΑΨΩΙΔΙΑ," 300–1.
57. See Andrew Ford, *The Origins of Criticism: Literary Culture and Poetic Theory in Classical Greece* (Princeton, NJ: Princeton University Press, 2002), in general: 272–93; these quotes: 273, 280.
58. Ford, *The Origins of Criticism*, 282–6.
59. One example mentioned in this context by Stephen Shennan is the replacement of snowshoes with snowmobiles among the Cree of northern Canada. See Stephen Shennan, *Genes, Memes and Human History* (London: Thames and Hudson, 2002), 56–7.
60. See Richard Dawkins, *The Selfish Gene*, 2nd ed. (1976; Oxford: Oxford University Press, 1989), 21–4; and *The Extended Phenotype: The Gene as a Unit of Selection* (Oxford: W.H. Freeman, 1982), 112.
61. See Richard Dawkins, *The God Delusion* (Boston, MA: Houghton Mifflin, 2006), 161–207.
62. Daniel Dennett, *Darwin's Dangerous Idea* (London: Allen Lane, 1995), 344, 348–9.
63. See Dawkins, *The Extended Phenotype*, 112; Dennett, *Darwin's Dangerous Idea*, 352–69.
64. W. G. Runciman, *The Theory of Cultural and Social Selection* (Cambridge: Cambridge University Press, 2009), 109, 92, 112.
65. See Maurice Bloch, "A Well-Disposed Social Anthropologist's Problems with Memes," in *Darwinizing Culture: The Status of Memetics as a Science*, ed. Robert Aunger (Oxford: Oxford University Press, 2000), 189–203; here: 192–4; see also Peter J. Richerson and Robert Boyd, *Not by Genes Alone: How Culture Transformed Human Evolution* (Chicago: University of Chicago Press, 2005), 63, 81–2.
66. For debates in this field, see the papers in Aunger, ed., *Darwinizing Culture: The Status of Memetics as a Science*. See also Runciman, *The Theory of Cultural and Social Selection*, 92–139.
67. Joseph Carroll, "Human Nature and Literary Meaning," in *The Literary Animal: Evolution and the Nature of Narrative*, ed. Jonathan Gottschall and David Sloan Wilson (Evanston, IL: Northwestern University Press, 2005), 76–106; here: 98.
68. See Karl Eibl, *Kultur als Zwischenwelt: Eine evolutionsbiologische Perspektive* (Frankfurt am Main: Suhrkamp, 2009). On the notion of 'prefiguration' see Chapter 8 of this volume.

69. On the notion of "guided" variation and "biased" transmission in cultural selection, see Robert Boyd and Peter J. Richerson, *Culture and the Evolutionary Process* (Chicago, IL: University of Chicago Press, 1985), 94–7, 133–7; and Richerson and Boyd, *Not by Genes Alone*, 66–72, 116.
70. Friedrich Max Müller *Lectures on the Science of Language, Second Series* (London: Longmans, Green and Co., 1864), 305–6; see also Müller's "Lectures on Mr. Darwin's Philosophy of Language, Third Lecture," in *Fraser's Magazine* [London] July (1873): 1–24; here: 2–3.
71. Aristophanes, *Birds and Other Plays*, ed. and trans. Stephen Halliwell (Oxford: Oxford University Press, 1998), 71.
72. Stanley Kubrick, dir., *2001: A Space Odyssey*, screenplay by Stanley Kubrick, and Arthur C. Clarke, (Los Angeles: Warner Bros. Pictures, 1968), motion picture. See also Arthur C. Clarke's novel of the same name (New York: New American Library, 1968), which contains slightly different plot elements to the film.
73. By 1972, *2001: A Space Odyssey* was ranked within the top twenty highest grossing films ever in the United States; in 2002, a *Sight & Sound* survey of around 150 international film critics listed *2001: A Space Odyssey* as the sixth best film of all time. See Peter Krämer, *2001: A Space Odyssey* (BFI Film Classics) (London: Palgrave Macmillan, 2010), 93, 10.

7 'After the Work on Myth'
The Political Reception of *Work on Myth*

In an undated one-page text from the *Nachlass* that appears to be a thought experiment of the 1980s or 1990s,[1] Hans Blumenberg addresses a subject that was not systematically treated in *Work on Myth*: that of political myth. That this text is explicitly political is revealed by its title: "No Myth of the Twentieth Century" ("Kein Mythos des XX. Jahrhunderts") which invokes Alfred Rosenberg's *Myth of the Twentieth Century* (*Mythus des 20. Jahrhunderts*, 1930). Blumenberg regards this would-be founding mythological text of National Socialism as having been a "glaring failure" (*eklatanter Mißerfolg*, KMZ), and the reasons for this will be explored in Chapter 8 of this volume. For now, it is worthwhile examining the statement with which he opens this text:

> That there is, after the work on myth, never the end of myth, does not have to be accounted for or proven by the continued production of mythical models. No less illuminating and demonstrative is the persistent bidding for the vacant position of myths, for the status and function of the mythical.
>
> (KMZ)[2]

This text comes 'after the work on myth' in two senses. First, it appears to be the late reflection of a thinker who rarely made political questions an explicit feature of his theory of myth, but for whom the political is nevertheless often a latent presence. In other words, it may be a case of Blumenberg dealing with the unfinished political business of *Work on Myth* in what is, for him, an unusually direct fashion. Second, the text addresses, once again, the questions as to whether there can in fact be an end to myth, whether myth can be brought to an end, or in what guises myth, or perhaps the manufactured simulacra of myth, persisted in the twentieth century.

Blumenberg's answer to these questions is ambiguous: the fact that "mythical models" (*mythische Muster*) continue to be produced does not necessarily mean that they are in fact successful in creating new myths. A *Muster* is a merely a formal design that may or may not be put into effect or activated, and in the case of myth, the question of 'activation' is determined not by the producers of a would-be myth but by its reception. Blumenberg's use of the term *Produktion* might also suggest that these models are consciously manufactured in order to conjure up significance, thereby making a bid for the vacant positions of earlier myths that may have lost their ability to captivate audiences within the surrounding culture. Here, of course, the implication is that not all such bids are successful—that not all would-be myths end up producing significance. But even if they fail to produce significance, this failure would still amount to the continuation of the work on myth: here 'work' is still being done in order to fill or reoccupy an empty space, regardless of whether it is effective or not.

The tenor of this text is, then, in part ironic. Precisely because any theory of myth will be marked by the finitude of its own historicity, it can never be written from the perspective of an 'after,' from the *terminus ad quem*. When seen in these terms, the phrase 'after the work on myth' would appear to refer to the apparent persistence of myth in a period—that of the early to mid-twentieth century—in which the most important theoretical positions were at least *thought* to have been occupied by rational, as opposed to mythical, arguments. The optimistic view that there can be an 'after' to the work on myth would accordingly have to be seen as a symptom of the *mythos* to *logos* narrative that Blumenberg so trenchantly criticises in *Work on Myth*.

This *Nachlass* fragment also suggests the lineaments, if not the finer details, of what might be called a theory of political myth: of mythical models made to order for political propaganda. The question as to whether Blumenberg *does* elaborate something resembling a theory of political myth, or whether he in fact neglected the question of political myth altogether, has been central to the reception of *Work on Myth*. As will be discussed here, through an analysis of correspondence recently published from Blumenberg's *Nachlass*, Blumenberg did in fact directly engage with a topic that was treated at length by Ernst Cassirer in *The Myth of the State*: the role played by myth in National Socialism. Indeed, this question is already obliquely addressed in *Work on Myth*, while also being more explicitly considered in parts of the *Work on Myth* manuscripts that Blumenberg chose, in the end, not to publish, and that will be examined in Chapter 8 of this volume. But now, in order to understand how and why Blumenberg addressed the subject of political myth, it will be necessary to examine his position within the landscape of post-war philosophy in West Germany.

PHILOSOPHY IN THE *BUNDESREPUBLIK*

It has been said of Blumenberg that he neither emerged from, nor himself founded, a particular philosophical 'school.'[3] While the latter part of this formulation is true, the former proposition is not strictly correct. If the phenomenology of Edmund Husserl can be characterised as a philosophical school or movement, then it can be claimed that Blumenberg was member of this school for his entire academic career, albeit an unorthodox and at times even heretical member. So too were his closest academic mentors during his years at Kiel: Ludwig Landgrebe (1902–91) had been an assistant to Husserl in Freiburg between 1923 and 1927, while Walter Bröcker (1902–92) wrote his doctorate in Marburg under Martin Heidegger before later working as Heidegger's assistant at Freiburg. In Landgrebe and Bröcker, Blumenberg was thus exposed to one former student of phenomenology's founding father, and to a former protégé of phenomenology's most iconoclastic and controversial child.

Just eighteen years separated the birth of Blumenberg (1920) from that of Landgrebe and Bröcker (1902), yet the biographical significance of these years should not be underestimated. While Landgrebe (PhD, 1927; *Habilitation* 1935) and Bröcker (PhD 1928; *Habilitation*, 1934) were both old enough to have completed their studies before 1939, Blumenberg belonged to a generation whose higher education was interrupted by the Second World War. Here a key biographical difference between Landgrebe and Bröcker must have stood out to Blumenberg. Having a Jewish wife and having studied under the Jewish Professor Edmund Husserl, Landgrebe had been unable to establish himself as a philosopher under National Socialism;[4] while Bröcker—who had been a member of both the paramilitary *Sturmabteilung* (SA) of the National Socialist Party (NSDAP) between 1933 and 1935, and of the NSDAP itself from 1940–5—rose from being Professor (in 1941) to Dean (in 1942) at the University of Rostock, before being appointed as Professor at Kiel in 1948.[5]

How did colleagues work together and deal with such disturbing injustices during the immediate post-war years? Given Blumenberg's reticence on this subject, his interpretation of 1933–45 can, at best, be reconstructed only in a speculative way. A case in point can be found in the obituary that Blumenberg wrote in 1966 for Erich Rothacker.[6] As Professor of philosophy at Bonn University from 1928, Rothacker publicly declared his support for Hitler as early as 1932, was a member of the NSDAP from 1933 until the end of the war, and during early 1933 was leader of the *Volksbildung* (peoples' education) section of the National Socialist Ministry for Peoples' Education and Propaganda (*Reichsministerium für Volksaufklärung und Propaganda*), before Joseph Goebbels fired him for unknown reasons in April 1933.[7] Despite this apparent falling out with the regime, Rothacker is said to have acted as a mediator between the German Student Organisation (*Deutsche Studentenschaft*) and Propaganda Minister Goebbels in the organisation of the National Socialist book burnings of May 1933.[8]

Volker Böhnigk has argued that Rothacker's fascination with National Socialism was not just confined to the early years of the regime, and can be found in the explicit links that he draws between race (*Rasse*) and the spirit of the people (*Volksgeist*) in his two main works of cultural anthropology:

Philosophy of History (*Geschichtsphilosophie*, 1934) and *Problems of Cultural Anthropology* (*Probleme der Kulturanthropologie*, 1942).[9] Others contend that Rothacker either was a convinced anti-Semite and National Socialist whose attempts to influence the regime in its early years failed,[10] or that he merely integrated a racial element into his early cultural anthropology in order to find favour with the regime, before later criticising some of its key ideologies and especially its academic politics.[11] Whatever the level of Rothacker's real commitment to the NSDAP might have been, he was suspended from all university duties from April 1945 until the winter semester of 1946–7. The decision to reinstate him was in part based on the fact that some of Rothacker's lectures had aroused the suspicions of the Gestapo, that he had publicly criticised the NSDAP in its later phases, and that he had retained contact with Jewish academics and had cited them in his works as late as 1941.[12] After the war, Rothacker would go on to teach two of the most important post-war German philosophers: Karl-Otto Apel (1922–) and Jürgen Habermas (1929–), before retiring in 1956.

Blumenberg's obituary presents Rothacker as a conservative defender of the Humboldtian model of the university, while remaining by and large silent about his activities between 1933 and 1945. Its only possible mention of Rothacker's political past can be found in Blumenberg's brief discussion of what Rothacker apparently referred to as the "pre-scientific virtue" of "curiosity." According to Blumenberg, Rothacker himself "embodied" (*verkörpert*) this pre-rational form of curiosity, which at times allowed him to "forget" the "systematics of his evaluations." [13] Here Blumenberg may be implying that it was precisely Rothacker's 'curiosity' that had undermined his political judgement. The fact that Rothacker had played a key role in the careers of some extremely important post-war German philosophers— including some associated with the 'left'—is apparently alluded to by a text from Blumenberg's *Nachlass* entitled "A Letter Still to be Written," in which he addresses the case of Rothacker in a typically indirect fashion, through the form of a fictional letter:

> You wrote your dissertation under E.R., and so attained academic legitimacy.
> Did you ever ask about all the things that he did between 1933 and 1945?
> I was a friend of E.R.'s. I liked him. I have asked about all of the things that he did between 1933 and 1945. Despite this I remained friends with him until his death.
> I did not want to be, what I did not need to be: the last judgement (*das Weltgericht*).[14]

Who is the addressee of this letter? Is it Rothacker's most prominent former doctoral student, Jürgen Habermas? And does this fragment directly express Blumenberg's own reluctance to make retrospective moral judgements concerning Rothacker's past? The text provides us with no clear answers to these questions, and resists any singular interpretation. The case of Rothacker is raised here not to make retrospective pronouncements about Blumenberg's own political judgement, but simply to underline the deeply ambivalent situation with which he was confronted during the immediate post-war years: a situation in which many of Blumenberg's most significant philosophical colleagues had collaborated, to a greater or lesser extent, with the regime that had so persecuted him. For his part, Blumenberg was also well aware that given his biography, his mere presence in post-war German philosophy must have been difficult precisely for those who did not want to be reminded of their own recent political histories.[15]

In this respect, Rothacker was far from being an isolated case. Although the Poetics and Hermeneutics group conceived of itself as a project of the post-war generation of scholars—notably not inviting the older doyen of hermeneutics, Hans-Georg Gadamer (1900–2002) to join its ranks—some of its founding members (such as Hans Robert Jauss and Clemens Heselhaus) had complicated political histories.[16] Among those figures with whom Blumenberg had lively correspondences, Jauss had been a member of the paramilitary Waffen SS (although this was not publicly known until the 1980s),[17] while Heselhaus joined the NSDAP in 1937 before working as a teacher of German in Italy for the NSDAP *Auslandsorganisation* (foreign organisation).[18] Helmut Schelsky, with whom Blumenberg worked on the commission that founded the University of Bielefeld, was an NSDAP member from 1937 onwards, and was at times given to making troubling and even offensive statements in favour of the National Socialist state.[19] Despite this, he was seen as being too liberal by one of the chief National Socialist philosophers: Alfred Baeumler (1887–1968).[20] Another important correspondent—Joachim Ritter, father of Blumenberg's later interlocutor Henning Ritter and Blumenberg's predecessor at Münster—had initially been watched over by the National Socialist authorities on account of his early interest in Marxism, his having studied under the Jewish Professor Ernst Cassirer, and because his first wife (who died in 1928) was Jewish. Ritter later signed the "Loyalty Oath" of German Professors to Adolf Hitler and the National Socialist State in 1933.[21] He then joined the NSDAP in 1937, probably to make himself employable as a philosopher, though there is no evidence of him having taken on the racialist ideologies of National Socialism.[22] Gadamer, with whom Blumenberg had worked in the Senate Commission for the History of Concepts, had been seen as politically indifferent by the National Socialist authorities and never joined the NSDAP, though he did sign the aforementioned "Loyalty Oath" of German Professors to Adolf Hitler, as well as attending an NSDAP education camp in 1935, both of which probably helped him to gain his first Professorial post in Leipzig in 1939.[23]

The legacy of National Socialism was thus a latent presence in the biographies of many key figures in post-war German philosophy, and given

Blumenberg's own experiences between 1933 and 1945, it is hardly surprising that this latency also comes to expression in his writings. In works published during Blumenberg's lifetime, these political moments are usually only fleeting and indirect, but in certain works from the *Nachlass* to be investigated in Chapter 8 of this volume, the relation between politics and myth becomes an explicit topic of examination.

PROFESSING LIBERAL CONSERVATISM

As Chiara Bottici has pointed out, Hans Blumenberg is not an explicitly political philosopher and his theory of myth is not an explicitly political theory. Unlike Ernst Cassirer's *Myth of the State* (1946), Blumenberg's *Work on Myth* makes no systematic attempt to deal with myth as a political or sociological phenomenon. Yet in its essential claim that myths are continually 'worked on' or adapted in order to meet the needs of new historical and cultural contexts, *Work on Myth* offers, according to Bottici, an "ideal platform for a theory of political myth," in that it shows how myths may function in particular political situations.[24] *Work on Myth*, while not elaborating an explicit theory of political myth, is certainly characterised by distinctive political moments, such as the following one in which Blumenberg addresses the student protests of 1968:

> When it was announced from the walls during May 1968 in Paris that the imagination should and now would come to power, it was immediately clear to the late grandchildren of aesthetic Idealism that this guaranteed that everything would become different and thus better. No one thought they needed to ask—no one would have been permitted to ask—what the imagination had to offer, what it had ever offered [. . .] No imagination could have invented what ethnology and cultural anthropology have collected in the way of regulations of existence, world interpretations, forms of life, classifications, ornaments, and insignia. All of this is the product of a process of selection that has been at work for a long time, and in that respect, in this analogy to the mechanism of evolution, approaches the stupendous variety and the convincingness of the forms of nature itself. No aesthetic theory would credit the imagination with having invented what has been developed in human history in the way of institutions.
>
> (WOM, 161–2; AM, 179–80)

Blumenberg's use of the word 'institutions' in this passage would have had a particular resonance in Germany upon the publication of *Work on Myth* in 1979, bringing to mind the theory of institutions outlined by Arnold Gehlen. A brief examination of Gehlen's theory of institutions and its later reception in post-war West German thought will provide the necessary context through which to understand Blumenberg's political argument in *Work on Myth*.

In post-war Germany, Gehlen was a tarnished figure, having joined the NSDAP in May 1933, having signed the "Loyalty Oath" of Professors to Adolf Hitler, and having allegedly intended to write a philosophy of National Socialism during the early 1930s.[25] Already during the early phases of Hitler's regime, Gehlen was elaborating a conservative theory of institutions that found favour with some party officials,[26] and versions of this theory were in turn elaborated, first in Gehlen's *Man* (1940), and later in *Primal Man and Late Culture* (1956). Gehlen's very broad notion of primordial institutions as "systems of shared habits,"[27] which was primarily derived from the analysis of 'primitive' societies, could scarcely be applied to the concrete political institutions of the new *Bundesrepublik*. Yet after the war, Gehlen's theory of institutions continued to exert an at least latent influence in West Germany. Jens Hacke has shown the extent to which liberal conservative philosophers such as Joachim Ritter (1903–74), Helmut Schelsky (1921–84), Hermann Lübbe (1926–) and Odo Marquard (1928–)—all of whom were important colleagues of Blumenberg during the 1960s—elaborated revised versions of Gehlen's theory of institutions.[28] Hacke makes a convincing case that Gehlen's pessimistic view of human beings as 'creatures of deficiency' places him in a line of conservative political philosophers such as Thomas Hobbes and Edmund Burke. While Hobbes sees the solution to human weaknesses and deficiencies as being the transferral of individual rights into the hands of the absolute sovereign, and while Burke urges the continuation of ancestral traditions as a bulwark against unfounded and potentially dangerous philosophical speculation, Gehlen argues for a continuity of rigid institutions as a means of channelling undetermined human affects.[29]

It is this notion of the continuity, stability and pragmatism of institutions that reappears, albeit under decidedly more liberal guises, in the writings of Ritter, Schelsky, and Marquard. Invoking the political philosophy of Aristotle, Ritter associates habits (*Gewohnheiten*) and institutions with the classical conception of *ethos*: the organic cultural practices, including ethical mores, of a particular group associated with a particular locale.[30] For Aristotle, institutions arise from human nature, but this does not mean that they are 'fixed' or beyond critique. It is precisely the purpose of the *polis*, according to Ritter's account of Aristotle, to expose institutions to reflection and critique, but with the realisation that any such discourse is always already inscribed by pre-existing institutional structures. For Ritter, human life, which also means ethical life and political discourse, would literally be impossible without institutions.[31] Helmut Schelsky—who was a former student of Gehlen in Leipzig and whom Hacke describes as the most important critic of Gehlen's theory of institutions[32]—was, like Ritter, troubled by Gehlen's notion that institutions are pre-reflective, fixed and constitutive of legal regulations rather than alterable through juridical interventions. If obedience to pre-existing institutions takes place prior to any rational analysis, then this would obviate one of the central processes of a liberal democracy, which is continually to inquire into the legitimacy and rationality of its institutional structures. Schelsky attributes this shortcoming in Gehlen's theory of institutions to Gehlen's preoccupation with practices found in so-called primitive cultures that were purportedly not subject to social change.[33] In Schelsky's view, the liberal democratic demand that institutions should be capable of open and rational self-reform entails, contra Gehlen, the very institutionalisation of such processes of reflection and their enshrinement in law.[34]

But these 'liberal' revisions of Gehlen did not go far enough for some. Jürgen Habermas has argued that this defence of institutions—insofar as it would rather optimistically require them to be self-regulating and self-transforming independently of external critique—is "hopelessly reactionary" and amounts only to a non-solution.[35] Odo Marquard, who in the early 1970s saw himself as maintaining a sceptical position somewhere in between Gehlen's notion of fixed or 'essential' human deficiencies on the one hand and the Frankfurt School's notion of an historically and culturally conditioned humanity capable of political self-emancipation on the other,[36] attempts a further liberal conservative refinement of Gehlen's theory of institutions. It is not enough, according to Marquard, for institutions simply to relieve (*entlasten*) humans from what Gehlen calls the pressure to decide (*Entscheidungsdruck*). They must also, and from the beginning, be constituted by normative content insofar as they offer relief to all humans and not just the chosen few.[37] The difficulty in deciding what exactly amounts to 'normative content' would presumably lead to the kinds of 'ideological' disputes that Gehlen's authoritarianism of institutions seeks to avoid. In response to this problem, Marquard—who sees Gehlen's theory of institutions, and especially the relief (*Entlastung*) that they provide, as being central to his own notion of compensation (*Kompensation*)[38]—proposes that liberal democracies must offer a 'polytheism' of myths and institutions that correct and limit one another.[39] The human being, now defined as the *homo compensator* who is confronted by the finitude of life, resorts to scepticism as the "amelioration of finitude through plurality," by way of recourse to a variety of "convictions, stories, myths, sacred powers, and political formations."[40]

In an extremely influential essay on Blumenberg, Marquard also invokes Gehlen's notion of *Entlastung* in order to define what he regards as the "foundational idea" (*Grundgedanke*) that runs through all of Blumenberg's works: "relief from the absolute" (*Entlastung vom Absoluten*). "Humans," according to Marquard's account of Blumenberg, "cannot endure the absolute."[41] Their way of coping with absolute threats to their survival, whether those posed by the arbitrary powers of the gods or those posed by the terrifyingly destructive forces of nature, is to achieve both a physical and a psychological distance from them. Although Marquard does not mention the name of Arnold Gehlen in this essay, to any audience reasonably well versed in post-war German philosophy, the importance of Gehlen for Blumenberg's thought would have been more than apparent. Blumenberg expresses his theoretical interest in Gehlen's notion of the human being as a 'creature of deficiencies' as early as 1951,[42] and again in the first (1966) edition of the *Legitimacy of the Modern Age*,[43] but he does not undertake an explicit engagement with 'philosophical anthropology' until the years immediately following 1968, when a programmatic essay (see AAR) was published in 1971.

This essay—which, as we shall see, might in some respects also be seen as undertaking a dialogue with the thought of Habermas—went some way to making Blumenberg's philosophical-political position in the *Bundesrepublik* clear, and this clarification also included a clear rejection of what he refers to as Gehlen's "absolutism of institutions" (AAR, 439; WWL, 115). As the ironic tone of the previous long quotation from *Work on Myth* demonstrates, Blumenberg saw the 1968 student movement as a vainglorious attempt to surmount the validity of long-standing institutions through a tendentious invocation of the political imagination. Blumenberg's defence of institutions does not countenance the naked authoritarianism of Gehlen's notion of pre-reflective obedience to "command-systems" (*Führungssysteme*) as elaborated in the early editions of *Man*.[44] But he does—in a similar way to Ritter, Schelsky, and Marquard—outline rules within which any debate about institutions should be framed:

> Arguments of the kind that assert that something can no longer be accepted because it has already been accepted for a very long time without examination do not have the rational plausibility that is granted to them at times. What the heading 'institutions' covers is, above all, a distribution of burdens of proof. Where an institution exists, the question of its rational foundation is not, of itself, urgent, and the burden of proof always lies on the person who objects to the arrangement the institution carries with it.
>
> (WOM, 166; AM, 184)

By dint of their very survival over epochs, longstanding institutions have, in Blumenberg's view, demonstrated their utility in meeting human needs. And even when they might seem to be only antiquated obstructions—such as the city gate (*Holstentor*) in Blumenberg's hometown of Lübeck, notorious for holding up traffic—they are preserved because human beings find in them a shared identity that provides them with orientation. Directly addressing the supposedly post-bourgeois student protesters (*die Nachbürgerlichen*) in a short discussion of this Lübeck landmark, Blumenberg offers a defence of cultural preservation as a form of "bourgeois historicism" (*bürgerlicher Historismus*).[45] In a similar way, myths are also—in Gehlen's broad sense of "systems of shared habits"—longstanding institutions. The question as to whether this account of myth could ever be in a position to address the calculated use of myth by political regimes would become a central issue in the reception of Work on Myth. And the fact that Blumenberg's theory of myth at least seemed to be reliant on the account of human nature outlined by Gehlen may also have suggested that it was essentially conservative it its political orientation.

In fact, it would be no exaggeration to suggest that by the late 1960s and the early 1970s, Gehlen had become the chief public opponent of the German philosophical left, represented first and foremost by the Frankfurt School and in particular by the writings of Adorno and Habermas. The conservatism of Gehlen's 'pre-reflexive' notion of institutions was anathema to a group of scholars who believed that reflection and critique were the essence of any progressive theory of society. This is why Habermas, in his review of Primal Man and Late Culture written in 1956, had accused Gehlen of countenancing the "liquidation" of the individual for sake of maintaining strong institutions.[46] And in response to Gehlen's renewed (post 1968) defence of institutions against what he regarded as the hypertrophied humanitarianism of the left—an unashamedly polemical argument outlined by Gehlen in Morality and Hypermorality (Moral und Hypermoral, 1969)[47]—Habermas accused Gehlen of proposing a return to "the ethos of great and opaque institutions." Alluding to the legacy of National Socialism, Habermas observed that: "during the time at which one could still nourish illusions concerning such recommendations, one called this a revolution from the right."[48] By now the reverberations of this debate were reaching the mainstream press, appearing in the pages of the popular news weekly Der Spiegel in 1970. Here the supposed archenemies of German philosophy were helpfully caricatured for the reading public: "the Marxist who does not take anthropology seriously" (Habermas), and "the anthropologist who does not want to know anything about Marx" (Gehlen).[49]

The reality of the situation was, of course, much more complicated than that. Habermas took philosophical anthropology very seriously indeed, to the extent that in 1958, while he was still Adorno's assistant and not yet a Professor in his own right, his article on "Anthropologie" written for a prominent philosophical lexicon, devoted significant attention to the ideas of Scheler, Plessner, Gehlen, and especially Rothacker.[50] As a former doctoral student of Rothacker, Habermas was well placed to assess the merits and shortcomings of philosophical anthropology. He begins his article by identifying the key arguments of Schelsky, Plessner, and Gehlen: the human being is, by comparison with animals, deficient or weak in terms of its lack of predetermined instincts and is therefore seen as being 'open,' 'unspecialised,' and 'eccentric' in its orientation. This deficiency of instincts is compensated for by human action (Handeln), which finds its expression in work, technology, culture, and social organisation. Habermas points out that according to Gehlen, this very openness of the human senses to the world is accompanied by a "flood of stimuli" (Reizüberflutung), of which the human being must be "relieved" (entlastet). The orienting characteristics of human culture—symbols, myths, and institutions—provide relief from this over-stimulation and make an ordered life possible.[51]

The problem with this approach, according to Habermas, is that while some proponents of philosophical anthropology (such as Scheler, Plessner, and Gehlen) have the tendency to make ahistorical claims about the "essence of the human being,"[52] others (namely, Rothacker) have shown that the human being is foremost an historical, cultural, and societal being. Rothacker, in Habermas's account, was successful in refining the arguments of Uexküll. It is not the case that human beings are simply open to the world, while animals are attuned to specific environmental habitats and signals; rather, humans create their own specific cultural environments, in which certain features are selectively endowed with more significance than others. Thus, to speak of *the* human being is just as reductive as speaking of *the* human language.[53] The fact that "man has history and only becomes what he is by being historical" is therefore a "disconcerting fact for an anthropology that deals with the 'nature' of the human being, with what all human beings have in common." And it is this very tendency of philosophical anthropology to proceed "ontologically," to ascribe to human beings an ahistorical essence, which leads to what Habermas refers to as the dogmatism of Gehlen's politically dangerous theory of institutions.[54] In this respect, Rothacker's version of philosophical anthropology (renamed as cultural anthropology or *Kulturanthropologie* in light of his important book of 1942, notably cited here by Habermas it its post-war edition of 1948),[55] is seen by Habermas as opening the way to a more differentiated and self-reflexive approach to human cultures, insofar as it situates them in their respective historical and societal contexts. And here Habermas reminds the proponents of philosophical anthropology that they too are historically and socially situated, to the extent that their own theories concerning the 'essence of the human being' may in fact be inscribed by contemporary political agendas. In short: according to Habermas, philosophical anthropology will only become truly "critical" (*kritisch*: perhaps *the* keyword of the Frankfurt School) when it enters into dialogue with a "theory of society."[56]

According to Joachim Fischer, Habermas's article is shot through with a "logic of destruction," its central aim being the self-unravelling of philosophical anthropology through an internal critique inspired by Rothacker.[57] Whether this profound and in many ways accurate critique, combined with the Gehlen-Habermas polemics arising from 1968, inspired Blumenberg openly to engage with philosophical anthropology in the early 1970s remains an open question. In his highly anecdotal account of his years working as Blumenberg's assistant at Gießen, Ferdinand Fellmann, writes that "Blumenberg's intellectual profile cannot be grasped without a consideration of his relation to Jürgen Habermas." Together with Dieter Henrich and Jacob Taubes, Blumenberg and Habermas were, during the late 1960s, the editors of the prestigious *Theorie* series of books published by Suhrkamp. Blumenberg is said by Fellmann to have resigned from this editorial post in response to Habermas's alignment of himself with the political aims of the student movement, though other more compelling explanations for this resignation have recently emerged.[58] Yet when it comes to Blumenberg, maintaining an abstract opposition between 'left' and 'right,' between a 'critical theory of society' and 'philosophical anthropology,' might turn out to be more misleading than insightful. As Christoph Jamme has argued, despite some important differences, no roughly contemporaneous theory of myth comes closer to Blumenberg's than that elaborated by Horkheimer and Adorno in part one of *Dialectic of Enlightenment* (*Dialektik der Aufklärung*, 1947), perhaps *the* central text of the Frankfurt School.[59] And others, such as Jacob Taubes, also detected thoroughgoing similarities between the thought of Blumenberg and Adorno.[60]

Regardless of whether or not Blumenberg actually knew of Habermas's critique of philosophical anthropology (and it is almost certain that he did), *Work on Myth* can, as we have seen, be read as a response to Habermas insofar as it elaborates an historicised philosophical anthropology that is significantly indebted not only to Rothacker, but also to Wilhelm Dilthey. Here it is necessary, once again, clearly to underline those aspects of Blumenberg's thought that depart from the 'creature of deficiencies' model outlined by Gehlen. The most obvious difference can be found in Blumenberg's refusal to make any definitive statement about the so-called essence of the human being. In Blumenberg's words: "What remains as the subject matter of anthropology is a 'human nature' that has never been 'nature' and never will be" (AAR, 456; WWL, 134). According to Blumenberg, philosophical anthropology is always already marked by two epistemological features that undermine any claim to have provided a definitive account of human nature: self-externality and belatedness. Although philosophical anthropology amounts to humans reflexively engaging in the act of observing themselves, Kant's analysis of consciousness showed, according to Blumenberg, that these acts of self-analysis can only have the structure of "self-externality." Once apprehensions of the self move beyond the level of intuitions and into the realm of discursive theoretical statements associated with what Kant called the understanding, the human being necessarily becomes an external object to himself (AAR, 456; WWL, 134), or in Kant's words: "the consciousness of oneself is [. . .] far from being a cognition of oneself."[61]

This sense of having theoretically to reconstruct a primordial intuition of the self is also endowed with a temporal character by Blumenberg. The 'beginning' of the human being, which would also presumably provide us with insight into its 'essence,' is a primal scene that can only ever be the subject of belated historical speculation. We therefore choose the speculative story of anthropogenesis that offers the most functional effectiveness (*Leistungsfähigkeit*) for a theory of culture (BDM, 575; HA, 22). And as the analysis of *Description of Man* outlined in Chapter 4 of this volume has demonstrated, Blumenberg ultimately favoured Paul Alsberg's account of the human being over that of Gehlen. According to Alsberg's account, the human being was not *constitutively* a 'creature of deficiencies'; rather, it *became* such a creature because its contingent mode of development ended up favouring technological compensations over bodily adaptations. The more bodily adaptation waned, the more cultural compensation became a necessity.

This choice also has implicit political consequences. If the human being only came to be human through a contingent act of technological compensation, then where the human being will end up must also be determined by a 'human nature' that is not 'nature' precisely because it is susceptible to cultural alteration. Human beings therefore have, and *must have*, some freedom to decide which myths and institutions are the most functionally effective for their interests. Indeed, if myths and institutions are always engaged in rhetorical competition with one another, as Blumenberg's theory of myth suggests, then this fact may enable what Blumenberg refers to not only as "selection," but also as a "process of optimization" (WOM, 165; AM, 183).

Blumenberg's final reckoning with Gehlen appears in *Cave Exits*, published in 1989 (see HA, 808–18). Here Blumenberg asks how Plato's allegory of the cave might look if it were required to describe present day societies. Blumenberg's answer is to reinterpret Plato's allegory in relation to Gehlen's philosophy of institutions. Blumenberg describes this reinterpretation as a "paradox," in the sense that it is a "deliberately conceived myth" (*ein erdachter Mythos*, HA, 810). Blumenberg "does not hesitate" to recount this myth as "*the* myth [. . .] that would speak of philosophy itself and of its function" (HA, 810). In this analogy—which seems to be situated in the industrialised West Germany that is the object of Gehlen's analysis in two essays quoted by Blumenberg[62]—the cave and the shadows that are projected onto its walls are state institutions that protect the 'poorly adapted' human beings and prevent them from being dazzled by the direct light of the sun, thereby enabling relief (*Entlastung*, HA, 811–12). Those responsible for projecting the shadows are the "beneficiaries of human stupidity and seducibility," providing their audience with entertainment, diversion, and most importantly, with a feeling of dependability (HA, 813).

For Blumenberg, the only hope in this arrangement lies in the excess (*Überschuss*) of mental energy that is made possible by the very relief that the institutions themselves provide (HA, 813–14). From this reserve of energy there emerges the possibility of examining and perhaps even resisting the present institutions by proffering new ones: by imagining either an outside to the cave, or another kind of cave. Here Blumenberg implies that it is precisely the security provided by the institutions of the cave that makes a critique of the cave possible (HA, 814). If one were historically to concretise Blumenberg's argument, the institution that might be foremost in his mind (albeit without being named), is the German *Grundgesetz* or Basic Law: the post-war political settlement of the *Bundesrepublik* which, in the wake of

National Socialism, guaranteed the freedom to critique and if necessary to resist the state.

The point is therefore not to *exit* the cave into a speculative realm of absolute truth or political fantasy, as in Plato's allegory, but rather to reflect upon it from within, to conceive of a myth "*of the* cave *from within* the cave" (HA, 810). After having searched in vain for this liberal myth of the cave in Gehlen's works, Blumenberg wrote it himself (HA, 811). Blumenberg's theory of myth could thus generally be described as a form of 'liberal conservatism' insofar as it recognises the value of long-standing institutions for the purposes of human orientation and security. But these institutions must also be susceptible of a rhetorical—if not 'critical,' a term that Blumenberg seems to have disliked and scrupulously to have avoided[63]—examination, selection, and transformation, even if they can never completely be 'exited,' or left behind.

The *Dialectic of Enlightenment* and the *Myth of the State*

Despite its length, density, and hyper-erudition, *Work on Myth* did manage to make waves beyond the academy. In fact, Rudolf Augstein—the founding editor of *Der Spiegel*—saw fit to review Blumenberg's volume in the most prominent political and cultural weekly of the *Bundesrepublik*.[64] Augstein's 'review' was, however, something of a non-event in academic terms, since it offered no real assessment of the actual argument of *Work on Myth*. Instead, it focused almost exclusively upon one of its most politically charged episodes: Blumenberg's analysis of Goethe's encounter with Napoleon on October 2, 1808. As we saw in Chapter 6 of this volume, on this day Napoleon is reported to have said to Goethe that "politics is fate"— apparently meaning that it is the great actors upon the stage of world history, and not the gods, who determine the course of events.[65] It was perhaps Augstein's nose for journalistic significance that allowed him to put his finger upon what is possibly the most directly political dimension of *Work on Myth*. At the same time, however, he does not draw any connection between the fall of Napoleon and the events of then recent German history—a connection which, as we shall see, Blumenberg himself subtly encouraged the readers of *Work of Myth* to make.

Of the reviews that appeared in German language newspapers, two in particular are politically significant in assessing *Work on Myth* in relation to Theodor Adorno's and Max Horkheimer's *Dialectic of Enlightenment*. Both Bernhard Lypp and W. Martin Lüdke commented on the similarities between Blumenberg's approach to myth and that of Adorno and Horkheimer, while also noting Blumenberg's reluctance directly to engage with the *Dialectic of Enlightenment*.[66] Lüdke even went so far as to associate *Work on Myth* with a potentially dangerous contemporary resurgence in myth or "remythicization" (*Remythisierung*), an assessment also offered by Karl Heinz Bohrer in an article published in January 1980:

That the "Work on Myth" is an illuminating endeavour that never comes to an end [. . .] this one can learn through reading Hans Blumenberg's recently published work of the same name. But is that a good thing? Is it not a dangerous reversion, which one should oppose with all available means?[67]

Bohrer even speculated that the contemporary "return of myth" might partially be attributed to the fact that the *Dialectic of Enlightenment* had been "badly read." Was Blumenberg also to be included among the 'bad readers' of Adorno and Horkheimer?

There is little doubt that Blumenberg had Adorno's and Horkheimer's approach to myth in his sights when writing *Work on Myth*. Blumenberg certainly knew of Adorno's work, and had even conducted a seminar on the latter's *Negative Dialectics (Negative Dialektik)* in the winter semester of 1967–8.[68] In fact, Christoph Jamme has even claimed that Blumenberg understood *Work on Myth* to be a "polemical response" to the *Dialectic of Enlightenment*.[69] But at least upon first glance, Blumenberg's theory of myth seems to share key theoretical positions with that of Adorno and Horkheimer. When Adorno and Horkheimer write that "myth is already enlightenment; and enlightenment reverts to mythology," and that "mythology itself set off the unending process of enlightenment,"[70] they seem to recognise precisely the rational and self-assertive aspect of myth that leads Blumenberg to declare that myth, in having provided humans with initial orientation, "is a piece of high-carat 'work of logos' " (WOM, 12; AM, 18). Both theories also see myth as a response to primordial fear concerning the forces of nature: Adorno's and Horkheimer's reading of the Sirens episode in Homer's *Odyssey* suggests that Homer's epic is a post-mythical organisation of prior mythical narratives, in that Odysseus has already distanced himself from the terrifyingly seductive powers of nature by restraining the instinctive elements within himself.[71] The notion that "consciously contrived adaptation to nature brings nature under the control of the physically weaker"—which is the essence of Adorno's and Horkheimer's reading of the Sirens episode—presents myth as the forerunner of instrumental reason.[72] Perhaps most crucially of all, both Blumenberg and also Adorno and Horkheimer derive their notions of instrumental reason and conceptual thought from Nietzsche,[73] to the extent that their modes of expression become, at times, almost interchangeable. Just as for Blumenberg reason is nothing more than "the organ of self-preservation [. . . and . . .] would be unnecessary, if the body did not need it in order to exist" (BDM, 166), so too for Adorno and Horkheimer does the concept "take the place of the physical adaption to nature."[74]

Yet while Blumenberg shares with Adorno and Horkheimer this emphasis upon a developmental continuity between myth and instrumental reason, the crucial difference between their theories of myth—as Christoph Jamme has shown—lies in the fact that Blumenberg is far more optimistic about the self-assertive features of human rationality than are Adorno and Hork-heimer, and also apparently far less concerned about the potential dangers of myth.[75] For Adorno and Horkheimer, myth is always potentially "false clarity," and for that reason both "obscure and enlightening,"[76] while for Blumenberg myth is an effective mode of dealing with the 'absolutism of reality' that is subsequently transformed into aesthetic play once such abso-lutisms have been put at an adequate distance. And although both theories agree that myth can never be brought to an end, they do so for very differ-ent reasons. In Adorno's and Horkheimer's account, enlightenment reverts to mythology because the fear of the outside—or of the Other—to which myth originally responded can never be excised from reason: the enlighten-ment becomes "mythic fear turned radical" when it attempts to subject all otherness to the law of the same that inheres in the concept.[77] If, according to this scenario, "nothing at all may remain outside, because the mere idea of outsideness is the very source of fear,"[78] then it becomes possible to see the events of (then) recent German history as a pathology of enlightenment, to the extent that—as Adorno later puts it in *Minima Moralia*—"the racial difference is raised to an absolute so that it can be abolished absolutely, if only in the sense that nothing that is different survives."[79]

Blumenberg's account of myth does point to the limits of rational thought and the concomitant need to resort to myth when such limits are reached, but he does not conjoin this position with a thoroughgoing critique of enlightenment akin to that of Adorno and Horkheimer. This is partly because Blumenberg presents conceptual thought as more flexible and for-giving than do Adorno and Horkheimer. For Blumenberg, concepts must be sufficiently loose so that they can anticipate, in the interests of survival, a range of possible phenomena within a particular class (TDU, 12), whereas for Adorno and Horkheimer, the concept, in being "fit to do service for everything," demands a conformity that enables the sheer domination of nature.[80] Thus, if Blumenberg does stand in polemical relation to Adorno and Horkheimer, then it is a polemic of nuances: enlightenment as self-assertion and liberation from fear that enables myth to be transformed into aesthetic play (Blumenberg); as opposed to enlightenment as the domination of nature and alienation from the self, with the ever-present possibility of a catastrophic relapse into myth (Adorno and Horkheimer). This opposition is perhaps best seen in the vastly different interpretations of Francis Bacon offered by Blumenberg, Adorno, and Horkheimer: namely, as the hero of theoretical curiosity and scientific self-assertion depicted in the *Legitimacy of the Modern Age*,[81] and as the father of the instrumental exploitation of nature in *Dialectic of Enlightenment*.[82]

But Blumenberg is also not overly optimistic about the Enlightenment. He alludes to the potential dark side of instrumental reason in *Description of Man* when he points out that since there is no halting of "instrumental" (as opposed to biological) evolution, then it is plausible to speculate that "man may finally go under as a consequence of his instrumental evolution"

(BDM, 552). Here it is also possible that myth cannot be brought to an end by instrumental reason precisely because reason—in the form of science—may itself create new absolutisms that will in turn require new mythic responses, as is suggested by the fictional scenario of *2001: A Space Odyssey*, in which human beings are oppressed and murdered by the technology of artificial intelligence. But *Work on Myth* offers no exploration at all of how technology—in the form of what Adorno and Horkheimer call the "culture industry," exemplified by radio as the "universal mouthpiece of the Führer"—may be deployed for the purposes of political propaganda or "phony Fascist mythology."[83] In this context, Christa Bürger has usefully described *Dialectic of Enlightenment* as a book of remembering and *Work on Myth* as a book of forgetting: while the former spans from Auschwitz back to the *Odyssey*, the latter is much more interested in the therapeutic distancing work done by the telling of stories (*Geschichten*) than it is in recent history (*Geschichte*).[84] Blumenberg's most direct reckonings with that history remained by and large in the *Nachlass*. And perhaps most tellingly of all: *Dialectic of Enlightenment* is not referred to even once in *Work on Myth*.

When it comes to the political reception of *Work on Myth* in German academic journals, three reviews are especially noteworthy in directly accusing Blumenberg of having neglected the subject of political myth. In *Das Argument*, Jürgen Maruhn accused Blumenberg of calling for a "rehabilitation" of myth, while at the same time failing to ask the question as to "how this undertaking is related to the political currents of our recent history, which wanted, in the name of the *Myth of the Twentieth Century*, to shape society and history and their conflicts with the help of mythical thought."[85] Hans-Ludwig Ollig elaborated a similar critique in *Theologie und Philosophie*. Ollig correctly identified the anti-Platonic tenor of Blumenberg's theory of myth, which is accompanied by his rehabilitation of rhetoric. But in Ollig's view, it is precisely these tendencies that lead Blumenberg to argue, "almost in the manner of Gehlen," for the institutional achievements of myth. By "immersing himself in the history of myth," Blumenberg is said completely to have neglected the "the pressing societal and political problems of contemporary history."[86]

But the most noteworthy academic review of all was that published by Götz Müller in the *Zeitschrift für deutsche Philologie* (now republished in PF, 67–78), not least because Blumenberg both read and responded to Müller's critique. Müller correctly points out that Blumenberg's theory emerged from his earlier ideas about metaphorology and the 'theory of non-conceptuality,' while also contrasting Blumenberg's Rothacker-inspired historicist approach with that found in psychoanalytic and ethnographic theories of myth (Freud and Levi-Strauss, respectively). Yet Müller also wonders whether Blumenberg's departure from the psychoanalytic and ethnographic approaches to myth may not simply be attributable to Blumenberg's selection of primary sources: whereas Freud's theory of myth emerges from an analysis of neuroses, and while Levi-Strauss is concerned with so called 'primitive human beings,' or *Naturvölker*, Blumenberg is said to elaborate an aesthetic theory of myth that is dominated by the literary reception of Prometheus.[87]

Here Müller showed himself to be better informed than many other reviewers of *Work on Myth*, since he points out that Blumenberg had already been accused of over-emphasising the aesthetic features of myth, and of neglecting its social and political dimensions, at the Poetics and Hermeneutics meeting of 1968 (PF, 76). Müller alludes to the comments of Jurij Striedter, who argued that Blumenberg's definition of myth as a form of "aesthetic play" was not able to account for "the more recent theories and practices of the so-called 'new myths' as conscious constructions aimed at mobilising individuals or the masses."[88] Striedter's essential claim was that Blumenberg overlooked explicitly political theories of myth such as that elaborated by Georges Sorel in his *Reflections on Violence* (*Refléxions sur la violence*, 1908), and Müller reiterated this critique when he compared Blumenberg's position unfavourably with that of Ernst Cassirer:

> This powerful effectiveness of modern social myths may have prompted Ernst Cassirer to warn that "the intrusions and encroachments of myth into the sphere of science" should be curbed—not least through an understanding of the legitimate field of validity of myths. Blumenberg obviously does not share these fears; he does not share Cassirer's conviction that myth is, and must be, that which has been overcome in modernity. The dangerous proliferation of modern myths is barely even mentioned. The consistent aestheticisation of myth in modernity, at the highest literary level, also removes the terrors from the new myths.[89]

In considering Müller's critique, it is useful to examine Blumenberg's brief but telling treatment of Cassirer's *Myth of the State* in *Work on Myth*. It appears in the context of Blumenberg's argument, familiar to us from Chapter 4 of this volume, in which Cassirer deals with myth only from the perspective of the *terminus ad quem*—namely, as something that has decisively been superseded by scientific rationality. Referring to the optimism of Cassirer's philosophy of history, Blumenberg remarks that

> it is not without irony that Cassirer, the theorist of myth, completed as the last in the long sequence of his works *The Myth of the State*, which appeared only in 1946, a year after his death. Naturally this was a domain for which the philosophy of symbolic forms had least of all made provision, a domain in which it was at a loss. What Cassirer registers is fundamentally a unique Romantic regression, which it does not seem possible to fit into any philosophy of history. The historian of philosophy, of science, of the cultural subject, of the consciousness of reality, cannot too generously overlook such Romantic thrusts—which

breach the image of reason that irresistibly secures its rights—so as to avoid being disturbed in his philosophy of history.

(WOM, 51; AM, 59–60)

This assessment of Cassirer's *Myth of the State* is not entirely fair. Cassirer had begun writing *The Myth of the State* in 1943–4 and completed the manuscript only shortly before his death in April 1945. Not unlike the *Dialectic of Enlightenment*—albeit with a completely take *on* the Enlightenment—Cassirer's book was an attempt to understand what had occurred in Europe between 1933 and 1945. It is simply not true to suggest that Cassirer's book generously overlooks the processes of remythizisation associated with political romanticism. In fact, the book begins by openly stating that the "preponderance of mythical thought over rational thought in some of our modern political systems" presents the theorist of myth with "quite new theoretical problems."[90]

These theoretical problems are tackled with the theory of myth that Cassirer had already developed in *Mythical Thought* (1925), volume two of the *Philosophy of Symbolic Forms*. What is new about the *Myth of State* is that Cassirer now revisits this theory in order to explain why, and despite the advances of "scientific knowledge and technical mastery of nature," in political life "the defeat of rational thought seems to be complete and irrevocable."[91] Cassirer's explanation amounts to a long narrative concerning the development of Western political thought. Plato, although one of the "greatest myth makers in human history," is said to have correctly recognised the political dangers inherent in myth, which led him favour an ethical and a legal (as opposed to a mythical) conception of the state. This meant that any myth—such as the myth of the cave—would need to be in the service of the theory of forms in order to gain admittance to the state.[92] Machiavelli then ushers in the modern conception of politics by divorcing political from religious legitimacy. Whereas Saint Augustine and Thomas Aquinas had essentially followed Plato by basing their conceptions of the state upon religious arguments—in Augustine, for example, the Platonic ideas become the "thoughts of God"—Machiavelli offers the first theoretical expression of the secular state in which the political world now "stands alone" in "empty space." This situation, according to Cassirer, was dangerous, in that the political had now decisively been divorced from the ethical: Machiavelli's concern was to find "the move that wins the game," rather than to ask the normative question as to what ends the game itself should achieve. *The Prince* is therefore neither a moral nor an immoral book. It simply introduced a purely technical "*art* of politics," which was "equally fit for the illegal and for the legal state."[93]

This sense of politics as technique stands at the centre of the final chapter of the *Myth of the State*, entitled "The Technique of the Modern Political Myths." The modern political myths of National Socialism are seen to combine Thomas Carlyle's notion of hero-worship with Arthur de Gobineau's ideas concerning the inequality of races. Neither of these neo-romantic nineteenth-century theories was, in Cassirer's view, expressly intended as a theory of fascism, but they were both tools that were ready to hand during the crisis period of the Weimar Republic. It is here where Cassirer turns to a functionalist explanation for the resurgence of myth in National Socialism. Invoking Bronislaw Malinowski's *The Foundations of Faith and Morals* (1936), he argues that in times of particular uncertainty or perceived danger, magical or mythical arguments may take precedence over scientific or rational thought: "in desperate situations man will always have recourse to desperate means," and the hour of myth comes "as soon as the other binding forces of man's social life [. . .] lose their strength and are no longer able to combat the demonic mythical powers." The difference here is that these new myths are not necessarily believed in by their progenitors, since in relation to the modern political myths, the human being appears simultaneously in two guises: as *homo magus* and as *homo faber*, as magical and as technical man. These new myths are therefore not unconscious products of the imagination; rather, they are "artificial things fabricated by very skilful and cunning artisans."[94]

It is true to suggest, as Blumenberg does in *Work on Myth*, that this new narrative did amount to a fundamental disruption of Cassirer's earlier attempt, outlined in *Mythical Thought*, to theorise myth from the perspective of the *terminus ad quem*. That such an apparently irrational outbreak was possible at all within a highly advanced technological society suggested that no amount of enlightenment could ever guarantee that the definitive *terminus ad quem* had been reached. And this was the spirit in which Eric Voegelin reviewed the *Myth of the State* in 1947, when he wrote that "Cassirer seems to assume that the human mind evolves historically from an early mythical phase towards an increasingly rational penetration of the world." In Voegelin's view, Cassirer does not recognise that the Platonic critique of myth was itself based on the "new myth of the Socratic soul," thereby suggesting that the historical movement is not one from irrational myth to rationality, from *mythos* to *logos*, but rather one in which new myths emerge from and displace the old ones. This position would also seem to be similar to Blumenberg's reading of the *Protagoras*, in which the apparent victory of philosophy over sophistry was only rhetorically and not epistemologically grounded (WOM, 331; AM, 362). Crucially for Voegelin, Cassirer demonstrates "no awareness" that myth "is an indispensable forming element of social order," and instead merely describes myth pejoratively as a form of "darkness."[95]

It is therefore plausible to suggest that Blumenberg, much like Voegelin, would not have seen the *Myth of the State* as a significant advance beyond the position that Cassirer had already outlined in *Mythical Thought*. But in order properly to critique Cassirer's account of the role played by myth in National Socialism, Blumenberg would have had directly to address this topic himself. The reason as to why he did not end up doing so is revealed in his response to Götz Müller's review of *Work on Myth*, which Müller had sent to him on July 11, 1981 (see PF, 61). Replying with great candour on July 20, Blumenberg observed

> It is always difficult for me to say anything about reviews. It is always too late. But I do feel stung by yours, and for good reason. The book is missing a chapter that was already present in the manuscript, but which completely and utterly spoiled my taste for the book. I held it back. After I am gone, one may do with it what one wants. It was called: Stalingrad as mythical consequence. It cost me more work than most of the other things in the book. This is how the conclusion came to be left up in the air.
>
> (PF, 62)

Blumenberg's response amounts only to a personal statement rather than to a theoretical justification concerning his failure, within the pages of *Work on Myth*, directly and systematically to confront the theme of political myth in National Socialism. And here one can only resort to biographical speculation concerning Blumenberg's reluctance to engage with such questions: given his experiences between 1933 and 1945, this reluctance could be seen as perfectly understandable. The fact that such questions were nevertheless pressing for Blumenberg, and that he did labour over them in parts of the *Work on Myth* manuscripts, will shortly be examined in Chapter 8 of this volume, through an interpretation of what is in all likelihood the chapter described by Blumenberg in his response to Müller.[96]

In the remainder of his letter to Müller, Blumenberg also responded to Müller's allegation that the aesthetic and diachronic theory of myth outlined in *Work on Myth* arose merely from a narrow selection of literary material relating predominantly to Prometheus:

> Methodologically I accept the reservation that it is only my material that allows the temporal perspective. But is that an objection? The ethnological anthropologist has no material for a diachronic reception of myth. He must perforce produce a synchronically structured theory. It is not his triumph, but rather the disadvantage of the one who does not want to allow himself to be accused of ethnocentrism. I do not shy away from the accusation that a story interests me more when it offers me more possibilities for understanding something that may also have existed elsewhere, but that has become inaccessible forever. We are slaves of the material; precisely because of this we must take advantage of the freedom that the best sites offer. That in addition to this it is Prometheus, and also on the basis of the material, I certainly take to be in itself a result of selection.
>
> (PF, 63)

The question raised both by Müller's critique and by Blumenberg's response is whether Blumenberg's theory of myth displays a circular structure. We have seen the extent to which the Prometheus mythologem shapes Blumenberg's theoretical approach to questions about the human sciences or 'human nature'—questions that for him are best answered by Paul Alsberg's speculative Promethean hero *Pithekanthropogoneous*, who survives through recourse to technological means. But is it also the distorting lens of this theoretical approach that leads Blumenberg to focus on aesthetic material relating to Prometheus, at the expense of other, perhaps equally pervasive, myths in Western culture? Blumenberg would be likely to answer that this allegation of circularity arises from a fundamental misunderstanding of the inherent nature of myth reception.

If, according to Blumenberg's account, our consciousness is always already shaped by the distancing work done by myth, then there is no sense in which a theory of myth could undertake a 'scientific' observation of myth from an external and objective point of view. Christoph Jamme has argued that the speculative palaeoanthropology upon which Blumenberg's theory of myth is based amounts to nothing more than "a myth about myth."[97] Similarly, Robert Segal also wonders whether a "grander speculation" than the palaeoanthropological story told in *Work on Myth* is imaginable.[98] These critiques are absolutely correct, but Blumenberg's response would be to ask whether anything more than this is possible for the culturally and historically situated observer. And this is also the essence of Blumenberg's self-defence in relation to Müller's critique. While the purportedly scientific ethnologist of myth engages in what he or she takes to be purely synchronic and non-ethnocentric observations of culture, presumably under the mistaken impression that it is possible to remove, control or (in Husserl's sense) 'reduce' one's own prejudices and pre-understandings when viewing another culture, the diachronic theorist of myth (namely Blumenberg) takes the prejudices of historicity to be constitutive of one's own approach to the tradition. If this position sounds rather like the arguments of Hans-Georg Gadamer in *Truth and Method*—another book that is never once cited in *Work on Myth*, but that certainly could have been[99]—then the key difference is that Blumenberg overlays such an account of historicity with a palaeoanthropological argument about cultural selection. The Prometheus mythologem is one of the main relics at our disposal precisely because it has proved itself to be adaptable for the purposes of helping the human being to cope with various historically conditioned absolutisms throughout the ages. The Promethean theory of cultural selection, according to which the human being only survives through technology and culture, thus justifies Blumenberg's predominant focus upon the Prometheus material. In this way, 'theory' and 'subject matter' are inextricably linked, and the circle closes itself.

CARL SCHMITT AND THE 'EXTRAORDINARY SAYING'

Before any examination of that highly political material from the original *Work on Myth* manuscripts that Blumenberg decided not to publish, it is necessary to point out that those early reviewers who had accused Blumenberg of neglecting the subject of political myth altogether were not reading him closely enough. None of them mention those sections of *Work on Myth* that engage in a dialogue with Germany's most prominent 'political theologian': Carl Schmitt. This aspect of *Work on Myth* would, however, become a prominent feature of its early reception, due to a colloquium on Carl Schmitt organised by Jacob Taubes in 1980. In three letters written in 1979, Taubes invited Blumenberg to contribute to a colloquium devoted to the hermeneutical interpretation of Schmitt's ideas on political theology.[100] Replying to Taubes for the first time on April 4, 1979, Blumenberg declined to participate, ostensibly on the grounds that this would require him to write a third edition of *The Legitimacy of the Modern Age*. Mentioning *Work on Myth*, which had at that time not yet been published, he remarks: "By the way [. . .] the myth book will contain a portion of the dispute [*Auseinandersetzung*] with C.S." In his second reply to Taubes, dated October 20, 1979, Blumenberg adds: "*Work on Myth* will be published on the 15th of November, and contains everything that I could ever still have to say at such a colloquium."[101] This colloquium—which at one point carried the working title of "Political Theology III" ("Politische Theologie III")[102]—was held in Bad Homburg between January 30 and February 2, 1980, which enabled the participants to include the newly published *Work on Myth* in their considerations.[103]

The context for Blumenberg's exchange with Schmitt was provided by another passage from Part Four (Book Twenty) of Goethe's *Poetry and Truth*, in which Goethe again deals with the theme of the daemonic:

The daemonic principle [. . .] is at its most fearful when it emerges predominantly in some individual. In the course of my life I have been able to observe several of these, either in proximity or at a distance. They are not always the most excellent men, either in minds or talents, and they seldom have kindness of heart to recommend them. But they radiate an enormous strength and exercise incredible power over all creatures, even over the elements, and who can say just how far such influence does extend? All the moral powers in unison can do nothing against them. In vain the brighter segment of the population tries to make them suspect as deluded men or deluders; still the masses are attracted to them. Seldom or never do contemporaries of this type encounter each other, and they cannot be conquered by anything less than the universe itself, which they have defied. And from such observations may well have arisen that strange but prodigious saying [*ungeheurer Spruch*]:

Nemo contra deum nisi deus ipse [No one (can stand) against a god unless he is a god himself].[104]

In light of evidence gleaned from Blumenberg's *Nachlass*, it appears that this saying—for which Goethe uses the adjective *ungeheuer*, which can mean 'extraordinary' and 'prodigious,' but also 'monstrous'—played a significant role in the genesis of *Work on Myth*. In a letter to his friend Ulrich Thoemmes written in 1984, Blumenberg claims that *Work on Myth* "emerged from a kind of 'wager' with Gershom Scholem and Hans-Georg Gadamer, which related to Goethe's 'extraordinary saying' and which was made on a hotel veranda in May 1970, nine years before the book."[105]

It is highly likely that this wager had something to do Carl Schmitt's *Political Theology II*, which was published in 1970, and which contained a politically motivated interpretation of Goethe's saying that was designed to refute Blumenberg's earlier critique of Schmitt in the *Legitimacy of the Modern Age*. Even before Schmitt's interpretation, this saying had already accumulated political significance in post-war Germany. Heidrun Kämper's lexicon on German war guilt between 1945 and 1955 has briefly demonstrated the ways in which National Socialist perpetrators and their defenders made retrospective use of the term daemonic (*dämonisch*)—in the sense of being possessed by a daemon, or under the power of a purportedly irresistible and inexplicable force embodied in the person of Adolf Hitler—in order to excuse their crimes.[106] One such example is the trial at Nuremberg of the former of *Reichsbankpräsident* (President of the German Federal Bank) between 1933 and 1939, Hjalmar Schacht.[107] Schacht's defence attorney, Rudolf Dix, made the following claim to the military court: "beyond all doubt, the daemonic embodied itself in Adolf Hitler to the calamity of Germany and the world." He then cited the entire passage above from *Poetry and Truth* in order to argue that any resistance to Hitler undertaken by his client would have been impossible.[108] In *Political Theology II*, Schmitt himself also remarked that Goethe's saying "was cited and interpreted by people intimate with Goethe's work in countless informal conversations during the last war, 1939–45."[109] Thus, if one takes even half seriously Blumenberg's claim that *Work on Myth* emerged from a wager concerning Goethe's saying, and if this wager related to its interpretation by the most intellectually significant jurist of National Socialism,[110] then *Work on Myth* is a much more political book than is usually assumed.

Schmitt proposes that this saying, which Goethe seems to have formulated himself,[111] was derived from a drama-fragment by Jakob Michael Lenz entitled "Catharina von Siena." The eponymous heroine of this drama-fragment, in flight from her father, who has rejected the man that she loves and whom she describes as "a loving/and aggrieved God," utters the following lines: "God against God/[. . .] Save, save me/My Jesus, whom I follow, from his arms!"[112] This proposed Christian derivation of Goethe's saying allows Schmitt to claim that it should be interpreted in a monotheistic and not a polytheistic context: "God against God" means that Catharina flees towards the Son, Jesus, and away from the Father.

In *Work on Myth*, Blumenberg initially considers Schmitt's Christological Father-Son explanation to be plausible in relation to Goethe's preoccupation with Prometheus. He points out that Goethe's reinterpretation of the Prometheus story in his Prometheus fragment, in which the relation between Zeus and Prometheus becomes one of Father to Son instead of god to titan, represents a precedent for Goethe blending classical myth with Christian theology (WOM, 533, 553–4; AM, 578, 601). Blumenberg even cites Goethe's famous syncretism—according to which one can be a pantheist with respect to nature, a polytheist with respect to poetry, and a monotheist with respect to morals[113]—in order to argue that these interpretations need not be mutually exclusive (WOM, 539; AM, 585). But Blumenberg ultimately rejects Schmitt's univocal Christological reading on the grounds that a scenario in which the Son completely subverts the spiritual authority of the Father cannot be seen as exclusively Christian (WOM, 554; AM, 602). Blumenberg writes: "The saying becomes fertile only if [. . .] it can be detached from the unequivocally monotheistic mysticism of intradivine dualization [. . .] and set in the more comprehensive reference system that includes pantheism and polytheism" (WOM, 531; AM, 576–7).

The broader context for this hermeneutical confrontation over Goethe's saying lies in an earlier debate between Blumenberg and Schmitt over political theology. This debate is to be found in the two editions of Blumenberg's *Legitimacy of the Modern Age*, in Schmitt's *Political Theology II*, and in the Blumenberg-Schmitt correspondence and related materials that have recently been published from Blumenberg's *Nachlass*.[114] It has become one of the most intensely researched aspects of Blumenberg's writings, with no fewer than three papers already having been devoted to it at the colloquium on Carl Schmitt organised by Jacob Taubes in 1980.[115]

Although the finer nuances of the Blumenberg-Schmitt debate cannot be entered into here,[116] its core is to be found in Blumenberg's full frontal critique of Schmitt's claim, outlined in *Political Theology* (1922), that "all significant concepts of the modern theory of the state are secularized theological concepts." Schmitt argues that the political legitimacy of monarchs, and later of the state as a Leviathan as imagined by Thomas Hobbes, was always grounded in a "metaphysical kernel" derived from the idea of God as the Sovereign. This notion of legitimacy was later taken over by the secularised state, which became sovereign in the lesser (and hence non-capitalised) sense of being the political entity that takes decisions under exceptional political circumstances, such as when public order is threatened. This idea was, according to Schmitt, lost in the later social contract theory of Rousseau, according to which the people themselves become identical with the sovereign. The problem with this new situation—and here Schmitt's critique of all forms of liberalism and parliamentarianism comes through—is that the people, or at least the parties that are contentiously said to represent them, talk too much and have too many different opinions.[117]

In the *Crisis of Parliamentary Democracy* (*Die geistesgeschichtliche Lage des heutigen Parlamentarismus*, first ed.: 1923; second ed.: 1926), Schmitt goes on to suggest that parliamentary democracy runs the risk of amounting to nothing more than an "eternal conversation" that kills the "genuine instincts and intuitions that produce a moral decision."[118] This critique is based upon a distinction, found in both *Political Theology* and in the *Crisis of Parliamentary Democracy*, between a so-called democratic general will one the one hand and authority on the other. Schmitt argues that the real conditions of mass democracy—secret party negotiations carried out through committees, along with popular opinion shaped by the vested interests of capital—mean that parliament cannot perform its representative function.[119] This inability of parliament legitimately to express the general will means that authority must be established by way of a non-rationalist political theory. Such a theory grants authority not to the conclusions arrived at by a naïve belief in the "outmoded" parliamentary principles of "discussion and openness,"[120] but rather to the sovereign itself. This non-rational move was already present in *Political Theology*, in Schmitt's implicit approval of the following dictum of Thomas Hobbes, which then reappears in the *Crisis of Parliamentary Democracy: Auctoritas, non veritas facit legem* (authority and not the truth makes the law).[121] This non-rational conception of political legitimacy is said to be a secularised form of religious authority.

In the first edition of *The Legitimacy of the Modern Age* (1966), Blumenberg took Schmitt's theory of secularisation to task. The modern age is not characterised by its secularised use of theological concepts, but by its own self-assertion in the face of the theological absolutism of the Middle Ages. In the realm of politics, this meant renouncing civil wars between various religious absolutisms through the creation of the nation-state, which defined itself more in national than in religious terms.[122] It is certainly true, notes Blumenberg, that modern nation-states may have used religious language or metaphors in order to establish their legitimacy. This vocabulary had for centuries played a role in shaping the horizon of human questions and expectations. Modern political ideologies *did* take up these questions and this vocabulary, but reoccupied them with totally different answers. "The uniformity of language," wrote Blumenberg in 1966, "indicates the uniformity of function for consciousness, but not the identity of meaning."[123] What Schmitt called political theology was in fact nothing more than political rhetoric.

Schmitt replied to these arguments in *Political Theology II* (1970), a book to which Blumenberg in turn responded in the revised edition of *The Legitimacy of the Modern Age* published in 1974.[124] Here Blumenberg asked the following rhetorical question of his opponent:

Is "political theology" only the sum of a set of metaphors, whose selection reveals more about the character of the situations in which use is made of them than about the origin of the ideas and concepts that are employed in dealing with such situations?

(LMA, 94; LDN, 104)[125]

As was the case in 1966, Blumenberg's answer to this question was affirmative. "Political theology" does not instantiate a secularised form of religious authority within the state. It merely uses theological metaphors as part of a rhetorical quest for legitimacy.

But back in 1970, in the 'Postscript' to *Political Theology II*, Goethe's 'extraordinary saying' had taken centre stage in Schmitt's critique of the 1966 edition of *The Legitimacy of the Modern Age*, and it is more than likely that Blumenberg was only drawn to focus on this section of *Poetry and Truth* through his encounter with Schmitt.[126] The critique offered by Schmitt is deeply abstruse and is intended to defend the plausibility of what he calls political theology. It relies upon Schmitt's interpretation of a statement by the fourth-century theologian Gregory of Nanzianus: "The One— to *Hen*—is always in uproar—*stasiazon*—against itself—*pros heauton*."[127] If the 'extraordinary saying,' when interpreted in relation to Gregory's statement, means that the only thing which can oppose God is God himself, and that enmity can only emerge by way of a discord from within the totality of the divine, then it showed that Christian monotheism contained the essence of the political as Schmitt defined it in his *Concept of the Political* (*Der Begriff des Politischen*, 1927)—namely, through the distinction between friend and enemy that is made by the sovereign state.[128] This distinction or 'decision' is irreducible, non-rational and therefore ultimately theological. It stands at the core of political legitimacy as Schmitt defined it, while also being serviceable as a means to establishing a so-called national will under National Socialism.[129] As we have seen, although Blumenberg remains open to the possibility that Goethe's saying is successful in producing monotheistic, polytheistic, and pantheistic resonances, the polytheistic interpretation nevertheless receives much more positive attention from him than do the other two options. And it does so, perhaps not only for philosophical or theological reasons, as some commentators have argued,[130] but rather for what seem, in the context of Goethe's writings about Napoleon, to be scarcely veiled political reasons that have everything to do with how Goethe's notion of the daemonic might best be interpreted in the *Bundesrepublik*.

If, Blumenberg argues, those people "intimate with Goethe's work" mentioned by Schmitt understood the 'extraordinary saying' in relation to Goethe's judgement of the fallen Napoleon who had failed to renounce his limitless ambitions in Russia—a context that, especially following the attempt to invade Moscow in the winter of 1941–2, along with the Battle of Stalingrad in 1942–3, displayed unmistakable parallels with the later phases of National Socialism—then it would have offered them "the secret comfort" that a political leader who purports to measure himself against God must ultimately be undone by powers of the universe of that will inevitably oppose him (WOM, 532; AM, 578). In Blumenberg's letter to Schmitt dated 7 August 1975 (that is, after the publication of *Political Theology II* and after the second edition of *Legitimacy of the Modern Age* in 1974, but before the publication of *Work on Myth* in 1979), this preference for a polytheistic interpretation of "God against God" becomes unmistakable:

> Goethe's apothegm seizes upon the generality of the meaning of polytheism as its separation of powers, its prevention of absolute power and of any religion as a feeling of unconditional dependence on this power. Gods, when there are many of them, always already stand one against the other. A god can only in turn be limited by a god.[131]

This position is restated in *Work on Myth*, when Blumenberg writes that Goethe's saying expresses "the structural principle of myth [. . .] the principle of mutual adjustment and of the separation of powers" (WOM, 538; AM, 584). As we saw in Chapter 2 of this volume, the notion that myth enacts a division of powers—a division that can, in turn, be interpreted as a form of tolerance—can already be found in Hume's *Natural History of Religion*.[132] Blumenberg's invocation of the "separation of powers" within the context of his theory of myth thus raises the question as to whether anything resembling a coherent theory of the political can be identified either in *Work on Myth*, or in his other writings.

POLITICAL POLYTHEISM?

Blumenberg's most explicitly political essay appeared in 1968.[133] Here he argues that the perceived political value of rhetoric is always bound up with conceptions of reality to be found in theories of the state, and some of his positions on this question closely resemble those of Cassirer in *The Myth of State*, which is cited throughout the essay. Blumenberg points out that since for Plato, reality lay in the realm of the ideas, politics was simply to be the realisation of the universal truths contained in them, a process portrayed in the allegory of the cave. Rhetoric, with its alleged substitution of appearance for Being, could in Plato's view only lead away from the just state, because it was not based on a real account of the cosmos and the nature of things (WST, 125–6). The key point of continuity between Blumenberg and Cassirer lies in the central position of Machiavelli in both of their conceptions of the political. The self-assertive modern age is for Blumenberg most obviously represented in the political thought of Machiavelli, which broke with Plato's conception of the state by arguing that political reality lies in the exercise of power and the "artificial" (*künstlich*) creation of legitimacy, rather than in the mere realisation of pre-existent utopian ideas that are in any case continually subject to dispute (WST, 124–5).

Herein lies the political role of rhetoric. Whereas Plato demonises sophi-sim as the use of mere words, Blumenberg argues—and here the Cold War context of his essay becomes clear—that a politics of words can be prefera-ble to one of deeds (WST, 128–9). This Blumenberg describes as the "return of Sophism" into the political sphere, in the guises of "institutionalised rhetoric" and of "political technique" (WST, 133, 138). In this context, it is Blumenberg's interpretation of Machiavelli that underlines his decisive departure from Cassirer. While Cassirer sees Machiavelli's "new science of politics" as a "powerful and dangerous weapon" precisely because it breaks the link between politics and ethics,[134] for Blumenberg "Machiavel-li's separation of ethics and politics" emerges from a "theory of the political minimum"—from a realistic politics of radically scaled down hopes. This would be a politics in which real "actions" (*Handlungen*) are "reoccupied" (*umbesetzt*) with "quasi-actions" (*Quasi-Handlungen*, WST, 138). Here the deployment of rhetoric means the forestalling of concrete interventions that may have far graver consequences than the merely *possible*—and in this sense rhetorical—courses of action suggested by a political technician such as Machiavelli. Blumenberg admits that such a rhetorical politics may open the way for "demagoguery and propaganda," but he sees this danger as compensated for by the advantages of a political technique in which speech is prioritised over action (WST, 138). The fitting motto for such a politics is then derived by Blumenberg from the title of a book by the speech act theo-rist J. L. Austin: not *How to do Things with Words*,[135] but in Blumenberg's reformulation: "How to do nothing with words" (WST, 138).

This melancholy conception of the political—perhaps best described as the politics of the 'least worst option'—is then repeated in the important anthropology essay of 1971, where rhetoric is said to create "institutions where evident truths are lacking" (AAR, 435; WWR, 110). To be a human being means to lack a strong pre-given orientation that can determine actions, and it also means to be situated outside of the ideas associated with Platonic *episteme* (AAR, 432; WWL, 107). An anthropology that has been subsumed by rhetoric is therefore described as the "last, and belated, discipline of philosophy" in that it is the chief means through which possible courses of action are debated and legitimised (AAR, 432; WWL, 107). And insofar as it can lead to what Blumenberg calls consensus and tolerance, to the avoidance of coercion, and to the deferment of action, it is the opposite of decisionism and of what Blumenberg sees as Gehlen's "absolutism of institutions" (AAR, 439; WWL, 115). Rhetoric is a tool for creating con-sensus, but also for questioning and exposing positions that are perceived to be problematic or inadequate: "rhetoric teaches us to recognize rhetoric, but it does not teach us to legitimate it" (AAR, 448; WWL, 126). What, then, does all of this have to do with Blumenberg's preference for the polytheistic interpretation of Goethe's 'extraordinary saying' in his debates with Carl Schmitt? A polytheistic scenario in which one god is opposed to another, and in which no single god is able to achieve absolute power, appears to be

Blumenberg's classical vision of a liberal conservatism in which competing rhetorical positions and institutions vie for legitimacy, and ideally achieve non-violent consensus.

Here it is highly likely that Blumenberg's emphasis on polytheism was also designed to refute Carl Schmitt's thoroughly positive reception of George Sorel's theory of political myth, outlined in Sorel's *Reflections on Violence*. According to Sorel,

> Men who are participating in great social movements always picture their coming action in the form of images of battle in which their cause is certain to triumph. I proposed to give the name of 'myths' to these constructions.[136]

By focusing on the function of images in myths, Sorel implies that they have a non-rational appeal that leads to direct action rather than mere deliberation. The context of this argument was Sorel's notion that while socialist *doctrine* would be open to discussion and therefore to compromise within the parliamentary system, the "myth of the general strike" was a call to *action* that would lead to "absolute revolution." For Sorel, myths are not "descriptions of things"; they are much more "expressions of a will to act," and because myth is primarily non-theoretical it "cannot be refuted since it is, at bottom, identical to the convictions of a group." While myths are not to be equated with utopias, it is often the case that utopian political doctrines cannot succeed without the support of myths. "French democracy," for example, is said to have been sustained by "myths which represented the struggle against the *ancien régime*," whereas "liberal political economy" will be likely to fail precisely because it is "a utopia free from any element of myth." Socialism, too, has often been "scarcely anything but a utopia," but through the "myth of the general strike" it will become "firmly established in the minds of workers."[137]

The reason that myths are superior to rational argument in securing direct political action is explained by Sorel's recourse to the thought of Henri Bergson.[138] While rational argument is associated with the external and logical sequence of mathematical time, myths can penetrate to the inner-self of duration, to the "essence of emotional life." By appealing to "*intuition alone*, before any considered analyses are made," myths are said to "give an aspect of complete reality to the hopes of immediate action." In the case of Christianity, it was the constant threat of the mythical apocalypse that inspired Christians to act in the hope of achieving the desired utopian outcome in "the return of Christ." It is such myths which condition political violence, defined not as physical acts of assault, but as the destruction of an existing authority in order to bring about a wholly new state of affairs. In this way, moral convictions are said to depend upon "a state of war in which men voluntarily participate and which finds expression in well-defined myths."[139]

Blumenberg knew this text by Sorel well, since a German translation of it appeared in 1969, in the Surhkamp book series *Theorie* that he co-edited with Habermas, Dieter Henrich and Taubes.[140] In *Work on Myth*, Blumenberg undertakes a brief consideration of Sorel's notion of social myths, arguing that Sorel "underestimates the dimension of the indeterminate past" in the function of myth. Instead of being directed *towards* future utopias, myths are for Blumenberg movements *away* from an essentially forgotten and horrific past associated with the state of nature (WOM, 223; AM; 247–8). Sorel's social myth (*gesellschaftlicher Mythos*) is for Blumenberg an example of the late function of myth, being the "minimum of what could still bear the title of myth." Here all stories about the past have been stripped of content and are no longer told. Instead, myth now corresponds solely with "what is not allowed to exist" under present conditions: namely, the utopia that political violence promises to deliver (WOM, 224; AM, 248). This rather cursory critique of Sorel displays a high level of abstraction and refuses even to consider what the term 'social myth' means. And as we have seen, this glaring shortcoming in Blumenberg's theory of myth—a theory in which 'society' rarely becomes an object of explicit inquiry—was underlined both by Jurij Striedter in 1968 and by Götz Müller in his 1981 review of *Work on Myth*. Yet here Müller could also have mentioned that Blumenberg's main confrontation with Sorel's theory of myth is actually *indirect*, proceeding via the roundabout route of Carl Schmitt's critique of parliamentarianism.

In *The Crisis of Parliamentary Democracy*, Sorel's ideas on myth meet with Schmitt's hearty approval, while also undergoing a thoroughly nationalist reinterpretation. For Schmitt, Sorel's theory of myth is a "theory of direct, active decision" and a "powerful contradiction" of liberal democratic notions such as public discussion and debate. But unlike Sorel, Schmitt saw this potential power of myth not in the general strike of the proletariat, but in the "national myth" that had helped Mussolini come to power in 1922. "A common spiritual enemy," wrote Schmitt, "can [. . .] produce the most remarkable agreements," and the way in which Italian fascism had demonised the communists was able to evoke "powerful emotions," thereby successfully creating a new national myth. In Schmitt's view "the theory of myth is the most powerful symptom of the decline of the relative rationalism of parliamentary thought." In this he saw both positive and negative potential. On the one hand, political myth might create "an authority based on the new feeling for order, discipline, and hierarchy." Yet on the other,

> The last remnants of solidarity and a feeling of belonging together will be destroyed in the pluralism of an unforeseeable number of myths. For political theology that is polytheism, just as every myth is polytheistic.[141]

While Schmitt saw this polytheism as a potential threat to order and national identity, Blumenberg appears to have taken up precisely the opposite position: to rehabilitate mythic polytheism as a guard against political absolutism. As we have seen, Odo Marquard contemporaneously developed an apparently similar political philosophy in essays entitled "In Praise of Polytheism" (1979), and "Enlightened Polytheism" (1983).[142] But Marquard arrives at far more concrete conclusions than does Blumenberg; or to paraphrase Richard Faber, Marquard makes explicit what is only implicit in Blumenberg's political polytheism.[143] At the Carl Schmitt colloquium held in May 1980, Marquard reformulated Goethe's saying as *nemo contra Deum nisi plures Dei*: no one (can stand) against a God unless it is many gods. Marquard proposes that liberal democracies must, through the modern political concept of the separation of powers (*Gewaltenteilung*), offer a polytheism of myths and institutions that hold one another in check. Precisely because the human being is incapable of providing absolute answers to political questions, all grand political narratives, whether of the left or the right, must be renounced in favour of the liberal democratic model: "a plurality of myths (*Polymythie*) is agreeable, a single myth (*Monomythie*) is bad."[144]

In order to find a similar political position in the writings of Blumenberg, one is forced to read between the lines. In fact, Blumenberg's writings on the political can in general be described as mere phenomenological descriptions of political situations—descriptions in which normative or emancipatory moments are few. One such normative moment occurs when Blumenberg invokes the term "democracy" in the essay on anthropology and rhetoric. Here Hobbes is said to have objected to democracy because it purportedly arrives at decisions *impetu animi* ("by a certain violence of the mind") rather than by *recta ratione*, or "right reason." This violence of the mind is seen to arise from rhetoric, because orators are guided by the "passions of their listeners." In this way, a pluralistic democracy made up of competing rhetorical points of view would, in Hobbes's view, lack the rational foundations of the social contract: the decision to give up the state of nature in exchange for the security provided by the absolutist state (AAR, 452–4; WWL, 130). This critique of the anti-democratic Hobbes within the context of a rehabilitation of rhetoric would appear to be Blumenberg's quiet way of staking a claim for liberal democracy in opposition to absolutism.

Blumenberg then revisits this theme in the *Nachlass* text "Political Theology III" (BSB, 167–74), which is thought to have been sent by Blumenberg to Jacob Taubes some time after Taubes had invited him to contribute to the 1980 colloquium on Carl Schmitt.[145] The tone of this text is ironic and weary: "who would still dare to doubt," asks Blumenberg "that theology can become political, and politics theological?" In answering this question he again returns to Napoleon's statement to Goethe that politics is fate. This statement was not, argues Blumenberg, "a piece of secularisation, not the replacement of the old 'destiny' by the new self-performance of historically potent action" as found in the "most evil demagogic rhetoric of the twentieth century." As is already pointed out in *Work on Myth*, if the context of this statement was a discussion of tragedy, then it merely referred to the position of the "defeated"—to those whose lives are ruined by the great political actors. But in the "following century" others—and here, Blumenberg would seem to include not only Carl Schmitt, but perhaps also Adolf Hitler—misread the statement in the active sense, as the opportunity "finally to take fate into one's own hands." The implication here is that within the absolutist state as envisioned by Hobbes and perhaps also Schmitt, and which Blumenberg sees as the "ideal realisation of a political theology," the polytheism of myth has been suppressed and is replaced with something resembling a would-be political monotheism founded upon nothing more than rhetoric and propaganda (BSB, 167–8, 170).

BLUMENBERG AND TAUBES ON MYTH AND DOGMA

If this does amount to a political position, then one of its central premises is "the antithesis of myth and dogma," which for Blumenberg emerges from the difference between originally oral mythic narratives on the hand and theological "images that are fixed in written form" on the other (WOM, 216; AM, 240). There can be no original, authentic or 'dogmatic' version of myth precisely because myth is always "already in the process of reception," which also means that it is subject to "variable freedom from writing" (WOM, 217–18; AM, 240–1). One of Blumenberg's paradigmatic cases of this transition from a polytheistic system of variable stories about gods to a fixed written story about God is the Areopagus sermon of St. Paul, where an unknown God is introduced as the only God. In Blumenberg's account of this speech,

> What matters is no longer to avoid incurring the displeasure of any of the established authorities in a system characterized by a separation of powers, but rather to satisfy the conditions posed by the one and hitherto unknown power that decides the fate of the world in accordance with justice.
>
> (WOM, 253; AM, 282)

Schmitt's 'political theology' would—in Blumenberg's implicit view—rhetorically attempt to reoccupy this position of the single power that must always decide in exceptional circumstances. The transition from myth to dogma thus takes on an air of absolutism, against which the free variation of myth appears to be liberal and polytheism becomes, at least in Odo Marquard's more explicit view, worthy of praise.[146]

This purported antithesis between myth and dogma is one of the most contested aspects of Blumenberg's theory of myth, and from the beginning its most persistent opponent was Jacob Taubes.[147] Already at the Poetics and Hermeneutics meeting of 1968, Taubes questioned whether there is "such a sharp separation between dogmatic and mythic traditions," while also suggesting that Blumenberg applied this opposition *a priori* to his materials rather than allowing for a sufficiently open analysis of them.[148] The chief exception to Blumenberg's thesis identified by Taubes was also the subject of Taubes's own paper at that 1968 meeting: "The Dogmatic Myth of Gnosticism" ("Der dogmatische Mythos der Gnosis"). Here Taubes alleges that Blumenberg ignores the extent to which the allegory found in Greek philosophy was itself a form of "translation" through which "mythic forms, names, and the destinies of mythic narrative" were transformed into concepts. Allegory is in this way "the triumph of a demythologized consciousness over mythic consciousness," but a triumph that nevertheless emerged from the body of myth that preceded it. This "allegorical method," always indebted to myth, is also said to reappear in "late ancient gnosticism" in the form of what Taubes refers to as "dogmatic myth." This myth is dogmatic because "in all of its variations it deploys only one 'true' doctrine."[149]

In *Work on Myth*, Blumenberg would come to reject this interpretation, albeit without even once referring to Taubes by name. Following the analysis of Hans Jonas, he reads late antique Gnosticism as a "fundamental myth" (*Grundmythos*), which is to say, as a "dynamic principle of the establishment of meaning" (WOM, 179; AM, 197–8).[150] This myth is not fundamental in the sense of being a 'master myth'—a purported origin or cause behind later variations—but in the sense that its lasting pregnance caused it to remain visible over time, which allows one to infer that it played a structuring or transcendental role during the period that Jonas refers to as the "Gnostic epoch" (WOM, 175, 179; AM, 192–3, 198). In the fundamental myth of Gnostic dualism, the miseries of this world are attributed to the world-creator or demiurge. This demiurge is seen as being opposed to a God of salvation, who is said to have played no role in the creation of the evil world.

In Blumenberg's view, this dualism gave rise to "problem-concerns" (*Problembesorgnisse*) that only later Christianity was able to resolve (WOM, 187; AM, 207). As Blumenberg argues at length in the *Legitimacy of the Modern Age*, Augustine's solution was to make fallen human beings, rather than the Gnostic demiurge, responsible for what is bad in the world (LMA, 132–3; LDN, 145–6). For Blumenberg, dualistic Gnosticism was never dogmatic precisely because two gods were always involved, about whom new stories could always be told (WOM, 179; AM, 198–9). Indeed, Gnosticism is said by him to have perished precisely "as a result of the abundance of its narrative contradictions and the discipline of the Roman Church's dogma" (WOM, 187; AM, 207). Blumenberg does concede that the "disjunction between the mythical and the dogmatic frame of mind is not complete," since the differences between them are more "matters of tendency" than they are essential or "eidetic." (WOM, 184, 218; AM, 204, 242). But these important differences in tendency cannot, he thinks, be overlooked. Gnosticism—as myth—told stories about why there were bad things in the world, whereas Christian dogma made these into an exclusive and single doctrine that purported to answer the theodicy question once and for all.

As a later (1983) paper by Taubes concerning polytheism demonstrates, this scholarly debate was not devoid of broader political consequences. Here Taubes's ostensible target was Odo Marquard's more explicit political polytheism, but he also openly admitted that Blumenberg's theory of myth, which Marquard had allegedly made into a "program," was also in his sights.[151] Here Taubes invokes Hermann Cohen's interpretation of Ezekiel 18 in his *Religion of Reason out of the Sources of Judaism* (*Religion der Vernunft aus den Quellen des Judentums* 1919). In Ezekiel, according to Taubes's reading of Cohen, the "mythical nexus of guilt and atonement" handed down by the tradition of myth is "transcended" by a new doctrine of individual responsibility for one's sins.[152] This, in Cohen's interpretation, leads to the birth of individual subjectivity: the ego or soul. In Cohen's words: "the sin before God leads us to man as I," and this development is a movement beyond what Cohen refers to as "the mythico-tragic view."[153] The neo-Kantian Cohen, like his successor Cassirer, presented myth as having been surpassed in a decisive way by the ethical progress of religious dogma. And not unlike Cohen, Cassirer went on to claim that in the context of the Second World War, the ethical core of Judaism might have been able to "break the power of the modern political myths." In Cassirer's view, one reason why the National Socialist regime was so opposed to the Jewish cultural tradition was precisely because it had taken the "decisive step that led from a *mythical* to an *ethical* religion."[154]

In this context, in which myth and dogma were always interrelated but in which the latter is seen to have progressed beyond the former, Taubes claims that a "recourse to mythology" in the form of political polytheism would mean "a suspension of the ethical, the dissolution of the I, whose ur-history we have sketched in Ezekiel."[155] The implication here is that political polytheism would amount only to relativism: to a politics with no normative moment other than the supposed virtues of pluralism. It is probably no coincidence that this essay appeared in a volume edited by Karl Heinz Bohrer, who had already associated *Work on Myth* with a purportedly dangerous "return of myth into culture." Thus, despite his more or less open critique of Carl Schmitt, Blumenberg, especially through his secondary association with the ideas of Arnold Gehlen and Odo Marquard, did not himself end up escaping allegations of political conservatism. But these allegations were made without access to the Blumenberg *Nachlass*. A concluding analysis of selected *Nachlass* materials relating to *Work on Myth* will provide a better understanding of Blumenberg as a theorist of political myth.

NOTES

1. The text appears in the fourth of four folders entitled "Götterschwund: Nach der Arbeit am Mythos" ("Fading of the Gods: After the Work on Myth"), which contains pieces that are thought to have been compiled and/or written between 1985 and 1991. See Blumenberg, "Kein Mythos des XX. Jahrhunderts," Hans Blumenberg Nachlass, *Deutsches Literaturarchiv* Marbach (hereafter DLA Marbach).

2. [Daß es nach der Arbeit am Mythos nie das Ende des Mythos gibt, muß nicht dadurch belegt oder bewiesen werden, daß die Produktion mythischer Muster fortgeht. Nicht minder aufschlußreich und beweiskräftig ist die fortbestehende Bewerbung um den vakanten Platz von Mythen, vom Rang und der Funktion des Mythischen.]

3. Franz Josef Wetz and Hermann Timm, "Vorwort," in *Die Kunst des Überlebens: Nachdenken über Hans Blumenberg* (Frankfurt am Main: Suhrkamp, 1999), 9–13; here: 10.

4. Christian Tilitzki, *Die deutsche Universitätsphilosophie in der Weimarer Republik und im Dritten Reich*, 2 vols. with continuous pagination (Berlin: Akademie Verlag, 2002), 2:780, footnote 43.

5. Tilitzki, *Die deutsche Universitätsphilosophie*, 2: 815–16.

6. Blumenberg, "Nachruf auf Erich Rothacker. Gehalten am 29. April 1966 in der öffentlichen Sitzung der Akademie der Wissenschaften und Literatur," in *Jahrbuch der Akademie der Wissenschaften und der Literatur in Mainz* (1966): 70–6.

7. See "Erich Rothacker," in Ernst Klee, *Das Personenlexikon zum Dritten Reich*, 4th ed. (Frankfurt am Main: S. Fischer, 2013), 510. For a detailed account of Rothacker's dealings with Goebbels and his other attempts to exert a cultural influence within the NSDAP, see Ralph Stöwer, *Erich Rothacker: Sein Leben und seine Wissenschaft vom Menschen* (Bonn: Bonn University Press, 2012), 13–17; 113–210.

8. See Gerhard Sauder, *Die Bücherverbrennung. Zum 10. Mai 1933* (Munich: Hanser, 1983), 80. See also Hildegard Brenner, *Die Kunstpolitik des Nationalsozialismus* (Hamburg: Rowohlt, 1963), 256.

9. See Volker Böhnigk, *Kulturanthropologie als Rassenlehre. Nationalsozialistische Kulturphilosophie aus der Sicht des Philosophen Erich Rothacker* (Würzburg: Königshausen and Neumann, 2002); "Die nationalsozialistische Kulturphilosophie Erich Rothackers," in *Philosophie im Nationalsozialismus*, ed. Hans Jörg Sandkühler (Hamburg: Felix Meiner, 2009), 191–217.

10. Michael Grüttner, "Das Scheitern der Vordenker. Deutsche Hochschullehrer und der Nationalsozialismus," in *Geschichte und Emanzipation: Festschrift für Reinhard Rürup* (Frankfurt am Main: Campus, 1999), 458–81; Tilitzki, *Die deutsche Universitätsphilosophie*, 2:930–4.

11. Stöwer, *Erich Rothacker*, 348–51.

12. Stöwer, *Erich Rothacker*, 289–300.

13. Blumenberg, "Nachruf auf Erich Rothacker," 73, 71.

14. Blumenberg, "Ein noch zu schreibender Brief," in VP, 144. Blumenberg's reference to *das Weltgericht* is probably an allusion to a line from Friedrich Schiller's poem of 1786, "Resignation": "Die Weltgeschichte ist das Weltgericht" (The history of the world is the last judgement). See Schiller, "Resignation" in Johann Christoph Friedrich Schiller, *Werke und Briefe*, ed. Otto Dann et al., 12 vols. (Frankfurt am Main: Deutscher KlassikerVerlag, 1992–2004), 1:168–71.

15. See Blumenberg to Taubes, March 22, 1965, in BTB, 46–50; here: 48.

16. Julia Wagner, "Anfangen. Zur Konstitutionsphase der Forschungsgruppe Poetik und Hermeneutik," in *Internationales Archiv für Sozialgeschichte der deutschen Literatur 35*, no. 1 (2010): 53–76; here: 61–2, 74.

17. See Hans Ulrich Gumbrecht, "Mein Lehrer, der Mann von der SS," in *Die Zeit*, April 7, 2011, 62; see also Ernst Klee, *Kulturlexikon zum Dritten Reich* (Frankfurt am Main: Fischer, 2009), 255.

18. Klee, *Kulturlexikon zum Dritten Reich*, 216.

19. See, for example, the statement quoted by Klee in *Das Personenlexikon zum Dritten Reich*, 529–30.

20. Tilitzki, *Die deutsche Universitätsphilosophie*, 1:727–9.

21. The full title of this 'oath' was "Loyalty Oath of the Professors at German Universities and Colleges to Adolf Hitler and the National Socialist State" ("Bekenntnis der Professoren an den deutschen Universitäten und Hochschulen zu Adolf Hitler und dem nationalsozialistischen Staat"). See Klee, *Das Personenlexikon zum Dritten Reich*, 499.

22. Tilitzki, *Die deutsche Universitätsphilosophie*, 2:826–31; Hans Jörg Sandkühler, "Joachim Ritter: Über die Schwierigkeiten, 1933–45 Philosoph zu sein," in *Philosophie im Nationalsozialismus*, ed. Hans Jörg Sandkühler (Hamburg: Felix Meiner, 2009), 219–52; here: 228–42.

23. Tilitzki, *Die deutsche Universitätsphilosophie*, 1:340, 698; Jean Grondin, *Hans-Georg Gadamer: A Biography* (New Haven, CT: Yale University Press, 2003), 158, 181; Klee, *Das Personenlexikon zum Dritten Reich*, 172.

24. Chiara Bottici, *A Philosophy of Political Myth* (Cambridge: Cambridge University Press, 2007), 7–8.

25. Christian Thies, *Gehlen zur Einführung* (Hamburg: Junius, 2000), 12, 15–19; Klee, *Das Personenlexikon zum Dritten Reich*, 176–7.

26. See Tilitzki, *Die deutsche Universitätsphilosophie*, 1:633–5.

27. Arnold Gehlen, *Urmensch und Spätkultur: Philosophische Ergebnisse und Aussagen* (Bonn: Athenäum, 1956), 25.

28. Jens Hacke, *Philosophie der Bürgerlichkeit: Die liberalkonservative Begründung der Bundesrepublik* (Göttingen: Vandenhoeck and Ruprecht, 2006), 135–61.

29. See Wolf Lepenies, "Anthropologie und Gesellschaftskritik. Zur Kontroverse Gehlen-Habermas," in *Kritik der Anthropologie. Marx und Freud, Gehlen und Habermas, Über Aggression* (Munich: Hanser, 1971), 77–102; here: 78. Quoted in Hacke, *Philosophie der Bürgerlichkeit*, 142.

30. Joachim Ritter, "Politik und Ethik in der praktischen Philosophie des Aristoteles (1967)," in *Metaphysik und Politik. Studien zu Aristoteles und Hegel* (Frankfurt am Main: Suhrkamp, 1988), 106–32; here: 110.

31. Ritter, "Politik und Ethik," 121–2, 124, 127–8.

32. Hacke, *Philosophie der Bürgerlichkeit*, 147.

33. See Helmut Schelsky, *Die Soziologen und das Recht. Abhandlungen und Vorträge zur Soziologie von Recht, Institution und Planung* (Opladen: Westdeutscher Verlag, 1980), 81–3.

34. See Schelsky, "Zur soziologischen Theorie der Institution," in *Zur Theorie der Institution* (Düsseldorf: Bertelsmann, 1970), 9–26. Quoted in Hacke, *Philosophie der Bürgerlichkeit*, 148–9.

35. See Jürgen Habermas, *Remarks on Discourse Ethics*, in *Justification and Application: Remarks on Discourse Ethics*, trans. Ciaran Cronin (Cambridge, MA: MIT Press, 1993), 19–111; here: 22; *Erläuterungen zur Diskursethik* (Frankfurt am Main: Suhrkamp, 1991), 122.

36. See Marquard, *Schwierigkeiten mit der Geschichtsphilosophie. Aufsätze* (Frankfurt am Main: Suhrkamp, 1982), 13–33.

37. Marquard, *Schwierigkeiten mit der Geschichtsphilosophie*, 136.

38. Marquard positions Gehlen's notion of compensation at the end of a long philosophical tradition of compensation theories that begins in the early modern period. See Marquard, "Kompensation" (1976) in *Historisches Wörterbuch der Philosophie*, ed. Joachim Ritter et al., 13 vols. (Basel: Schwabe, 1971–2007), 4: 912–18, and: "Kompensation. Überlegunen zu einer Verlaufsfigur geschichtlicher Prozesse," in *Aesthetica und Anaesthetica: Philosophische Überlegungen* (Paderborn: Schönigh, 1989), 64–81. In this last essay Marquard defines compensation, in terms that are redolent of Gehlen, as "the balancing out (*Ausgleich*) of deficient circumstances (*Mangellagen*)" (67). Maquard also points, however, to another line of compensation theory, namely that elaborated by Joachim Ritter, in which art is seen to compensate

for the objectification of the world undertaken by the natural sciences. See Marquard, "Kompensationstheorien des Ästhetischen," in *Studien zur Ästhetik und Literatur der Kunstperiode*, ed. Dirk Grathoff (Frankfurt am Main: Peter Lang, 1985), 103–20; here: 113.

39. Odo Marquard, "Lob des Polytheismus. Über Monomythie und Polymythie," in *Philosophie und Mythos. Ein Kolloquium*, ed. Hans Poser (Berlin: De Gruyter, 1979), 40–58. This essay appeared in the same year as Blumenberg's *Work on Myth*, but already displays the influence of Blumenberg's ideas about myth as they were outlined at the *Poetik und Hermeneutik* meeting of 1968. See Blumenberg, WWM.
40. Odo Marquard, *Skepsis als Philosophie der Endlichkeit* (Bonner philosophische Vorträge und Studien), ed. Wolfram Hofgrebe (Bonn: Bouvier, 2002), 5, 9–10.
41. Odo Marquard, "Entlastung vom Absoluten," in *Die Kunst des Überlebens: Nachdenken über Hans Blumenberg*, ed. Franz Josef Wetz and Hermann Timm (Frankfurt am Main: Suhrkamp, 1999), 17–27; here: 20.
42. See Blumenberg, "Das Verhältnis von Natur und Technik als philosophisches Problem," (1951), in ÄMS, 253–65; here: 253–4.
43. Blumenberg, *Die Legitimität der Neuzeit* (Frankfurt am Main: Suhrkamp, 1966), 91.
44. Arnold Gehlen, *Der Mensch: Seine Natur und seine Stellung in der Welt* (1940; Berlin: Junker und Dünnhaupt, 1941), 448.
45. Hans Blumenberg, "Warum reißen wir das Holstentor in Lübeck nicht ab?" in VP, 36.
46. Jürgen Habermas, "Der Zerfall der Institutionen," in *Frankfurter Allgemeine Zeitung*, April 7, 1956.
47. Arnold Gehlen, *Moral und Hypermoral: Eine pluralistische Ethik* (Frankfurt am Main: Athenäeum, 1969).
48. Jürgen Habermas, "Arnold Gehlen: Imitation Substantiality," in *Philosophical-Political Profiles*, trans. Frederick G. Lawrence (London: Heinemann, 1983), 111–28; here: 121–2 (translation altered); "Nachgeahmte Substantialität. Eine Auseinandersetzung mit Arnold Gehlens Ethik," *Merkur* 24, no. 264 (1970): 313–27; here: 322.
49. Rudolf Augstein, "Wir Mundwerkburschen. Arnold Gehlens antiintellektuelle Wissenschaft," in *Der Spiegel* 23 (1970): 164–73.
50. Jürgen Habermas, "Anthropologie," in *Das Fischer Lexikon Philosophie*, ed. Alwin Diemer and Ivo Frenzel (Frankfurt am Main: Fischer, 1958), 18–35.
51. Habermas, "Anthropologie," 22–7.
52. Habermas, "Anthropologie," 18.
53. Habermas, "Anthropologie," 31–2. See also Erich Rothacker, *Geschichtsphilosophie* (Munich: Oldenbourg, 1934), 91–9; Rothacker, *Probleme der Kulturanthropologie* in *Systematische Philosophie*, ed. Nicolai Hartmann (Stuttgart: Kohlhammer, 1942), 54–198; here: 157–78.
54. Habermas, "Anthropologie," 32–3.
55. Erich Rothacker, *Probleme der Kulturanthropologie* (Bonn: Bouvier, 1948). The first edition appeared alongside Arnold Gehlen's *Zur Systematik der Anthropologie* in a volume edited by Nicolai Hartmann and titled *Systematische Philosophie* (Stuttgart: Kohlhammer, 1942). I have not been able to identify notable differences between the 1942 and 1948 editions.
56. Habermas, "Anthropologie," 33–4.
57. Joachim Fischer, *Philosophische Anthropologie. Eine Denkrichtung des 20. Jahrhunderts* (Freiburg: Alber, 2008), 320.
58. Ferdinand Fellmann, "Blumenberg, Hans," in *Information Philosophie*, http://www.information-philosophie.de/?a=1&t=857&n=2&y=1&c=63 (accessed

May 22, 2012). The recent publication of Blumenberg's correspondence with Jacob Taubes suggests that the reason for Blumenberg's resignation lay in his financial disagreements with Siegfried Unseld, the head of Suhrkamp Verlag. See Blumenberg to Taubes, January 19, 1971, in BTB 161; see also Blumenberg to Habermas, September 11, 1970, reproduced in the commentary in BTB, 161–2.

59. Christoph Jamme, *"Gott an hat ein Gewand." Grenzen und Perspektiven philosophischer Mythos-Theorien der Gegenwart* (Frankfurt am Main: Suhrkamp, 1999), 95–105.
60. Taubes expressed to Blumenberg his opinion that Adorno's *Negative Dialectics* (*Negative Dialektik*) and Blumenberg's *Legitimacy of the Modern Age*, published by Suhrkamp in the same year (1966), were both examples of ideology critique. See Taubes to Blumenberg, December 14, 1966, in BTB, 109–11. See also Taubes's letter to Siegfried Unseld dated December 14, 1966 (quoted in BTB, 112–13), in which he opines that Adorno and Blumenberg have more in common than they themselves recognise.
61. See Immanuel Kant, *Critique of Pure Reason*, ed. and trans. Paul Guyer and Allen W. Wood (Cambridge: Cambridge University Press, 1998), 260; *Kritik der reinen Vernunft* (B150–6), in *Werke in sechs Bänden*, ed. Wilhelm Weischedel, 7th ed., 6 vols. (Darmstadt: Wissenschaftliche Buchgesellschaft, 2011), 2:153.
62. Arnold Gehlen, "Arbeiten—Ausruhen—Ausnützen. Wesensmerkmale des Menschen" (1974), and "Unsere persönliche Freiheit—morgen" (1966), in *Gesamtausgabe*, vol. 7, *Einblicke*, ed. Karl-Siegbert Rehberg (Frankfurt am Main: Klostermann, 1978), 20–33, 79–87.
63. On Blumenberg's antipathy toward the term *Kritik*, see his letter to Taubes dated May 24, 1977, in BTB, 171–5; here: 172–3.
64. Rudolf Augstein, "Mit Napoleon: Die Politik ist das Schicksal," *Der Spiegel* 35, no. 6 (February 2, 1981): 171–9.
65. Goethe, "Unterredung mit Napoleon," in *Werke* (Hamburger Ausgabe), ed. Erich Trunz, 14 vols. (Munich: Deutscher Taschenbuch Verlag, 2000), 10:543–7; here: 546.
66. Bernhard Lypp, "Dasein am Mythos," *Neue Zürcher Zeitung*, March 22–3, 1980; W. Martin Lüdke, "Ein Lebenswerk: *Arbeit am Mythos*," *Frankfurter Rundschau*, July 11, 1981, section "Bücher von Heute," 4.
67. Karl Heinz Bohrer, "Rückkehr des Mythos?" *Frankfurter Allgemeine Zeitung*, January 26, 1980.
68. Blumenberg read *Negative Dialectics* on the suggestion of Taubes. See Blumenberg to Taubes, September 20, 1967, in BTB, 134–6.
69. Jamme, *"Gott an hat ein Gewand,"* 100.
70. Theodor W. Adorno and Max Horkheimer, *Dialectic of Enlightenment*, trans. John Cumming (1947; London: Verso, 1997), xvi, 11; *Dialektik der Aufklärung* (Amsterdam: Querido, 1947), 10, 22.
71. Adorno and Horkheimer, *Dialectic of Enlightenment*, 46–7; *Dialektik der Aufklärung*, 61–2.
72. Adorno and Horkheimer, *Dialectic of Enlightenment*, 57; *Dialektik der Aufklärung*, 73.
73. On the importance of Nietzsche for the argument of *Dialectic of Enlightenment*, see Jürgen Habermas, "The Entwinement of Myth and Enlightenment: Re-Reading *Dialectic of Enlightenment*," *New German Critique* 26 (1982): 13–30; here: 22–8; "Die Verschlingung von Mythos und Aufklärung. Bemerkungen zur *Dialektik der Aufklärung*—nach einer erneuten Lektüre," in *Mythos und Moderne. Begriff und Bild einer Rekonstruktion*, ed. Karl

Heinz Bohrer (Frankfurt am Main: Suhrkamp, 1983), 405–31; here: 419–26. On the importance of Nietzsche for Blumenberg's theory of metaphorology, see my remarks on Nietzsche's "On Truth and Lie in an Extra-Moral Sense" in Chapter 5 of this volume.

74. Adorno and Horkheimer, *Dialectic of Enlightenment*, 181; *Dialektik der Aufklärung*, 213.

75. Jamme, *"Gott an hat ein Gewand,"* 100.

76. Adorno and Horkheimer, *Dialectic of Enlightenment*, xiv; *Dialektik der Aufklärung*, 8.

77. Adorno and Horkheimer, *Dialectic of Enlightenment*, 16; *Dialektik der Aufklärung*, 27.

78. Adorno and Horkheimer, *Dialectic of Enlightenment*, 16; *Dialektik der Aufklärung*, 27.

79. Theodor W. Adorno, *Minima Moralia: Reflections on a Damaged Life*, trans. E.F.N. Jephcott (1951; London: Verso, 2005), 103; *Minima Moralia: Reflexionen aus dem beschädigten Leben* (Frankfurt am Main: Suhrkamp, 1951), 130.

80. Adorno and Horkheimer, *Dialectic of Enlightenment*, 39; *Dialektik der Aufklärung*, 54.

81. See LMA, 239–40, 383; LDN, 274, 447.

82. Adorno and Horkheimer, *Dialectic of Enlightenment*, 3–5; *Dialektik der Aufklärung*, 13–15.

83. Adorno and Horkheimer, *Dialectic of Enlightenment*, 159, 13; *Dialektik der Aufklärung*, 189, 24.

84. Christa Bürger, "Arbeit an der Geschichte," in *Mythos und Moderne*, 493–507; here: 493–5.

85. See Jürgen Maruhn, "Hans Blumenberg, *Arbeit am Mythos*," *Das Argument* 124 (1980): 883–4.

86. H. L. Ollig, "Hans Blumenberg, *Arbeit am Mythos*," *Theologie und Philosophie* 10, no. 1 (1981): 148–52; here: 151.

87. Götz Müller, "Hans Blumenberg, *Arbeit am Mythos*," *Zeitschrift für deutsche Philologie* 100 (1981): 314–18; republished in PF, 67–78 (references are to the PF edition); here: 69–71, 74–6.

88. See the comments of Jurij Striedter in "Mythos und Dogma," in *Terror und Spiel. Probleme der Mythenrezeption* (Poetik und Hermeneutik 4), ed. Manfred Fuhrmann (Munich: Fink, 1971), 527–47; here: 540.

89. Müller in PF, 77–8; Müller is quoting from the Preface to Ernst Cassirer's *Philosophy of Symbolic Forms*, vol. 2, *Mythical Thought*, trans. Ralph Manheim (New Haven, CT: Yale University Press, 1955), xvi (translation altered); *Philosophie der symbolischen Formen. Zweiter Teil: Das mythische Denken*, ed. Klaus Rosenkranz (1925; Hamburg: Felix Meiner, 2002), xiv.

90. Ernst Cassirer, *The Myth of the State* (New Haven, CT: Yale University Press, 1946), 3.

91. Cassirer, *The Myth of the State*, 3.

92. Cassirer, *The Myth of the State*, 71–2.

93. Cassirer, *The Myth of the State*, 98, 140, 143, 154–5.

94. Cassirer, *The Myth of the State*, 277, 278–80, 282.

95. Eric Voegelin, "The Myth of the State," *The Journal of Politics* 9, no. 3 (1947): 445–7. Also discussed by Peter E. Gordon in *Continental Divide: Heidegger, Cassirer, Davos* (Cambridge, MA: Harvard University Press, 2010), 314.

96. The chapter in question, now published from the *Nachlass* in PF, does not carry the title referred to in Blumenberg's letter, that of "Stalingrad als mythische Konsequenz." It is nevertheless highly probable that the text "Präfiguration" is the chapter to which Blumenberg refers in his letter to Müller dated July 20, 1981. For further discussion see the "Editorische Notiz" in PF, 79–81, and also note 15 in Chapter 8 of this volume.

97. Jamme, *"Gott an hat ein Gewand,"* 94.
98. Robert A. Segal, "Hans Blumenberg as a Theorist of Myth," in *Theorizing about Myth* (Amherst: University of Massachusetts Press, 1999), 143–52; here: 152.
99. See Hans-Georg Gadamer, *Truth and Method*, 2nd ed., trans. Joel Weinsheimer and Donald G. Marshall (1960; New York: Continuum, 2003), 271–85; *Wahrheit und Methode*, in *Gesammelte Werke*, vol. 1 (Tübingen: Mohr, 1986), 276–90. The recently published correspondence between Blumenberg and Taubes reveals the extent to which Blumenberg's antipathy towards Gadamer was probably both political and philosophical, having to do with Gadamer representing the on-going tradition of Martin Heidegger in German philosophy. Blumenberg ironically dubbed Gadamer "the pope of German philosophy." See Blumenberg to Taubes, March 22, 1965, in BTB, 46–50; here: 47–8. Taubes responded by reassuring Blumenberg that "even popes are mortal," see Taubes to Blumenberg, March 25, 1965, in BTB, 53–6; here: 55.
100. Jacob Taubes to Hans Blumenberg, February 7, 1979, and August 15, 1979, October 26, 1979, in BTB, 195, 199–200, 204–5.
101. Hans Blumenberg to Jacob Taubes, April 4, 1979, and October 20, 1979, in BTB, 196–7, 203.
102. See Taubes to Blumenberg, August 15, 1979, in BTB, 199–200. The title was the suggestion, not of Carl Schmitt, but of Taubes's colleague Wolfgang Hübener (see the commentary in BTB, 200). A text carrying this title and written by Blumenberg appears in BSB (167–74), and is discussed further on.
103. The colloquium papers, edited by Taubes, were later published as *Religionstheorie und Politische Theologie*, vol. 1, *Der Fürst dieser Welt. Carl Schmitt und die Folgen* (Munich: Fink, 1983).
104. Goethe, *From My Life, Poetry and Truth, Part Four*, trans. Robert R. Heitner, notes by Thomas P. Saine, *Goethe's Collected Works*, vol. 5 (New York: Suhrkamp, 1987), 598; *Dichtung und Wahrheit* in Goethe, *Sämtliche Werke, Briefe, Tagebücher und Gespräche* (Frankfurter Ausgabe), 2 parts, 40 vols., ed. Hendrik Birus et al. (Frankfurt am Main: Deutscher Klassiker Verlag, 1985–2003), 1,14:841–2. The translation of the Latin saying is that of Robert M. Wallace in WOM, 524.
105. [ist aus einer Art 'Wette' mit Gershom Scholem und Hans-Georg Gadamer enstanden, die sich auf Goethes 'ungeheuren Spruch' bezog und im Mai 1970 auf einer Hotelterasse zustande kam, neun Jahre vor dem Buch.] Hans Blumenberg to Ulrich Thoemmes, February 3, 1984, Hans Blumenberg Nachlass, DLA Marbach.
106. Heidrun Kämper, *Opfer—Täter—Nichttäter. Ein Wörterbuch zum Schulddiskurs 1945–1955* (Berlin: De Gruyter, 2007), 30–1.
107. For an account of Schacht's trial at Nuremberg, see Christopher Kopper, *Hjalmar Schacht. Aufstieg und Fall von Hitlers mächstigtem Bankier* (Munich: Hanser, 2006), 359–70.
108. See Dix's speech under the entry for Monday July 15, 1946, in *Der Nürnberger Prozeß. Das Protokoll des Prozesses gegen die Hauptkriegsverbrecher vor dem internationalen Militärgerichtshof, 14. November 1945–1–Oktober 1946* (CD-ROM), ed. Mathias Bertram (Berlin: Directmedia, 1999), 23416–18.
109. Carl Schmitt, *Political Theology II: The Myth of the Closure of Any Political Theology*, trans. Michael Hoelzl and Graham Ward (Cambridge: Polity, 2008), 126; *Politische Theologie II. Die Legende von der Erledigung jeder politischen Theologie* (Berlin: Duncker and Humblot, 1970), 122.
110. See Reinhard Mehring, *Carl Schmitt. Aufstieg und Fall* (Munich: C.H. Beck, 2009), especially 304–436.

111. Both of the recent scholarly editions of Goethe's works have found no prior source for the saying. See the commentaries in FA, 1/14: 1295, and in Goethe, *Sämtliche Werke nach Epochen seines Schaffens* (Münchner Ausgabe), ed. Karl Richter, Herbert G. Göpfert, Norbert Miller, and Gerhard Sauder, 21 vols. in 31 (Munich, 1985–98), 16:1073 (hereafter cited as MA followed by volume and page numbers).

112. Schmitt, *Political Theology II*, 127; *Politische Theologie II*, 123.

113. See Goethe, *Maximen und Reflexionen*, (no. 807), in MA, 17:863.

114. See Hans Blumenberg, *Legitimität der Neuzeit* (Frankfurt am Main: Suhrkamp, 1966), 57–61; Schmitt, *Political Theology II*, 116–30; *Politische Theologie II*, 109–26; Blumenberg, *Säkularisierung und Selbstbehauptung. Erweiterte und überarbeitete Neuausgabe von 'Die Legitimität der Neuzeit', erster und zweiter Teil* (Frankfurt am Main: Suhrkamp, 1974), 103–18; and BSB.

115. See Wolfgang Hübener, "Carl Schmitt und Hans Blumenberg oder über Kette und Schuß in der historischen Textur der Moderne," 57–76; Odo Marquard, "Aufgeklärter Polytheismus—auch eine politische Theologie," 77–84; Richard Faber, "Von der 'Erledigung jeder Politischen Theologie' zur Konstitution politischer Polytheologie," 85–99; all in Taubes, ed., *Der Fürst dieser Welt*.

116. On this question, see also: Ruth Groh, *Arbeit an der Heillosigkeit der Welt. Zur politisch-theologischen Mythologie und Anthropologie Hans Blumenbergs* (Frankfurt am Main: Suhrkamp 1998), 156–85; Jan-Werner Müller, *A Dangerous Mind: Carl Schmitt and Post-War European Thought* (New Haven, CT: Yale University Press, 2003), 156–68; Heidenreich, *Mensch und Moderne bei Hans Blumenberg* (Munich: Fink, 2005), 192–7; Oliver Müller, *Sorge um die Vernunft. Hans Blumenbergs phänomenologische Anthropologie* (Paderborn: Mentis, 2005), 288–91.

117. Carl Schmitt, *Political Theology: Four Chapters on the Concept of Sovereignty*, trans. and introd. George Schwab (Chicago: University of Chicago Press, 2005), 36, 51, 5–6, 47–9; *Politische Theologie. Vier Kapitel zur Lehre von der Souveränität*, 2nd ed. (1922; Munich: Duncker and Humblot, 1934), 49, 65, 11–12, 61–2.

118. Carl Schmitt, *The Crisis of Parliamentary Democracy*, trans. Ellen Kennedy (Cambridge, MA: MIT Press, 1988), 47, 71; *Die geistesgeschichtliche Lage des heutigen Parlamentarismus*, 5th ed. (1923; Berlin: Duncker and Humblot, 1979), 58, 83.

119. Schmitt, *The Crisis of Parliamentary Democracy*, 20, 29; *Die geistesgeschichtliche Lage*, 28–9, 38.

120. Schmitt, *The Crisis of Parliamentary Democracy*, 2; *Die geistesgeschichtliche Lage*, 5.

121. See Schmitt, *Political Theology*, 52; *Politische Theologie*, 66; *The Crisis of Parliamentary Democracy*, 43; *Die geistesgeschichtliche Lage*, 54.

122. Hans Blumenberg, *Die Legitimität der Neuzeit* (1966 ed.), 60–1.

123. Blumenberg, *Die Legitimität der Neuzeit* (1966 ed.), 58–9.

124. See Blumenberg, *Säkularisierung und Selbstbehauptung*, 103–18.

125. Blumenberg, *Säkularisierung und Selbstbehauptung*, 108–9. This passage remained unchanged in the later revised edition of *Säkularisierung und Selbstbehauptung*, published in 1983, upon which Robert M. Wallace's translation is based.

126. As Richard Faber suggests in "Von der 'Erledigung jeder Politischen Theologie' zur Konstitution Politischer Polytheologie," 92.

127. Schmitt, *Political Theology II*, 122; *Politische Theologie II*, 116.

128. Carl Schmitt, *The Concept of the Political*, trans. and introd. George Schwab (Chicago: University of Chicago Press, 1996), 25–7; *Der Begriff des Politischen* (1927; Berlin: Duncker and Humblot, 1979), 26–8.

129. See Jan-Werner Müller, *A Dangerous Mind*, 30–2.
130. See, in particular, Groh, *Arbeit an der Heillosigkeit*, 156–84.
131. Hans Blumenberg to Carl Schmitt, August 7, 1975, in BSB, 133.
132. Hume writes that "polytheism, claiming no single truth about a unique god, is more tolerant than monotheism." See David Hume, *The Natural History of Religion*, in *Dialogues and Natural History of Religion*, ed. J.C.A. Gaskin (Oxford: Oxford University Press, 2008), 195.
133. Hans Blumenberg, "Wirklichkeitsbegriff und Staatstheorie," *Schweizer Monatshefte* 48 (1968–9): 121–46, (WST).
134. Cassirer, *The Myth of the State*, 116.
135. J.L. Austin, *How to do Things with Words: The William James Lectures Delivered at Harvard University in 1955*, ed. James O. Urmson (Oxford: Clarendon Press, 1962).
136. Georges Sorel, *Reflections on Violence*, ed. and trans. Jeremy Jennings (Cambridge: Cambridge University Press, 2009), 20.
137. Sorel, *Reflections on Violence*, 24, 28, 29, 30.
138. Sorel cites Bergson's *Time and Free Will: An Essay on the Immediate Data of Consciousness* (*Essai sur les données immédiates de la conscience*) (Paris: Alcan, 1889), 175–6.
139. Sorel, *Reflections on Violence*, 26, 113, 115, 165–6, 208.
140. Georges Sorel, *Über die Gewalt*, mit einem Nachwort von George Lichtheim, übersetzt von Ludwig Oppenheimer (Frankfurt am Main: Suhrkamp, 1969).
141. Schmitt, *The Crisis of Parliamentary Democracy*, 68, 75–6; *Die geistesgeschichtliche Lage*, 80, 88–9.
142. See Marquard, "Lob des Polytheismus" and Marquard, "Aufgeklärter Polytheismus."
143. Faber, "Von der 'Erledigung jeder Politischen Theologie' zur Konstitution Politischer Polytheologie," 97.
144. Marquard, "Aufgeklärter Polytheismus," 83–4.
145. See the commentary in BSB, 174.
146. See Marquard, "Lob des Polytheismus."
147. For further context, see Herbert Kopp-Oberstebrink, "Between Terror and Play: The Intellectual Encounter of Hans Blumenberg and Jacob Taubes," *Telos* 158 (Spring, 2012): 119–34.
148. See Taubes's remarks in the first discussion in *Terror und Spiel. Probleme der Mythenrezeption* (Poetik und Hermeneutik 4), ed. Manfred Fuhrmann (Munich: Fink, 1971), 534, 539–40. Similar arguments were also made against Blumenberg in an unpublished response to Blumenberg's paper written by Taubes, now published in BTB, 252–4. Blumenberg's own private and previously unpublished note on the discussions at the Poetics and Hermeneutics meeting in 1968 also appears in BTB (255–7), and will be analysed in Chapter 8 of this volume.
149. Jacob Taubes, "The Dogmatic Myth of Gnosticism," trans. William Rauscher, in *From Cult to Culture: Fragments Towards a Critique of Historical Reason*, ed. Charlotte Elisheva Fonrobert and Amir Engel (Stanford, CA: Stanford University Press, 2010), 61–75; here: 62, 69; "Der dogmatische Mythos der Gnosis," in *Terror und Spiel*, 145–56; here: 145–6, 151.
150. For the interpretation of Gnosis as a *Grundmythos*, see Hans Jonas, *Gnosis und spätantiker Geist*, part 2, *Von der Mythologie zur mystischen Philosophie* (Göttingen: Vandenhoeck and Ruprecht, 1954), 1. Blumenberg reviewed this volume in 1958. See Blumenberg, "Epochenschwelle und Rezeption," *Philosophische Rundschau* 6 (1958): 94–119. On the importance of Jonas in relation to Blumenberg's reception of Gnosticism, see Benjamin Lazier, "Overcoming Gnosticism: Hans Blumenberg, Hans Jonas and the Legitimacy of the Natural World," *Journal of the History of Ideas* 64, no. 4 (2003): 619–37.

151. Jacob Taubes, "On the Current State of Polytheism," in *From Cult to Culture*, 302–14; here: 313; "Zur Konjunktur des Polytheismus," in *Mythos und Moderne*, 457–70; here: 468–9.
152. Taubes, "On the Current State of Polytheism," in *From Cult to Culture*, 302–14; here: 306; "Zur Konjunktur des Polytheismus," in *Mythos und Moderne*, 406.
153. Hermann Cohen, *Religion of Reason out of the Sources of Judaism Alone*, trans. Simon Kaplan (New York: F. Ungar, 1972), 189–91; *Religion der Vernunft aus den Quellen des Judentums* (Leipzig: Fock, 1919), 222–4.
154. See Ernst Cassirer, "Judaism and the Modern Political Myths," in *Contemporary Jewish Record* 7, no. 2 (1944): 115–26; reprinted in *Symbol, Myth and Culture: Essays and Lectures of Ernst Cassirer, 1935–45*, ed. Donald Phillip Verene (New Haven, CT: Yale University Press, 1979), 233–41; here: 241, 240. Also contextualised in Peter E. Gordon, *Continental Divide: Heidegger, Cassirer, Davos* (Cambridge, MA: Harvard University Press, 2010), 317–22.
155. Taubes, "On the Current State of Polytheism," 307; "Zur Konjunktur des Polytheismus," 462.

8   Conclusion
Political Myth in the Blumenberg *Nachlass*

In this Conclusion, two parts of the *Work on Myth* manuscripts—the first unpublished, the second recently published[1]—will be examined. Both texts explicitly deal with the role played by myth in National Socialism.

REMYTHICIZATION

The first of these—which carries the handwritten title of "Remythicizations" (*Remythisierungen*) and the signature 'AMY IV,' designating that it was part of the *Work on Myth* manuscripts—returns us to the subject of Alfred Rosenberg's *Myth of the Twentieth Century*.[2] Blumenberg already deals with the question of remythicization in *Work on Myth*, which is for him bound up with issues relating to mythic polytheism and 'dogmatic' monotheism. This argument stretches across an arc from antiquity to modernity. It begins with Aristotle's attribution to Thales of Miletus of the view that "everything is full of gods" (*De Anima* 411a 18), which Blumenberg interprets as a declaration of "the exhaustion of the mythical mode of thought" (WOM, 25; AM, 31), presumably in the sense that the gods referred to by Thales are now taken by him—or at least in Aristotle's presentation of his views—to be immanent causes resident in nature rather than supernatural beings. But in Blumenberg's view, the gods referred to by Thales were nevertheless part of "that millenniums-long work of myth itself, which told of the monstrous as something that is far in the past," thereby making possible the mode of self-assured theoretical observation that Thales announces at the so-called birth of philosophy. Thales, the "protophilosopher," merely "takes over the office" once held by myth: that of depleting superior powers by naming and explaining them (WOM, 26; AM, 32–3).

The modern point in this arc is in turn occupied by Friedrich Nietzsche's complaint that since the apparent triumph of monotheism (or as the world-weary Nietzsche dubs it, "monotono-theism") in the Western tradition, there has been "not a single new God!" This is followed by the exclamation: "And how many new gods are still possible!"[3] According to Blumenberg, these two sentences written by Nietzsche designate a new threshold situation that, seen as a need, comes under the heading of "remythicization." What makes Nietzsche's suggestive observation alarming is the further consideration that the new gods would not have to have the names and stories of the old ones again, and would exercise their superior power in unknown ways. Do we feel the danger that lies in such a generous promise of something totally different, from the mouth of the man who affirmed the eternal recurrence of the same?

(WOM, 29–30; AM, 36).

Blumenberg does not further investigate this text from Nietzsche's *Nachlass*, but even a cursory examination of it shows what retrospective dangers Blumenberg, as a survivor of National Socialism, would doubtless have found within its lines. When Nietzsche describes the Christian God as an "unnatural castration"—as a God of "the little people," and as a God who has been stripped of the ability to wreak terror—he also maintains that such a God "can no longer represent the aggressive and power-thirsty soul of a people, its will to power."[4] Here 'remythicization' appears to be an historical anachronism akin to that which Cassirer identifies in the 'modern political myths': namely the desire, within an age that is both technologically advanced and thereby post-mythical (in the sense of 'enlightened' and monotheistic) to create "totally different" gods with unknown powers.

Later in *Work on Myth*, Blumenberg refines precisely what he means by 'remythicization' by arguing that the new gods called for in such situations must paradoxically be both new and also purportedly capable of restoring an order which is already familiar and therefore susceptible of being dealt with. The story told by myth, writes Blumenberg,

says that some monsters have already disappeared from the world, monsters that were even worse than those that lie behind what is present; and it says that things have always been the way, or almost the way, that they are now. That makes ages that are characterized by high rates of change of their system-conditions eager for new myths, for remythicizations, but also ill adapted for giving themselves what they desire. For nothing permits them to believe what they would very much like to believe—that the world has always been or has once before been the way it now promises or threatens to become.

(WOM, 35; AM, 41)

Remythicization is therefore an expression of the desire for both difference and repetition: because the historical circumstances to which the new myth is required to respond are novel and perhaps disturbing, a so-called new myth is called for. But since the function of such a myth can only be imagined on the basis of its being compared to prior models, it must at the same time be old. Its function is also both revolutionary and restorative. The changes in the 'system-conditions' of the age are seen to require wholly new measures or 'answers' that will purportedly make these destabilising changes manageable, but the entire purpose of these measures is not to create a new set of arrangements, but simply to restore the familiarity of an old one. Here the notion that instability acts as a precondition for remythicization can be seen as a point of commonality between Blumenberg and Cassirer.

But in the *Nachlass* text entitled "Remythicizations," Blumenberg then sharpens the contours of this concept in a way that, in its reference to the relation between myth and Enlightenment, takes issue with Cassirer's *Myth of the State*:

> Remythicizations emerge from the longing to be relieved from questions more than from the longing for answers to questions. Thus, the archaic mythical appears as an idyll, because it did not know of the burden of the questions which the Enlightener regards as so obviously arising, that he always views myths and religions in terms of their deceptive preparedness to provide answers. But precisely this, the prehistoric absence of questions, cannot be restored by any myth.
>
> (RMY, 5)[5]

In this passage and elsewhere in "Remythicizations" (see RMY, 2–3), Blumenberg provides an explanation for the resurgence of myth in National Socialism that departs from Cassirer's analysis. Blumenberg's point of departure consists in his taking the view that a National Socialist *technique* or *theory* of myth could never be effective in creating a new myth. A consciously formulated *theory* of myth—or a mythic-historical justification for the existence of National Socialism akin to that offered by Alfred Rosenberg in *The Myth of the Twentieth Century*—would make the mistake of supposing that myth consists in providing answers to theoretical questions, while also failing to realise that the chief attraction of myth consists precisely in its being pre-theoretical: in telling stories in such a way that the relevant questions do not even need to be posed within a theoretical frame in the first place. As Blumenberg writes in *Work on Myth*: "myth does not need to answer questions; it makes something up, before the question becomes acute and so that it does not become acute" (WOM, 197; AM, 219).

Blumenberg already identifies this aspect of myth in the note that he made following the Poetics and Hermeneutics meeting held in 1968. Here he addresses one of the most controversial issues in his theory of myth: whether or not myth answers questions or provides explanations. Blumenberg claims that myth *does* seductively promise to answer all questions, but only because "it does not aim to serve the function of answering at all, which means: it is not capable of producing a controlled relation between question and answer." It is precisely this contradiction in myth—that of refusing to answer questions but nevertheless forestalling them and in that sense 'resolving' them in a non-transparent fashion—that in Blumenberg's opinion makes the so-called new myths so dangerous.[6] The attraction of myth in a supposedly enlightened age therefore consists in its ability to gratify human needs that cannot be satisfied by reason alone. It is not a regression to an earlier or 'primitive' stage of mental functioning as in the account of Cassirer. It is much more a taking of recourse to potentially dangerous pre-theoretical 'answers' in situations where the answers provided by reason cannot, or can no longer, suffice.

This argument also provides Blumenberg with an explanation for his claim, outlined in *Nachlass* fragment "No Myth of the Twentieth Century," that Rosenberg's *Myth of the Twentieth Century* was a "glaring failure." In "Remythicizations," Blumenberg refers to a passage dated May 24, 1946, from the American psychologist G. M. Gilbert's *Nuremberg Diary* (1947, see RMY, 1). The context is the trial of Baldur von Schirach, the former Head of the Hitler Youth. During his trial, Rosenberg's attorney asked Schirach whether he had ever read Rosenberg's *Myth of the Twentieth Century*. Schirach responded by saying that "he had never been able to read" Rosenberg's seven hundred page tome. This, according to Gilbert's account,

> made Rosenberg furious and he scolded his attorney for having asked such a stupid question. As they [i.e., those on trial] filed out of the courtroom to go to lunch, I asked each one if he had ever read Rosenberg's *Myth*. None of them had. Most of them laughed at it, and only [Julius] Streicher[7] claimed that it was a very profound study which was a little "too deep" for him. I told Rosenberg that he could console himself that none of the defendants had read the *Myth*. "But I don't write books for nobody to read them! Who asked that stupid attorney to ask that question?" Rosenberg fumed.[8]

Blumenberg regards this as the moment in which Rosenberg realised just how ineffectual *The Myth of the Twentieth Century* had been, despite its having benefited from the propaganda networks of the National Socialist state (RMY, 1).

Here it is remarkable that Blumenberg seems to credit Rosenberg—a man not renowned for his clarity of thought—with having himself had insight into why his supposedly great work ended up being little more than a laughing stock at Nuremberg (see RMY, 2–3). In 1939, notes Blumenberg, Rosenberg was asked to write a short version of his 'worldview' for mass consumption. This document can be found as a supplement to Rosenberg's *Political Diaries*, published posthumously in 1956.[9] In this text, Rosenberg is said by Blumenberg to have identified the fatal contradiction at the heart of the *Myth of the Twentieth Century*: the misconception that a myth should ever need to be justified by so-called research. Mythic images, according to Rosenberg as directly quoted by Blumenberg, are

> *allegories* (symbols) of an internal intuition of the world that has been externalised. Every true allegory [*Gleichnis*] is a self-contained and

definitive answer to the question of a period, or of a people. Allegories [*Gleichnisse*] are images, never dogmas. Great *races* live in their images, ideologues through schematic principles of enforced faith [*Zwangsglaubensätze*].[10]

Blumenberg implies that Rosenberg was correct in his realisation that successful myths—as opposed to the confected 'new myths'—operate through images rather than arguments or consciously deployed propaganda strategies. Nevertheless, and as Rosenberg notes, myths still 'answer' questions, albeit in a completely non-theoretical manner. In this Rosenberg's position resembles Georges Sorel's claim that myths function by way of intuitive images rather than through theoretical propositions.[11] Thus, in Blumenberg's words, "if myths were to be products of the will, then every theoretical effort to provide them with a foundation was as unnecessary as it was contemptible" (RMY, 3).[12] The shorter version of this argument then reappears in "No Myth of the Twentieth Century": Rosenberg, writes Blumenberg, "was, despite the dissemination of his book, not the chief ideologue of the NS-system," precisely because "the 'myth' of NS was Hitler himself" (KMZ).[13]

PREFIGURATION

If Hitler himself was the central myth of National Socialism, as a study by Ian Kershaw has also suggested,[14] then it remains to be seen how this myth was constituted. Blumenberg undertakes this task in a text that fits the description of the 'missing chapter' from *Work on Myth* referred to in his letter to Götz Müller (see Chapter 7 of this volume and PF, 62). There is, to the best of my knowledge, no text in the Blumenberg *Nachlass* that carries the title "Stalingrad as Mythical Consequence" ("Stalingrad als mythische Konsequenz") referred to by Blumenberg in that letter. But there is a very polished and thematically unified text which deals with the mythical dimensions of Hitler's decision to invade Stalingrad, and which is also marked with the "AMY" signature (in this case "AMY II"). The title of this text is "Präfiguration: Napoleon und Hitler/Napoleon und Alexander,"[15] now published with related materials as *Prefiguration: Work on Political Myth* (*Präfiguration: Arbeit am politischen Mythos*, 2014).

Unlike the aforementioned study by Kershaw, in this text Blumenberg is not explicitly interested in exploring how the propaganda machine of National Socialism constructed a myth of the '*Führer*.' It is Blumenberg's phenomenological approach to myth that leads him to consider the case of Hitler in terms of the apparently mythical decision processes within Hitler's own individual subjectivity, and also the ways in which he and Goebbels justified such decisions to those around them. Here the key concept is that of *Präfiguration*. The verb *präfigurieren*—a cognate of the English 'to prefigure'—generally means to imagine or to anticipate something in advance of it occurring. As Erich Auerbach has shown in his dense and rich essay on "Figura,"[16] the most common usage of prefiguration was a theo-logical one associated with the lines from the Gospel of Luke 21:22 quoted by Blumenberg: "all things which are written may be fulfilled" (see PF, 11).[17] This refers to the theological principle of typology. "The aim of this sort of interpretation," according Auerbach,

> was to show that the persons and events of the Old Testament were prefigurations of the New Testament and its history of salvation [. . .] Figural interpretation establishes a connection between two events or persons, the first of which signifies not only itself but also the second, while the second encompasses or fulfills the first. The two poles of the figure are separate in time, but both, being real events or figures, are within time, within the stream of historical life.[18]

The origin of this mode of interpretation is found most prominently, accord-ing to Auerbach, in the Pauline Epistles, in which, to cite just one of many examples (1 Corinthians, 15:21) "Adam appears as the *typos* of the future Christ." Similarly, in the thought of St. Augustine, Moses is a prefiguration of Jesus (*figura Christi*) and Noah's Ark prefigures the Christian Church (*praefiguratio ecclesiae*).[19] Blumenberg would have been familiar with such notions from his time spent at Catholic philosophical-theological Colleges in Paderborn and Frankfurt am Main from 1939 to 1940, which is why he emphasises that prefigurations are always "made" retrospectively rather than "born" (PF, 11). The act of rhetorical persuasion consists in convincing the audience that the second event or figure was somehow latent in the first, thereby establishing a sense of law-like continuity and authority.

But for Blumenberg prefiguration is not only associated with biblical typology. In the *Theory of Non-Conceptuality* he also uses the term in a more strictly phenomenological and anthropological sense, associating it with the survival function of the concept as a form of *actio per distans*. The subject, unsure of what particular phenomena may lay ahead either spatially or temporally, takes recourse to the concept as something that combines the definitiveness of that which has already been experienced with sufficient flexibility in order to prefigure (*präfigurieren*), to prepare for (*präperieren*), and if necessary to bring about the prevention (*Prävention*) of that which may be to come (TDU, 12, see also PF, 9). Here orientation in relation to the unknown is derived from patterns or models with which the subject is already familiar. The basic expectation is that these models will be repeated, or perhaps, in some cases, reversed, which is simply the negative form of repetition.

In *Work on Myth*, prefiguration is briefly discussed in relation to the top-ics of significance (*Bedeutsamkeit*) and temporality, but no formal definition of the term is offered and its precise function is never explained (see WOM, 95, 100; AM, 109, 114). We are told, for example, that because myth works "toward evidentness in the articulation of time," it makes use not only of "beginnings and ends" but also of "simultaneity and prefiguration, imitative execution and the recurrence of the same" (WOM, 100; AM, 114). But in *Prefiguration*, this term is now charged with the task of explaining the function of myth in a supposedly post-mythical age. Blumenberg claims that if myth does still have a function to play in the supposedly enlightened or post-mythical age, then its function is that of prefiguration, which combines a sense of 'theological' authority with the anthropological need for orientation in times of confusion or crisis:

> The phenomenon of prefiguration presupposes that the mythical form of thought, as a disposition towards particular modes of functioning, is still or once again virulent. In prefiguration, mythicization approaches or even oversteps the border of magic as soon as the explicit act of repeating a 'prefigurate' [*Präfigurat*] is associated with the expectation of producing the identical effect. To begin with, however, prefiguration is only something like a decision-making aid: under the presupposition of a constancy of conditions, what has already been done once does not require renewed deliberation, confusion or cluelessness, it is predecided by the paradigm.
>
> (PF, 9)

A clear example of the mythical decision-making function of prefiguration is provided by Blumenberg's account of the Arab-Israeli Yom Kippur War of 1973, which follows that of Chaim Herzog.[20] Here Blumenberg claims that the decision made by the Egyptian and Syrian armies to invade Israel on October 6, the tenth day of Ramadan, was 'prefigured' by the fact that the Prophet Mohammed had also begun his preparations for the Battle of Badr in 623 on the same day: the tenth day of the month of fasting (PF, 10). This prefiguration is said to be based on the mythic idea of repetition: the date of an important battle in the history of Islam was seen as being an auspicious day upon which to launch an invasion of Israel. Prefiguration is therefore rhetorical in that it "lends legitimacy to a decision that may be of the most extreme contingency and therefore unjustifiability" (PF, 10).

What specifically does prefiguration have to do with myth? Like myth, it relies upon significance in order to establish its legitimacy:

> The actuality becomes potential for prefiguration through precisely the characteristic that must be attributed to myth, namely through significance. First and foremost because prefiguration is a singular instrument of justification in situations in which taking action is weakly justified, it depends upon the pregnance of the figure being invoked [...] the relation to prefiguration should guarantee to the action an assuredness of decision making, the commitment to the impossibility of breaking off, but also magical protection; and because the action is barred from running off course along the paths of personal capriciousness, the definitiveness

of its outcome is warranted. A trail that has already been blazed is used, and nothing excludes that it can be trodden in the opposite direction.

(PF, 14, 16–17)

It is this notion of a "trail that has already been blazed" (*ein schon gebahnter Weg*) that Blumenberg uses in order to examine what he takes to be the mythic decision making processes that led Hitler to invade Stalingrad. And here it is easy to see how this material could have been integrated into *Work on Myth*: Hitler would in these terms be the final part of a political Prometheus-programme that begins with Goethe's 'extraordinary saying' and extends into Napoleon's statement that 'politics is fate,' which then took on a new meaning after the failed Russian campaign of 1812. Napoleon's Russian campaign would in turn function as one of the important 'prefigurates' for the German attempt to take Moscow in the winter of 1941-2, and for the Battle of Stalingrad in 1942-3. Hence the construction in the title of Blumenberg's text: "Napoleon and Hitler."

That these 'prefigurates' may exist in an historical sequence is demonstrated by the other component of Blumenberg's title: "Napoleon and Alexander." Napoleon is said to have drawn upon the example of Alexander the Great's success in Egypt in order rhetorically to legitimate his own campaign there (PF, 23–4). And Napoleon, along with others who had also foundered in Russia, would in turn serve as a negative 'prefigurate' in relation to Hitler's Stalingrad campaign, as can be seen in the following passage:

Hitler initiated the turning point of the war with his order to attack Stalingrad. For this purpose he travelled especially to Poltava, where the prototype of the northern conflict with the east, Charles XII [i.e., Charles of Sweden], had been defeated in 1709. This defeat was to be made up for. There no historical experiences applied, rather what was to be made as history, and where, had its prior impression [*Vorprägung*]. This prior impression had to allow itself to be reversed in order to proceed in the opposite direction, provided one had only taken the correct *point de départ*. This could not appear in the prescribed official terminology and accordingly not in the German newspapers, since that which was to be significant for the victory could only have been so through the victory. Hitler alone, it seems, trusted in the identifications that he sought. Among the many around him who engaged in mythicization, he was the only one who gave himself over to the archaic compulsion to repeat, so long as the omen did not stand against him. This did not serve the cause of realism. When his armies became bogged down outside of Moscow in the early arriving winter of 1941, he appealed, in opposition to the manifest parallels that were being whispered all around, to the principle that history does not repeat itself.

(PF, 31–2)

Those manifest parallels were of course to be found in the defeats of Charles XII at Poltava and of Napoleon in Russia. But while Hitler may indeed have seen an historical parallel with Charles XII when visiting the German planning headquarters of Army Group South at Poltava,[21] the more compelling 'prefigurate' was that of Napoleon, who—like the German army attempting to invade Moscow in 1941—had been brought undone by the Russian mud and snow. In Blumenberg's view, these historical circumstances forced Hitler to perceive the case of Napoleon only as a negative 'prefigurate' after "his relation to Napoleon" had become "ominous" following the German defeat outside of Moscow in the winter of 1941–2 (PF, 36). This is also why—according to Blumenberg in another text already published from the *Nachlass*—Hitler eventually came to forbid the comparison between himself and Napoleon, a comparison that he feared as "the devil fears holy water."[22]

If this recourse to negative prefiguration was already radically at odds with the military realities confronted by the German army in 1942, then "Hitler's final choice of prefiguration, that of Frederick the Great is, in its total loss of contact with reality, to be described as almost magical" (PF, 36). The final pages of *Prefiguration* quote liberally from the diaries of Joseph Goebbels in order to demonstrate how, in the last few months of the war, Hitler and Goebbels desperately clung to the positive 'prefigurate' of Frederick the Great in order to provide themselves with some form of mythical orientation (PF, 37–49). Of interest here is the way in which this historical setting leads to a subtle change in the 'work of myth,' a change that Blumenberg does not expose to critical analysis. Hitler's wholly opportunistic vacillations between negative and positive 'prefigurates' (Napoleon and Frederick the Great respectively) in order lend legitimacy to the myth of the '*Führer*' demonstrate that prefiguration can lead to an individual and even to a collective loss of contact with reality. "The self-mythicisation," according to Blumenberg, "functions on the condition that the others also put it into effect for themselves. What develops in this way is a world which stands in opposition to realism" (PF, 33). Whereas in *Work on Myth* Blumenberg describes myth as being always already rational in terms of helping the subject come to terms with reality, the examples of Hitler and Goebbels seem, in the end, to tip the scales completely in the direction of magical thinking and irrationality, a complete "contempt for realism" (PF, 44). In so doing, they would also seem also to underline the "preponderance of mythical thought over rational thought" identified by Cassirer in his analysis of National Socialism.[23]

It may, therefore, be the case that the subject matter of National Socialism led Blumenberg onto theoretical ground not altogether distant from that occupied by Cassirer in the *Myth of the State*. Most crucially, Blumenberg is unable to identify an operational point at which the pragmatic and orienting function of myth tips over into a completely debilitating descent into irrationality. It was perhaps this theoretical factor—combined with the likelihood that confronting this subject matter may have been deeply traumatic for Blumenberg—which meant that an explicit treatment of National Socialism within the pages of *Work on Myth* would have "completely and utterly spoiled" his taste for his own book.[24] Faced with this trauma, Blumenberg seems to have resorted to 'detours' or 'roundabout routes' (*Umwege*). This approach is seen in the text entitled "A Detour" ("Ein Umweg," UNF 812/813) that is referred to on the cover page of *Prefiguration* manuscript,[25] in which Blumenberg's treatment of the relation between Napoleon and Hitler takes on a much more personal dimension:

> Reflectiveness permits discretionary digressions. To look away from that which "the issue" could be, or even would have to be, is one of the great auxiliary tools in intellectual quandaries, such as that of being reminded in this ninth decade, because of an interval of half a century, and in addition always and again, of Hitler. Napoleon is the man who preoccupies me more and more, the less I can reflect upon Hitler.
>
> (PF, 53)

In this late biographical admission from the *Nachlass*,[26] Blumenberg offers his most candid explanation for his failure directly to confront the 'Hitler myth' in *Work on Myth*. Here, as in *Work on Myth*, Blumenberg's focus on the 'prefigurate' of Napoleon acts as a detour that enables the 'real issue' to be kept at an adequate distance, thereby allowing it to be 'worked on' and perhaps also 'worked through' indirectly.

By February 28, 1945, the date of the following passage from Goebbels's diary that is quoted verbatim by Blumenberg in *Prefiguration* (see PF, 37–8), Hitler and Goebbels were in the so-called *Führerbunker* in Berlin, and the war was irredeemably lost. In this hopeless situation, the example of Frederick the Great is invoked by Goebbels:

> We must be as Frederick the Great was and act as he did. The Führer agrees with me entirely [. . .] The stoic philosophical attitude to people and events adopted by the Führer today is very reminiscent of Frederick the Great [. . .] Who knows when the moon may not crash into the earth and this whole planet go up in flame and ashes. Nevertheless, he says, it must be our mission to do our duty to the last. In these matters the Führer too is a stoic and a complete disciple of Frederick the Great.[27]

According to Blumenberg, this fantastic scenario, in which the moon would crash into the earth, allows Hitler and Goebbels to see the imminent demise of the National Socialist state as a mere trifle within the cosmic scheme of things (PF, 38). Here the 'prefigurate' of Frederick the Great seems to authorise this so-called stoicism, which is actually a form of megalomania that subscribes to the following absolutist maxim: if the National Socialist state must end, then the world, which is in any case insignificant, may just as well end, too.

Blumenberg identifies a similar 'logic' in Hitler's thinking in one of the most significant of his various reflections on Hitler.[28] This appears in *Lifetime and World-Time* (1986), a volume that explores a disjunction that emerges from the phenomenological analysis of time: once the human being leaves the pre-theoretical and pre-reflective comforts of the life-world, he or she begins to realise that there is a vast difference between the span of one's lifetime and that of so-called world time. "To step out of the life-world means that lifetime and world-time fall into divergence," observes Blumenberg (LZ, 99). After one dies, the world will go on, just as it had existed before one was born. Though the awareness of the gulf between lifetime and world-time, the subject is confronted by "the indifference of the world in relation to him" (LZ, 75). This indifference can be experienced as an "annoyance" or an "offence" (*Ärgernis*), since one is forced to realise that the world has in store further pleasures that will lie beyond the limits of one's own lifetime (LZ, 78).

One of the human mechanisms for coping with this disjunction is to create institutions which are passed on from one generation to the next: "Institutions are based precisely on the notion that the lifetime is not the measure of all things, but rather that provisions must be made and traditions put in place and recognized beyond its borders" (LZ, 83). Institutions provide orientation not only by helping us to decide what to do in the present, but also by reassuring us that something of which we have partaken will continue to exist once we are gone. In short: institutions help us to cope with the gap between lifetime and world-time.

Another reaction to the disjunction between lifetime and world-time is one that Blumenberg associates with "delusion" (*Wahn*):

> In the borderline case of paranoia, the one and only life that an individual has becomes the condition for the realisation of historical and political meaning, so that he can make the non-attainment of his life-goal into the failure of the world to realise its purpose: if, due to whichever actual disturbances of his life-conception, he is condemned to go under, then everything else is condemned to be at an end [. . .] In an extension of the language of Freud, one would be permitted to call this 'absolute narcissism.'
>
> (LZ, 80)

The case to which Blumenberg is referring is of course Hitler, and for this purpose he makes use of another internal National Socialist witness concerning the final stages of the war: the memoirs of the Luftwaffe adjutant, Nicolaus von Below (published in 1980, one year after *Work on Myth*). Of direct relevance to the subject of 'prefiguration' is the fact that in early December 1944, prior to the Ardenne Offensive that began on December 16, Hitler attempted to convince his generals that the Allies would break apart by making the following appeal: "He reminded them of how Frederick the Great, in the darkest hours of his war, had stood alone and triumphed (*durchgehalten*)."[29] Blumenberg does not cite these lines in *Lifetime and World-Time*, but we can see how this material could also have fed into his ideas about 'prefiguration' as a rhetorical method that is deployed in order to justify highly precarious military decisions. The key lines quoted in *Lifetime and World-Time* (see LZ, 80–1) are in fact those that Hitler is reported to have uttered to Below after the Ardenne Offensive had failed: "we will not capitulate, ever. We may go down. But we will take a world with us [*wir werden eine Welt mitnehmen*]."[30] Blumenberg takes interest in Hitler's use of the indefinite article in relation to "world," which is said to mean that "Hitler did not have a world" (LZ, 84). This is not to suggest that Hitler had lost touch with reality completely. Rather, he simply had no conception of *the* objective world of history that had existed before him and which would continue to exist after him (LZ, 84). This also meant that Hitler had no understanding of, or at least no respect for, the political and social institutions that predated National Socialism (LZ, 83).

The fact that Hitler had no conception of *the* world as the continuity of history also meant, in Blumenberg's interpretation, that contrary to Napoleon's statement to Goethe, politics for Hitler was *not* fate, and it was not about the fame or glory (*Ruhm*) associated with the great political actor who makes history. This is simply because "to think of fame, to speak of fame, depends upon the continuance of the world." Politics was not to be *equated* with fate, but was rather seen as the complete "replacement of fate" (*Schicksalsersatz*) in such a way that if the political goals in question were in fact not to be realised, then history, and with it fate, would have to come to an end. This "forcible reduction of the world-time back into the dimensions of a life-time" would in this way be "a most extreme act of violence [. . .] against the basic condition of human existence" (LZ, 84).

Here the continuity with *Work on Myth* in the treatment of Hitler in both *Prefiguration* and in *Lifetime and World-Time* consists in showing how Hitler brings the Prometheus problem to its most extreme and drastic conclusion. The earlier polytheistic scenario of God against God has been replaced by one in which the end of the supposedly 'one and only God' must also, and of necessity, mean the end of existence itself. Despite this continuity, it is also possible that Blumenberg would have struggled to integrate the *Prefiguration* material into the chronological structure of *Work on Myth*. The fifth and last part of *Work on Myth* ends at the beginning of the twentieth-century, with Franz Kafka's rewriting of the Prometheus myth. Bridging the chronological and cultural gap between Kafka and Germany of the Third Reich would no doubt have required Blumenberg to add a lengthy sixth part to an already extensive volume.

THE ABSOLUTISM OF WISHES

Blumenberg's 'diagnosis' of the narcissistic Hitler points to a feature of his theory of myth that has, up until now, gone unexamined within the pages of this volume: its significant debt to Freud.[31] An exploration of this debt is an instructive way in which to conclude this study precisely because Blumenberg's considerations of Freud in *Work on Myth* are enlightening with respect to what I will call not the 'theory of myth' but rather the 'myth of theory' within the field of the human sciences.

At the level of theory construction, Blumenberg himself underlines this debt with reference to the notion—or perhaps metaphor—of 'absolutism' and the two limit concepts that he conjoins with it. In the opening chapter of *Work on Myth*, Blumenberg observes: "the absolutism of reality is opposed by the absolutism of images and wishes" (WOM, 8; AM, 14). The 'absolutism of reality' is associated with Freud's notion of the reality principle, since for Freud 'reality' always presents itself as that which intrudes upon and potentially thwarts the wishes of the subject. The formation of the reality principle emerges from the "non-occurrence" of an "expected satisfaction." When this non-occurrence arises, the subject must "decide to form a conception of the real circumstances in the external world and to endeavour to make a real alteration in them."[32] Disappointed expectations give rise to questions. Thus, in early childhood, reality—in the sense of an object-world differentiated from the self—only emerges when the infant begins to realise that the mother's breast, in not always being present when the infant demands it, is not an extension of the infant's own subjectivity.[33]

The absolutism of wishes, or what Freud terms the "omnipotence of thoughts" (*Allmacht der Gedanken*), is in turn associated by Blumenberg with the purely theoretical hypothesis of a completely intact and undisturbed life-world in which all needs are satisfied and in which no questions arise. This would amount to the "absolute dominion of the wish, of the pleasure principle," as imagined by the more subjective strains of German idealism (WOM, 269; AM, 298). Although this is not precisely the sense in which Freud uses the phrase 'omnipotence of thoughts' in *Totem and Taboo* (*Totem und Tabu*, 1913), it is easy to see how Blumenberg has adapted it for his own purposes. Freud relates the "omnipotence of thoughts" to animism, which is for him coterminous with myth, and with what Wilhelm Wundt refers to as "mythopoeic consciousness." The background hypothesis that informs this notion of primitive animism is to be found in the ideas of Tylor and Frazer discussed in Chapter 2 of this volume: like these thinkers, Freud too believes that humanity passes through three developmental stages. The first of these is "animistic (or mythological)," while the second and third are "religious and scientific," respectively. The "omnipotence of thoughts" appears predominantly in the animistic stage, and corresponds with the human desire to "obtain mastery over men, beasts and things—or rather, over their spirits." This mastery is to be achieved by way of "magic," and here Freud simply repeats Frazer's ideas concerning similarity and contiguity: one might make it rain through a ritual that imitates the rain, or cause harm to one's foe by destroying a piece of his clothing.[34]

What Freud adds to Frazer's account is the psychoanalytic conception of the wish, since "primitive man had an immense belief in the power of his wishes."[35] The "omnipotence of thoughts" is nothing more than the human being's projection of its wishes onto the external world, and it is a feature not only of 'primitive' beliefs but can also be encountered among children and neurotics. For Freud,

> Primitive men and neurotics [. . .] attach a high valuation—in our eyes an *over*-valuation—to psychical acts. This attitude may plausibly be brought into relation with narcissism and regarded as an essential component of it.[36]

Blumenberg makes selective use of these ideas in both *Work on Myth* and in *Cave Exits*. While he ignores the colonial distinctions made by Tylor, Frazer and Freud between so-called primitive and advanced cultures, he at the same time applies Freud's basic dualism of 'reality' and 'wishes' to the primal scene of anthropogenesis. The realm of the wish, of myth, is said by Blumenberg to have been made possible by "the division of life between caves and open hunting grounds" after our pre-human ancestors left the rainforest and were confronted by the harsh realities of the open savannah. The comparative safety of the cave provides a "closed space" that "allows what the open space prohibits: the power of the wish, of magic, of illusion, and the preparation of effects by thought" (WOM, 8; AM, 14; see also HA, 25–6). The cave is the sanctum in which the human being gains the necessary respite in order to conceive of imaginary methods or "procedures" through which to influence the course of things outside of its confines (WOM, 8; AM, 14). The opportunity to reflect upon past experiences allows the subject to 'prefigure' and prepare for forays onto the open ground.

That these 'prefigurations' could continue to be a feature of thinking within the modern age—even to the extent that political leaders deploy them—might at least heuristically be explained by what Blumenberg refers to, in *Cave Exits*, as "species memory" (*Erinnerung der Gattung*, see HA, 23). The 'species memory' of having prepared for future confrontations by 'prefiguring' them in relation to past experiences would in these terms be a primeval form of orientation that is never fully left behind, and which is resorted to in times of extreme crisis. Here the similarity between Freud and Blumenberg also extends to their respective deployments of Ernst Haeckel's 'biogenetic law' in order to achieve their own speculative theoretical ends: just as Freud claims that the "omnipotence of thoughts" found in the animism of 'primitive' peoples resembles the mental lives of children,[37] so too does Blumenberg claim, at least heuristically or metaphorically, that leaving the rainforest for the open savannah was akin to a birth trauma that demanded new cultural compensations (WOM, 5; AM, 10–11). This is also why, in *Cave Exits*, the retreat into the cave is explicitly associated with a return to the safety of an artificial womb (HA, 20).

FREUD AND THE MYTH OF THEORY

For Blumenberg, myth does its work in-between the theoretical poles of the 'absolutism of reality' and the 'absolutism of wishes': its function is to repair life-worlds that have been torn by intrusions of reality that give rise to questions which, even if they cannot (or cannot yet) be answered theoretically, at least need to be explained away or put at a distance by the telling of stories. But the need to respond to such questions, if not to answer them directly and theoretically, does not belong to myth alone. It also belongs to that which emerged after it, but which cannot, in Blumenberg's view, be separated from it: namely, the *theory* of myth. That there should even have to be a distinction between myth and its theory is something that Blumenberg seems to accept only with reluctance. "It is part of the modern age's consciousness of itself," according to Blumenberg, "that it is always 'getting serious' anew with new (theoretical, practical, aesthetic) realisms" (WOM, 178; AM, 197). This notion of 'getting serious' may raise the expectation that a theory should be grounded in a realist—in the sense of empirically verifiable—account of the objects or phenomena that it attempts to explicate.

In a passage from *Work on Myth* that sounds like the coded position-statement of an academic who enjoys toying with the expectations of the academy, Blumenberg writes:

> We have become accustomed to the 'rule of the game' of professionalism in the realm of theory that also promotes those who are only able to invent questions, and still more those who only act as critics of the answers and who even equip them with the quasi-ethical pretension according to which being criticized is part of the immanent intention of all supposed answers. To expose oneself to criticism with a bearing expressive of the enjoyment of suffering thus becomes a professional faculty, just as being a good loser once was one of the duties of the so-called good sportsman. Such burdens are unknown to myth, which is why it was necessary to speak of them here.
>
> (WOM, 184; AM, 204)

One thing that attracts Blumenberg to Freud is precisely the fact that Freud was hyper-aware of these 'rules of the game' as delineated by the natural sciences, but was forced by his human subject matter to transgress them time and again with speculative or even mythical arguments. This tendency occurs whenever Freud is required to give an account of origins, and it begins with his earliest attempt to establish psychoanalysis as a materialist science: his "Project for a Scientific Psychology" ("Entwurf einer Psychologie") of 1895.

There we are told that psychoanalysis will be a "natural science" that will "represent psychical processes as quantitatively determined states of specifiable material particles."³⁸ This ambitious beginning, in which we find Freud's 'will to science' in full flight, was soon undermined by the fact that the main objects of Freud's 'natural science'—the unconscious in general and instincts in particular—do not have a physical status. Both could only be inferred by way of their effects, as Freud later admitted in the essay on "Instincts and Their Vicissitudes" ("Triebe und Triebschicksale") of 1915. This essay begins with the proposition that "even at the stage of description" within a science, "it is not possible to avoid applying certain abstract ideas to the material in hand, ideas derived from somewhere or other but certainly not from the new observations alone."³⁹ Thus, although the "source" of an instinct is thought to be a "somatic process which occurs in an organ or part of the body," and which may be associated with what Freud refers to as "chemical" or "mechanical" processes, in the end we can know instincts "only by their aims," and not by their sources or origins.⁴⁰ This method of argument—in which a concept or name stands in for something that is inferred but which cannot be experienced as an empirical object—is duly noted by Blumenberg in the *Theory of Non-Conceptuality*, where he observes that some "concepts are not only based on objects, rather concepts also constitute objects." For Blumenberg, the paradigmatic case of this function of the concept is the unconscious, which, far from being clear and distinct, is an "auxiliary concept" (*Hilfsbegriff*) that allows the technical operations of psychoanalysis to be performed by way of inference (TDU, 40–3).

If giving a name to something that cannot be experienced directly, but which is thought to influence the trajectory of one's life, means to deplete the power of that something and render it approachable, then psychoanalysis, with its series of names for unseen forces, is a perfect example of the work *of* myth. One name that Freud did use in order to describe the feeling of being subject to an unknown power was the same one that Goethe had used in *Poetry and Truth*: daemonic (*dämonisch*). In *Beyond the Pleasure Principle* (*Jenseits des Lustprinzips*, 1920), those who experience repeated misfortunes in life are said to have the impression of being "possessed by some 'daemonic' power."⁴¹ But Freud did not only invoke the old names for such forces; he was also adept at creating new ones. In Blumenberg's words: "no success in hitting on names can be compared to Freud's" (WOM, 55; AM, 64). Already by the time of the *Interpretation of Dreams* (*Die Traumdeutung*) in 1900, Freud's "system of the ego and the unconscious, the superego and the id" is said to be "that of a vertical imagination, which as such would already have an affinity to myth" (WOM, 56; AM, 65–6). Blumenberg even points to the fact that Freud, in a letter to Wilhelm Fliess dated December 12, 1897, coins the expression "endopsychic myths" in order to explain the way in which the subject attempts to represent its own "psychic apparatus" to itself in the form of a personal mythology (WOM, 55–6; AM, 64–5).⁴² It is this endogenous or personal mental topography—first 'discovered' in the mythical founding act of Freud's 'self-analysis' undertaken during the first

half of the 1890s—which would later be 'objectified' in the formal categories of psychoanalysis.

That the later Freud still openly admitted that these categories are mythical is something that seems to have escaped even Blumenberg's awareness.
In the *New Introductory Lectures on Psychoanalysis* (*Neue Folge der Vorlesungen zur Einführung in die Psychoanalyse*) written in 1932, Freud's at
least momentary renunciation of the 'will to science' can be found in his
admission that

> The theory of instincts is so to say our mythology. Instincts are mythical
> entities, magnificent in their indefiniteness. In our work we cannot for a
> moment disregard them, yet we are never sure that we are seeing them
> clearly [*nie sicher, sie scharf zu sehen*].[43]

Here the language used by Freud gives expression to the fundamental contradiction inherent in the 'human science' of psychoanalysis: namely, to treat
something that is fundamentally non-empirical as though it were empirical.
Freud's use of the verb 'seeing' (*sehen*) has the rhetorical effect of endowing something that is merely *inferred* with the status of an actual thing that
would be susceptible to direct observation under optimal conditions and if
the correct theoretical orientation were in place. The admission of mythical
indefiniteness is in this way quickly withdrawn through the assertion that
instincts are actual things. Freud's 'realist' proposition is that although we
cannot see them, these things are actually there, just as *the* unconscious,
expressed in the form of a substantive, is thought to be a universal attribute
of human subjectivity rather than a merely theoretical tool. Here the 'mythical' mode of argumentation is invoked only in order to talk about those
aspects of the 'science' of psychoanalysis that are thought to be based on
plausible inferences, but which can never be proven or falsified. Here too,
myth responds to a question without directly answering it.

Mythical plausibility, we have noted, is also a feature of Blumenberg's
story of anthropogenesis, as outlined in the opening section of *Work on Myth*.
This story is not told with the expectation that it can be proven or disproven,
but rather in order to demonstrate its effectiveness or *Leistungsfähigkeit* in
illuminating the kind of work that myth was originally able to do. Here our
interest is not in Blumenberg's *interpretations* of Freud—for example, the
notion that Freud attempted to formulate a "countermyth" to Prometheus in
Civilization and its Discontents (*Das Unbehagen in der Kultur*, see WOM,
621–5; AM, 674–8)[44]—but rather in how Freud's use of 'mythical plausibility' might be compared with Blumenberg's own speculative account of
hominisation. Both thinkers are aware—Freud implicitly, Blumenberg much
more explicitly and ironically—that any theory of the human being will have
to tell a story about the origin, which also means that any theory of the
human being that claims to be based upon the 'empirical facts' alone would
itself be a rhetorical construction and perhaps even a myth.

The clearest case of such a story in Freud's writings is that of the "primal horde," first outlined in *Totem and Taboo*: a speculative account of an early human society in which a despotic father-ruler is killed and devoured by his sons, who then expiate their guilt by establishing exogamy and then by worshipping him as their god. This narrative is forced to shoulder a huge theoretical burden, explaining nothing less than the origins of "social organization, of moral restrictions and of religion."[45] In a later publication, *Group Psychology and the Analysis of the Ego* (*Massenpsychologie und Ich-Analyse*, 1921), Freud describes this narrative as a "conjecture" (*Vermutung*) and even as a "scientific myth" (*wissenschaftlicher Mythus*) but he defends its use on grounds that might remind us of Blumenberg: "It is creditable to such a hypothesis," Freud argues, "if it proves able to bring coherence and understanding into more and more new regions."[46]

An even more extreme instance of such speculation can be found in Freud's hypothesis, outlined in *Beyond the Pleasure Principle*, that "*an instinct is an urge inherent in organic life to restore an earlier state of things* which the living entity has been obliged to abandon under the pressure of external disturbing forces.*" This hypothesis is based on an account of the origins of consciousness which Freud introduces with the following lines: "What follows is speculation, often far-fetched speculation [. . .] it is further an attempt to follow out an idea consistently, out of curiosity to see where it will lead." The hypothesis is that consciousness first arose in simple organisms in order to "discover the direction and nature" of "external stimuli" so that the organism could develop mechanisms for "protection against excessive amounts of stimulation and for excluding unsuitable kinds of stimuli." In other words: consciousness emerged only in order to deal with external disturbances to the organism. Since consciousness is a system, and since any system prefers a state of rest and stability to one of tension and disturbance, then the purpose of conscious life is nothing other than to return to the original state of stability that existed prior to consciousness, or in Freud's dramatic phrasing: "*the aim of all life is death.*"[47]

Blumenberg describes Freud's theory of the death-drive (*Todestrieb*) as "the total myth." This is a myth of

> the final return home to the original state. To promise this is the great temptation of comprehensive theories, the temptation to equal myth in the production of totality. The death instinct completes this story of history [*Geschichte von der Geschichte*] and permeates it with the tenor of the contingency of life.
>
> (WOM, 91; AM, 103–4)

Of interest here is Blumenberg's failure to reflect upon why this 'total myth' of psychoanalysis became necessary for Freud at all. Blumenberg claims that it was not invented by Freud, but simply emerged "in the process of interrogating the instincts with regard to their functional meaning" (WOM, 91; AM, 103). Freud's biographer, Peter Gay, by and large agrees with this interpretation by arguing that Freud had already identified aggressive instincts as part of the Oedipus complex in 1905, and that his later "reclassification of the drives" emerged from "problems internal to psychoanalytic theory." But Gay does not completely discount another more historically contingent factor: namely, that "the great slaughter of 1914 to 1918 [. . .] had also forced Freud to assign enhanced stature to aggression."[48] Seen in this way, the death-drive was not merely developed 'out of curiosity.' Its functional effectiveness consisted in telling a story that could make the horrors of the Great War comprehensible. In other words, it is an example of both 'working through' and the 'work *of* myth.'

Is Blumenberg's theory of myth also a 'comprehensive theory' that succumbs to the 'temptation to equal myth in the production of totality'? The basic premise of Blumenberg's theory of myth—that it assisted human beings in dealing with the biological crisis of the 'absolutism of reality,' and that 'human nature' is nothing more than the contingent emergence of culture out of these crisis conditions—is self-consciously hypothetical. It could perhaps be claimed that this hypothesis is framed by a rhetoric of *negative totality*: that is, by a total renunciation of the attempt to answer Kant's fourth question in a definitive or 'scientific' fashion. But even this explanation would not be adequate. Blumenberg's position is *not* one of negative totality, since he also insists that the question concerning the human being must convincingly be answered, at least provisionally, in order to provide an orienting account of where we have come from and where we might be going. Here the fundamental difference between Freud and Blumenberg can be discerned: both of them attempt to answer Kant's fourth question, which is *the* question of the human sciences. But whereas Freud still seems to think that psychoanalysis will one day be a 'science' capable of delivering definitive answers, Blumenberg expresses a preference for provisional answers selected only according to their explanatory effectiveness. Freud's 'will to science' never abated. In Blumenberg's theory of myth, the 'will to science' lives on, but only as the memory of an impossible to fulfil expectation.

If Freud's theory—or myth—of the death instinct did emerge from a need to understand the war that had ended only two years before the publication of *Beyond Pleasure Principle*, then what are we to make of Blumenberg's interpretation of National Socialism in "Remythicizations," in *Prefiguration* and in *Lifetime and World-Time*? These texts could only claim to explain the resurgence of myth in National Socialism in phenomenological terms, which is to say, predominantly through an analysis of Hitler's individual subjectivity. Although Blumenberg does suggest, in *Work on Myth*, that 'remythicizations' emerge from the attempt to deal with rapid changes in the 'system-conditions' of a society, the 'system-conditions' that prevailed in Germany leading up to and during the period 1933–45 never become an object of explicit analysis either in that work, or in the aforementioned texts from the *Nachlass*. And if Blumenberg *has* anything resembling a theory of society at all, then it can only be found in his liberal conservative vision of institutions that develop through long and slow processes of cultural selection, and which engage in rhetorical competition with one another. Blumenberg sees these processes as having been completely uprooted by Hitler's violent attempt to force world-time into the confines of his lifetime.

The story with which *Prefiguration* closes is accordingly that of Hitler's individual pathology and magical thinking, not the collective reversion to myth diagnosed by Cassirer in *The Myth of State* or by Adorno and Horkheimer in the *Dialectic of Enlightenment*. It is taken from the memoirs of Henriette von Schirach—Baldur von Schirach's wife—who reports upon the account of the last days in the *Führerbunker* related to her by Hitler's former pilot, Hans Baur (paraphrased in PF, 49). Hitler is said to have owned a small portrait of Frederick the Great painted by Anton Graff, which he "took with him as a talisman into the bunker-underworld." Hitler, according to Baur, identified with Frederick, comparing his own defeats with the disaster of the Seven Years' War, his loneliness with the embitterment of the great King, and his German shepherd, Blondi, with Frederick's Italian greyhound named Biche. This identification seems to have been Hitler's last psychological resort. "In his final desperation," reports Baur, Hitler "screamed at the portrait, demanding that the King help him."[49]

NOTES

1. Hans Blumenberg, *Präfiguration: Arbeit am politischen Mythos*, ed. Angus Nicholls and Felix Heidenreich (Berlin: Suhrkamp, 2014), cited as PF.
2. Two versions of this loosely structured forty-three-page text can be found in the Hans Blumenberg *Nachlass*. The first is untitled and can be found in the second of four folders of paralipomena relating to *Work on Myth* (catalogued as 'AMY Paralipomena'). The second, which is a hand-corrected version of the first and which carries the handwritten title "Remythisierungen" lies in the fourth of four folders entitled "Götterschwund: Nach der Arbeit am Mythos" (Fading of Gods: After the Work on Myth), which are thought to have been compiled between 1985 and 1991. References are to the second of these two versions. See Blumenberg, "Remythisierungen," Hans Blumenberg *Nachlass*, *Deutsches Literaturarchiv* Marbach (hereafter DLA Marbach).
3. Friedrich Nietzsche, "Zur Geschichte des Gottesbegriffs," *Kritische Studienausgabe*, ed. Giorgio Colli and Mazzino Montinari, 15 vols. (Berlin: De Gruyter, 1967–77), 13:523–6; here: 525.
4. Nietzsche, "Zur Geschichte des Gottesbegriffs," 523.
5. [Remythisierungen entstehen aus dem Verlangen nach der Entlastung von Fragen mehr als aus dem nach Antwort auf Fragen. Deshalb erscheint die archaische Mythizität als Idylle, weil sie die Last der Fragen nicht kannte, die der Aufklärer für so selbstverständlich vorgegeben hält, dass er Mythen und Religionen unter dem Aspekt ihrer trügerischen Antwortbereitschaft sieht. Aber gerade dies, die vorgeschichtliche Fraglosigkeit, ist durch keinen Mythos wiederherzustellen.]
6. See Blumenberg, "Notiz zur Diskussion um 'Wirklichkeitsbegriff und Wirkungspotential des Mythos (1968),'" in BTB, 255–7; here: 256.

7. Founder and publisher of the National Socialist propaganda paper *Der Stürmer*.
8. G. M. Gilbert, *Nuremberg Diary* (1947; New York: Da Capo Press, 1995), 349–50.
9. See "Dokument PS—1749," in Alfred Rosenberg, *Das politische Tagebuch Alfred Rosenbergs*, ed. Hans-Günther Seraphim (Göttingen, 1956), 197–212.
10. Rosenberg, *Das politische Tagebuch*, 211 (emphasis in the original).
11. Georges Sorel, *Reflections on Violence*, ed. and trans. Jeremy Jennings (Cambridge: Cambridge University Press, 2009), 20.
12. [wenn Mythen Produkte des Willens sein sollten, war jede theoretische Anstrengung zu ihrer Begründung so überflüssig wie verächtlich].
13. [Rosenberg war trotz der Verbreitung seines Buches nicht der Chefideologe des NS-Systems [. . .] der 'Mythos' des NS war Hitler selbst].
14. Ian Kershaw, *The "Hitler Myth": Image and Reality in the Third Reich* (New York: Oxford University Press, 1998).
15. Two almost identical versions of this thirty-page chapter can be found in the *Nachlass*. The first lies in the third of four folders entitled "Paralipomena zu Arbeit am Mythos," the second in the first of four folders entitled "Götterschwund" and referred to in note 2 of this chapter. The second version carries a cover page with the following information: "AMY II, MYTHOLOGICA MINORA, PRÄFIGURATION: NAPOLEON UND HITLER / NAPOLEON UND ALEXANDER, UNF 812/813." The first "Götterschwund" folder also contains a draft contents page upon which "x/1984 (rev.)" is written. The eleventh chapter title on this contents page is "Poltava und Stalingrad/Wiederholung und keine Wendung" ("Poltava and Stalingrad / Repetition and No Change"). This suggests that Blumenberg may have considered including a revised version of the "Präfiguration" essay in a second book devoted to myth under the title of "Götterschwund." It therefore seems likely that "Präfiguration" was begun as part of the original *Work on Myth* manuscript, and was then reworked and reconsidered by Blumenberg for other possible projects during the early 1980s. The "UNF 812/813" that appears on the cover page of "Präfiguration" is Blumenberg's own reference to another *Nachlass* text entitled "Ein Umweg" ("A Detour") to be discussed below and also published in PF, 54–8. The numbering of this text (812/813) suggests that it was written sometime between May 25, 1981, and October 1, 1984 (I thank Dorit Krusche of the DLA Marbach for her advice on this matter). The signature "UNF" can be found on many other texts in the *Nachlass*, and indicates that Blumenberg may have considered this text for future use in a later context, and is normally taken to mean work which is unfinished ("unfertig"), or "unerlaubte Fragmente" (forbidden or unauthorised fragments)—perhaps, in this case, fragments which Blumenberg deliberately held back due to their personal nature. See the comments of Ulrich von Bülow and Dorit Krusche in QSE, 282–3. For further details on "Präfiguration" see the "Editorische Notiz" in PF, 79–81.
16. Erich Auerbach, "Figura," trans. Ralph Manheim, in *Scenes from the Drama of European Literature* (New York: Meridian, 1959), 11–76.
17. *The Bible, Authorized King James Version with Apocrypha*, introd. Robert Carroll and Stephen Prickett (Oxford: Oxford University Press, 1988), New Testament, 107.
18. Auerbach, "Figura," 30, 53.
19. See Augustine, *City of God*, 18, 11 and 15, 27, quoted in Auerbach, "Figura," 50, 38.
20. Chaim Herzog, *The War of Atonement* (London: Weidenfeld and Nicholson, 1975), 33; the German edition cited by Blumenberg is entitled *Entscheidung in der Wüste* (Berlin: Ullstein, 1975), 48.

21. See Anthony Beevor, *Stalingrad* (London: Penguin, 2011), 52.
22. See "Vergleichsverbot," in BG, 221–3; here: 221.
23. Ernst Cassirer, *The Myth of the State* (New Haven, CT: Yale University Press, 1946), 3.
24. Hans Blumenberg to Götz Müller, July 20, 1981, in PF, 62.
25. See note 15 in this chapter.
26. Blumenberg's reference to the "ninth decade" suggests that this text was written in the 1980s and probably in 1983, to mark the fiftieth anniversary of Hitler coming to power. See the "Editorische Notiz" in PF, 79–81; here: 80.
27. Joseph Goebbels, *The Goebbels Diaries: The Last Days*, ed. Hugh Trevor-Roper, trans. Richard Barry (London: Secker and Warburg, 1978), 1; *Tagebücher*, ed. Ralf Georg Reuth, 5 vols. (Munich: Piper, 1992), 5:2127 (the date of this entry in the English edition is listed as February 27, 1945).
28. For an overview, see the "Nachwort der Herausgeber," in PF, 83–146; here: 128–36.
29. Nicolaus von Below, *At Hitler's Side: The Memoirs of Hitler's Luftwaffe Adjutant 1937–1945*, trans. Geoffrey Brooks (London: Greenhill Books, 2001), 222; *Als Hitlers Adjutant, 1937–45* (Mainz: Hase and Koehler, 1980), 397.
30. Below, *At Hitler's Side*, 223 (translation altered); *Als Hilters Adjutant*, 398.
31. On Blumenberg's complex relation to Freud, see Rüdiger Zill, "Zwischen Affinität und Kritik. Hans Blumenberg liest Sigmund Freud," in *Hans Blumenberg beobachtet. Wissenschaft, Technik und Philosophie*, ed. Cornelius Borck (Freiburg: Alber, 2013), 126–48.
32. Sigmund Freud, "Formulations on the Two Principles of Mental Functioning," in *The Standard Edition of the Complete Psychological Works of Sigmund Freud*, 24 vols. ed. James Strachey and Anna Freud (London: The Hogarth Press, 1953–74), 12:218–26; here: 219. The *Standard Edition* of Freud's works will hereafter be cited as SE followed by volume and page numbers; "Formulierungen über die zwei Prinzipien des psychischen Geschehens," in *Gesammelte Werke*, ed. Anna Freud (London: Imago, 1948), 8: 230–8; here: 231. Freud's *Gesammelte Werke* will hereafter be cited as GW, followed by volume and page numbers.
33. Freud, *An Outline of Psychoanalysis*, in SE, 23:141–207; here: 188; "Abriss der Psychoanalyse," in GW, 17:67–138; here: 115.
34. Freud, *Totem and Taboo: Some Points of Agreement between the Mental Lives of Savages and Neurotics*, in SE, 13: 1–162; here: 77, 78, 79–85; *Totem und Tabu: Einige Übereinstimmungen im Seelenleben der Wilden und der Neurotiker*, vol. 9 of GW, 95, 96–7, 98–106.
35. Freud, *Totem and Taboo*, SE, 13:83; *Totem und Tabu*, GW, 9:103.
36. Freud, *Totem and Taboo*, SE, 13:89; *Totem und Tabu*, GW, 9:110.
37. Freud, *Totem and Taboo*, SE, 13:90; *Totem und Tabu*, GW, 9:111.
38. Freud, "Project for a Scientific Psychology," in *The Origins of Psycho-Analysis. Letters to Wilhelm Fliess, Drafts and Notes: 1887–1902*, ed. Marie Bonaparte, Anna Freud, and Ernst Kris (London: Imago, 1954), 349–445 here: 355; "Entwurf einer Psychologie," in GW, *Nachtragsband*, 387–477; here: 387.
39. Freud, "Instincts and their Vicissitudes," in SE, 14:117–40; here: 117; "Triebe und Triebschicksale," in GW, 10: 210–32; here: 210.
40. Freud, "Instincts and their Vicissitudes," in SE, 14:123; "Triebe und Triebschicksale," in GW, 10: 215–16.
41. Freud, *Beyond the Pleasure Principle*, in SE, 18:7–64; here: 21; *Jenseits des Lustprinzips*, in GW, 13: 3–66; here: 20.

42. See Sigmund Freud to Wilhelm Fliess, December 12, 1897, in *The Complete Letters of Sigmund Freud to Wilhlem Fliess*, ed. and trans. Jeffrey Moussaieff Masson (Cambridge, MA: Harvard University Press, 1985), 285–6; *Briefe an Wilhlem Fließ, 1887–1904*, ed. Jeffrey Moussaieff Masson and Michael Schröter (Frankfurt am Main: S. Fischer, 1986), 311.

43. Freud, "Anxiety and Instinctual Life," in *New Introductory Lectures on Psychoanalysis*, in SE, 22:5–182; here: 95; "Angst und Triebleben," in *Neue Folge der Vorlesungen zur Einführung in die Psychoanalyse*, in GW, 15: 101.

44. See also Blumenberg's reflections on Freud in VP, 163–79.

45. Freud, *Totem and Taboo*, in SE, 13:141–2; *Totem und Tabu*, in GW, 9: 171–2.

46. Freud, *Group Psychology and the Analysis of the Ego*, in SE, 18:64–143; here: 122, 135, 122; *Massenpsychologie und Ich-Analyse*, in GW, 13:73–161; here: 136, 151, 136.

47. Freud, *Beyond the Pleasure Principle*, in SE, 18: 36, 24, 27–8, 38 (emphasis in the original); *Jenseits des Lustprinzips*, in GW, 13: 38, 23, 27, 40.

48. Peter Gay, *Freud: A Life for Our Time* (New York: Norton, 1998), 397, 395.

49. Henriette von Schirach, *Der Preis der Herrlichkeit. Erlebte Zeitgeschichte* (Munich: Herbig, 1975), 239; Blumenberg cites the 1978 edition (Munich: Herbig, 1978), 239.

Index